VOLUME 7

BY RIE TAKADA

LOS ANGELES • TOKYO • LONDON • HAMBURG

ALSO AVAILABLE FROM TOKYOPOP®

You want it? We got it!
A full range of TOKYOPOP
products are available now at:
www.TOKYOPOP.com/shop

04.23.04T

ALSO AVAILABLE FROM

MANGA

.HACK//LEGEND OF THE TWILIGHT
@LARGE
ABENOBASHI: MAGICAL SHOPPING ARCADE
A.I. LOVE YOU
AI YORI AOSHI
ANGELIC LAYER
ARM OF KANNON
BABY BIRTH
BATTLE ROYALE
BATTLE VIXENS
BRAIN POWERED
BRIGADOON
B'TX
CANDIDATE FOR GODDESS, THE
CARDCAPTOR SAKURA
CARDCAPTOR SAKURA - MASTER OF THE CLOW
CHOBITS
CHRONICLES OF THE CURSED SWORD
CLAMP SCHOOL DETECTIVES
CLOVER
COMIC PARTY
CONFIDENTIAL CONFESSIONS
CORRECTOR YUI
COWBOY BEBOP
COWBOY BEBOP: SHOOTING STAR
CRAZY LOVE STORY
CRESCENT MOON
CROSS
CULDCEPT
CYBORG 009
D•N•ANGEL
DEMON DIARY
DEMON ORORON, THE
DEUS VITAE
DIABOLO
DIGIMON
DIGIMON TAMERS
DIGIMON ZERO TWO
DOLL
DRAGON HUNTER
DRAGON KNIGHTS
DRAGON VOICE
DREAM SAGA
DUKLYON: CLAMP SCHOOL DEFENDERS
EERIE QUEERIE!
ERICA SAKURAZAWA: COLLECTED WORKS
ET CETERA
ETERNITY
EVIL'S RETURN
FAERIES' LANDING
FAKE
FLCL
FLOWER OF THE DEEP SLEEP
FORBIDDEN DANCE
FRUITS BASKET
G GUNDAM

GATEKEEPERS
GETBACKERS
GIRL GOT GAME
GIRLS' EDUCATIONAL CHARTER
GRAVITATION
GTO
GUNDAM BLUE DESTINY
GUNDAM SEED ASTRAY
GUNDAM WING
GUNDAM WING: BATTLEFIELD OF PACIFISTS
GUNDAM WING: ENDLESS WALTZ
GUNDAM WING: THE LAST OUTPOST (G-UNIT)
GUYS' GUIDE TO GIRLS
HANDS OFF!
HAPPY MANIA
HARLEM BEAT
I.N.V.U.
IMMORTAL RAIN
INITIAL D
INSTANT TEEN: JUST ADD NUTS
ISLAND
JING: KING OF BANDITS
JING: KING OF BANDITS - TWILIGHT TALES
JULINE
KARE KANO
KILL ME, KISS ME
KINDAICHI CASE FILES, THE
KING OF HELL
KODOCHA: SANA'S STAGE
LAMENT OF THE LAMB
LEGAL DRUG
LEGEND OF CHUN HYANG, THE
LES BIJOUX
LOVE HINA
LUPIN III
LUPIN III: WORLD'S MOST WANTED
MAGIC KNIGHT RAYEARTH I
MAGIC KNIGHT RAYEARTH II
MAHOROMATIC: AUTOMATIC MAIDEN
MAN OF MANY FACES
MARMALADE BOY
MARS
MARS: HORSE WITH NO NAME
MINK
MIRACLE GIRLS
MIYUKI-CHAN IN WONDERLAND
MODEL
MY LOVE
NECK AND NECK
ONE
ONE I LOVE, THE
PARADISE KISS
PARASYTE
PASSION FRUIT
PEACH GIRL
PEACH GIRL: CHANGE OF HEART
PET SHOP OF HORRORS
PITA-TEN

04.23.04T

Translator - Beni Axia Hirayama
English Adaptation - Marion Brown
Copy Editor - Suzanne Waldman
Retouch and Lettering - Eva Han
Cover Layout - Patrick Hook
Graphic Designer - Yoohae Yang

Editor - Julie Taylor
Digital Imaging Manager - Chris Buford
Pre-Press Manager - Antonio DePietro
Production Managers - Jennifer Miller, Mutsumi Miyazaki
Art Director - Matt Alford
Managing Editor - Jill Freshney
VP of Production - Ron Klamert
President & C.O.O. - John Parker
Publisher & C.E.O. - Stuart Levy

E-mail: info@TOKYOPOP.com
Come visit us online at www.TOKYOPOP.com

A  Manga

TOKYOPOP Inc.
5900 Wilshire Blvd. Suite 2000
Los Angeles, CA 90036

Wild Act Vol. 7

ISBN: 1-59182-565-2

First TOKYOPOP printing: July 2004

10 9 8 7 6 5 4 3 2 1
Printed in the USA

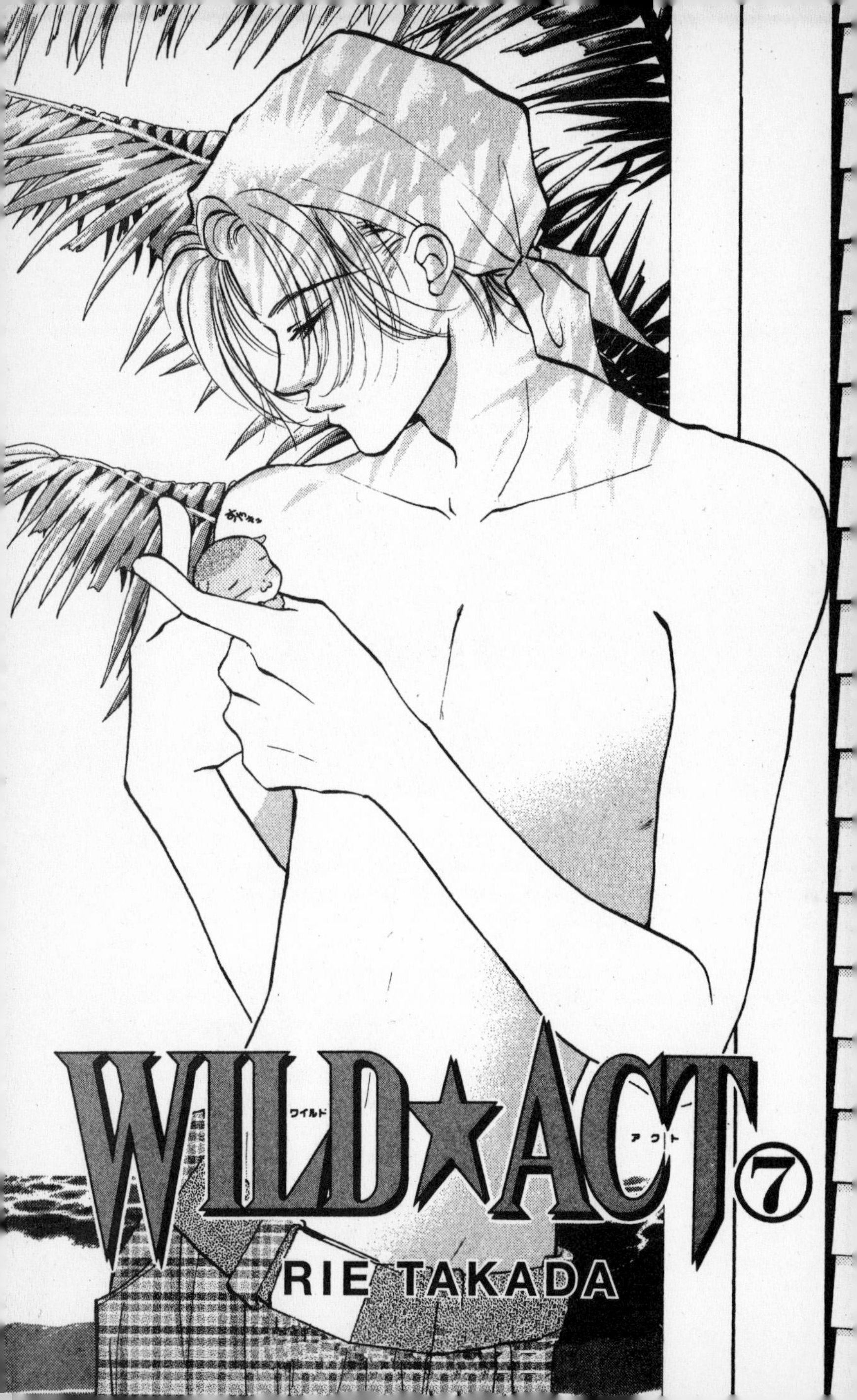
WILD★ACT
ワイルド
アクト
7
RIE TAKADA

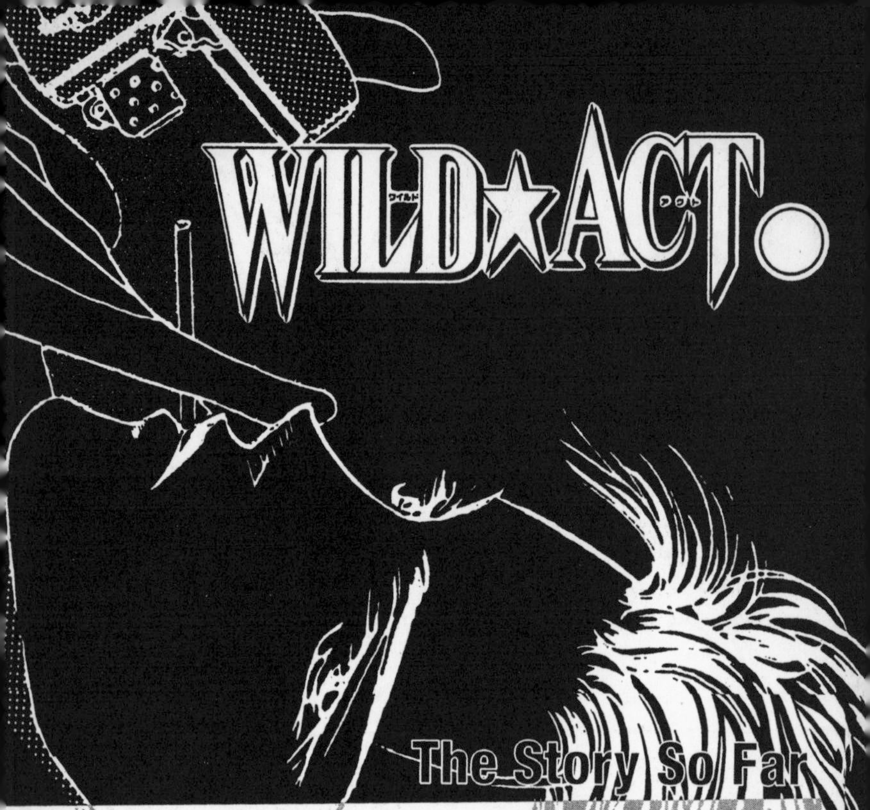
WILD★ACT.
The Story So Far

Yuniko Sakuraba is a 15-year-old girl. She's the daughter of the late, great actor Akira Nanae—and is also his biggest fan. In fact, she's so obsessed with him that she even resorts to stealing his long-lost mementos. She met the popular actor Ryu Eba during one of her heists and is now his girlfriend.
One day, people begin to suspect that Ryu and Yuniko are siblings. To make this rumor disappear, Yuniko and Ryu do everything they can to help Yuniko's amnesic mother, Maiko Sakura, regain her memory. To aid in this mission, they collect items pictured in Akira and Maiko's treasured photographs hoping to jog her memory.
One of these mementos leads Yuniko and Ryu to Bob Parker, who was Akira Nanae's agent at one time. Bob invites Ryu to move to Hollywood so he can make him an even bigger star, and Ryu accepts. Yuniko can't decide whether to support Ryu's dream or freak out over the fact she's going to be separated from him.
When the former paparazzi pest Maki consoles Yuniko, Ryu explodes in a fit of rage. Yuniko runs away into the city and is assaulted by a group of hooligans, but the one who saved her was not Ryu, but Maki...

Akira Nanae
The first Japanese actor
to star in a Hollywood movie.
He died in a tragic accident
when he was only 25.

Yuniko Sakuraba
The daughter of Akira
Nanae—and his biggest fan.
She is currently stealing back
her deceased father's
mementos, which were
stolen by zealous fans.

Ryu Eba
A popular 17-year-old actor.
He is called "the new Akira,"
but he hates it when people
call him that!

Maki Tatsumi
He was after a scoop about
Yuniko and Ryu to try to raise
money for his mother's surgery.
As of now, he's quit being a
member of the paparazzi.

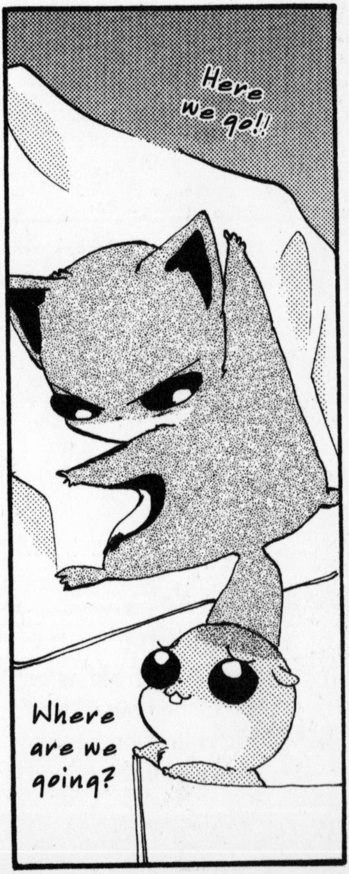
Here we go!!
Where are we going?

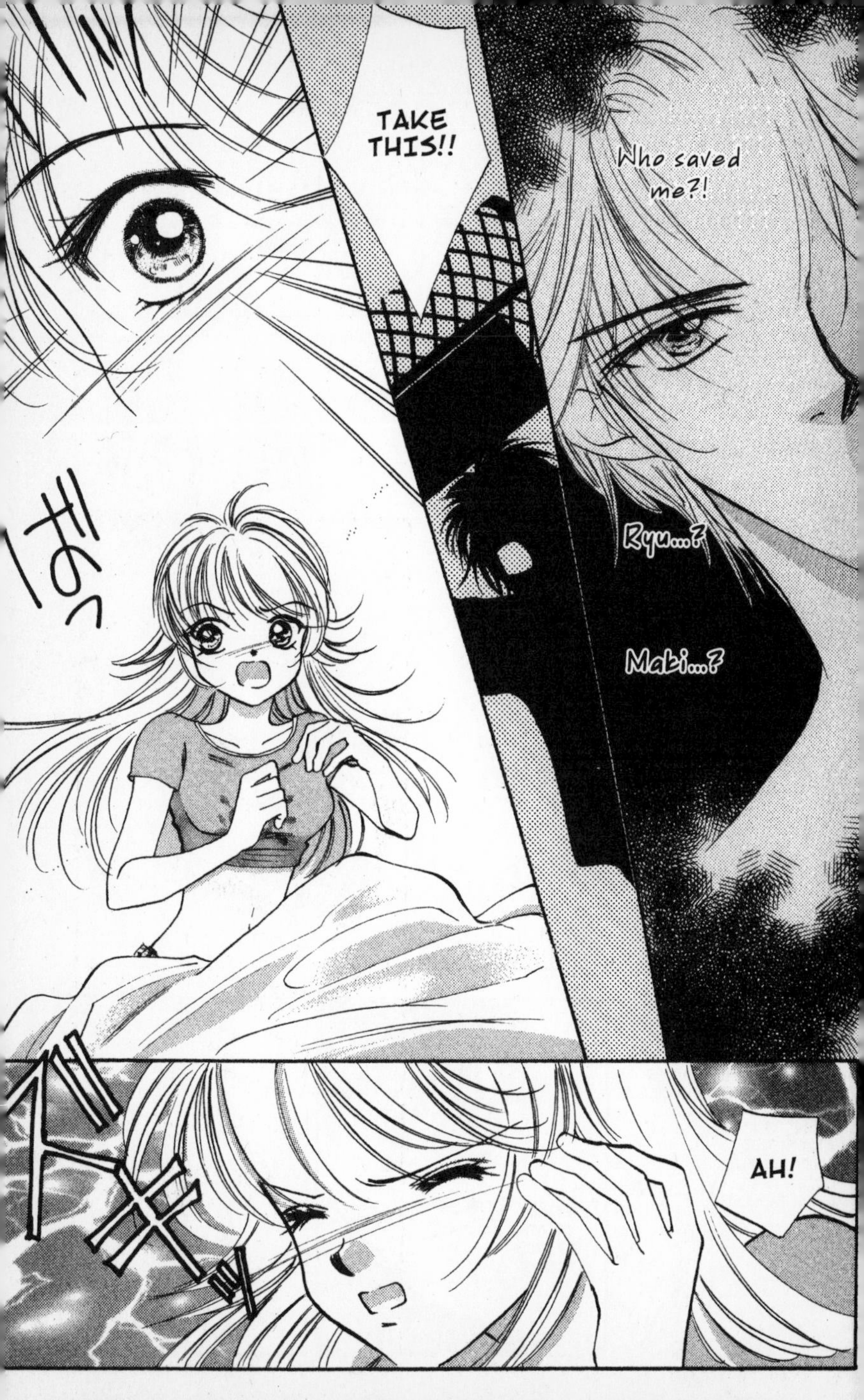
Who saved me?!
Ryu...?
Maki...?
TAKE THIS!!
ぱっ
AH!

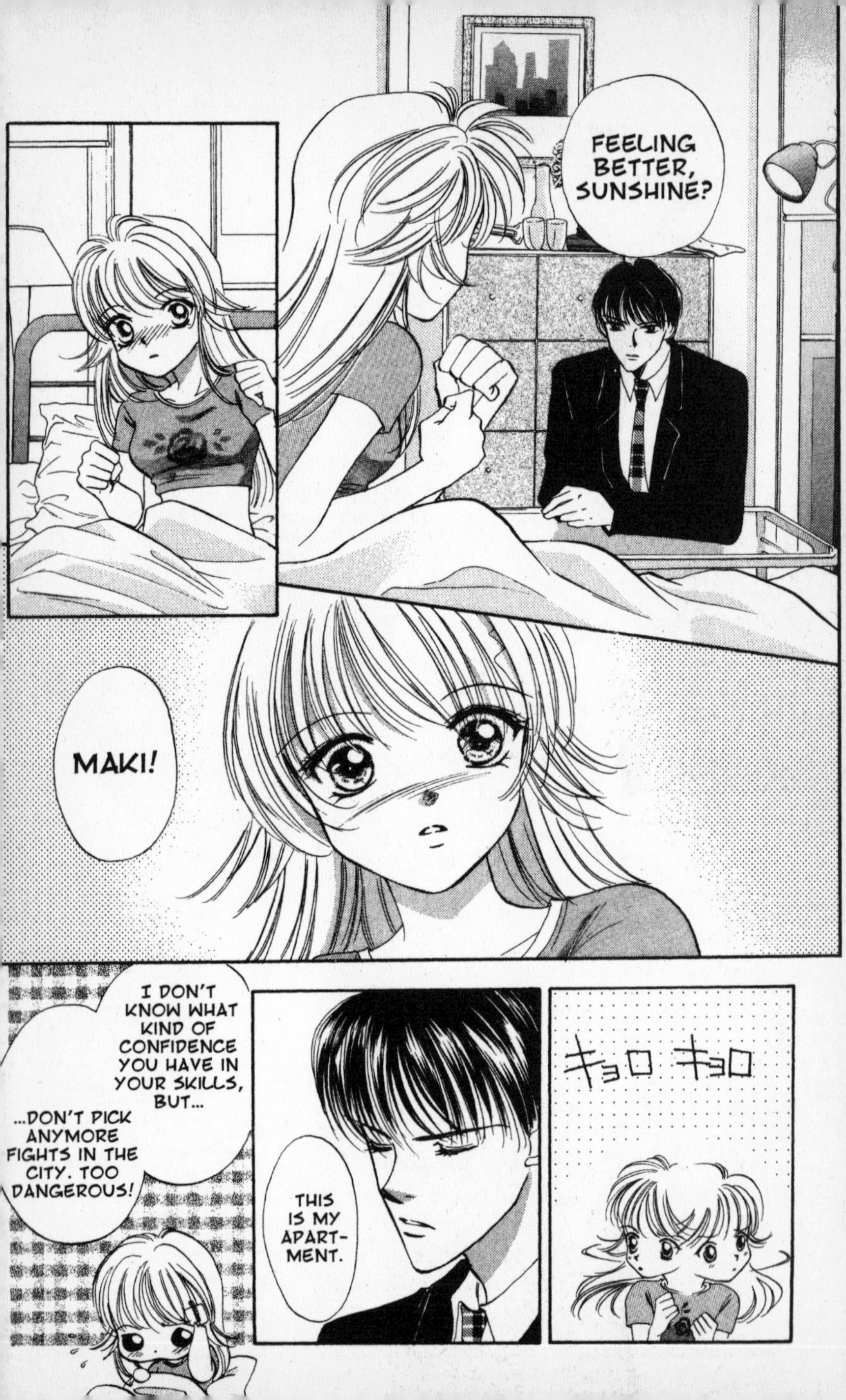
FEELING BETTER, SUNSHINE?
MAKI!
キョロ キョロ
THIS IS MY APARTMENT.
I DON'T KNOW WHAT KIND OF CONFIDENCE YOU HAVE IN YOUR SKILLS, BUT...
...DON'T PICK ANYMORE FIGHTS IN THE CITY. TOO DANGEROUS!

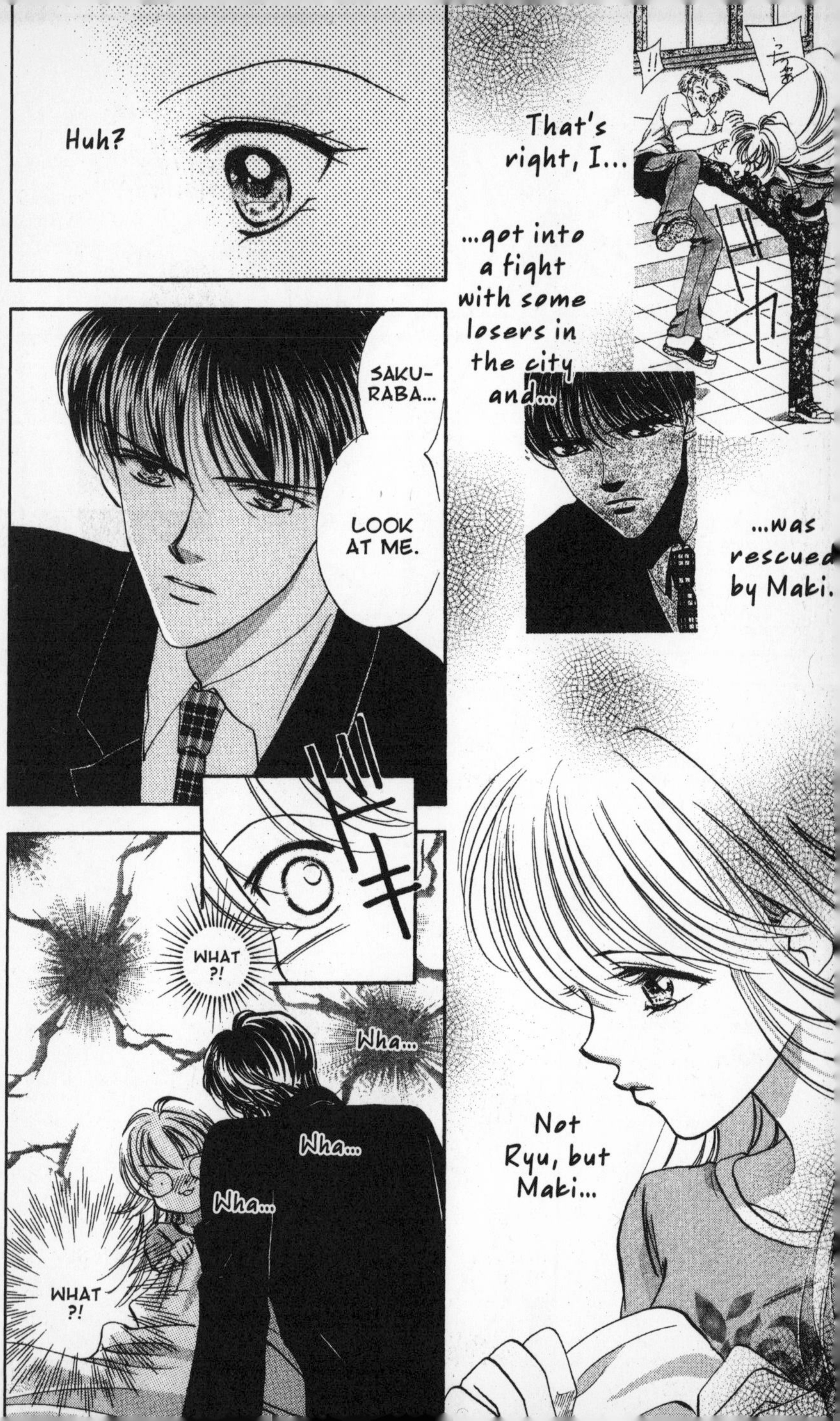

That's right, I...
...got into a fight with some losers in the city and...
...was rescued by Maki.
Not Ryu, but Maki...
Huh?
SAKURABA...
LOOK AT ME.
WHAT ?!
Wha...
Wha...
Wha...
WHAT ?!

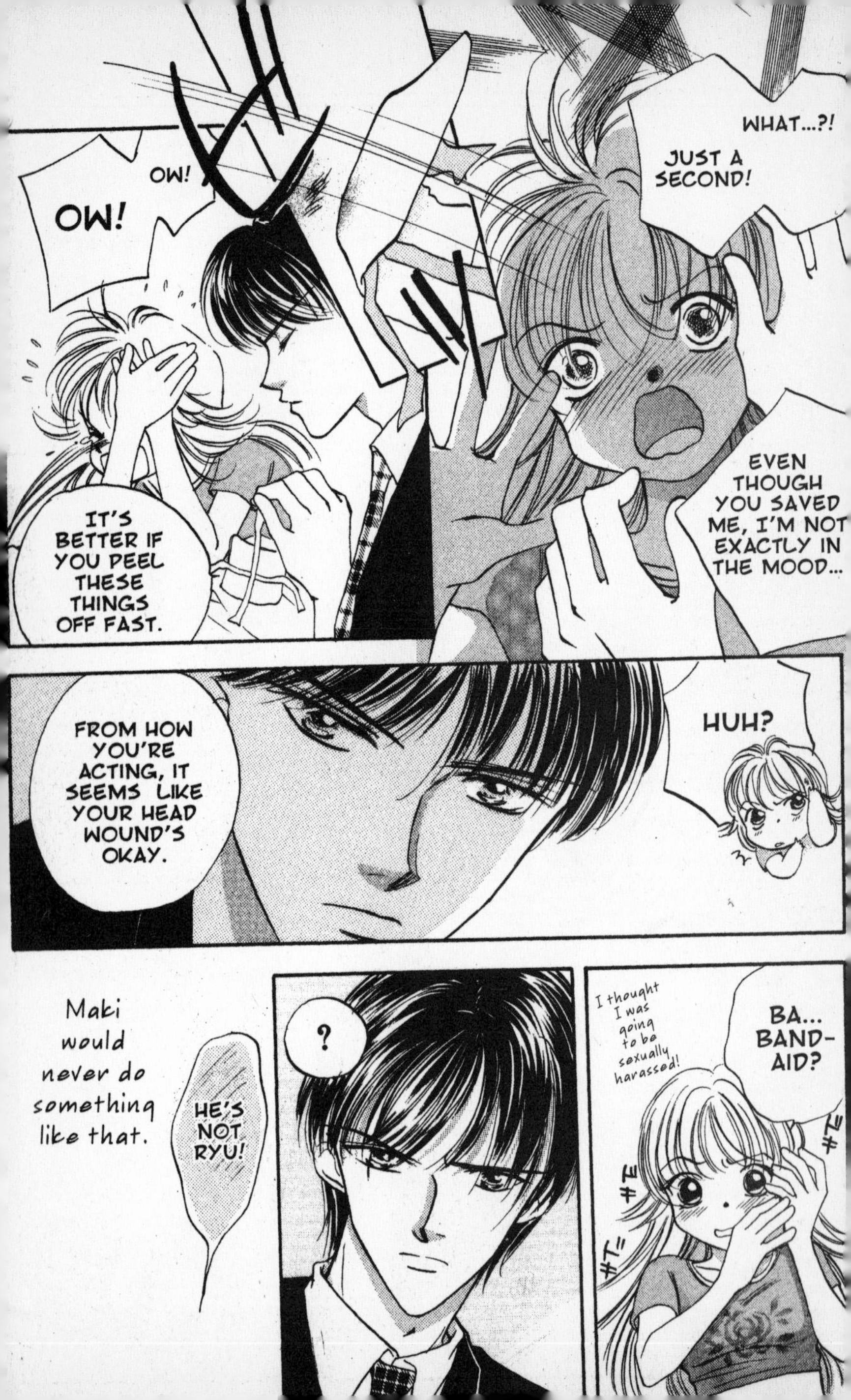
WHAT...?!
JUST A SECOND!
EVEN THOUGH YOU SAVED ME, I'M NOT EXACTLY IN THE MOOD...
OW!
OW!
IT'S BETTER IF YOU PEEL THESE THINGS OFF FAST.
HUH?
FROM HOW YOU'RE ACTING, IT SEEMS LIKE YOUR HEAD WOUND'S OKAY.
BA... BAND-AID?
I thought I was going to be sexually harassed!
?
HE'S NOT RYU!
Maki would never do something like that.

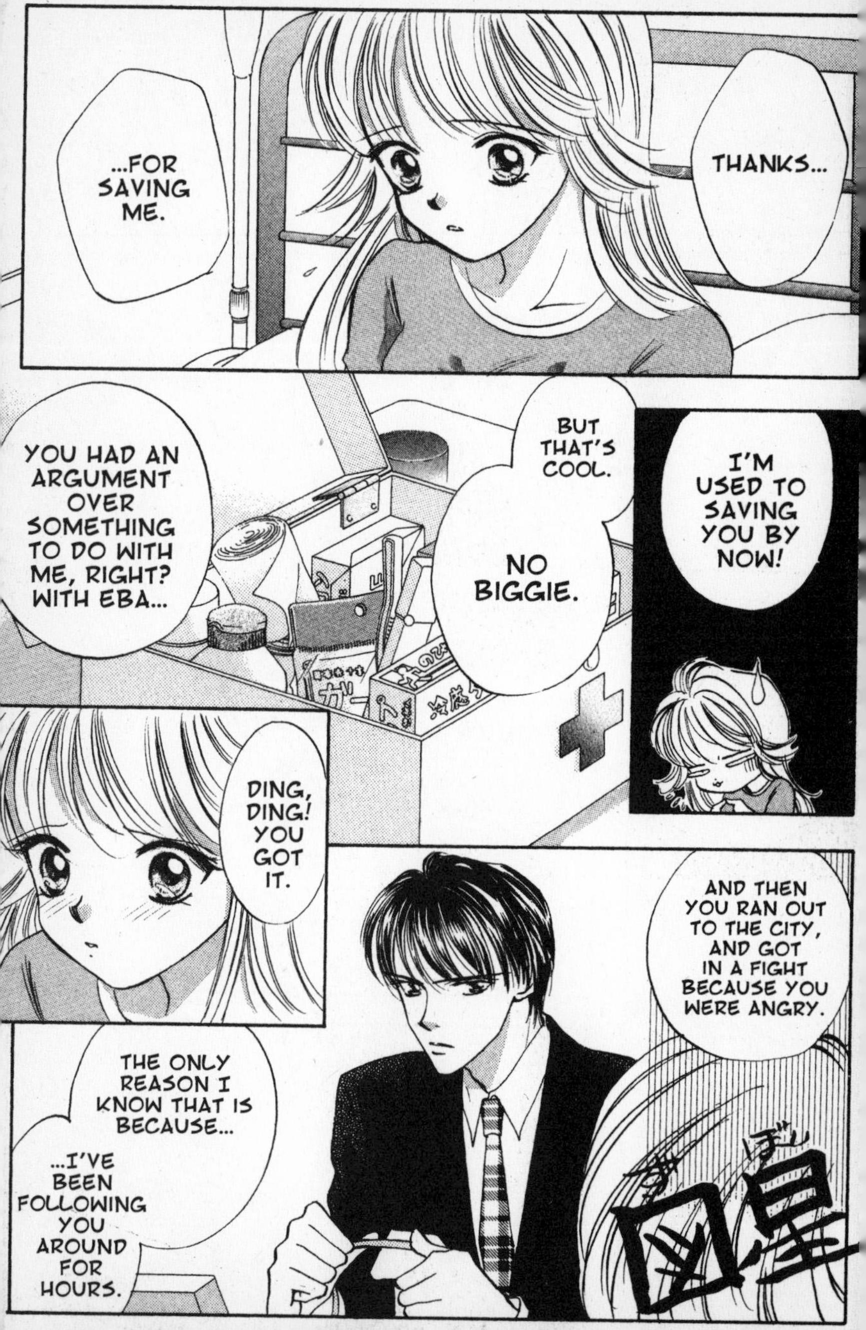
THANKS...
...FOR SAVING ME.
I'M USED TO SAVING YOU BY NOW!
BUT THAT'S COOL.
NO BIGGIE.
YOU HAD AN ARGUMENT OVER SOMETHING TO DO WITH ME, RIGHT? WITH EBA...
DING, DING! YOU GOT IT.
AND THEN YOU RAN OUT TO THE CITY, AND GOT IN A FIGHT BECAUSE YOU WERE ANGRY.
THE ONLY REASON I KNOW THAT IS BECAUSE...
...I'VE BEEN FOLLOWING YOU AROUND FOR HOURS.

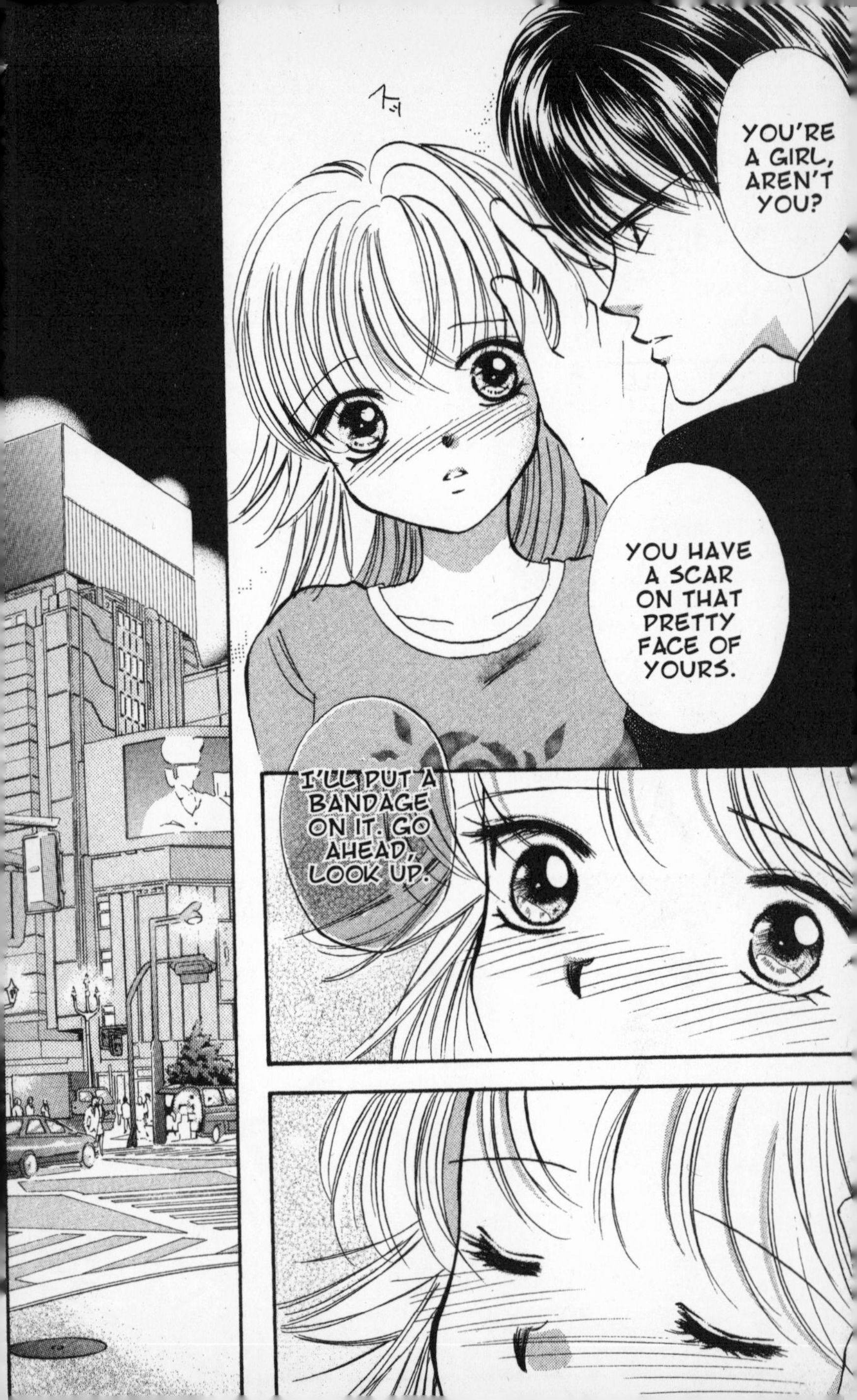
YOU'RE A GIRL, AREN'T YOU?
YOU HAVE A SCAR ON THAT PRETTY FACE OF YOURS.
I'LL PUT A BANDAGE ON IT. GO AHEAD, LOOK UP.

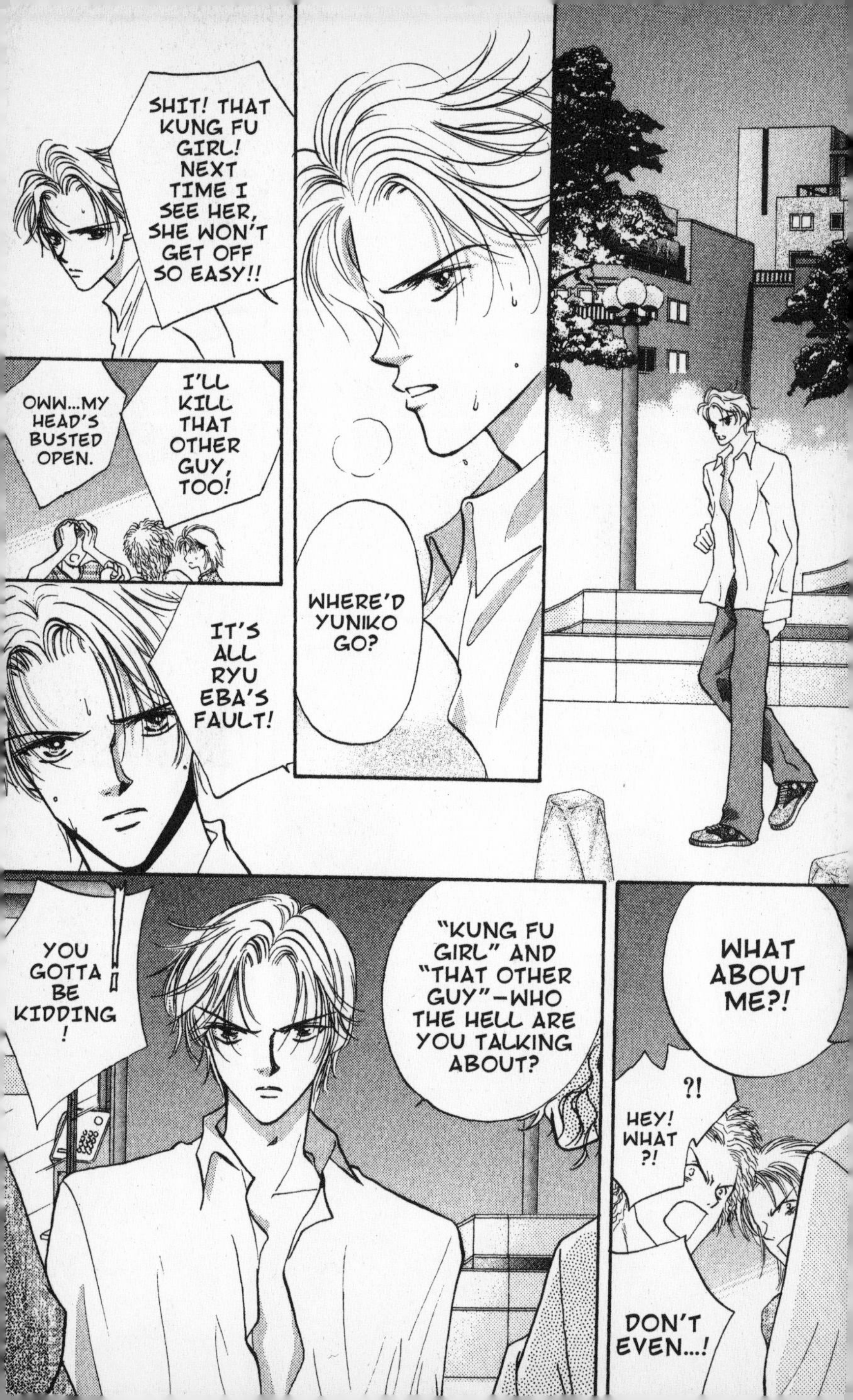
WHERE'D YUNIKO GO?
SHIT! THAT KUNG FU GIRL! NEXT TIME I SEE HER, SHE WON'T GET OFF SO EASY!!
I'LL KILL THAT OTHER GUY, TOO!
OWW...MY HEAD'S BUSTED OPEN.
IT'S ALL RYU EBA'S FAULT!
WHAT ABOUT ME?!
?!
HEY! WHAT?!
DON'T EVEN...!
"KUNG FU GIRL" AND "THAT OTHER GUY"—WHO THE HELL ARE YOU TALKING ABOUT?
YOU GOTTA BE KIDDING!

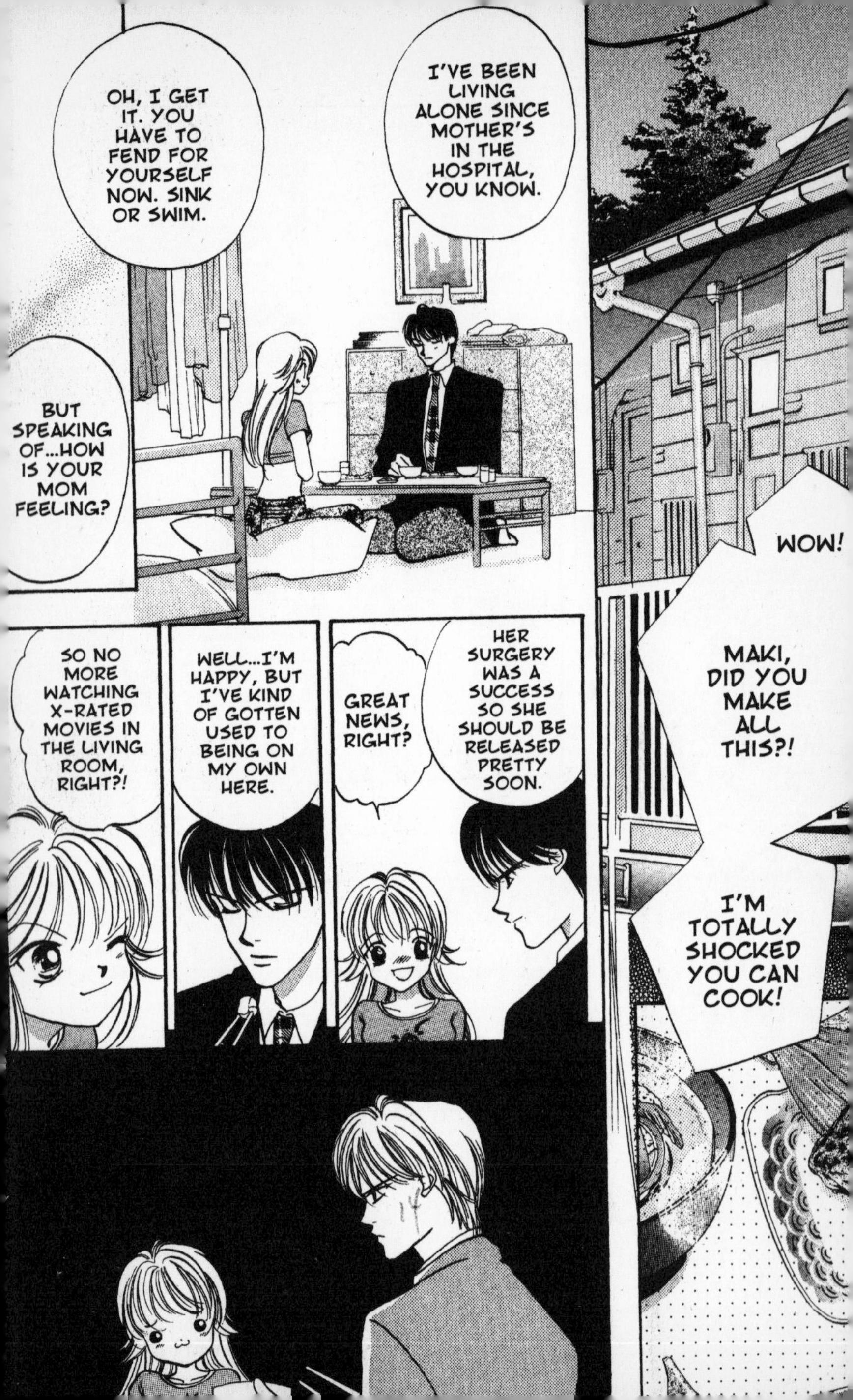
WOW!
MAKI, DID YOU MAKE ALL THIS?!
I'M TOTALLY SHOCKED YOU CAN COOK!
I'VE BEEN LIVING ALONE SINCE MOTHER'S IN THE HOSPITAL, YOU KNOW.
OH, I GET IT. YOU HAVE TO FEND FOR YOURSELF NOW. SINK OR SWIM.
BUT SPEAKING OF...HOW IS YOUR MOM FEELING?
HER SURGERY WAS A SUCCESS SO SHE SHOULD BE RELEASED PRETTY SOON.
GREAT NEWS, RIGHT?
WELL...I'M HAPPY, BUT I'VE KIND OF GOTTEN USED TO BEING ON MY OWN HERE.
SO NO MORE WATCHING X-RATED MOVIES IN THE LIVING ROOM, RIGHT?!

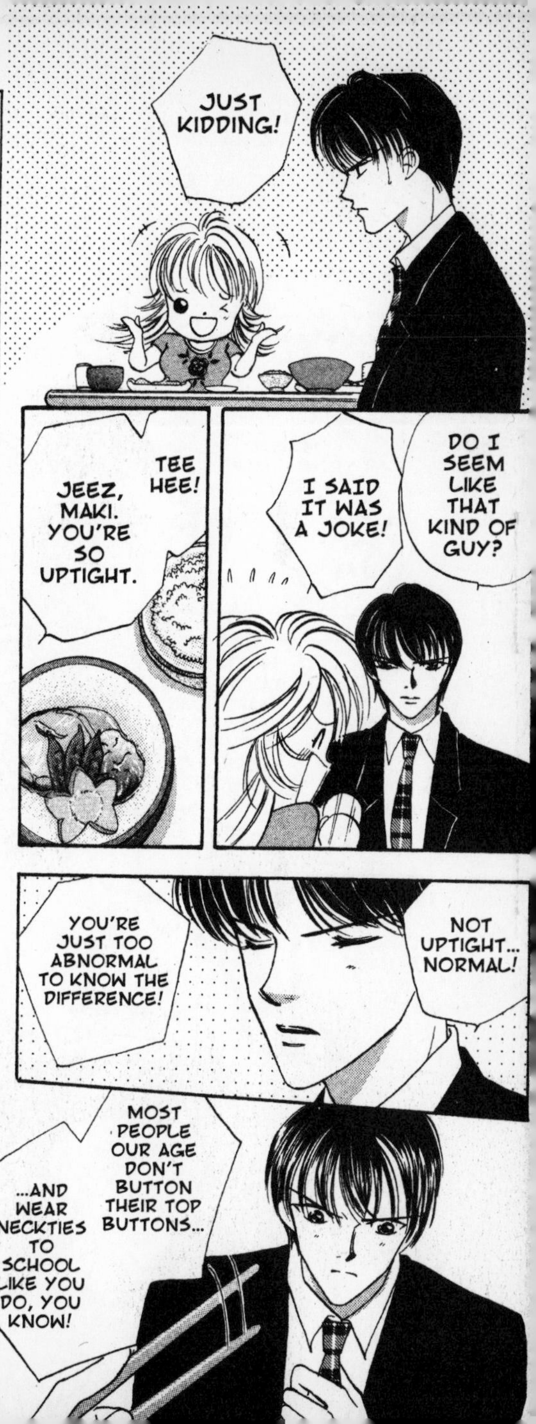
JUST KIDDING!
DO I SEEM LIKE THAT KIND OF GUY?
I SAID IT WAS A JOKE!
TEE HEE!
JEEZ, MAKI. YOU'RE SO UPTIGHT.
NOT UPTIGHT... NORMAL!
YOU'RE JUST TOO ABNORMAL TO KNOW THE DIFFERENCE!
MOST PEOPLE OUR AGE DON'T BUTTON THEIR TOP BUTTONS...
...AND WEAR NECKTIES TO SCHOOL LIKE YOU DO, YOU KNOW!

The Thing I Like Best About Myself:

My legs.

They're long and slender.

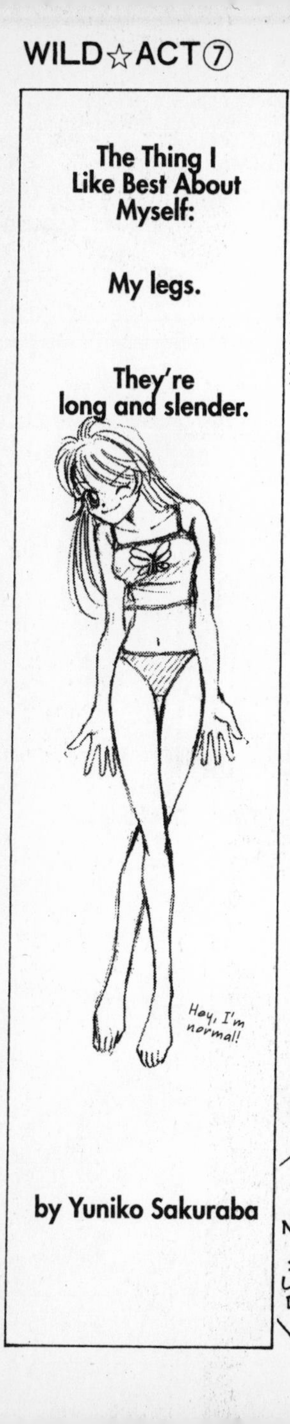
Hey, I'm normal!

by Yuniko Sakuraba

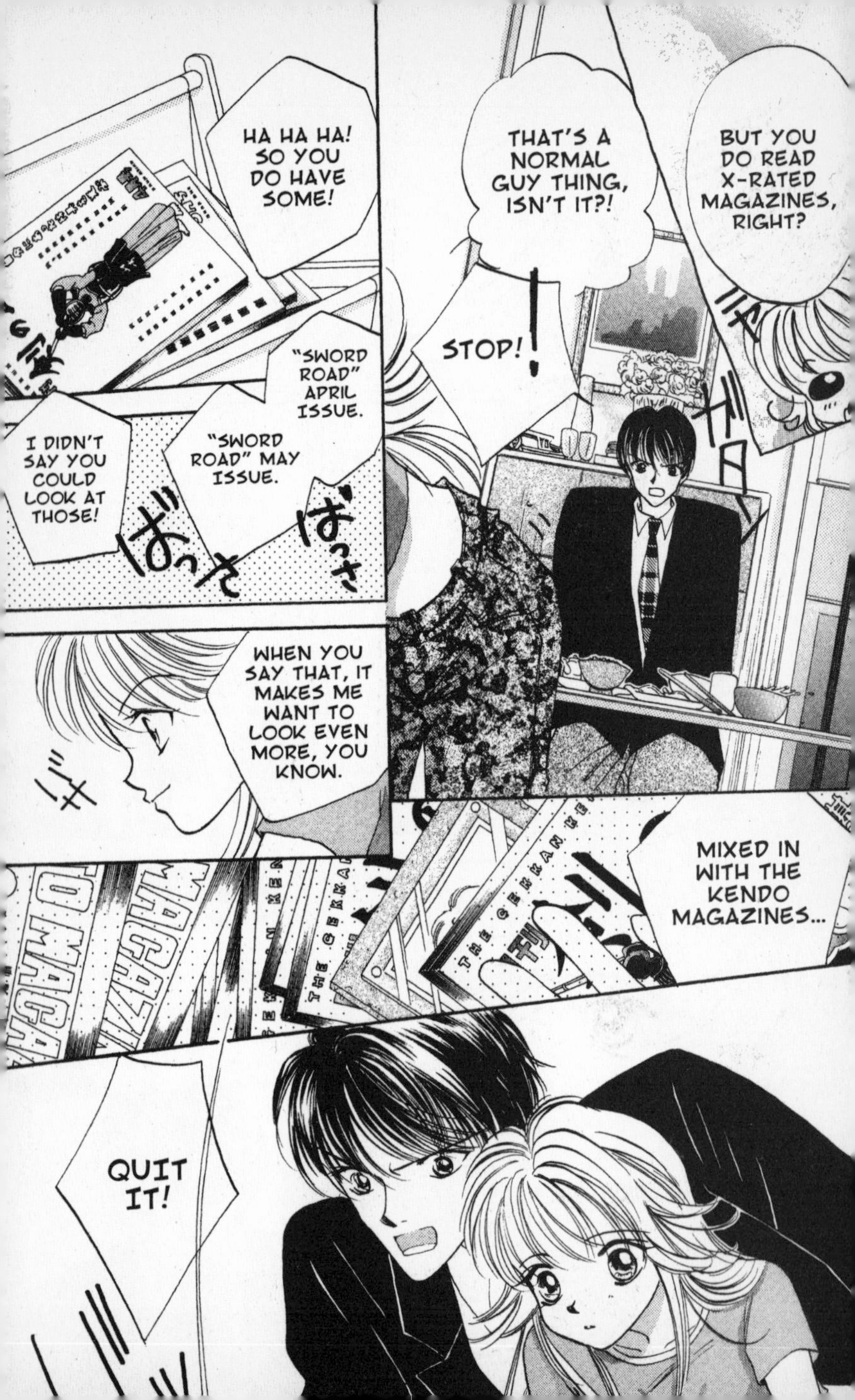
BUT YOU DO READ X-RATED MAGAZINES, RIGHT?
THAT'S A NORMAL GUY THING, ISN'T IT?!
STOP!
HA HA HA! SO YOU DO HAVE SOME!
"SWORD ROAD" APRIL ISSUE.
"SWORD ROAD" MAY ISSUE.
I DIDN'T SAY YOU COULD LOOK AT THOSE!
ばっさ
ばっさ
WHEN YOU SAY THAT, IT MAKES ME WANT TO LOOK EVEN MORE, YOU KNOW.
MIXED IN WITH THE KENDO MAGAZINES...
QUIT IT!

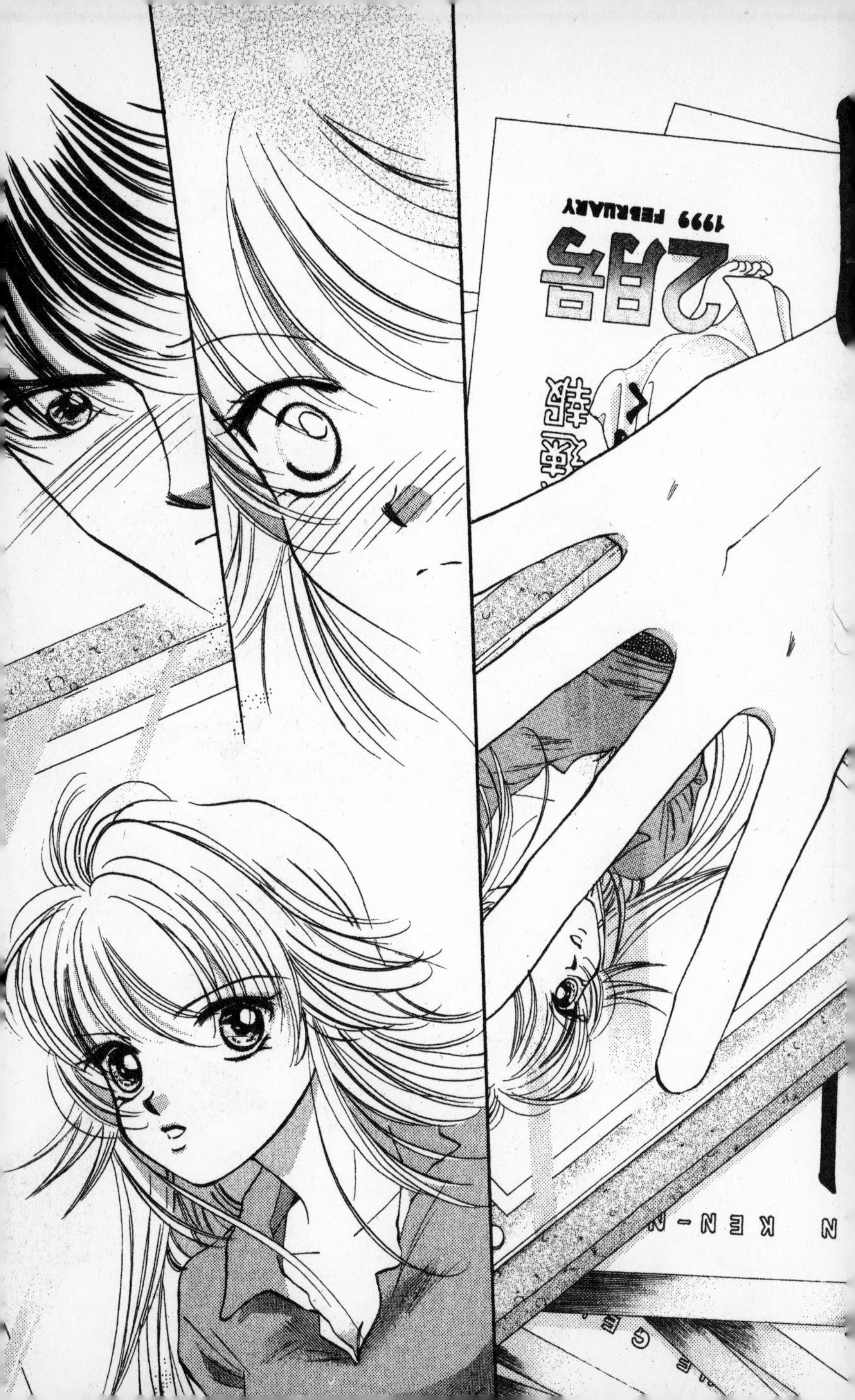
速報
2月号
1999 FEBRUARY
N KEN-N

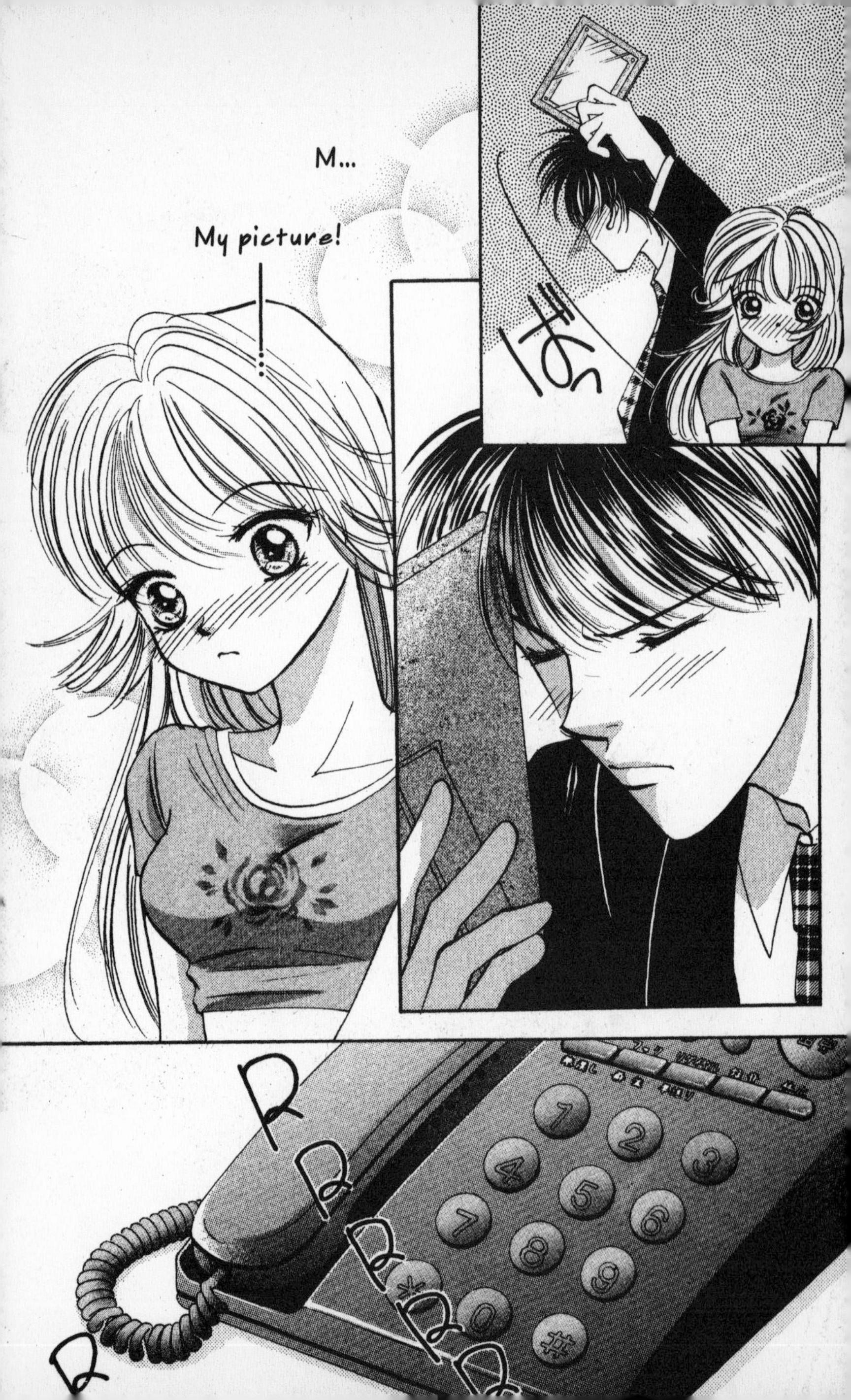
M...
My picture!
R R R R RRR R

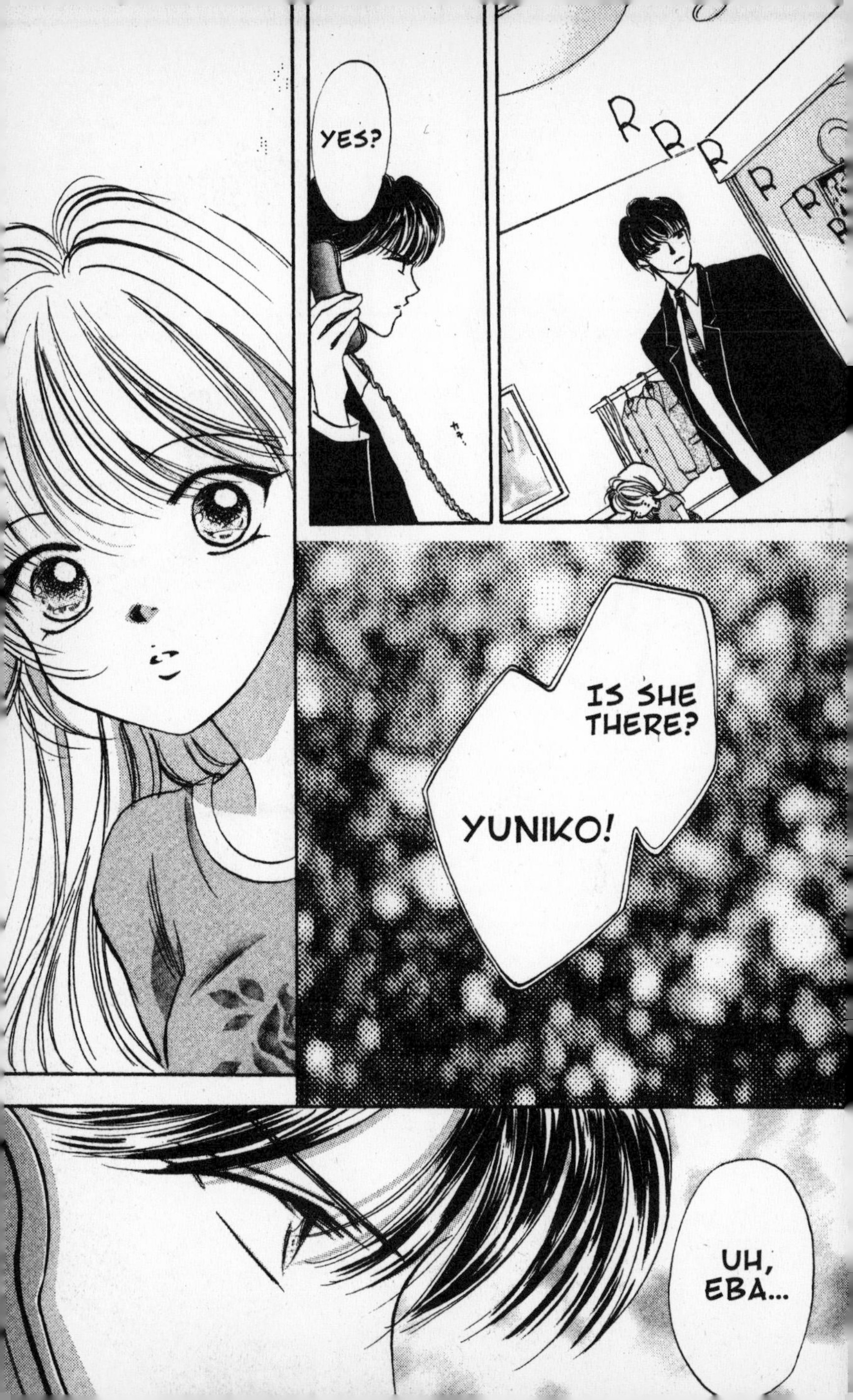
RRRRRR
YES?
IS SHE THERE?
YUNIKO!
UH, EBA...

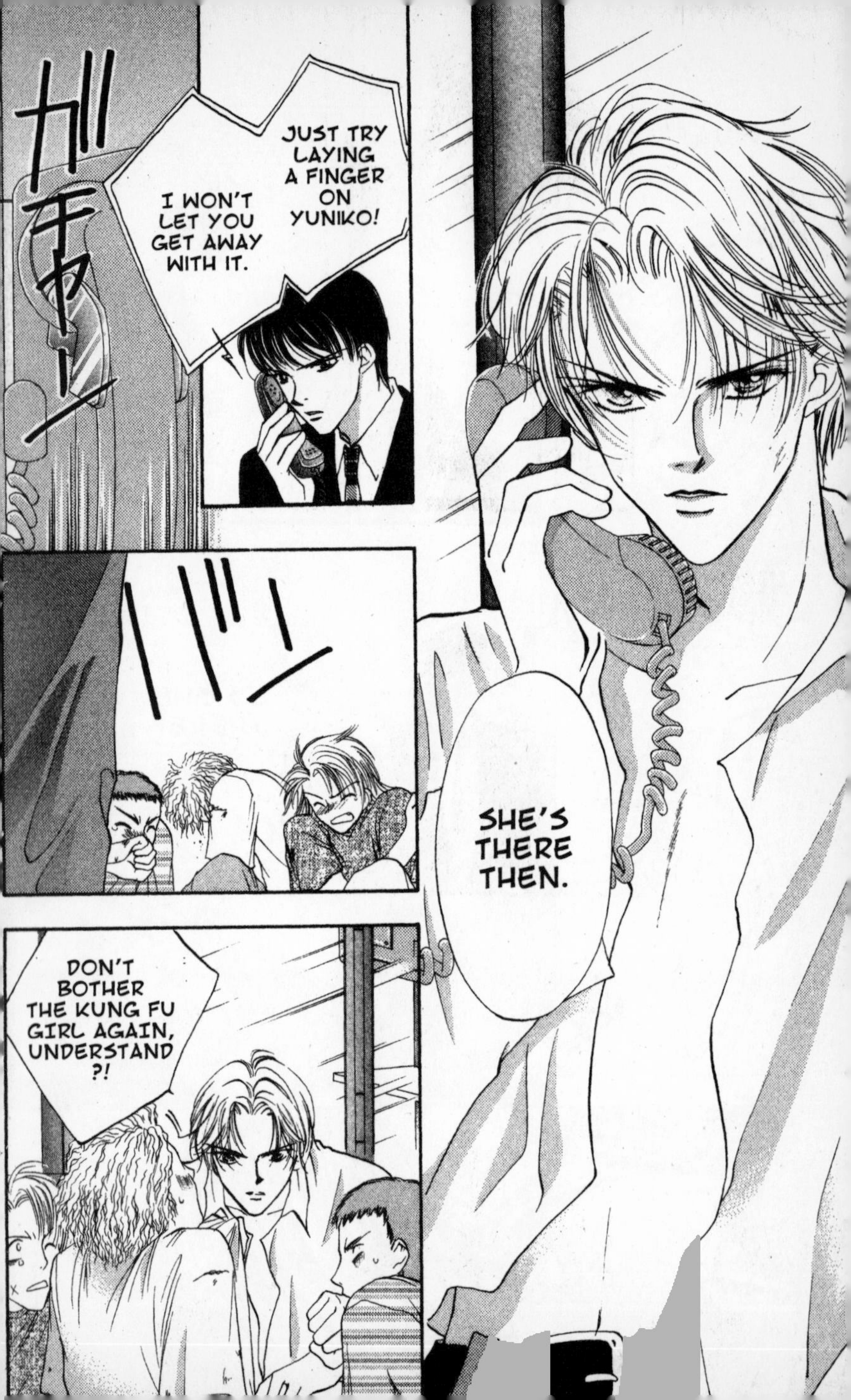
SHE'S THERE THEN.
JUST TRY LAYING A FINGER ON YUNIKO!
I WON'T LET YOU GET AWAY WITH IT.
ガチャーン
DON'T BOTHER THE KUNG FU GIRL AGAIN, UNDERSTAND ?!

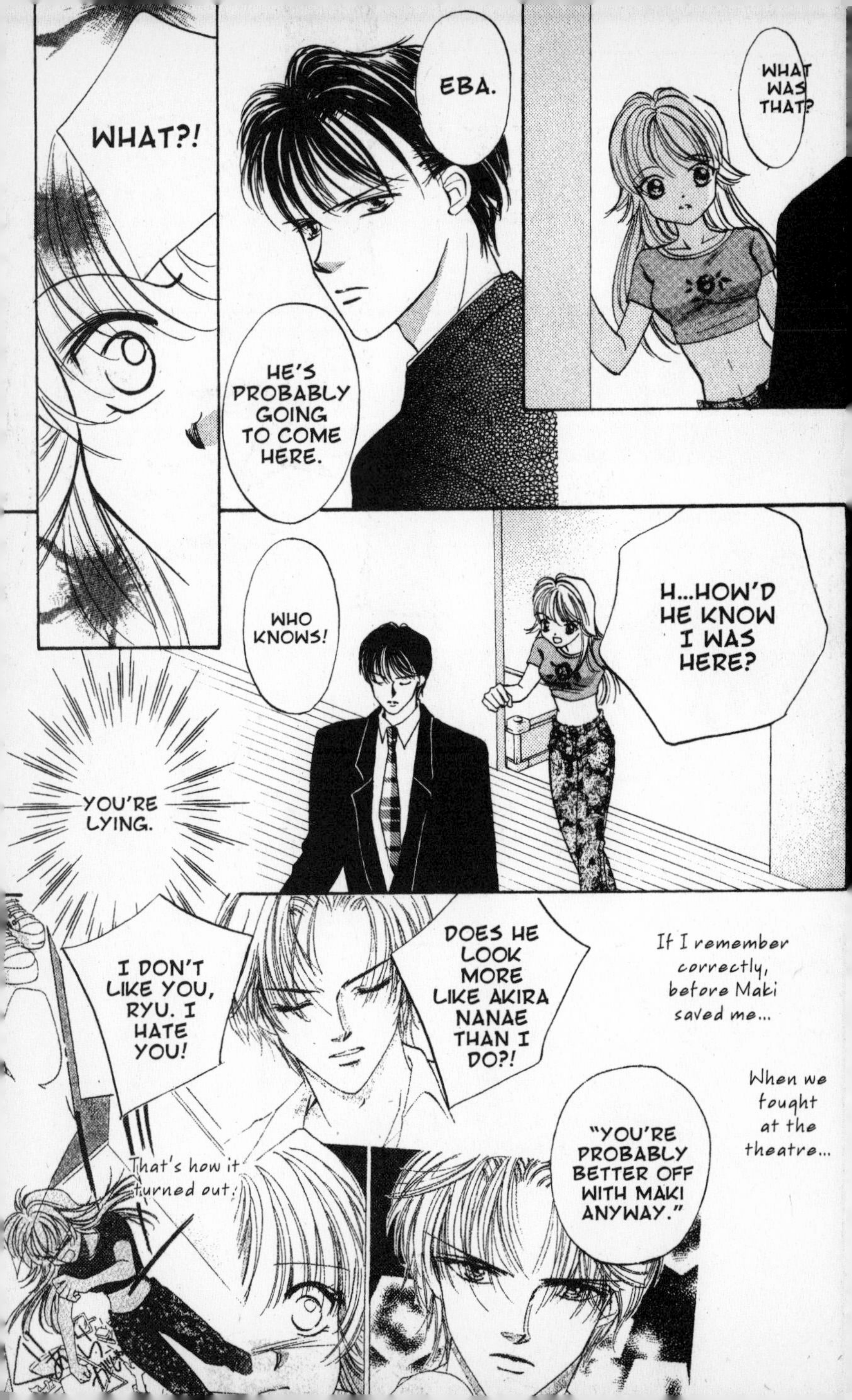
WHAT WAS THAT?
EBA.
HE'S PROBABLY GOING TO COME HERE.
WHAT?!
H...HOW'D HE KNOW I WAS HERE?
WHO KNOWS!
YOU'RE LYING.
If I remember correctly, before Maki saved me...
DOES HE LOOK MORE LIKE AKIRA NANAE THAN I DO?!
When we fought at the theatre...
I DON'T LIKE YOU, RYU. I HATE YOU!
"YOU'RE PROBABLY BETTER OFF WITH MAKI ANYWAY."
That's how it turned out.

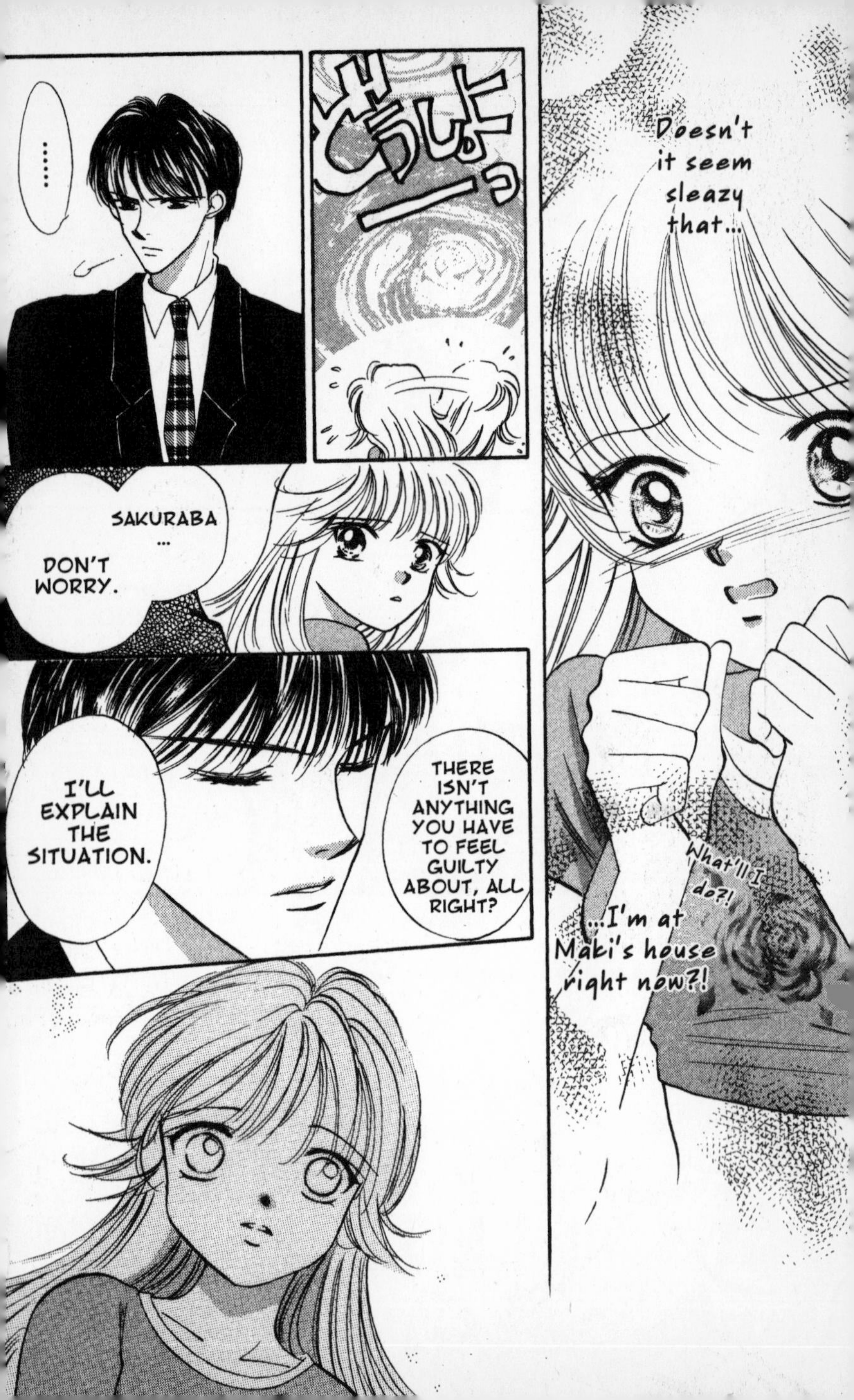

Doesn't it seem sleazy that...
...I'm at Maki's house right now?!
What'll I do?!
どうしよーっ
......
SAKURABA ...
DON'T WORRY.
THERE ISN'T ANYTHING YOU HAVE TO FEEL GUILTY ABOUT, ALL RIGHT?
I'LL EXPLAIN THE SITUATION.

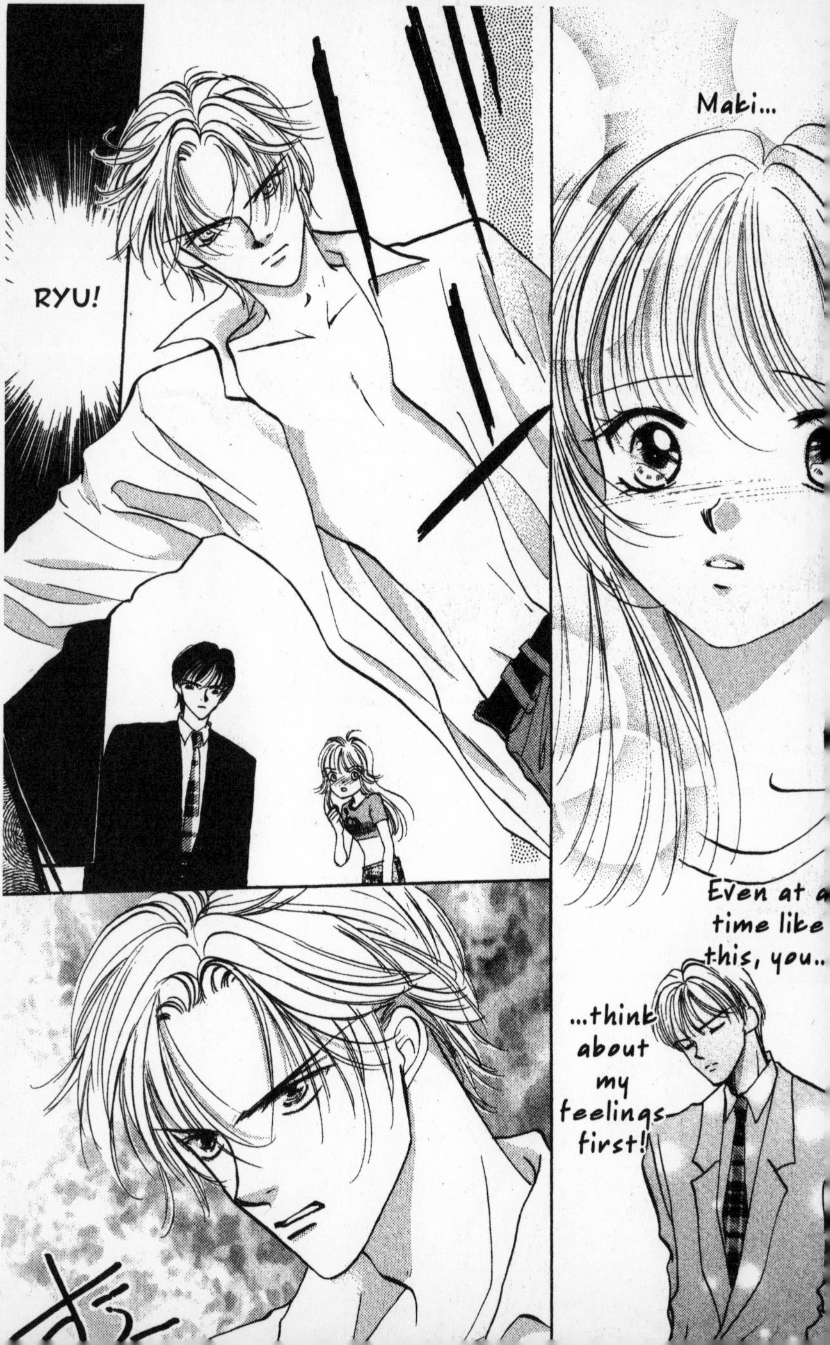

Maki...
Even at a time like this, you..
...think about my feelings first!
RYU!

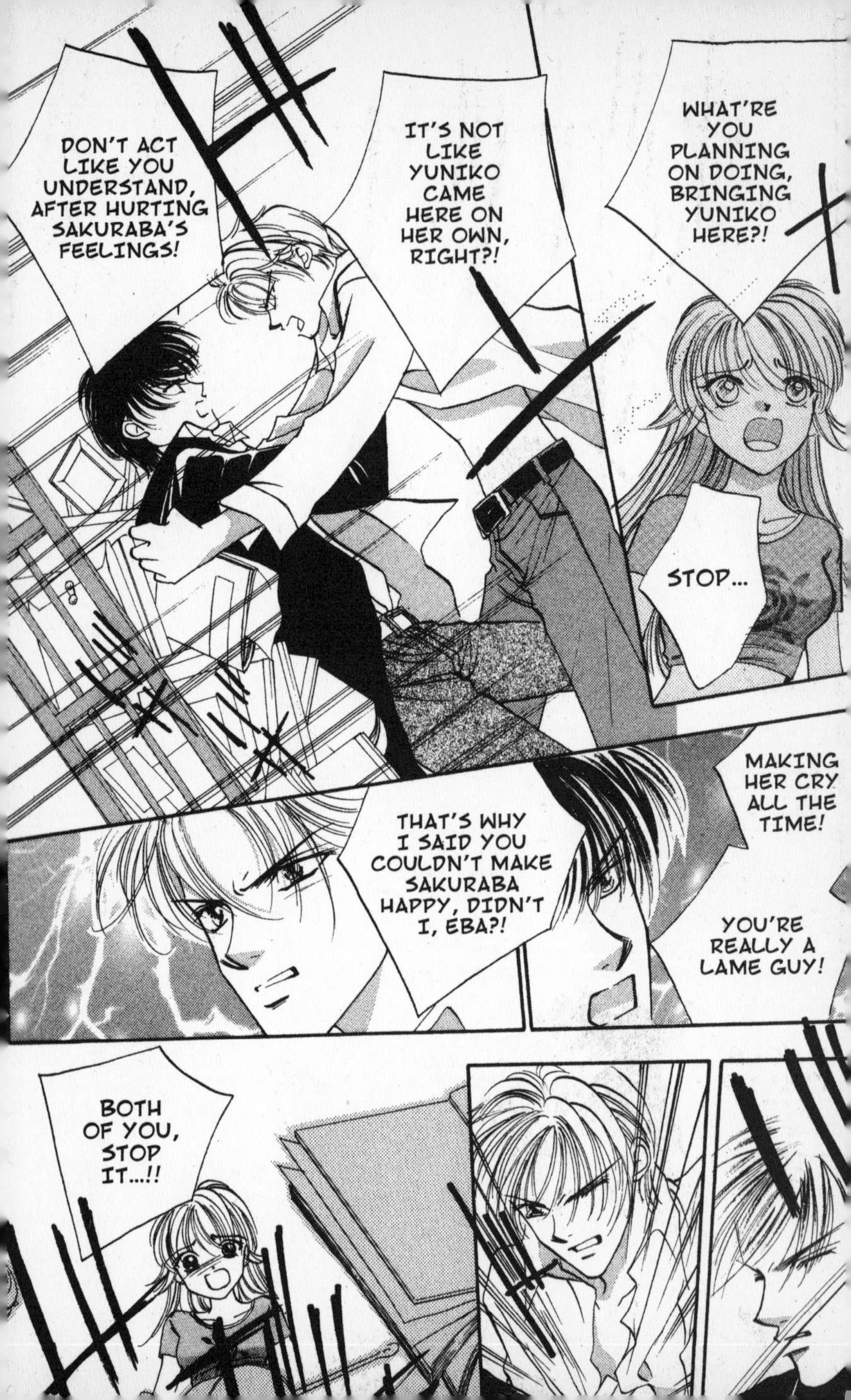
WHAT'RE YOU PLANNING ON DOING, BRINGING YUNIKO HERE?!
STOP...
IT'S NOT LIKE YUNIKO CAME HERE ON HER OWN, RIGHT?!
DON'T ACT LIKE YOU UNDERSTAND, AFTER HURTING SAKURABA'S FEELINGS!
MAKING HER CRY ALL THE TIME!
YOU'RE REALLY A LAME GUY!
THAT'S WHY I SAID YOU COULDN'T MAKE SAKURABA HAPPY, DIDN'T I, EBA?!
BOTH OF YOU, STOP IT...!!

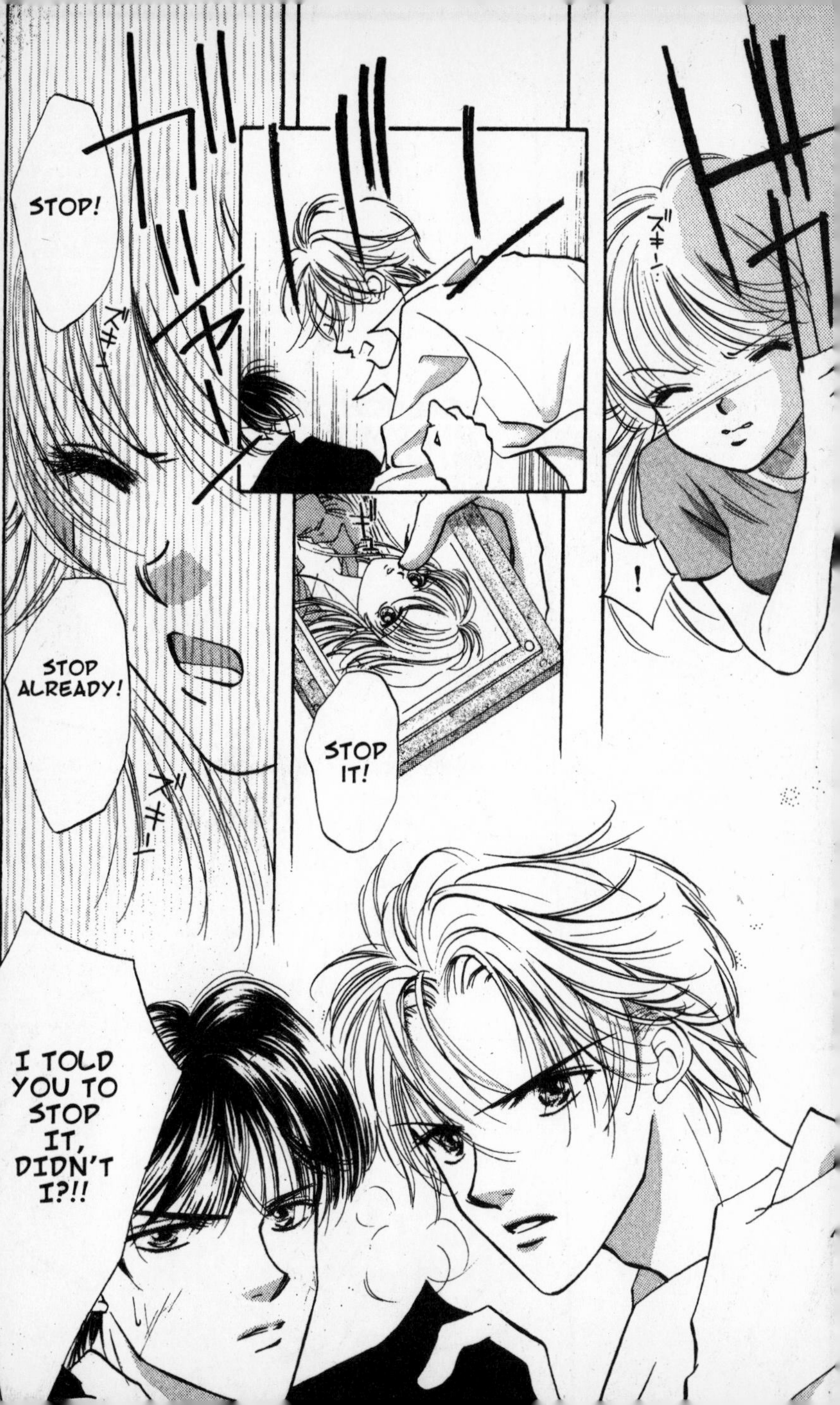
!
STOP IT!
STOP!
STOP ALREADY!
I TOLD YOU TO STOP IT, DIDN'T I?!!

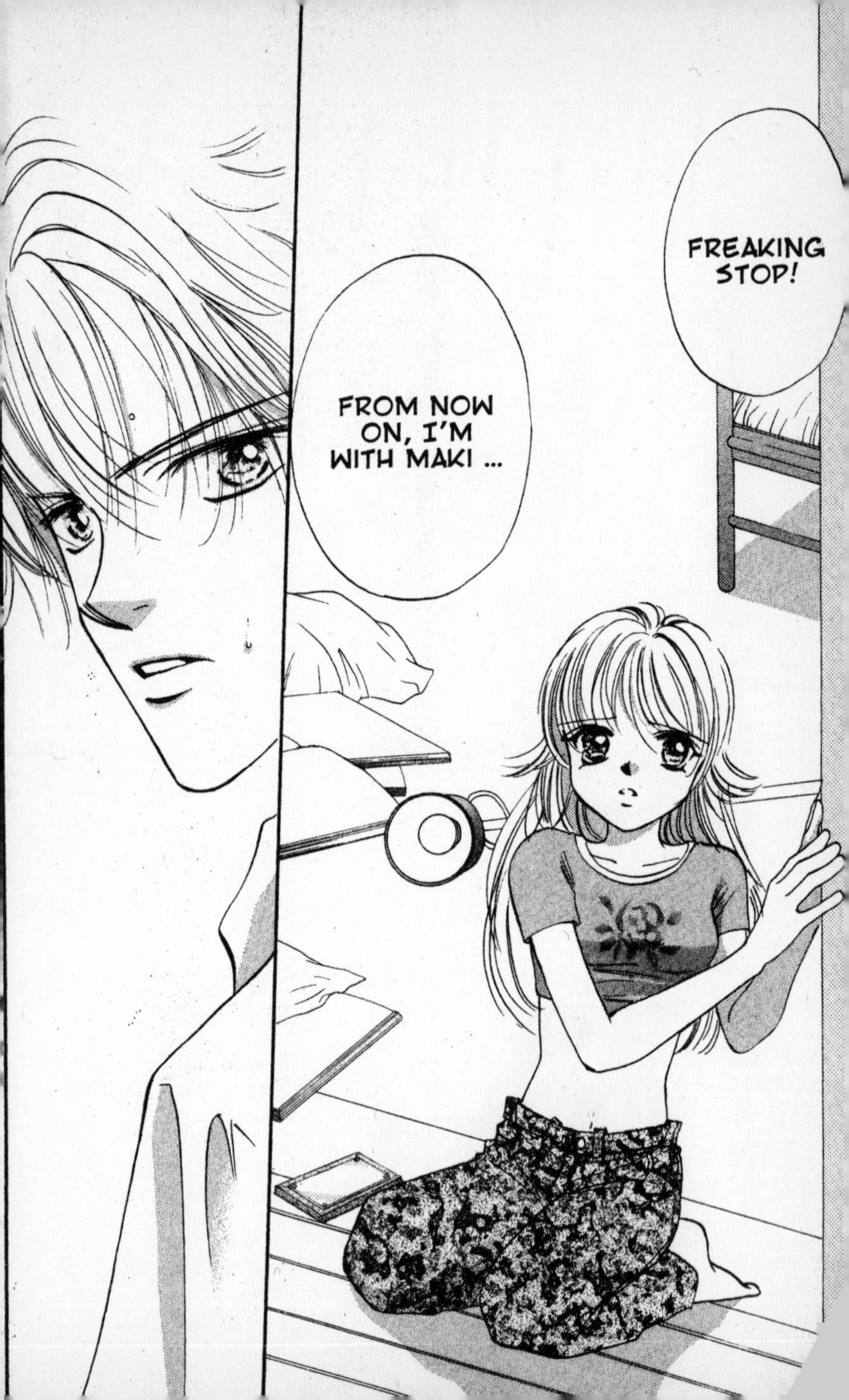
FREAKING STOP!
FROM NOW ON, I'M WITH MAKI ...

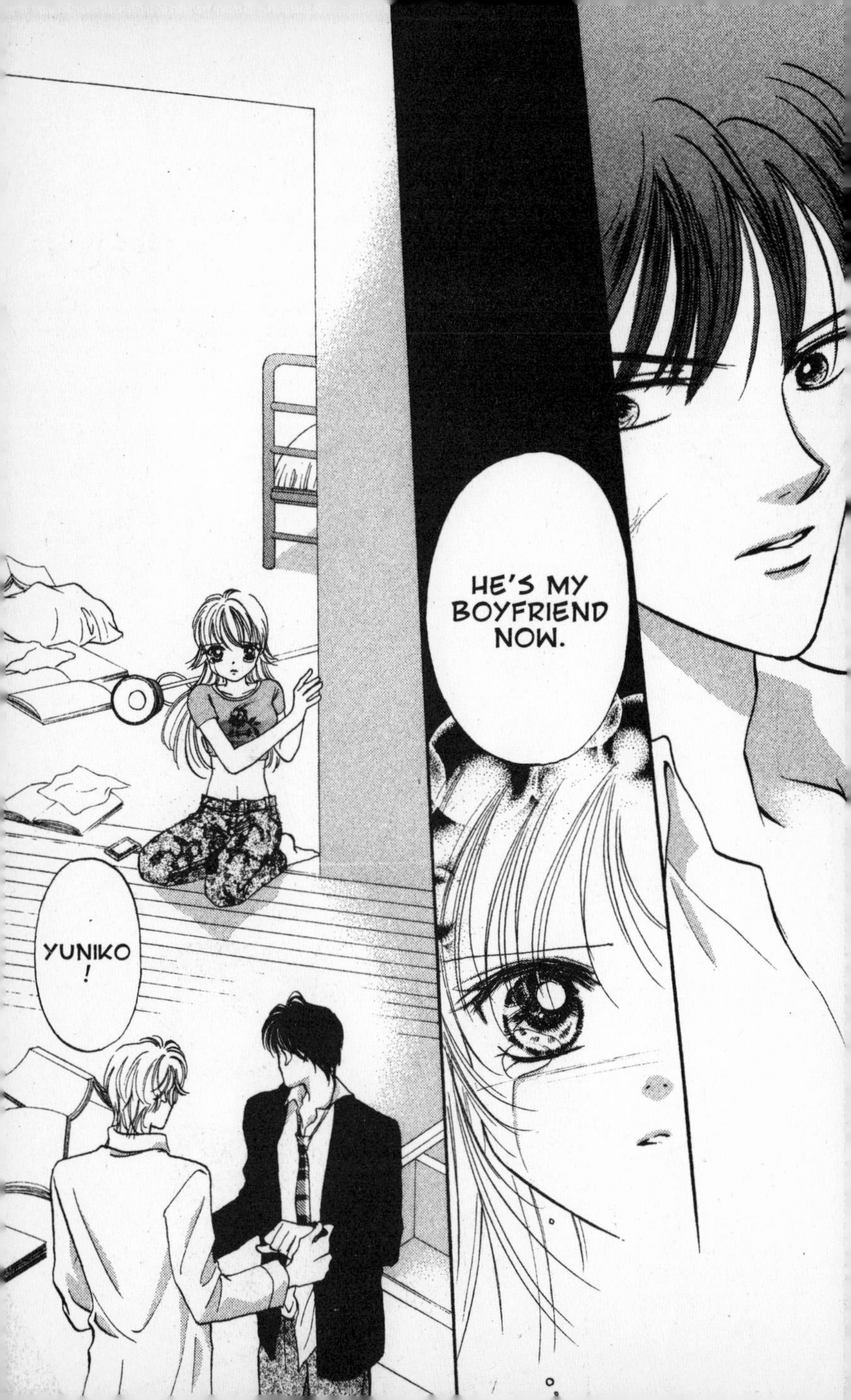
HE'S MY BOYFRIEND NOW.
YUNIKO!

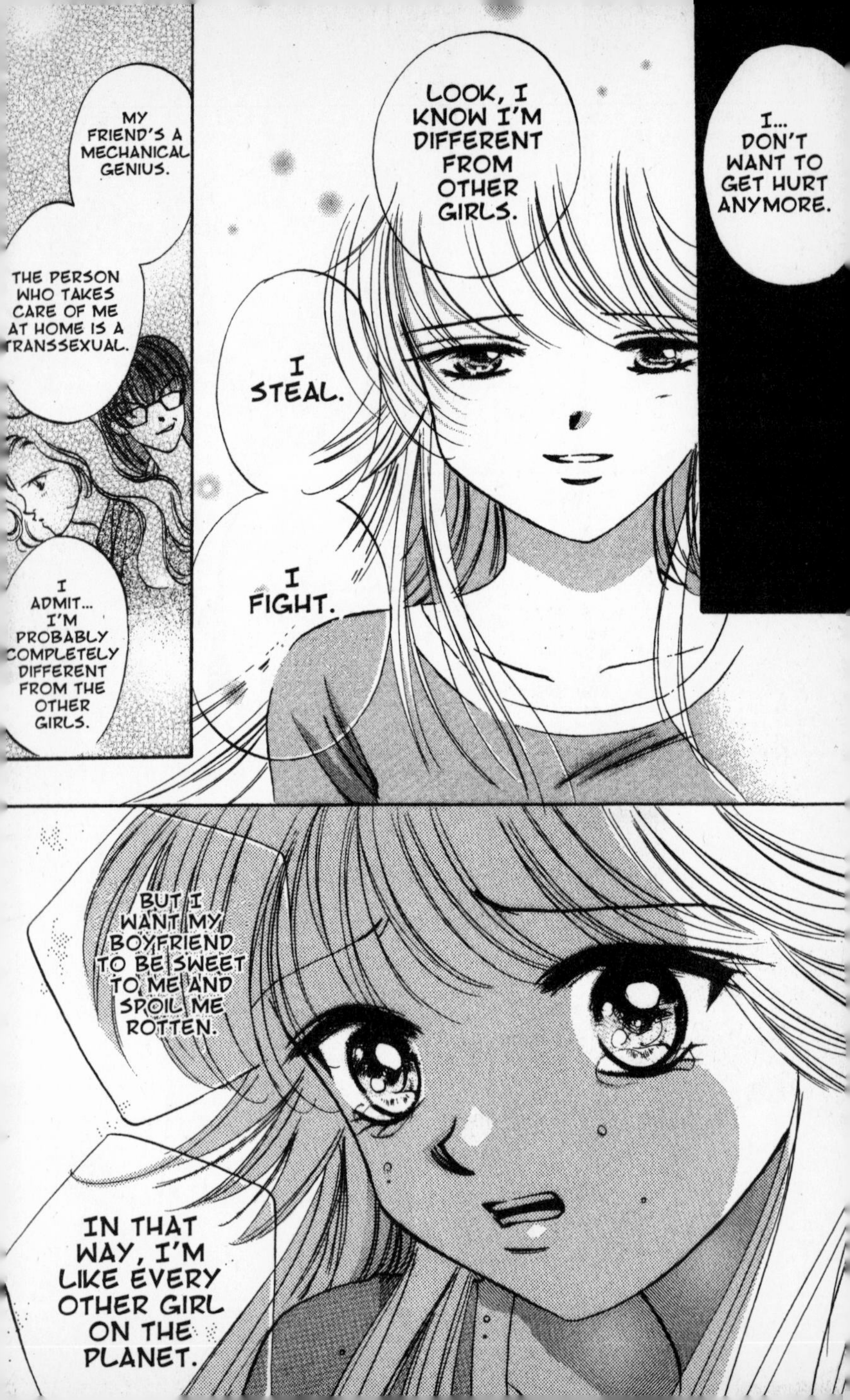

I... DON'T WANT TO GET HURT ANYMORE.
LOOK, I KNOW I'M DIFFERENT FROM OTHER GIRLS.
I STEAL.
I FIGHT.
MY FRIEND'S A MECHANICAL GENIUS.
THE PERSON WHO TAKES CARE OF ME AT HOME IS A TRANSSEXUAL.
I ADMIT... I'M PROBABLY COMPLETELY DIFFERENT FROM THE OTHER GIRLS.
BUT I WANT MY BOYFRIEND TO BE SWEET TO ME AND SPOIL ME ROTTEN.
IN THAT WAY, I'M LIKE EVERY OTHER GIRL ON THE PLANET.

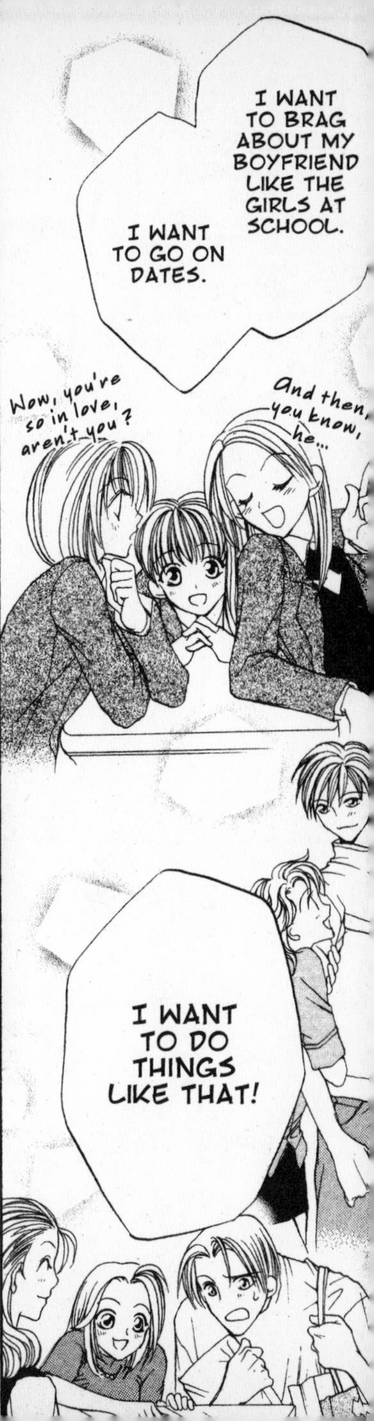
I WANT TO BRAG ABOUT MY BOYFRIEND LIKE THE GIRLS AT SCHOOL.
I WANT TO GO ON DATES.
And then, you know, he...
Wow, you're so in love, aren't you?
I WANT TO DO THINGS LIKE THAT!

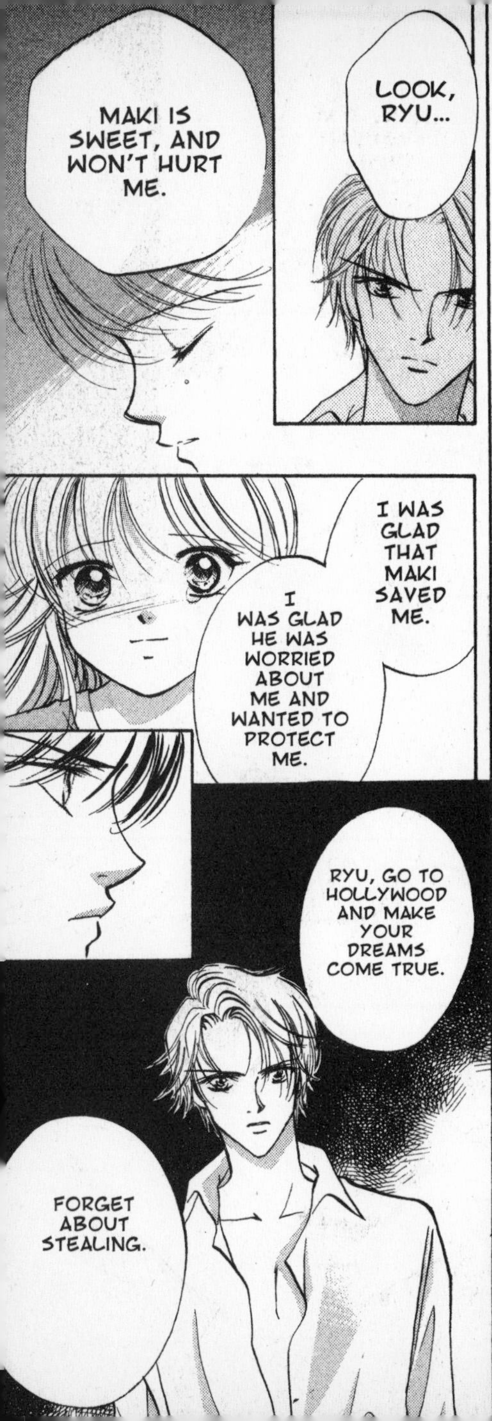
LOOK, RYU...
MAKI IS SWEET, AND WON'T HURT ME.
I WAS GLAD THAT MAKI SAVED ME.
I WAS GLAD HE WAS WORRIED ABOUT ME AND WANTED TO PROTECT ME.
RYU, GO TO HOLLYWOOD AND MAKE YOUR DREAMS COME TRUE.
FORGET ABOUT STEALING.

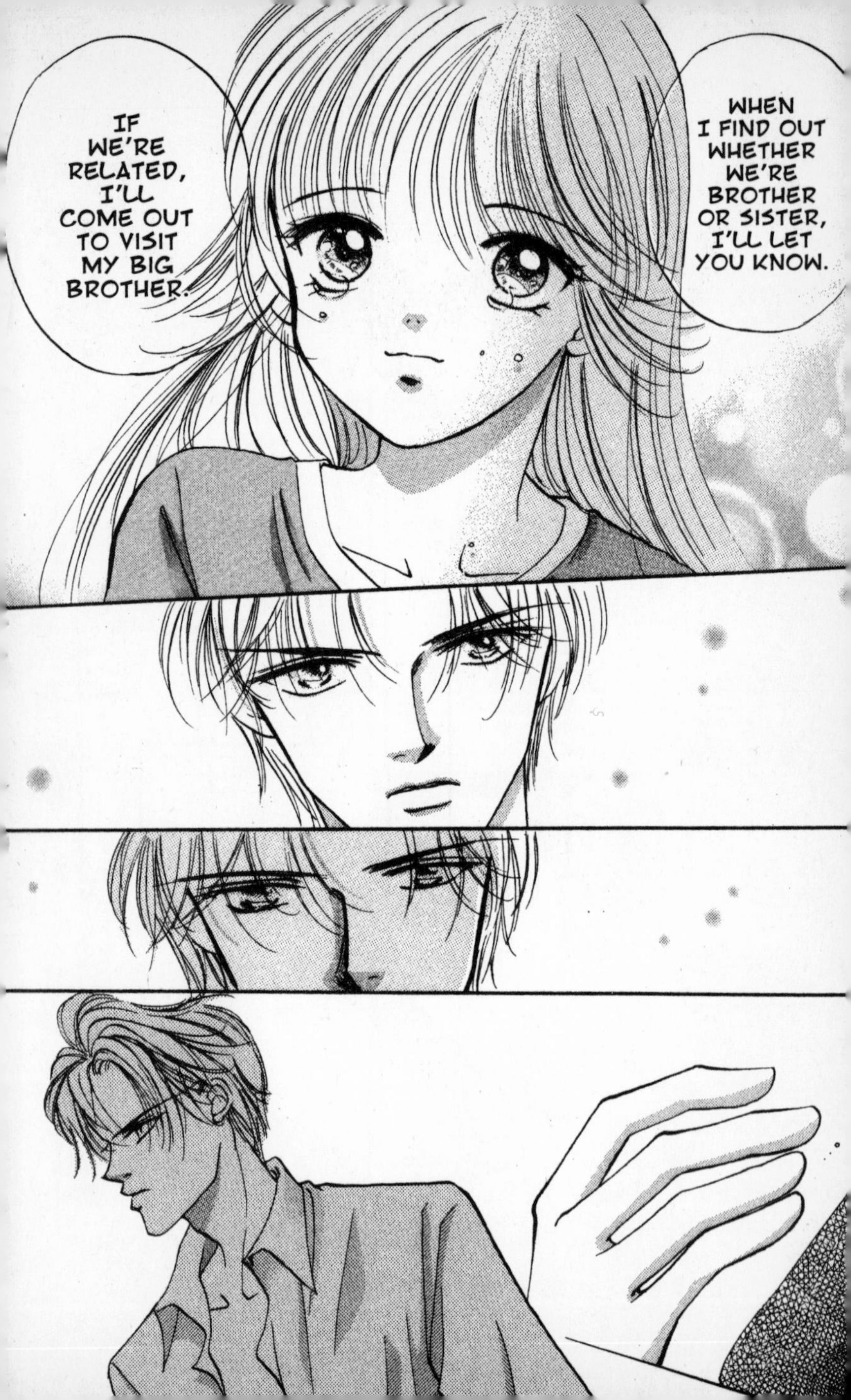
WHEN I FIND OUT WHETHER WE'RE BROTHER OR SISTER, I'LL LET YOU KNOW.
IF WE'RE RELATED, I'LL COME OUT TO VISIT MY BIG BROTHER.

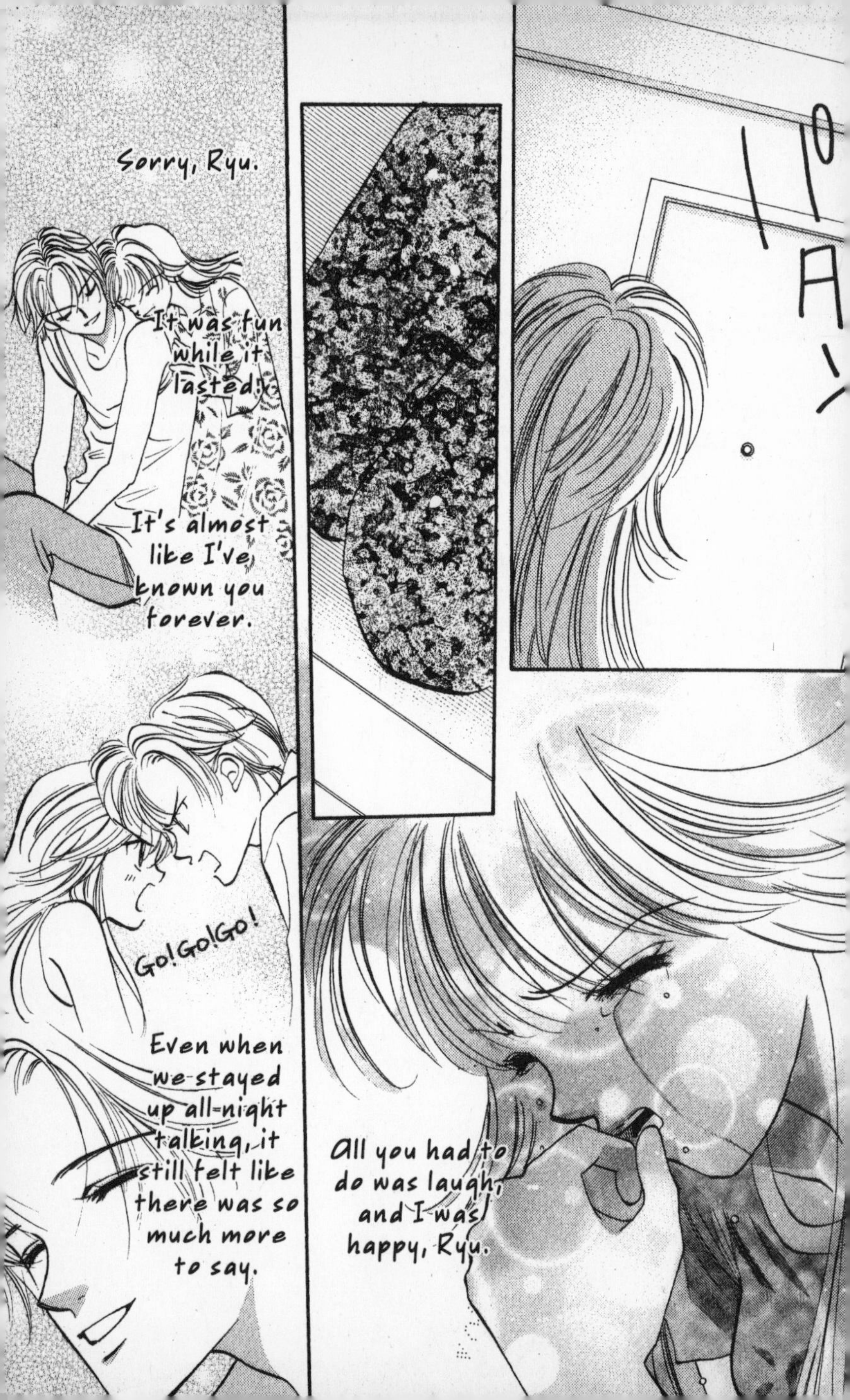
All you had to do was laugh, and I was happy, Ryu.
Sorry, Ryu.
It was fun while it lasted!
It's almost like I've known you forever.
Go!Go!Go!
Even when we stayed up all night talking, it still felt like there was so much more to say.

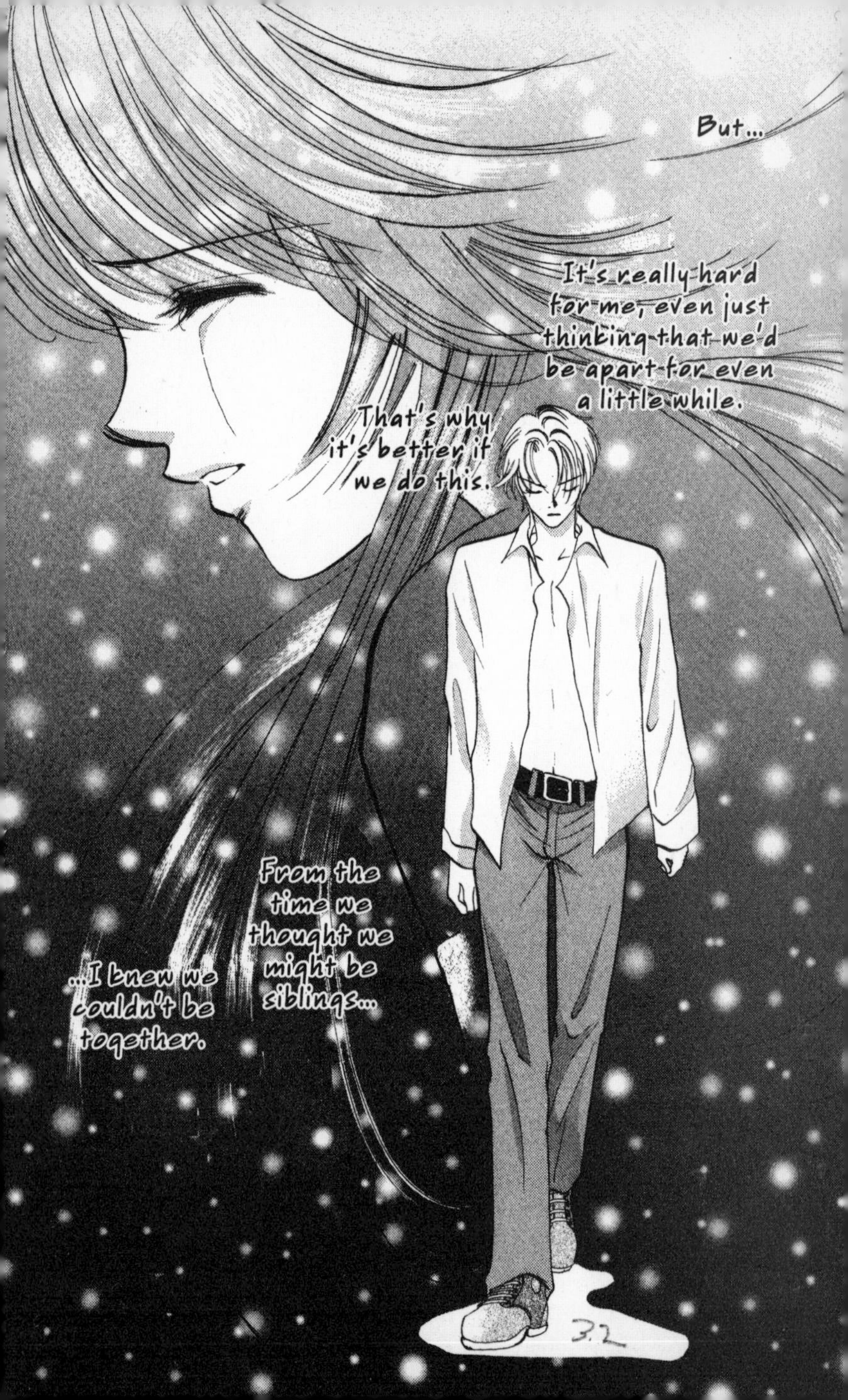
But...
It's really hard for me, even just thinking that we'd be apart for even a little while.
That's why it's better it we do this.
From the time we thought we might be siblings...
...I knew we couldn't be together.

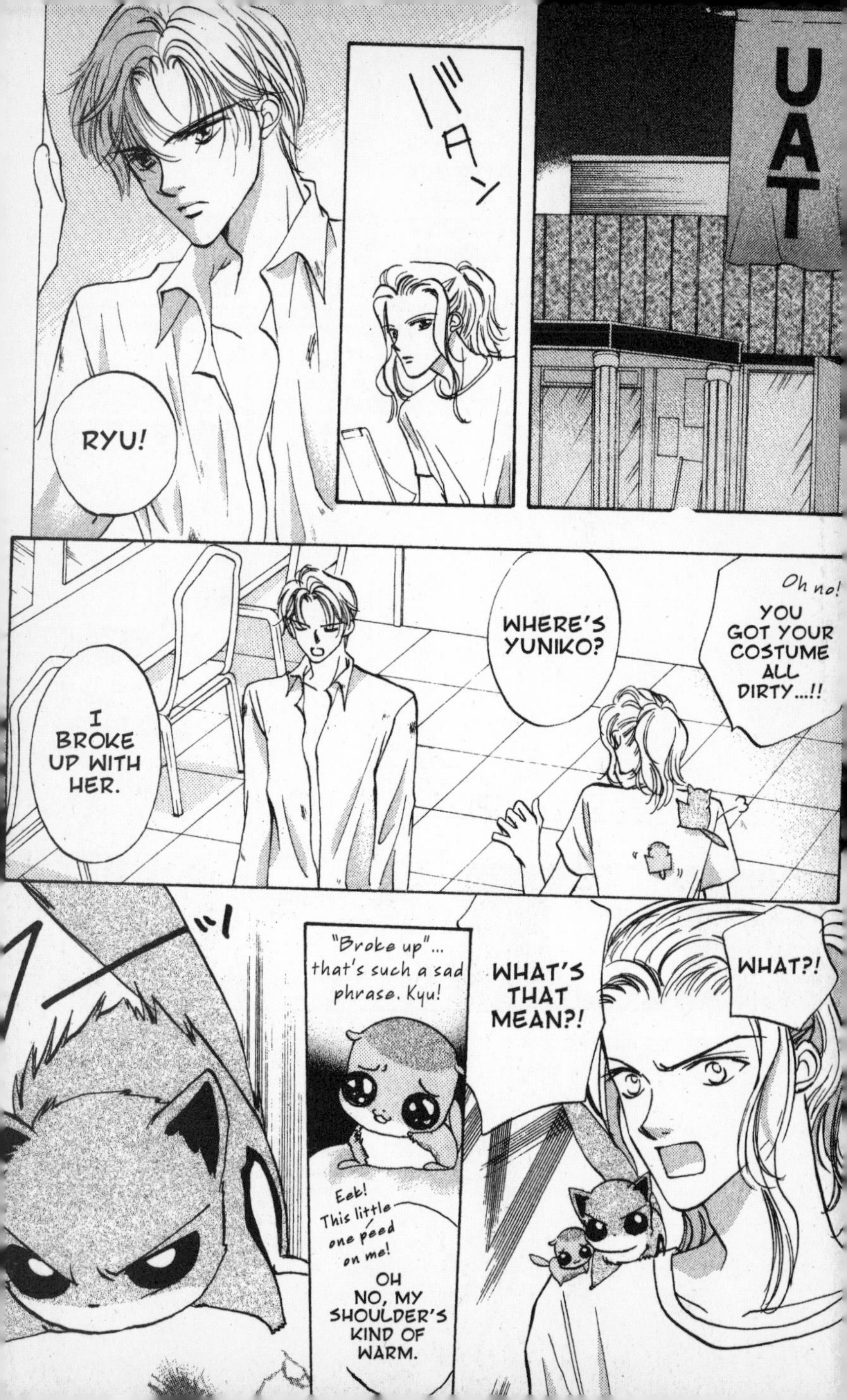

UAT
RYU!
Oh no!
YOU GOT YOUR COSTUME ALL DIRTY...!!
WHERE'S YUNIKO?
I BROKE UP WITH HER.
WHAT?!
WHAT'S THAT MEAN?!
"Broke up"... that's such a sad phrase. Kyu!
Eek! This little one peed on me!
OH NO, MY SHOULDER'S KIND OF WARM.

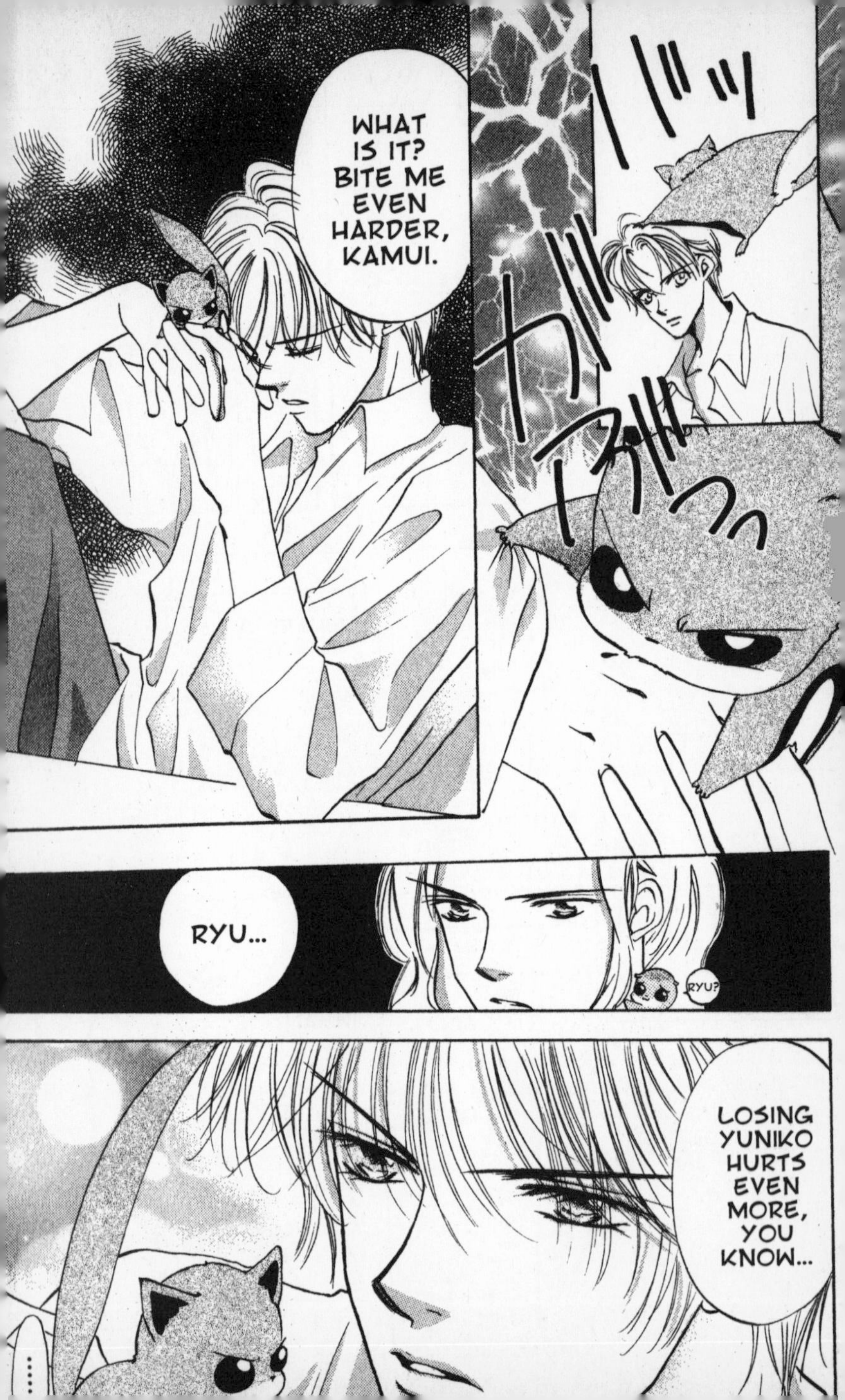
WHAT IS IT? BITE ME EVEN HARDER, KAMUI.
RYU?
RYU...
LOSING YUNIKO HURTS EVEN MORE, YOU KNOW...

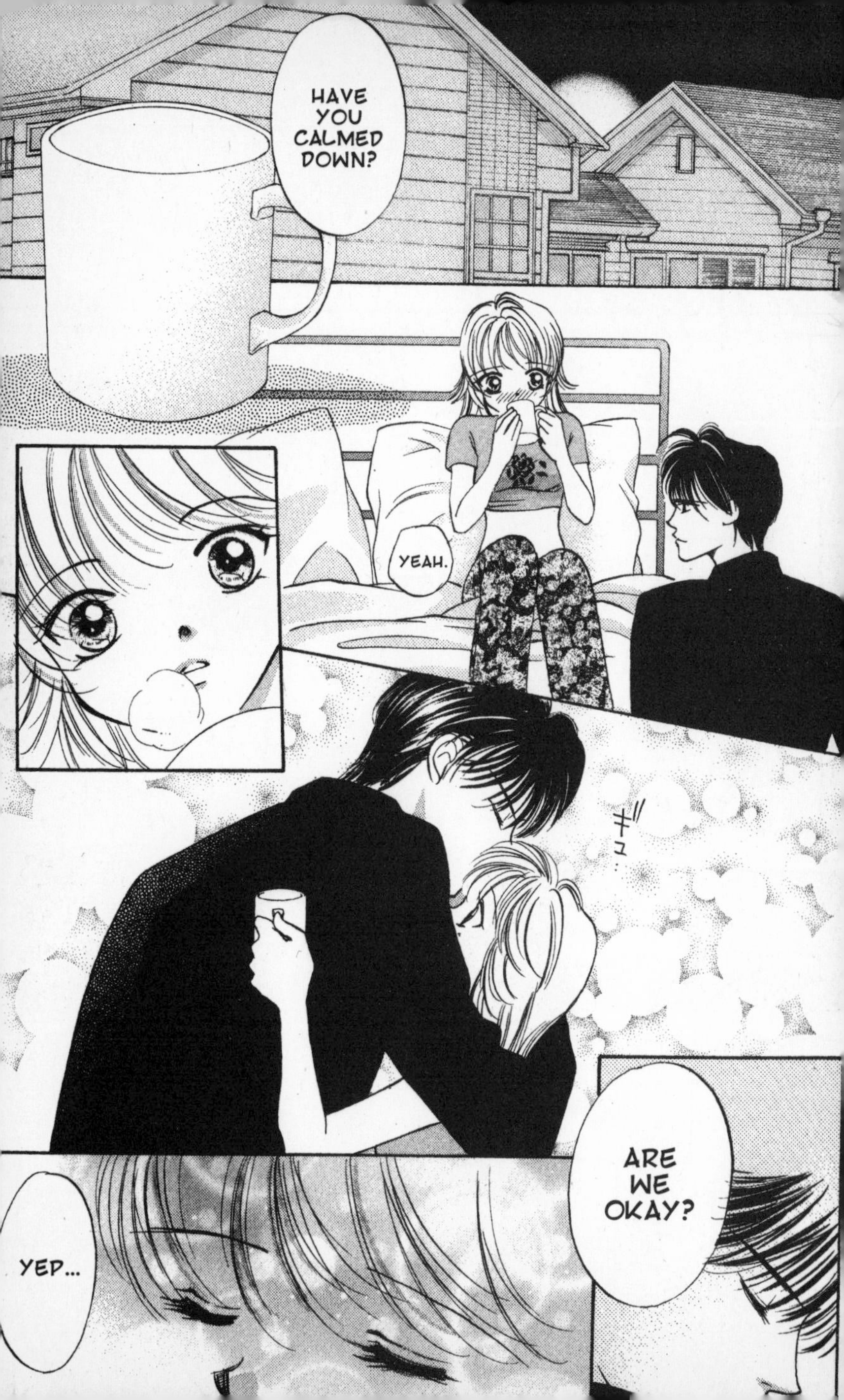
HAVE YOU CALMED DOWN?
YEAH.
ギュ…
ARE WE OKAY?
YEP...

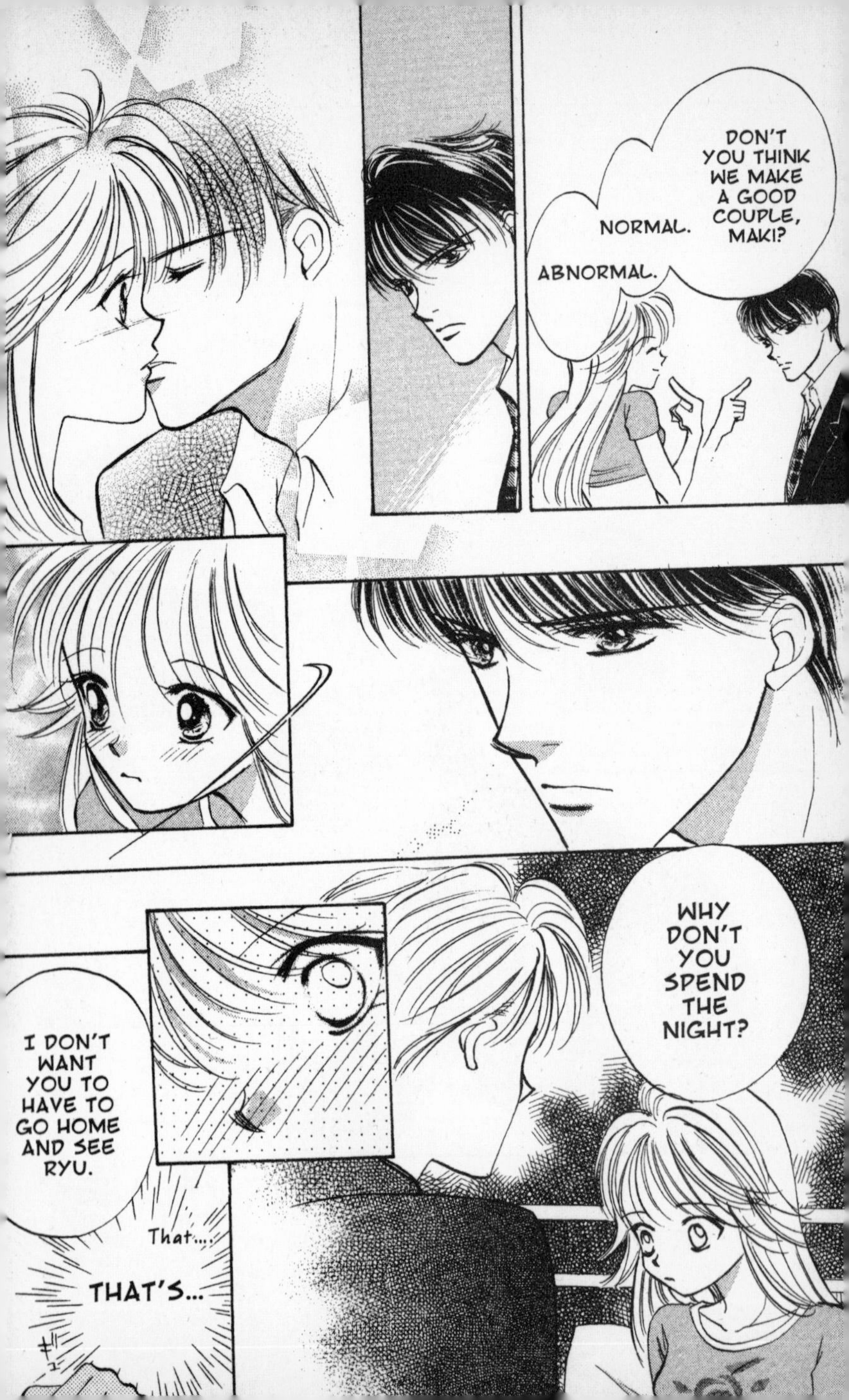
DON'T YOU THINK WE MAKE A GOOD COUPLE, MAKI?
NORMAL.
ABNORMAL.
WHY DON'T YOU SPEND THE NIGHT?
I DON'T WANT YOU TO HAVE TO GO HOME AND SEE RYU.
That....
THAT'S...

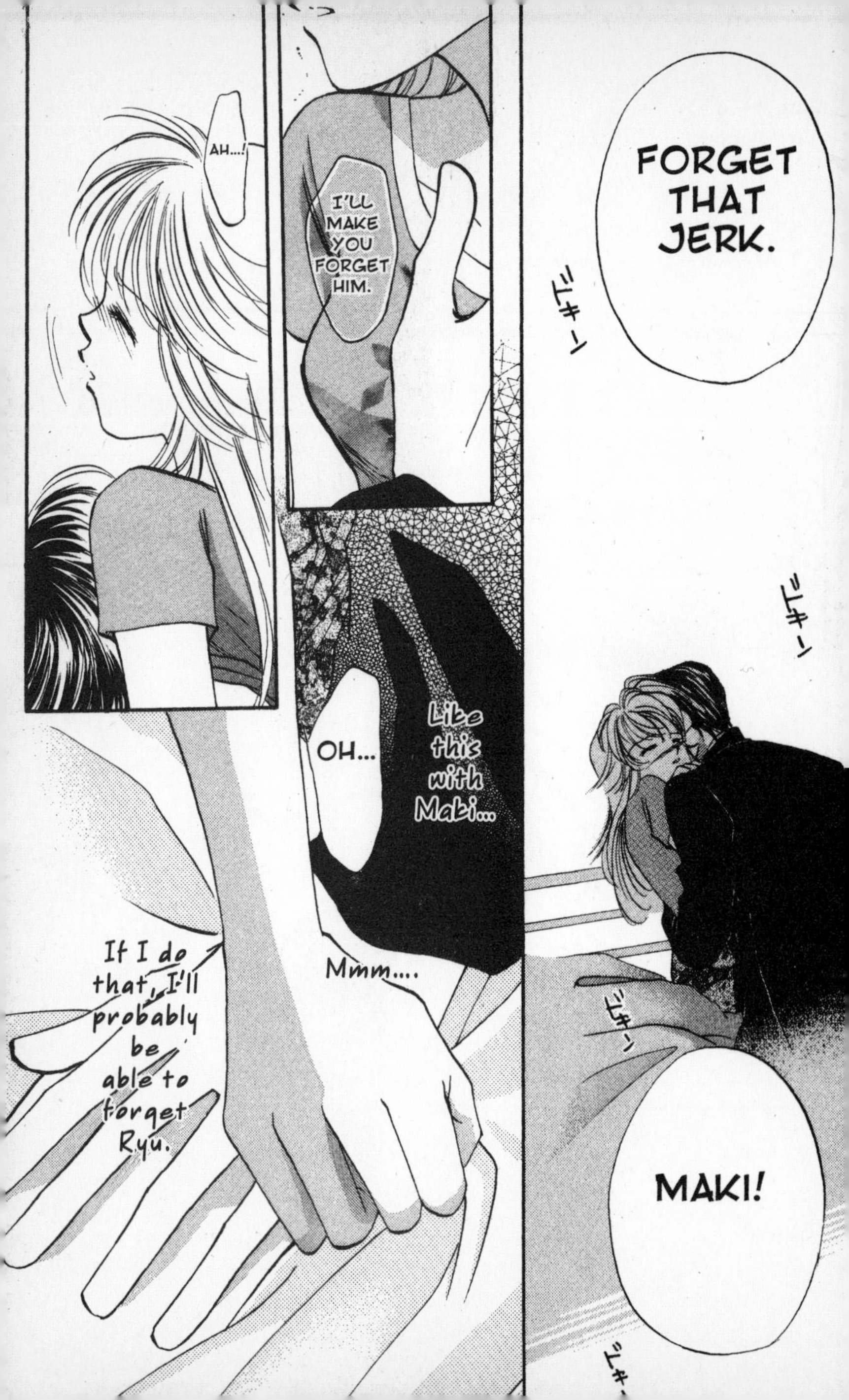
FORGET THAT JERK.
ドキーン
ドキーン
ドキーン
MAKI!
ドキー
I'LL MAKE YOU FORGET HIM.
AH...!
Like this with Maki...
OH...
Mmm....
If I do that, I'll probably be able to forget Ryu.

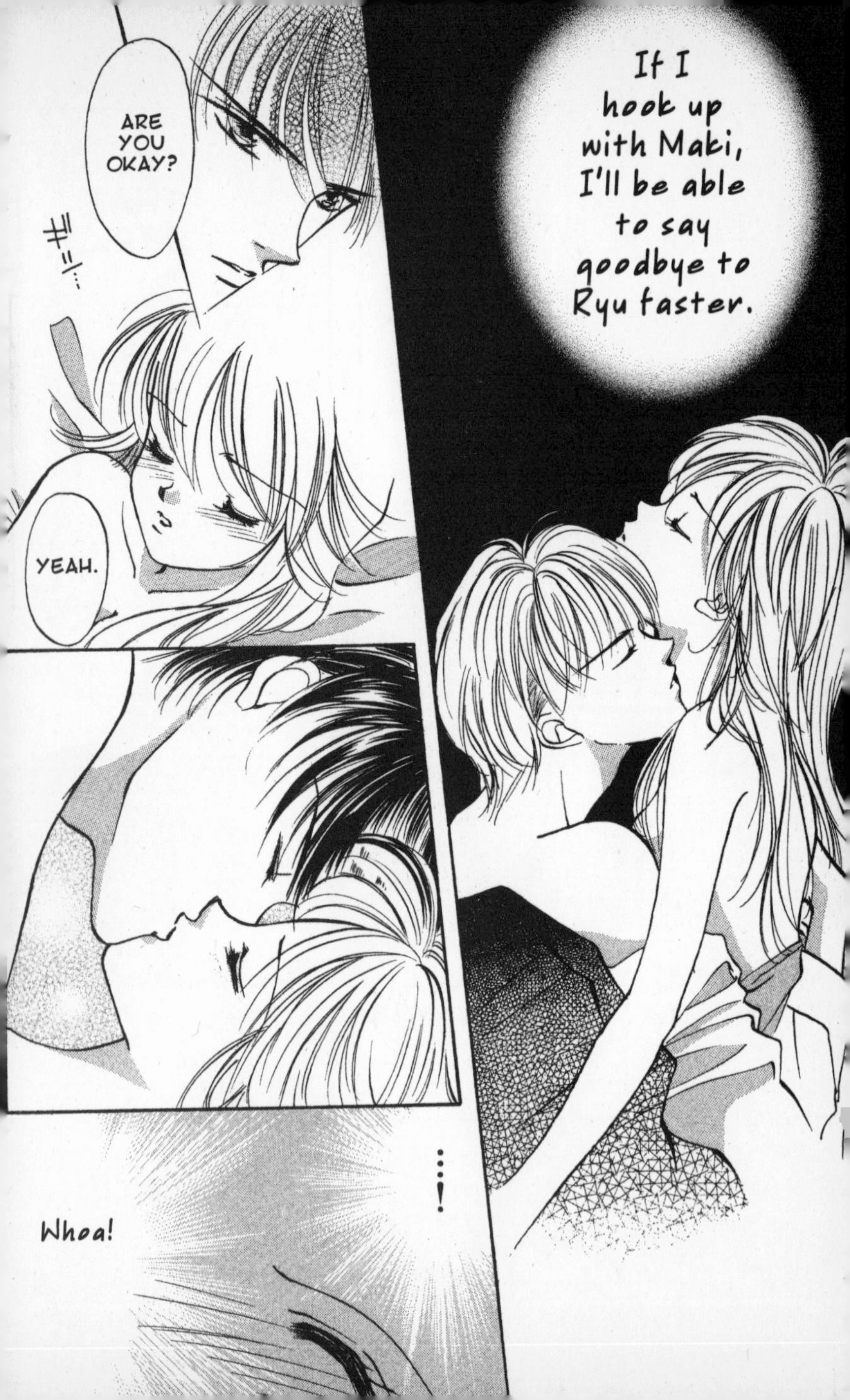
If I hook up with Maki, I'll be able to say goodbye to Ryu faster.
ARE YOU OKAY?
YEAH.
...!
Whoa!

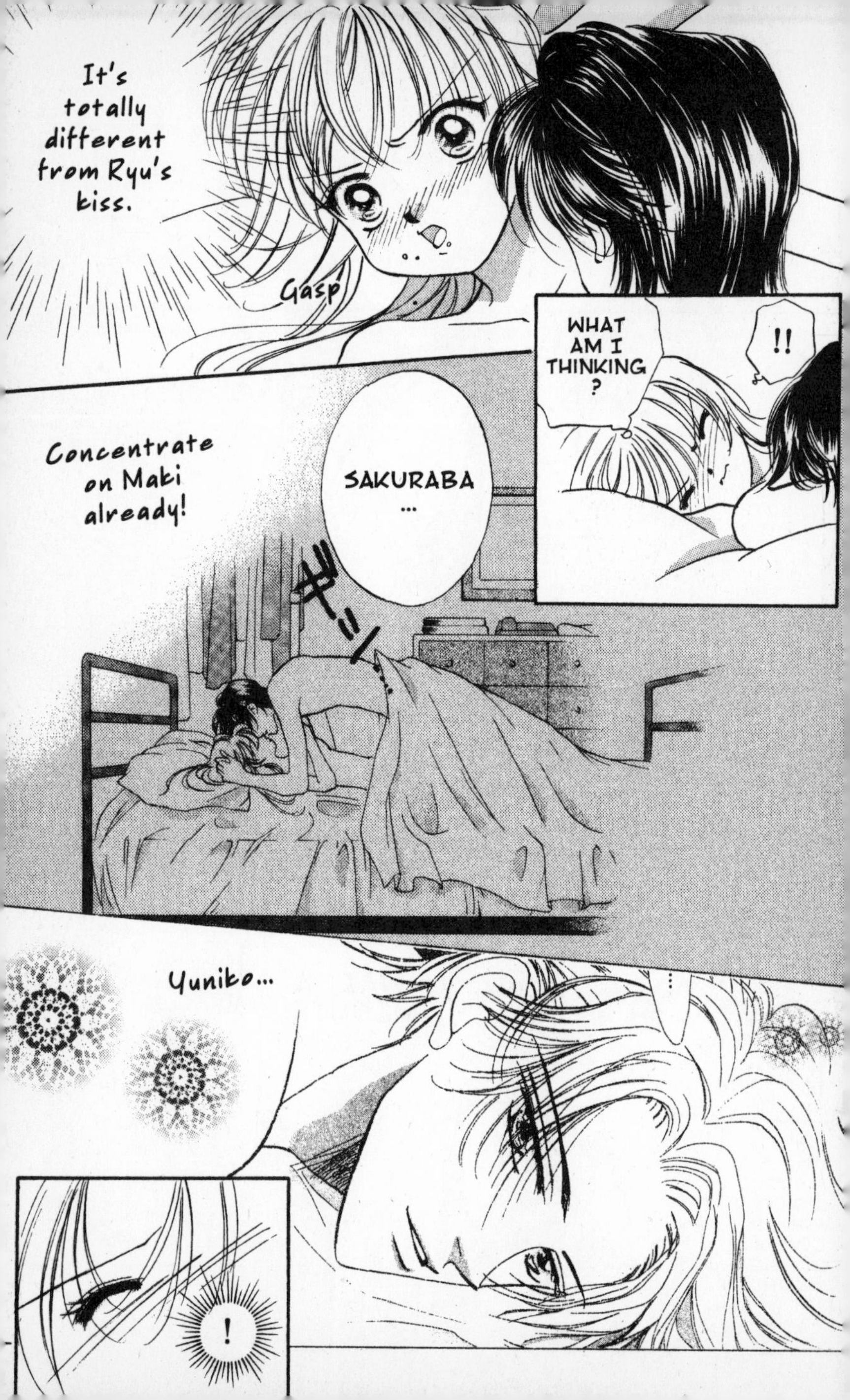
It's totally different from Ryu's kiss.
Gasp
!!
WHAT AM I THINKING?
Concentrate on Maki already!
SAKURABA ...
...
Yuniko...
!

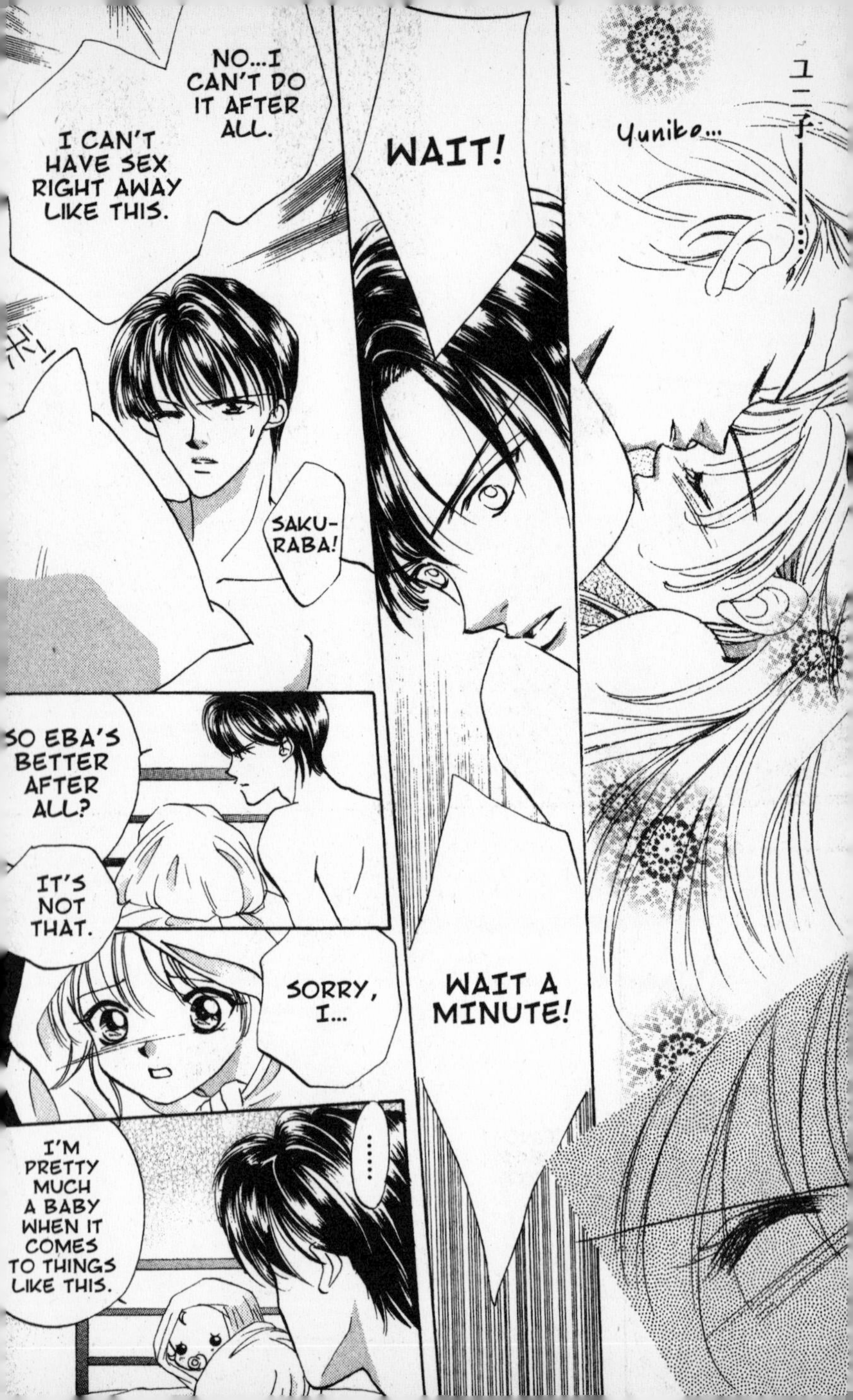
Yuniko...
ユニ子ーー…
WAIT!
WAIT A MINUTE!
NO...I CAN'T DO IT AFTER ALL.
I CAN'T HAVE SEX RIGHT AWAY LIKE THIS.
SAKU-RABA!
SO EBA'S BETTER AFTER ALL?
IT'S NOT THAT.
SORRY, I...
......
I'M PRETTY MUCH A BABY WHEN IT COMES TO THINGS LIKE THIS.

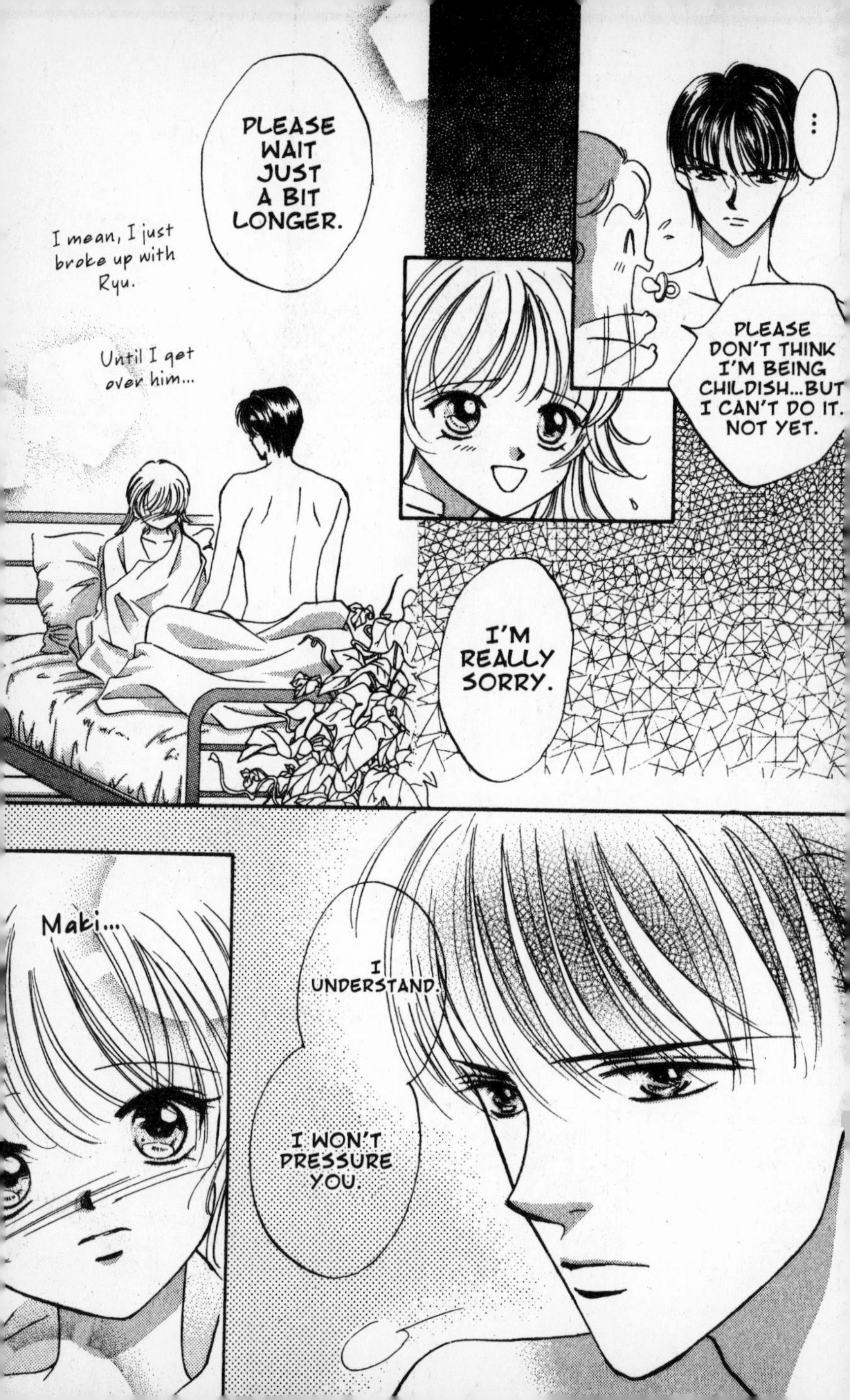

...
PLEASE DON'T THINK I'M BEING CHILDISH...BUT I CAN'T DO IT. NOT YET.
I'M REALLY SORRY.
PLEASE WAIT JUST A BIT LONGER.
I mean, I just broke up with Ryu.
Until I get over him...
I UNDERSTAND.
I WON'T PRESSURE YOU.
Maki...

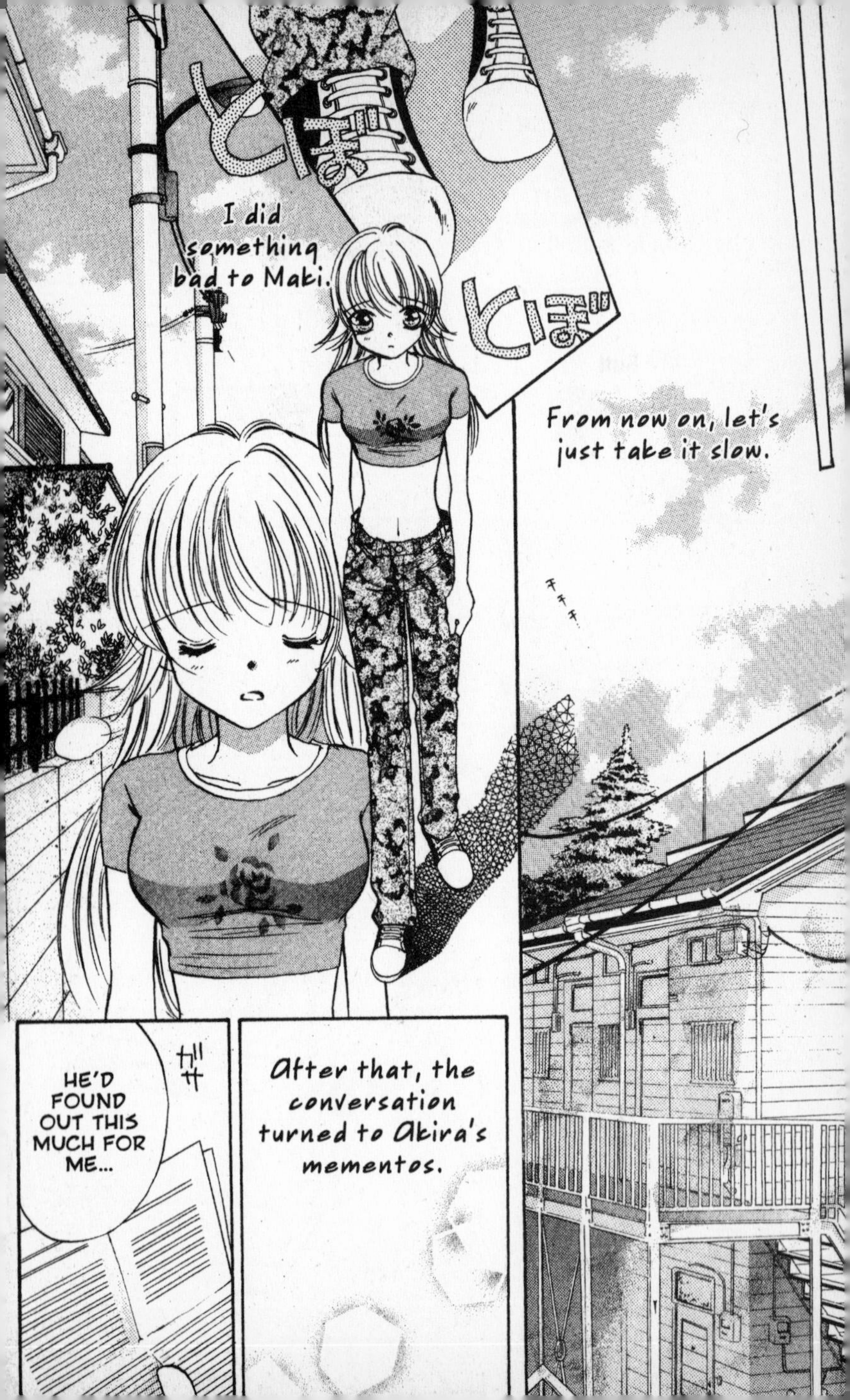
From now on, let's just take it slow.
チチチ
とぼ
とぼ
I did something bad to Maki.
After that, the conversation turned to Akira's mementos.
ガサ
HE'D FOUND OUT THIS MUCH FOR ME...

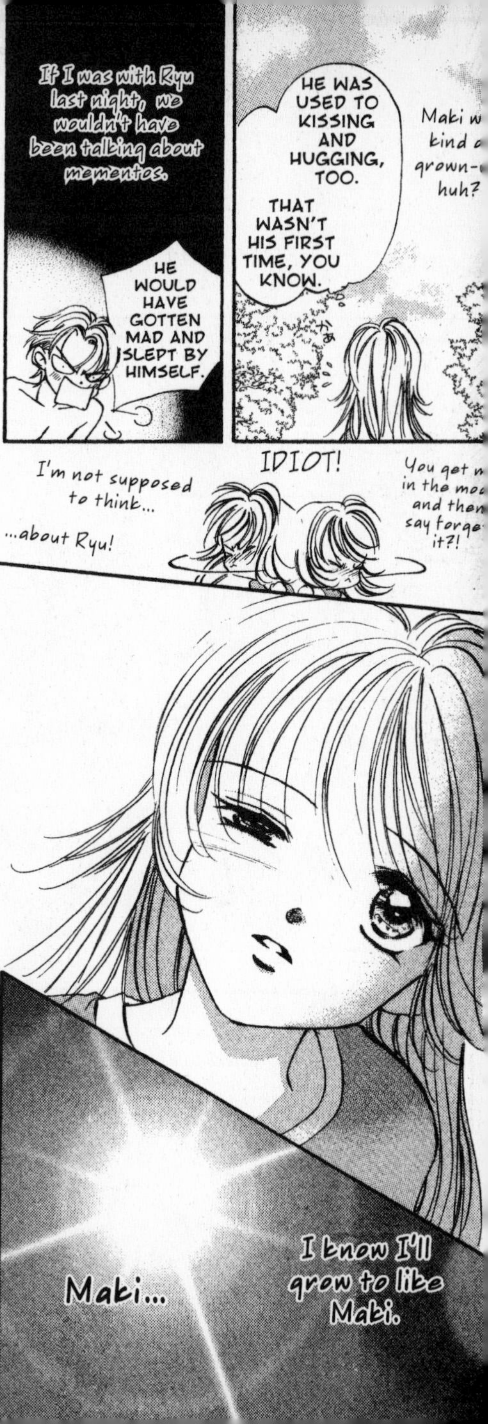
Maki w
kind o
grown-
huh?
HE WAS USED TO KISSING AND HUGGING, TOO.
THAT WASN'T HIS FIRST TIME, YOU KNOW.
If I was with Ryu last night, we wouldn't have been talking about mementos.
HE WOULD HAVE GOTTEN MAD AND SLEPT BY HIMSELF.
You get m
in the moo
and then
say forge
it?!
IDIOT!
I'm not supposed to think...
...about Ryu!
I know I'll grow to like Maki.
Maki...

The Thing I Like Best About Myself:

My Butt

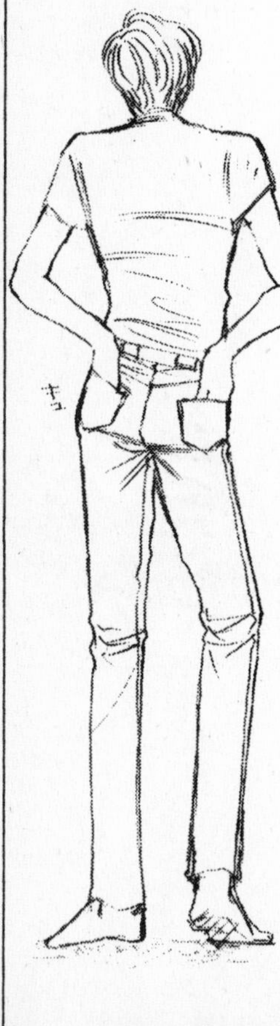

By Ryu Eba

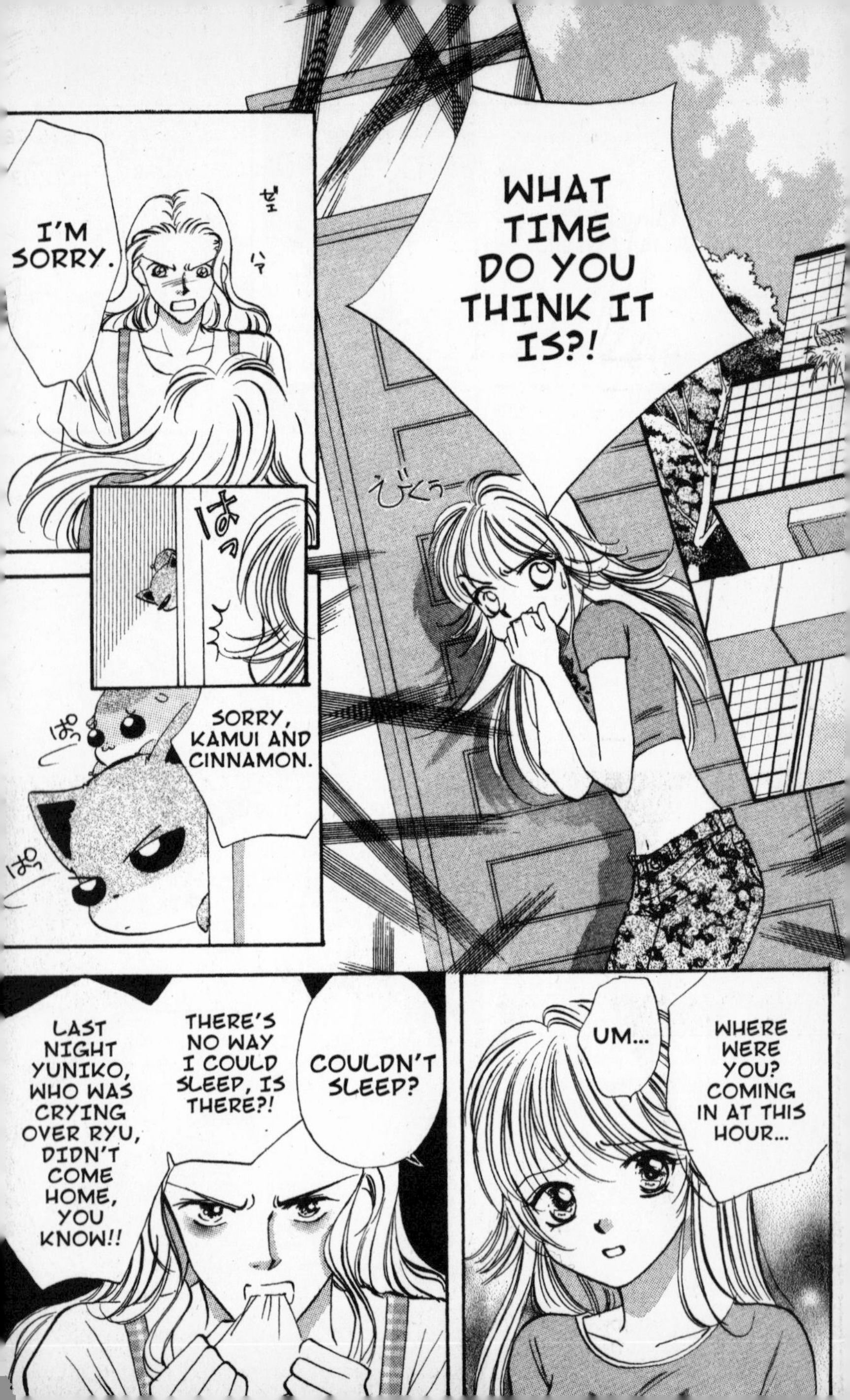
WHAT TIME DO YOU THINK IT IS?!
びくぅ
I'M SORRY.
ゼェ
ハァ
はっ
ぱっ
ぱっ
SORRY, KAMUI AND CINNAMON.
WHERE WERE YOU? COMING IN AT THIS HOUR...
UM...
COULDN'T SLEEP?
THERE'S NO WAY I COULD SLEEP, IS THERE?!
LAST NIGHT YUNIKO, WHO WAS CRYING OVER RYU, DIDN'T COME HOME, YOU KNOW!!

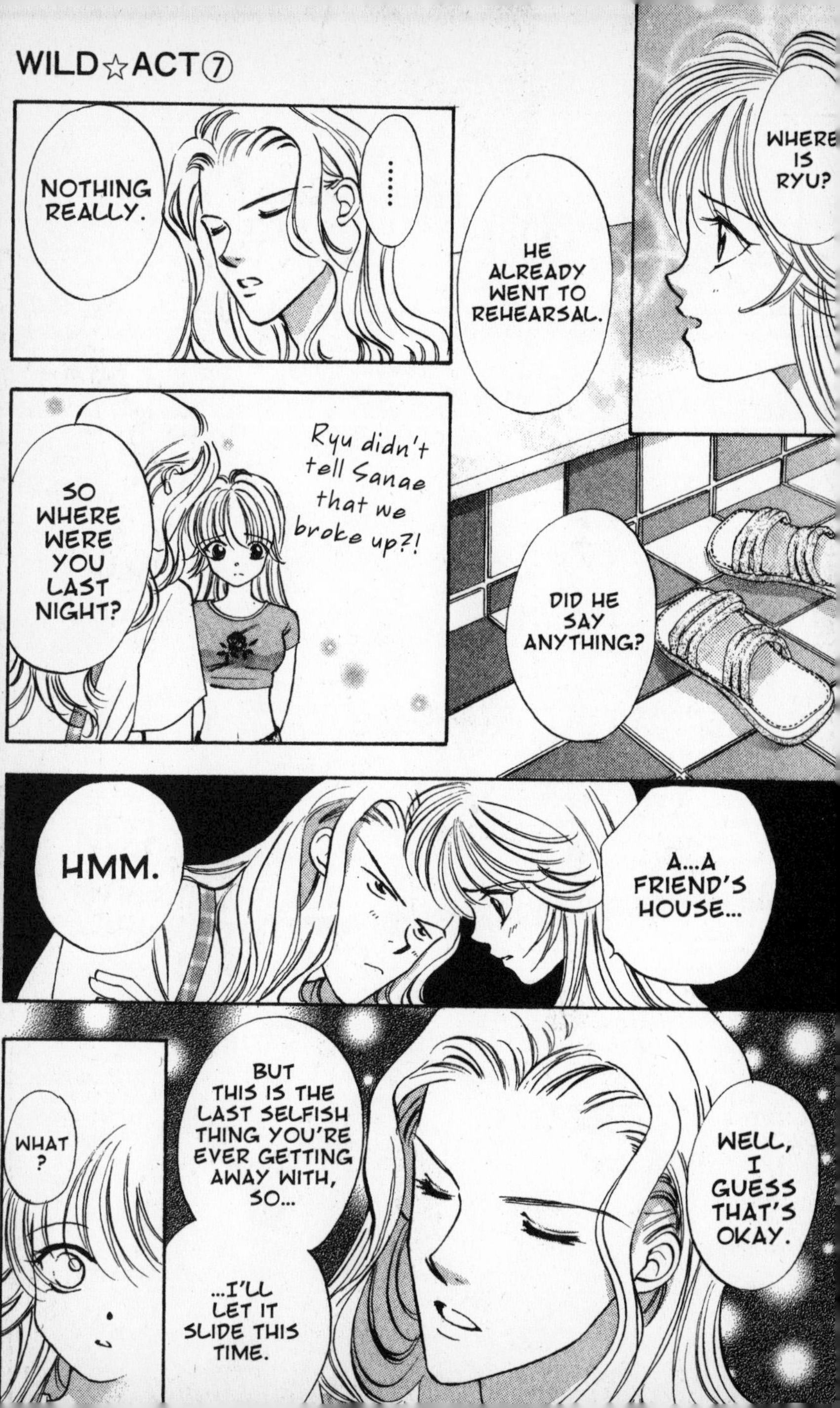
WHERE IS RYU?
HE ALREADY WENT TO REHEARSAL.
DID HE SAY ANYTHING?
......
NOTHING REALLY.
Ryu didn't tell Sanae that we broke up?!
SO WHERE WERE YOU LAST NIGHT?
A...A FRIEND'S HOUSE...
HMM.
WELL, I GUESS THAT'S OKAY.
BUT THIS IS THE LAST SELFISH THING YOU'RE EVER GETTING AWAY WITH, SO...
...I'LL LET IT SLIDE THIS TIME.
WHAT?

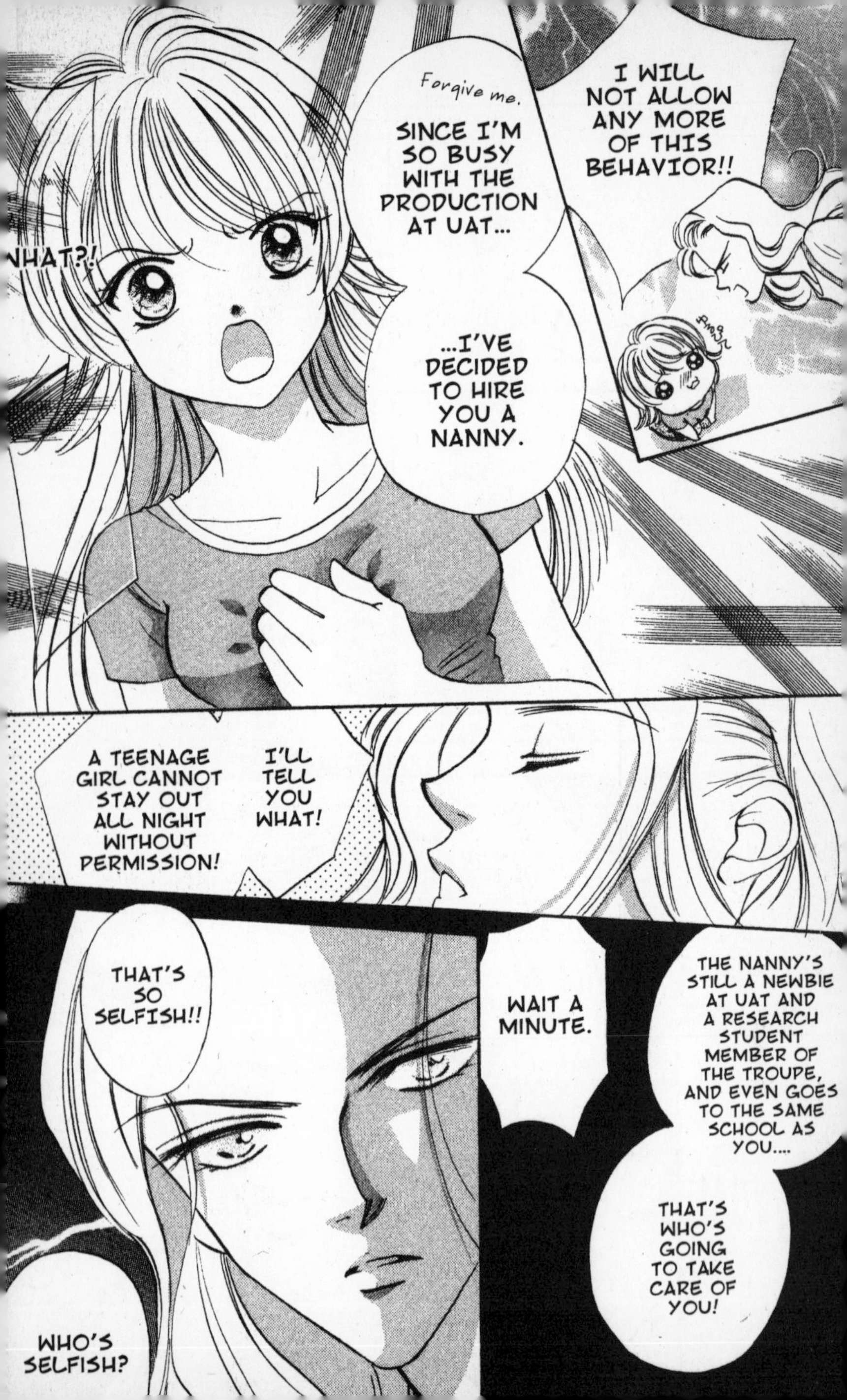
I WILL NOT ALLOW ANY MORE OF THIS BEHAVIOR!!
Forgive me.
SINCE I'M SO BUSY WITH THE PRODUCTION AT UAT...
...I'VE DECIDED TO HIRE YOU A NANNY.
WHAT?!
I'LL TELL YOU WHAT!
A TEENAGE GIRL CANNOT STAY OUT ALL NIGHT WITHOUT PERMISSION!
THE NANNY'S STILL A NEWBIE AT UAT AND A RESEARCH STUDENT MEMBER OF THE TROUPE, AND EVEN GOES TO THE SAME SCHOOL AS YOU....
WAIT A MINUTE.
THAT'S WHO'S GOING TO TAKE CARE OF YOU!
THAT'S SO SELFISH!!
WHO'S SELFISH?

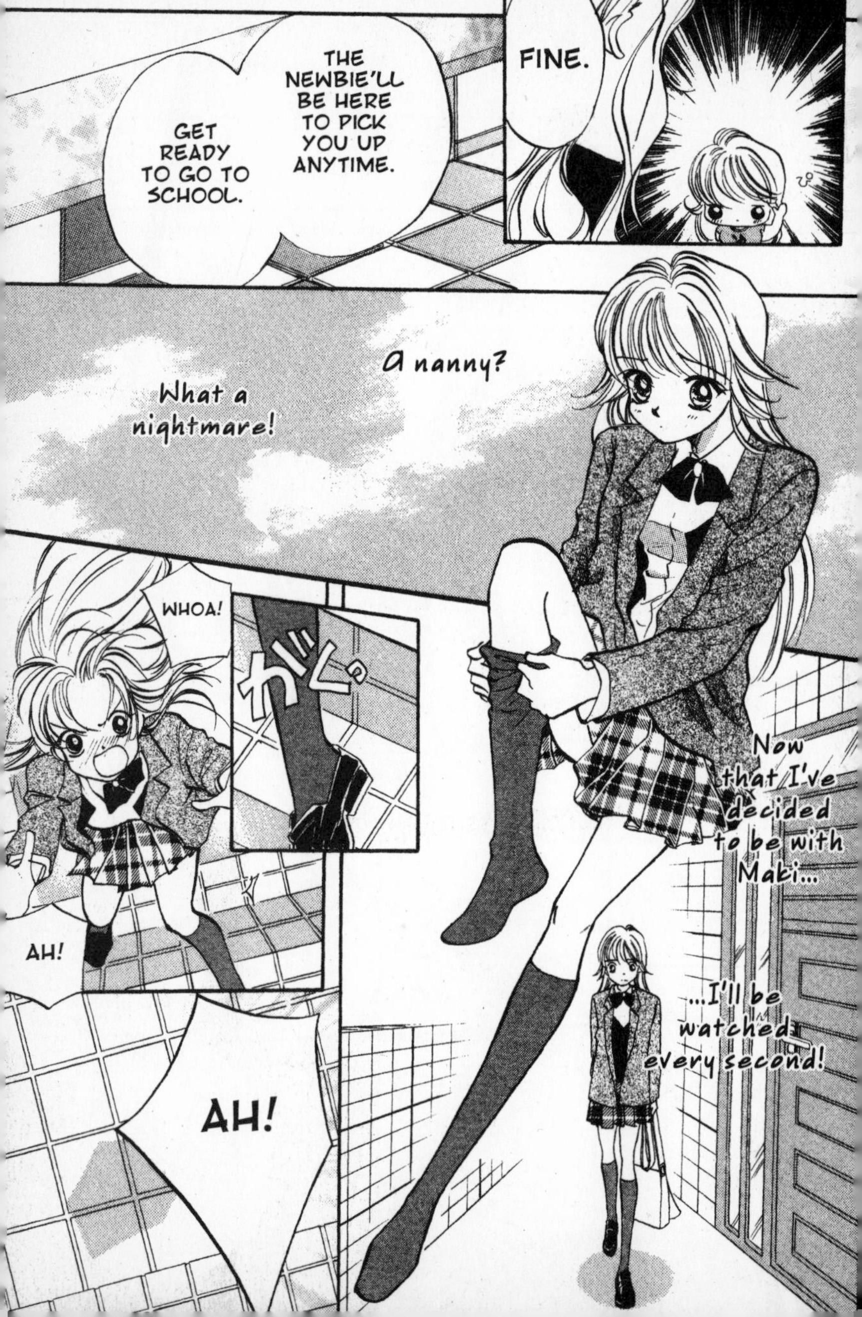
FINE.
ぴ
THE NEWBIE'LL BE HERE TO PICK YOU UP ANYTIME.
GET READY TO GO TO SCHOOL.
A nanny?
What a nightmare!
Now that I've decided to be with Maki...
...I'll be watched every second!
わぐ
WHOA!
AH!
AH!

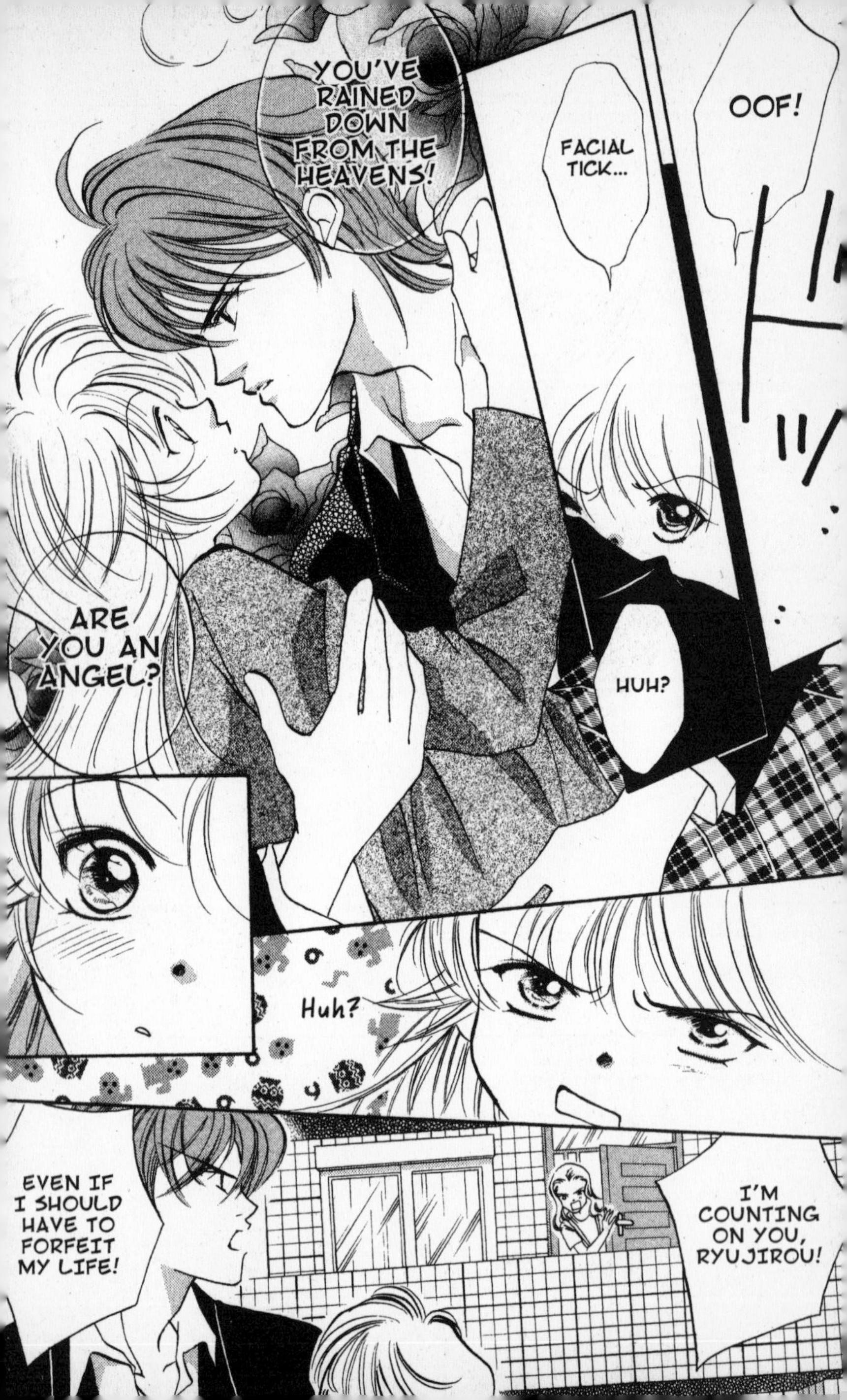
OOF!
FACIAL TICK...
HUH?
YOU'VE RAINED DOWN FROM THE HEAVENS!
ARE YOU AN ANGEL?
Huh?
I'M COUNTING ON YOU, RYUJIROU!
EVEN IF I SHOULD HAVE TO FORFEIT MY LIFE!

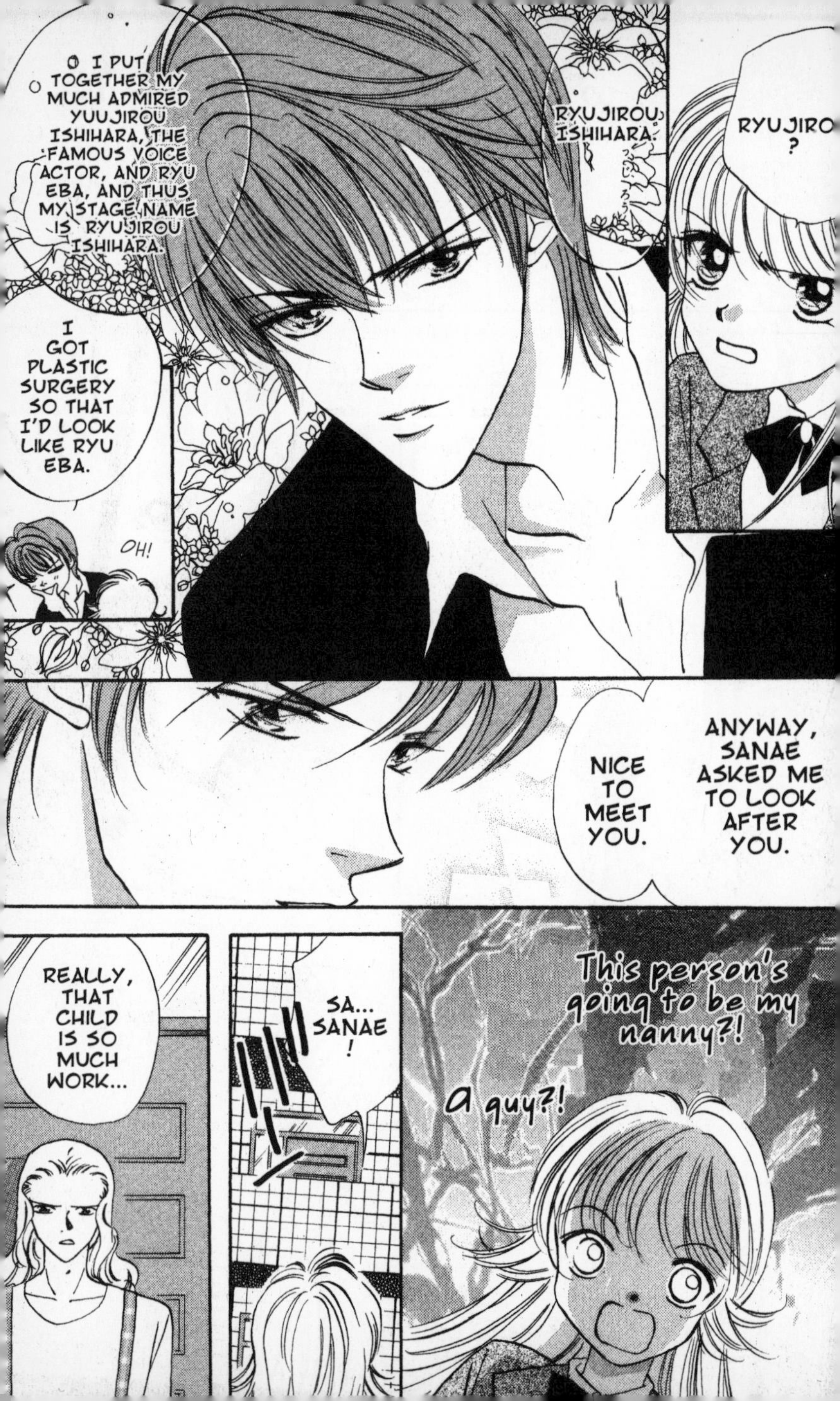
RYUJIRO ?
RYUJIROU ISHIHARA.
I PUT TOGETHER MY MUCH ADMIRED YUUJIROU ISHIHARA, THE FAMOUS VOICE ACTOR, AND RYU EBA, AND THUS MY STAGE NAME IS RYUJIROU ISHIHARA.
I GOT PLASTIC SURGERY SO THAT I'D LOOK LIKE RYU EBA.
OH!
ANYWAY, SANAE ASKED ME TO LOOK AFTER YOU.
NICE TO MEET YOU.
This person's going to be my nanny?!
A guy?!
SA... SANAE !
REALLY, THAT CHILD IS SO MUCH WORK...

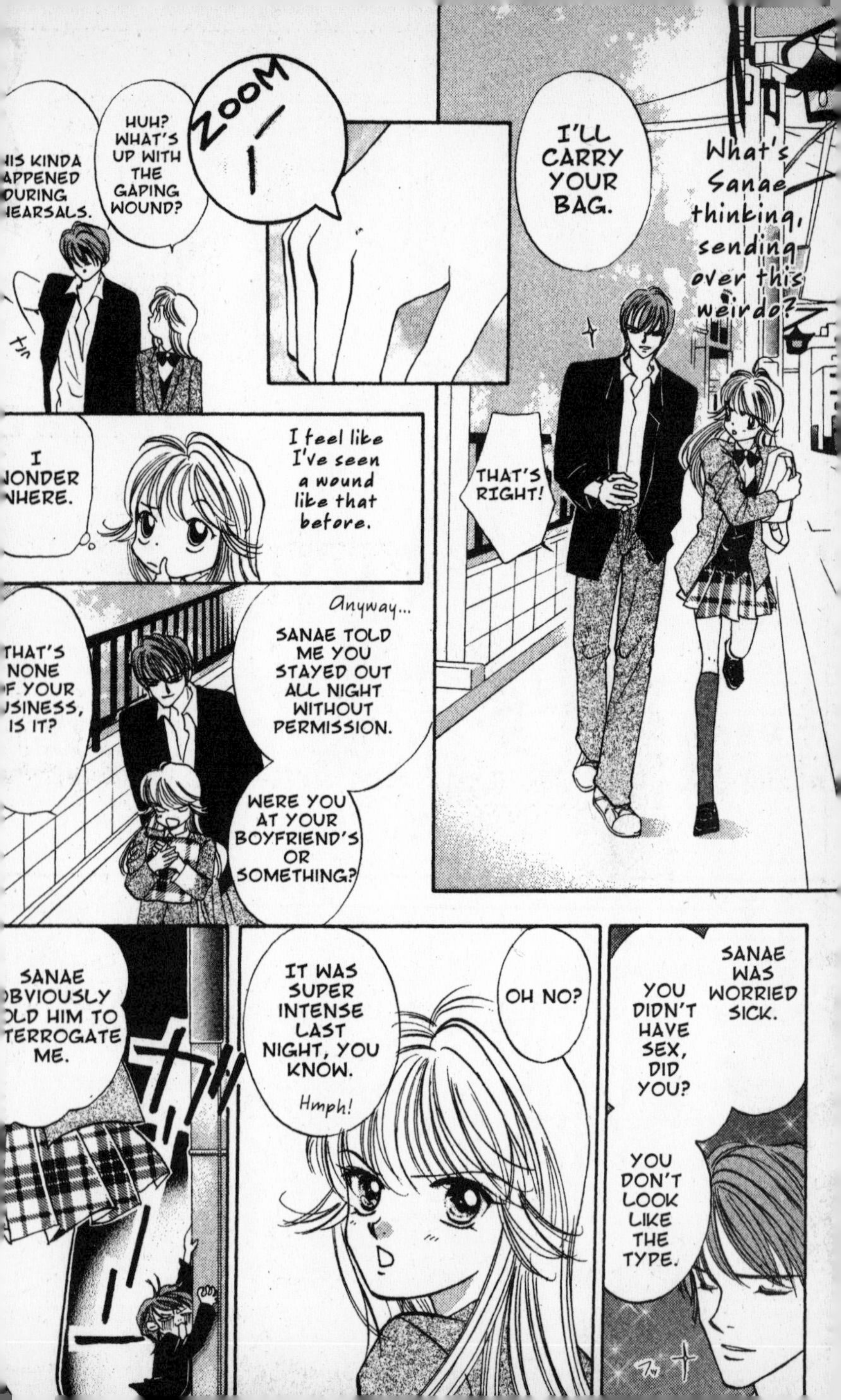
I'LL CARRY YOUR BAG.
What's Sanae thinking, sending over this weirdo?
THAT'S RIGHT!
ZOOM
HUH? WHAT'S UP WITH THE GAPING WOUND?
HIS KINDA APPENED DURING HEARSALS.
I feel like I've seen a wound like that before.
I ONDER HERE.
Anyway...
SANAE TOLD ME YOU STAYED OUT ALL NIGHT WITHOUT PERMISSION.
WERE YOU AT YOUR BOYFRIEND'S OR SOMETHING?
THAT'S NONE F YOUR USINESS, IS IT?
SANAE WAS WORRIED SICK.
YOU DIDN'T HAVE SEX, DID YOU?
YOU DON'T LOOK LIKE THE TYPE.
OH NO?
IT WAS SUPER INTENSE LAST NIGHT, YOU KNOW.
Hmph!
SANAE BVIOUSLY OLD HIM TO TERROGATE ME.

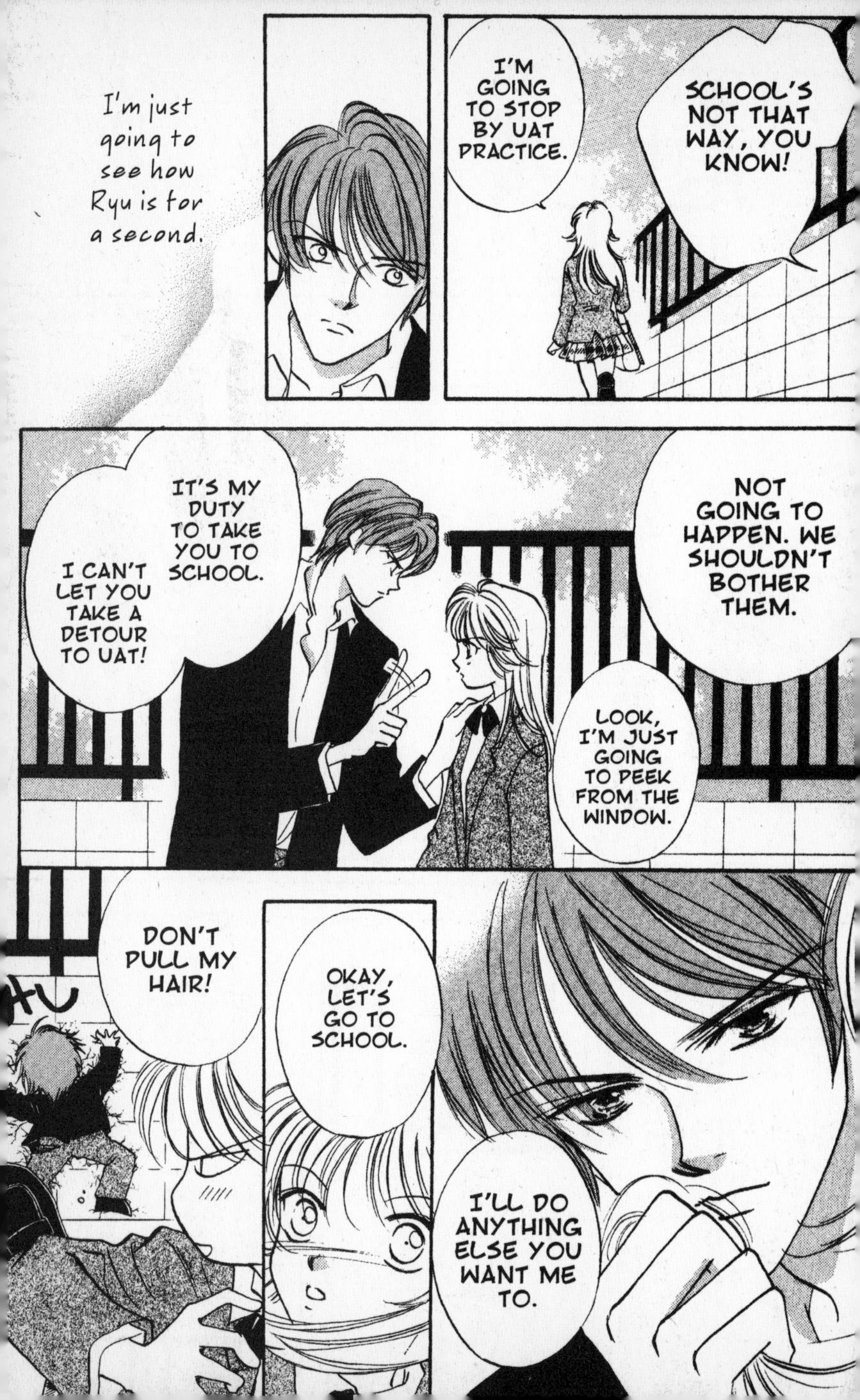
SCHOOL'S NOT THAT WAY, YOU KNOW!
I'M GOING TO STOP BY UAT PRACTICE.
I'm just going to see how Ryu is for a second.
NOT GOING TO HAPPEN. WE SHOULDN'T BOTHER THEM.
LOOK, I'M JUST GOING TO PEEK FROM THE WINDOW.
IT'S MY DUTY TO TAKE YOU TO SCHOOL.
I CAN'T LET YOU TAKE A DETOUR TO UAT!
I'LL DO ANYTHING ELSE YOU WANT ME TO.
OKAY, LET'S GO TO SCHOOL.
DON'T PULL MY HAIR!

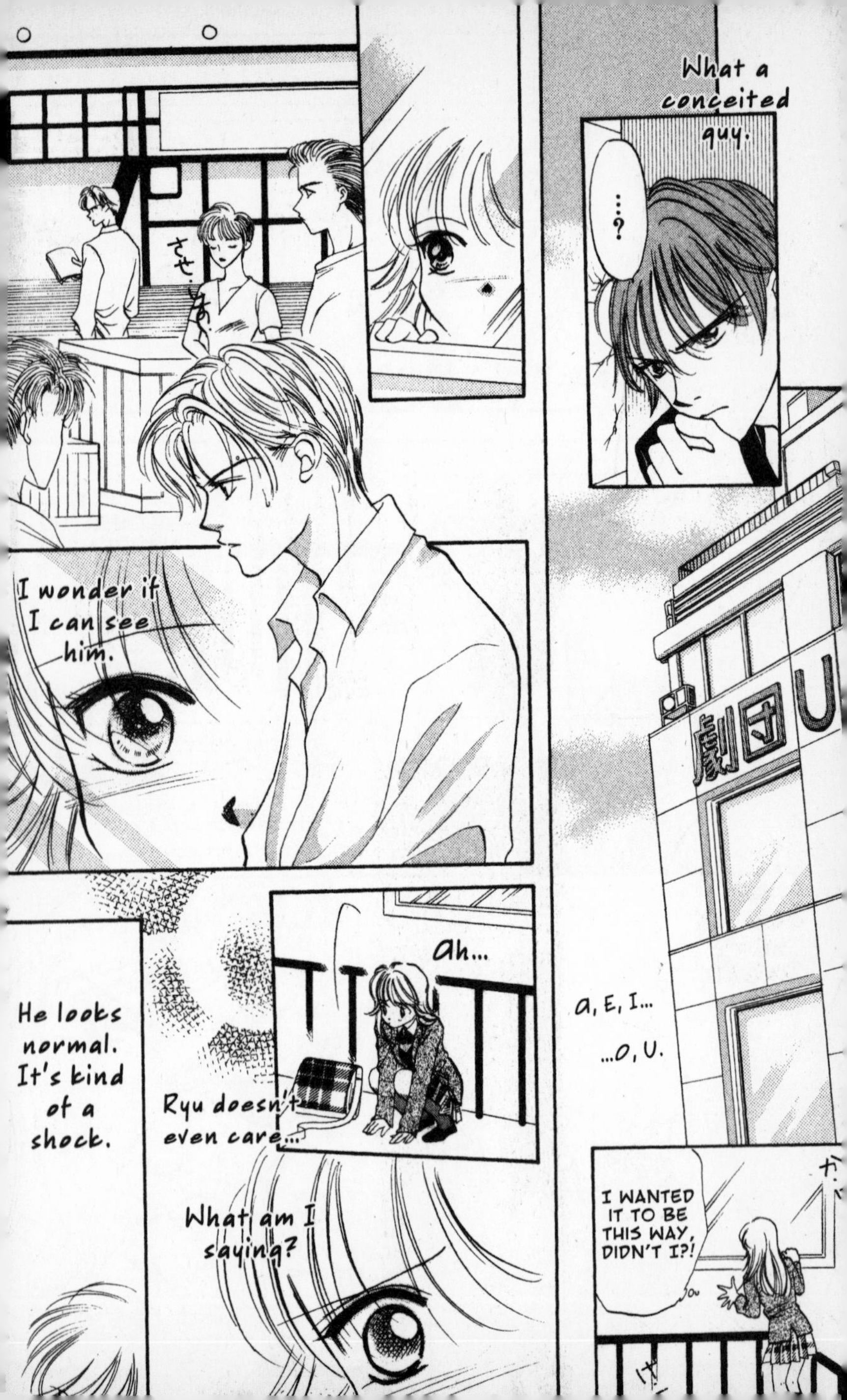
What a conceited guy.
...?
a, E, I...
...O, U.
I WANTED IT TO BE THIS WAY, DIDN'T I?!
I wonder if I can see him.
ah...
Ryu doesn't even care...
What am I saying?
He looks normal. It's kind of a shock.

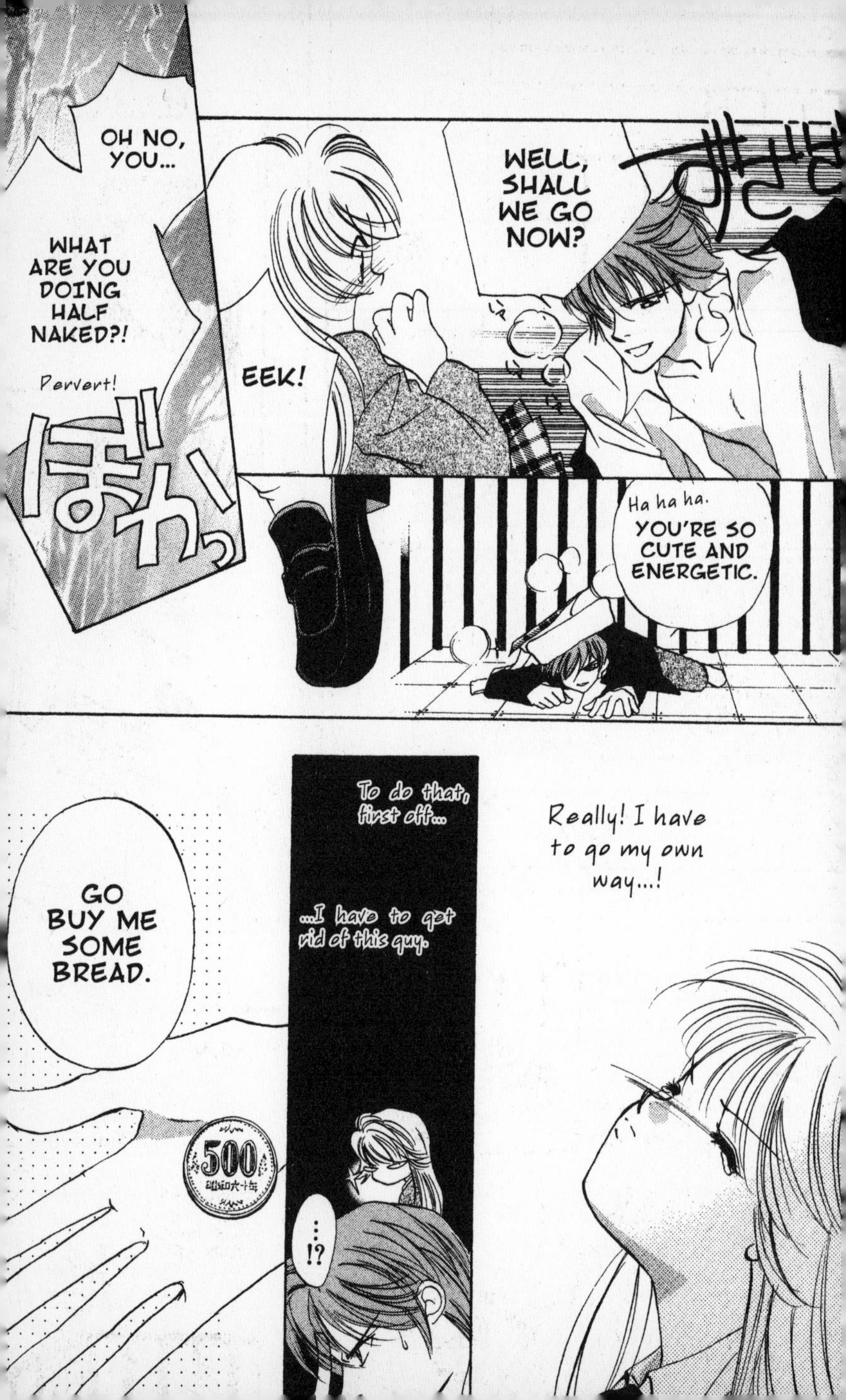
WELL, SHALL WE GO NOW?
OH NO, YOU...
WHAT ARE YOU DOING HALF NAKED?!
Pervert!
EEK!
Ha ha ha.
YOU'RE SO CUTE AND ENERGETIC.
Really! I have to go my own way...!
To do that, first off...
...I have to get rid of this guy.
...!?
GO BUY ME SOME BREAD.
500

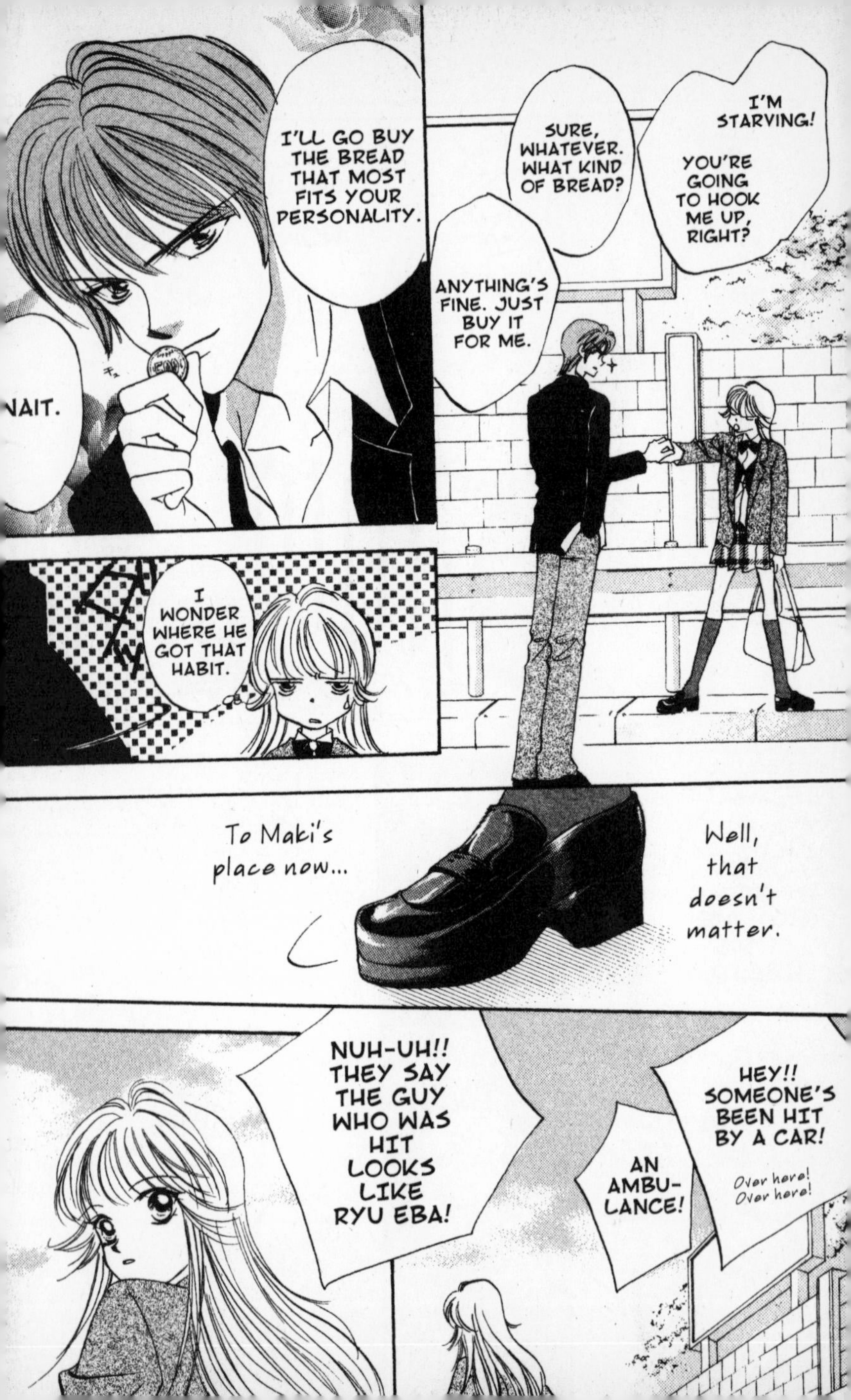
I'M STARVING!
YOU'RE GOING TO HOOK ME UP, RIGHT?
SURE, WHATEVER. WHAT KIND OF BREAD?
ANYTHING'S FINE. JUST BUY IT FOR ME.
I'LL GO BUY THE BREAD THAT MOST FITS YOUR PERSONALITY.
NAIT.
I WONDER WHERE HE GOT THAT HABIT.
Well, that doesn't matter.
To Maki's place now...
HEY!! SOMEONE'S BEEN HIT BY A CAR!
Over here! Over here!
AN AMBU-LANCE!
NUH-UH!! THEY SAY THE GUY WHO WAS HIT LOOKS LIKE RYU EBA!

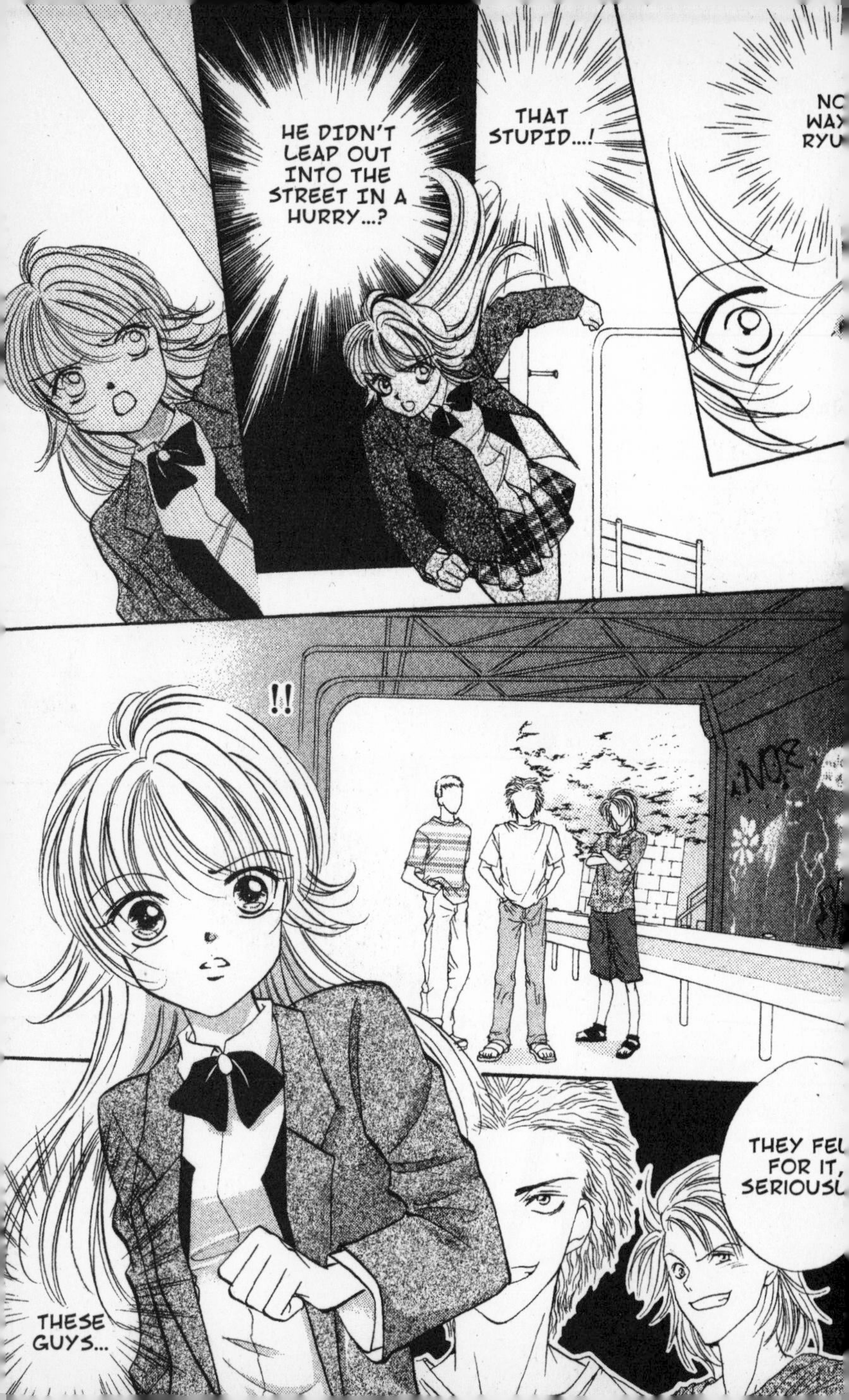
NO WAY RYU
THAT STUPID...!
HE DIDN'T LEAP OUT INTO THE STREET IN A HURRY...?
!!
THEY FEL FOR IT, SERIOUSL
THESE GUYS...

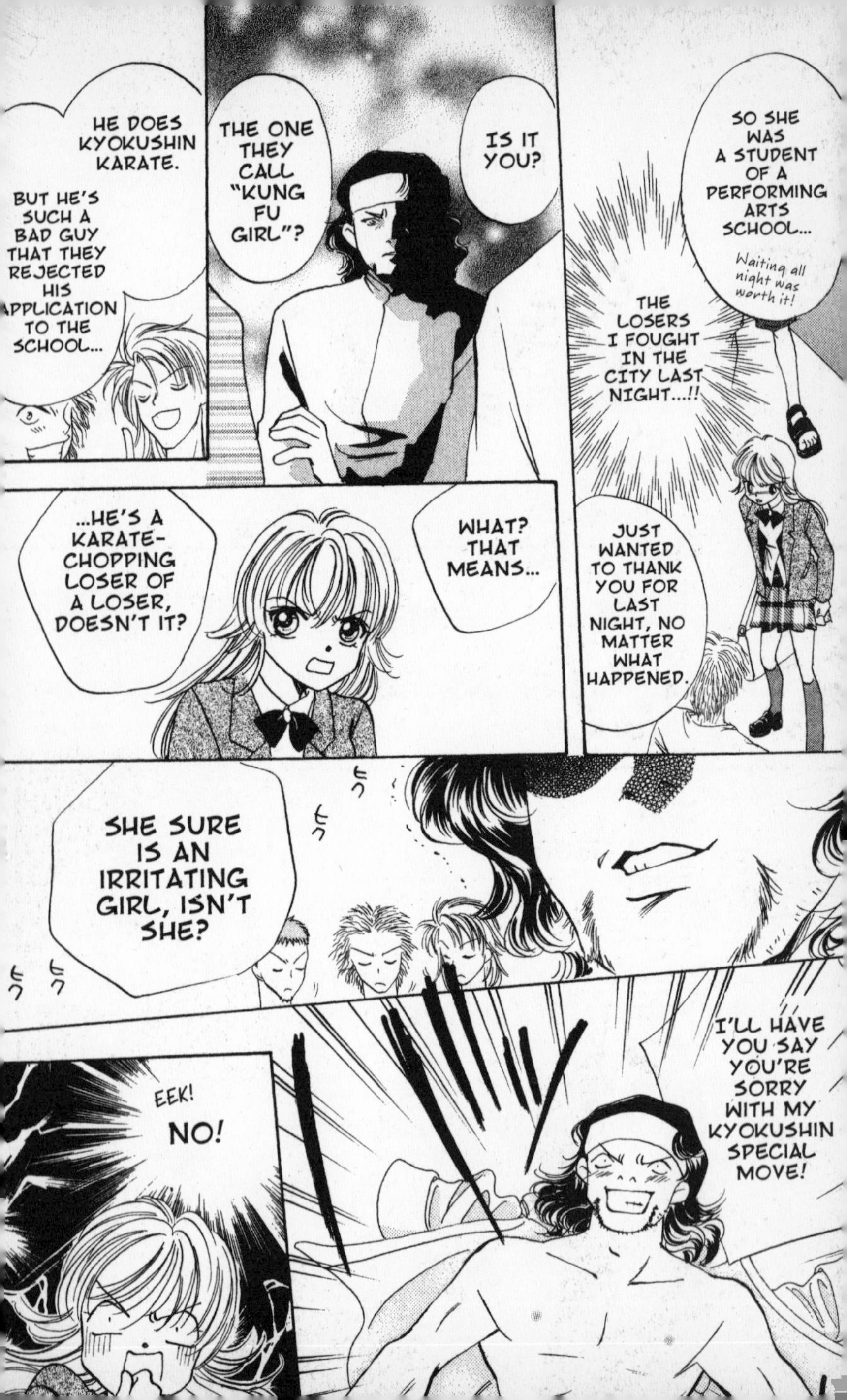
SO SHE WAS A STUDENT OF A PERFORMING ARTS SCHOOL...
Waiting all night was worth it!
THE LOSERS I FOUGHT IN THE CITY LAST NIGHT...!!
JUST WANTED TO THANK YOU FOR LAST NIGHT, NO MATTER WHAT HAPPENED.
IS IT YOU?
THE ONE THEY CALL "KUNG FU GIRL"?
HE DOES KYOKUSHIN KARATE.
BUT HE'S SUCH A BAD GUY THAT THEY REJECTED HIS APPLICATION TO THE SCHOOL...
WHAT? THAT MEANS...
...HE'S A KARATE-CHOPPING LOSER OF A LOSER, DOESN'T IT?
SHE SURE IS AN IRRITATING GIRL, ISN'T SHE?
I'LL HAVE YOU SAY YOU'RE SORRY WITH MY KYOKUSHIN SPECIAL MOVE!
EEK!
NO!

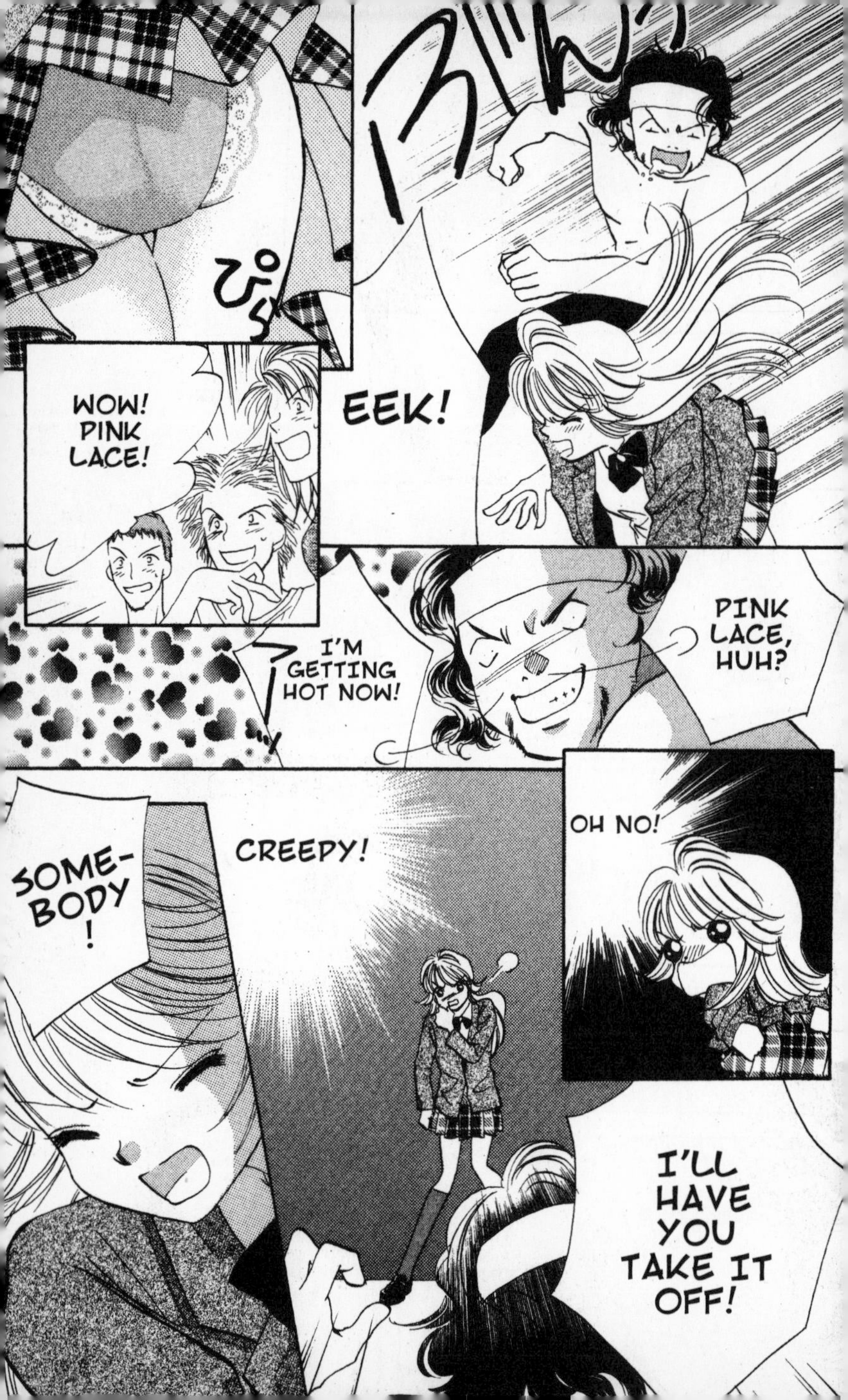
EEK!
WOW! PINK LACE!
PINK LACE, HUH?
I'M GETTING HOT NOW!
OH NO!
I'LL HAVE YOU TAKE IT OFF!
CREEPY!
SOME-BODY!

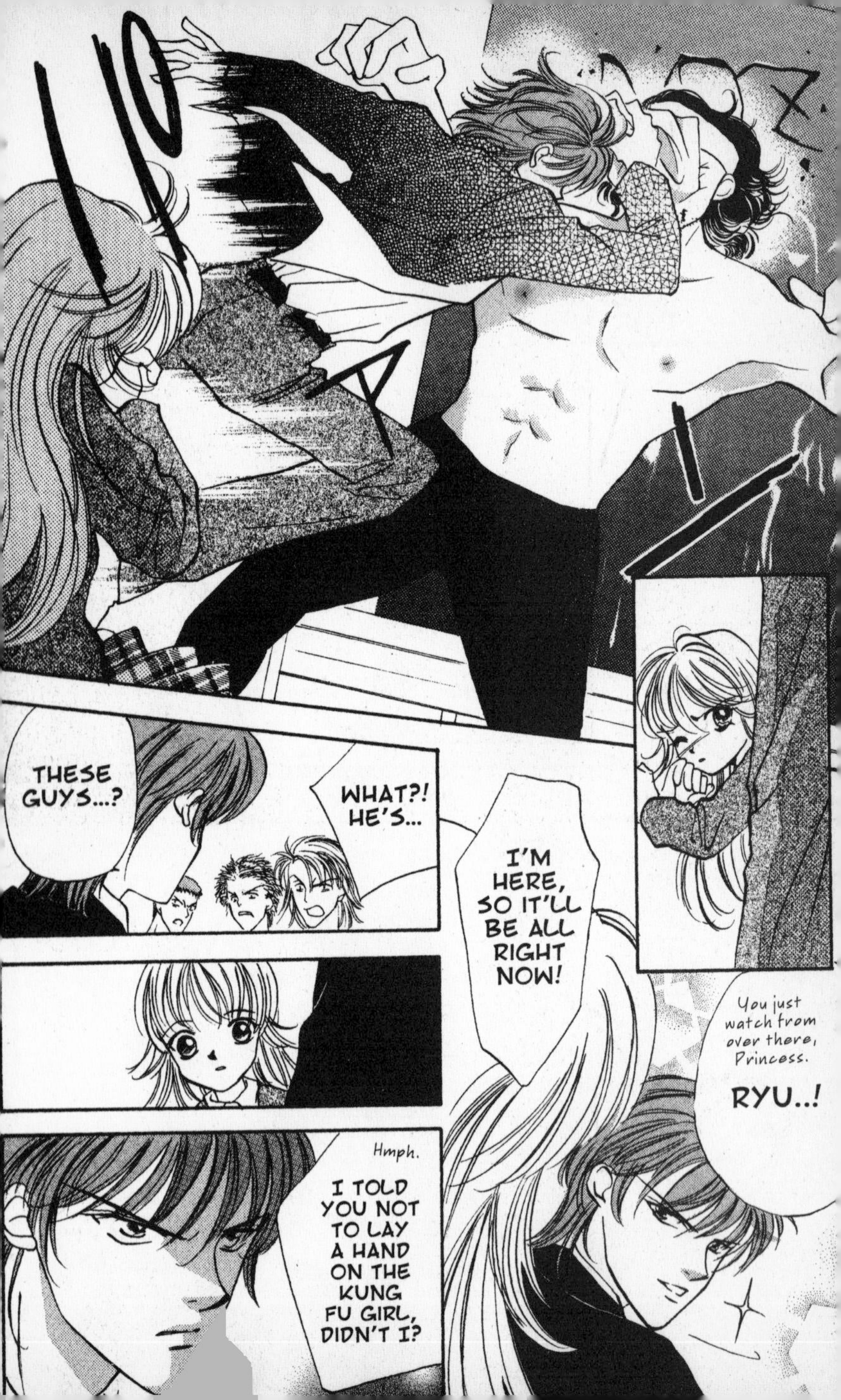
I'M HERE, SO IT'LL BE ALL RIGHT NOW!
You just watch from over there, Princess.
RYU..!
WHAT?! HE'S...
THESE GUYS...?
Hmph.
I TOLD YOU NOT TO LAY A HAND ON THE KUNG FU GIRL, DIDN'T I?

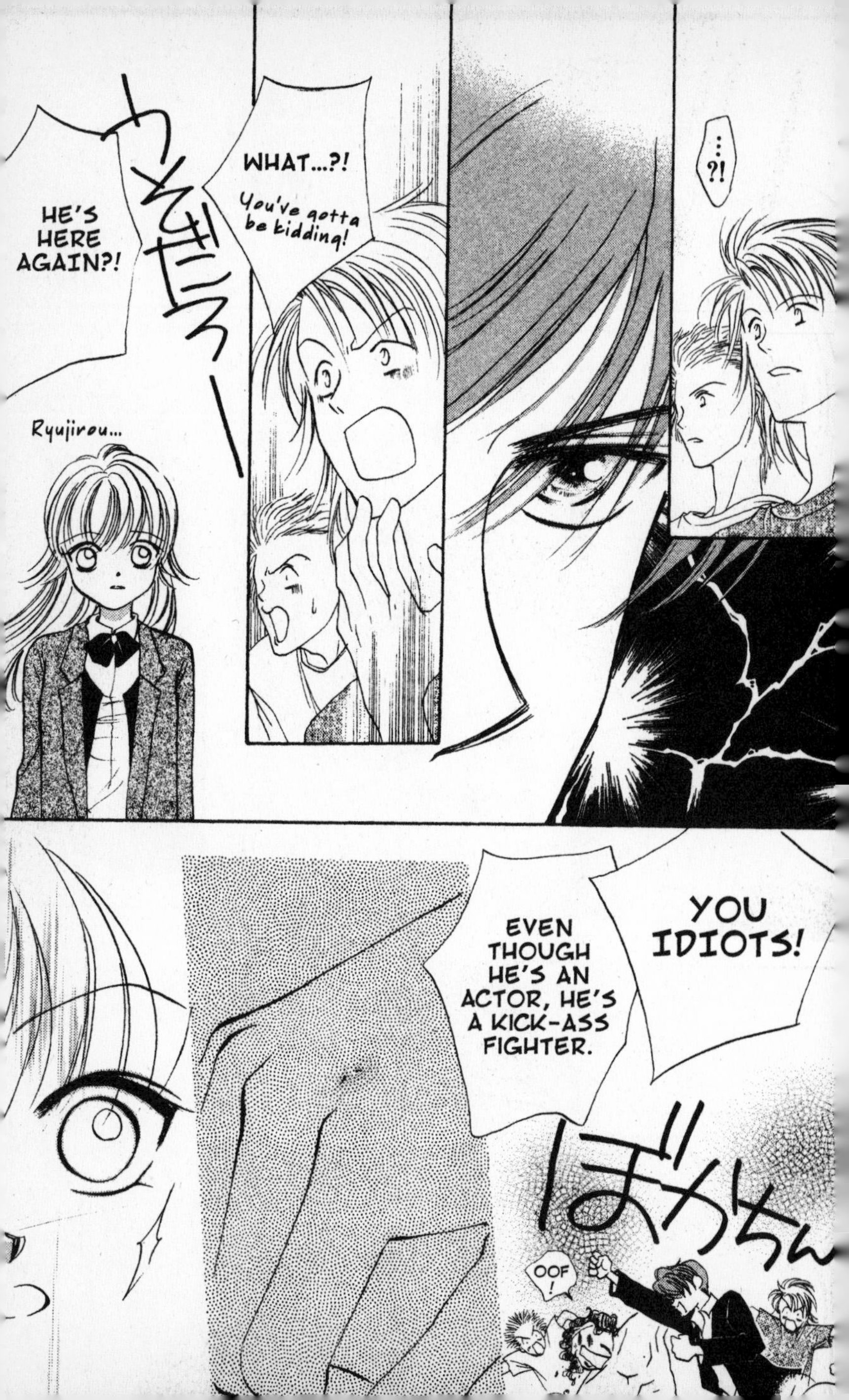
…?!
WHAT…?!
You've gotta be kidding!
HE'S HERE AGAIN?!
Ryujirou…
YOU IDIOTS!
EVEN THOUGH HE'S AN ACTOR, HE'S A KICK-ASS FIGHTER.
OOF!

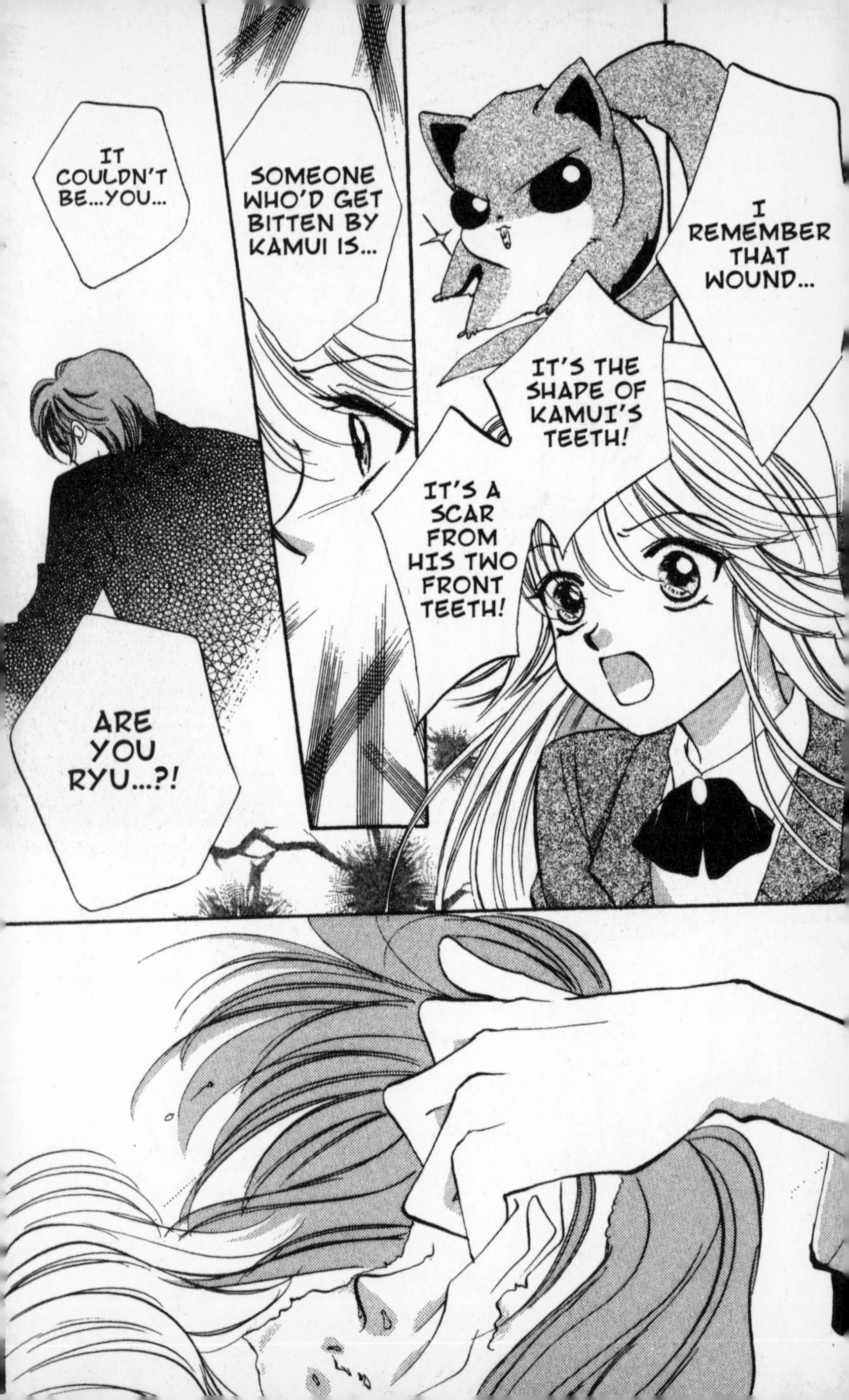
I REMEMBER THAT WOUND...
IT'S THE SHAPE OF KAMUI'S TEETH!
IT'S A SCAR FROM HIS TWO FRONT TEETH!
SOMEONE WHO'D GET BITTEN BY KAMUI IS...
IT COULDN'T BE...YOU...
ARE YOU RYU...?!

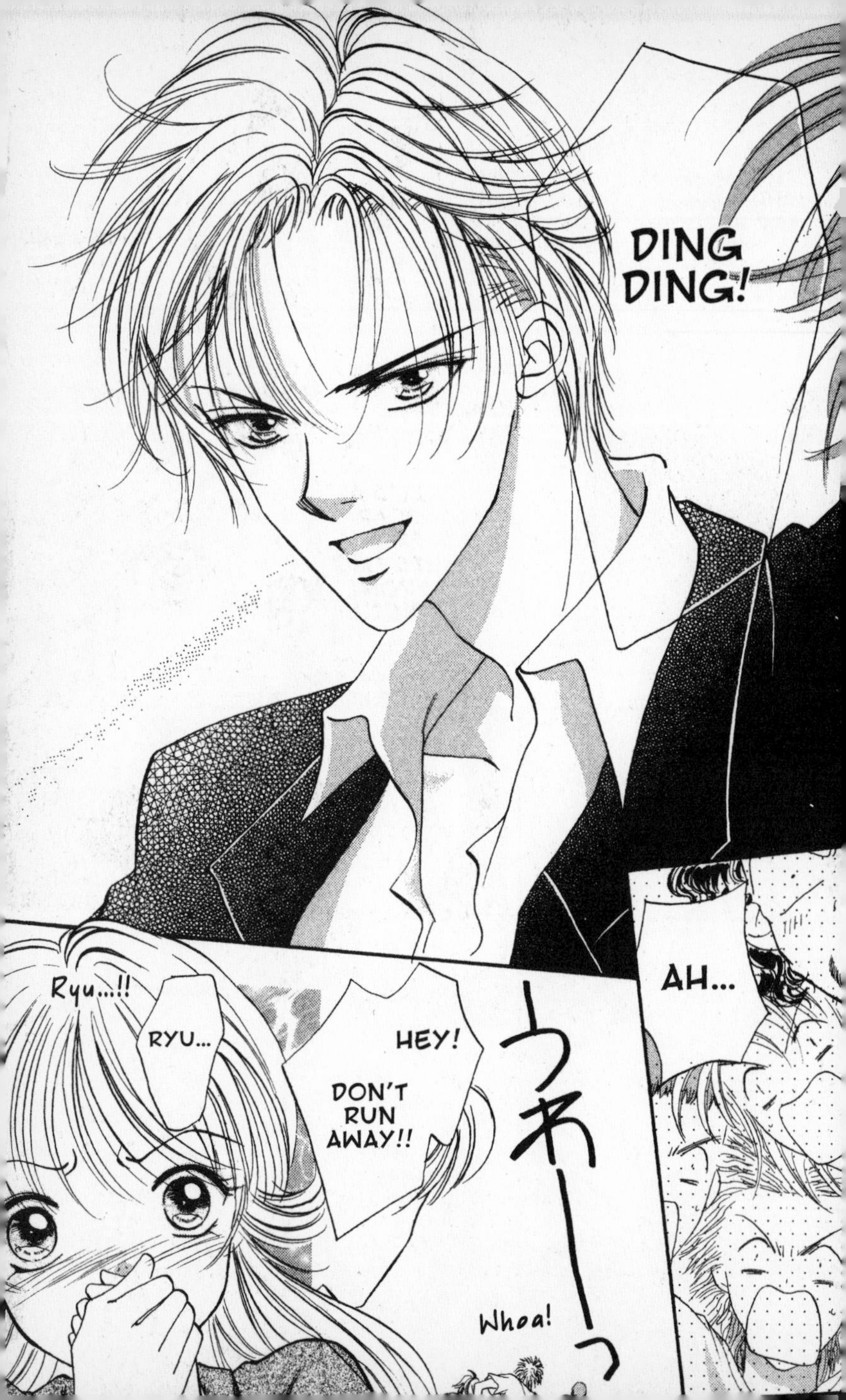
DING DING!
AH...
うわーっ
HEY!
DON'T RUN AWAY!!
RYU...
Ryu...!!
Whoa!

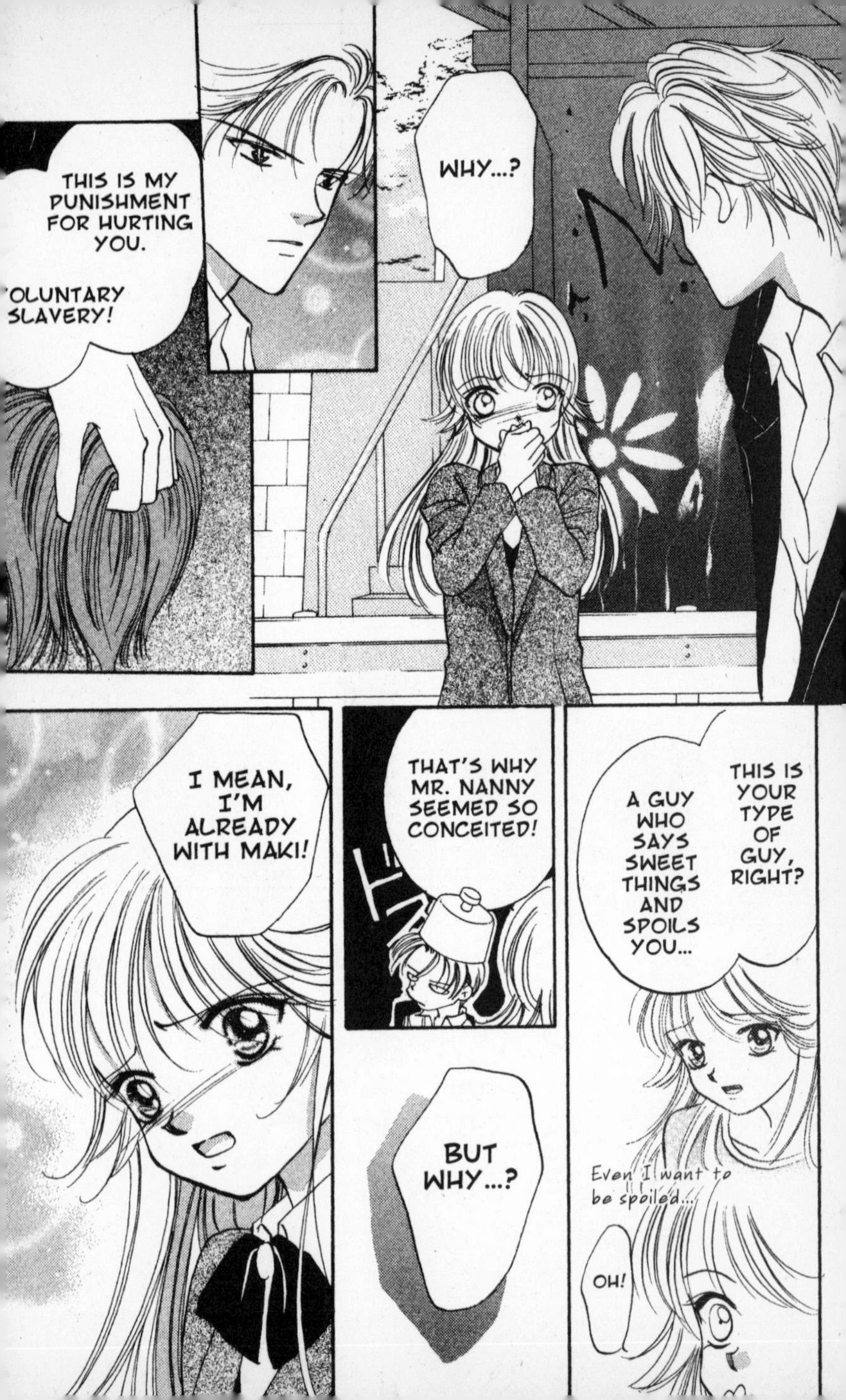
WHY...?
THIS IS MY PUNISHMENT FOR HURTING YOU.
OLUNTARY SLAVERY!
THIS IS YOUR TYPE OF GUY, RIGHT?
A GUY WHO SAYS SWEET THINGS AND SPOILS YOU...
Even I want to be spoiled...
OH!
THAT'S WHY MR. NANNY SEEMED SO CONCEITED!
BUT WHY...?
I MEAN, I'M ALREADY WITH MAKI!

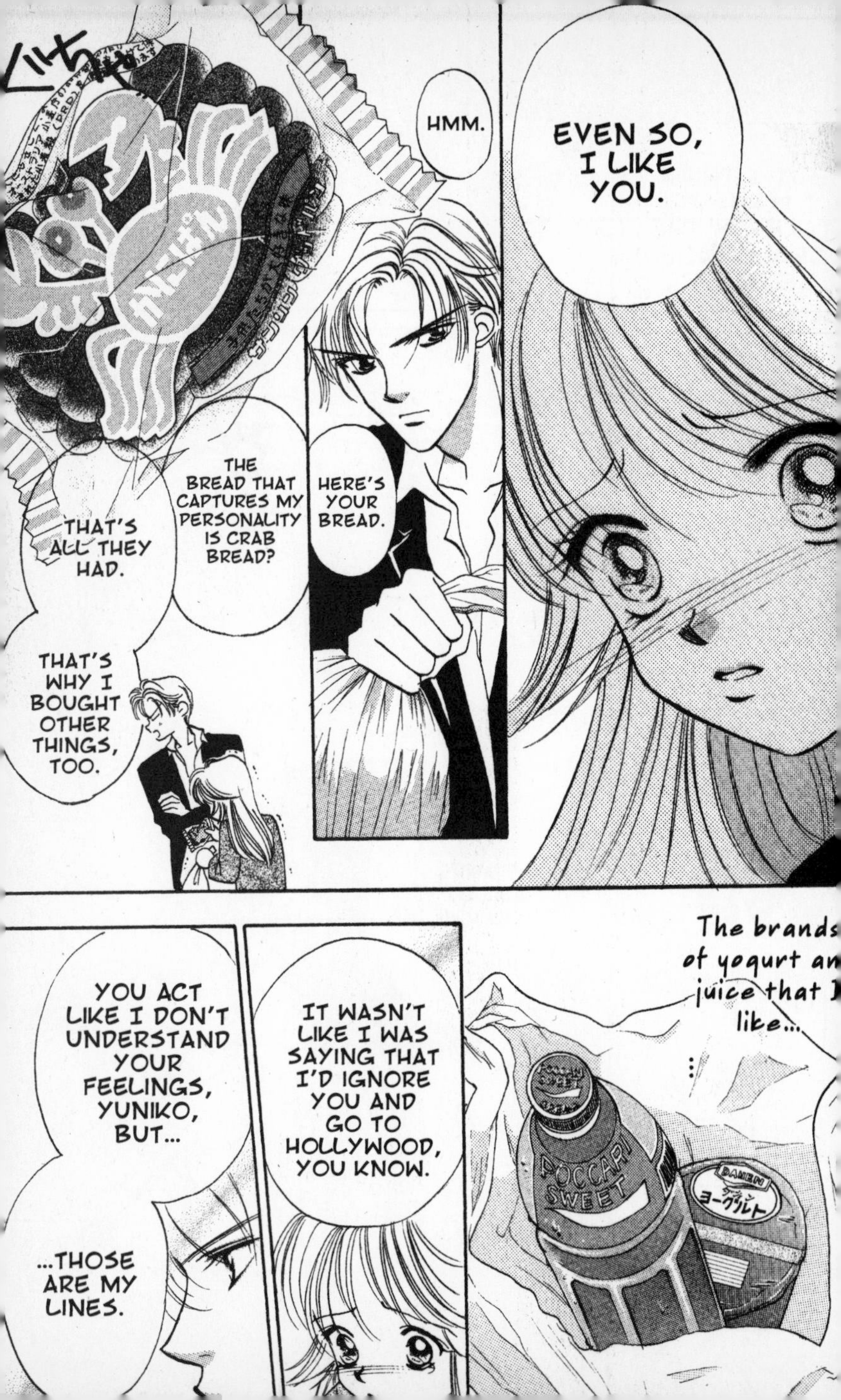
EVEN SO, I LIKE YOU.
HMM.
HERE'S YOUR BREAD.
THE BREAD THAT CAPTURES MY PERSONALITY IS CRAB BREAD?
THAT'S ALL THEY HAD.
THAT'S WHY I BOUGHT OTHER THINGS, TOO.
The brands of yogurt an juice that I like...
...
POCCARI SWEET
ヨーグルト
IT WASN'T LIKE I WAS SAYING THAT I'D IGNORE YOU AND GO TO HOLLYWOOD, YOU KNOW.
YOU ACT LIKE I DON'T UNDERSTAND YOUR FEELINGS, YUNIKO, BUT...
...THOSE ARE MY LINES.

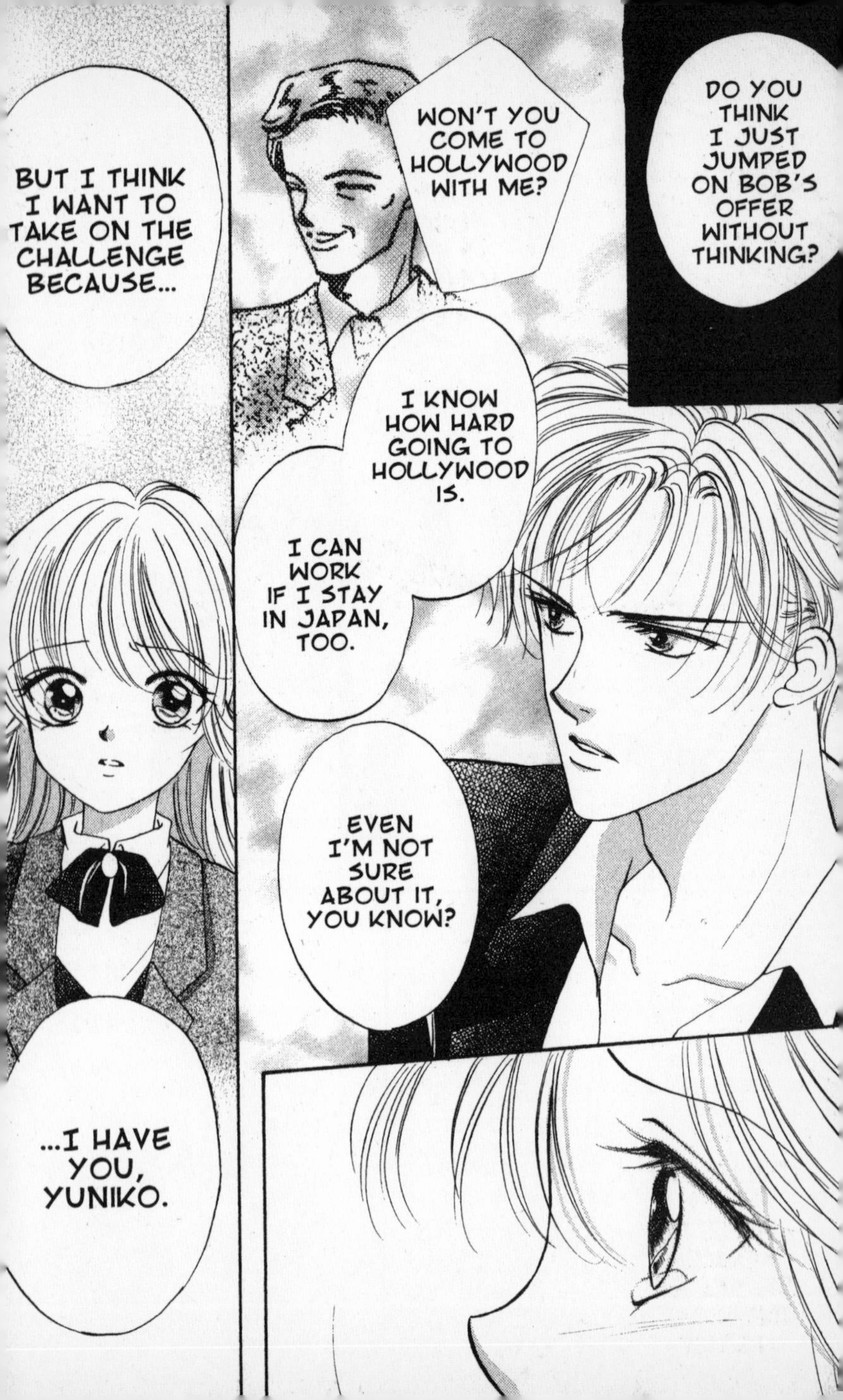
DO YOU THINK I JUST JUMPED ON BOB'S OFFER WITHOUT THINKING?
WON'T YOU COME TO HOLLYWOOD WITH ME?
I KNOW HOW HARD GOING TO HOLLYWOOD IS.
I CAN WORK IF I STAY IN JAPAN, TOO.
EVEN I'M NOT SURE ABOUT IT, YOU KNOW?
BUT I THINK I WANT TO TAKE ON THE CHALLENGE BECAUSE...
...I HAVE YOU, YUNIKO.

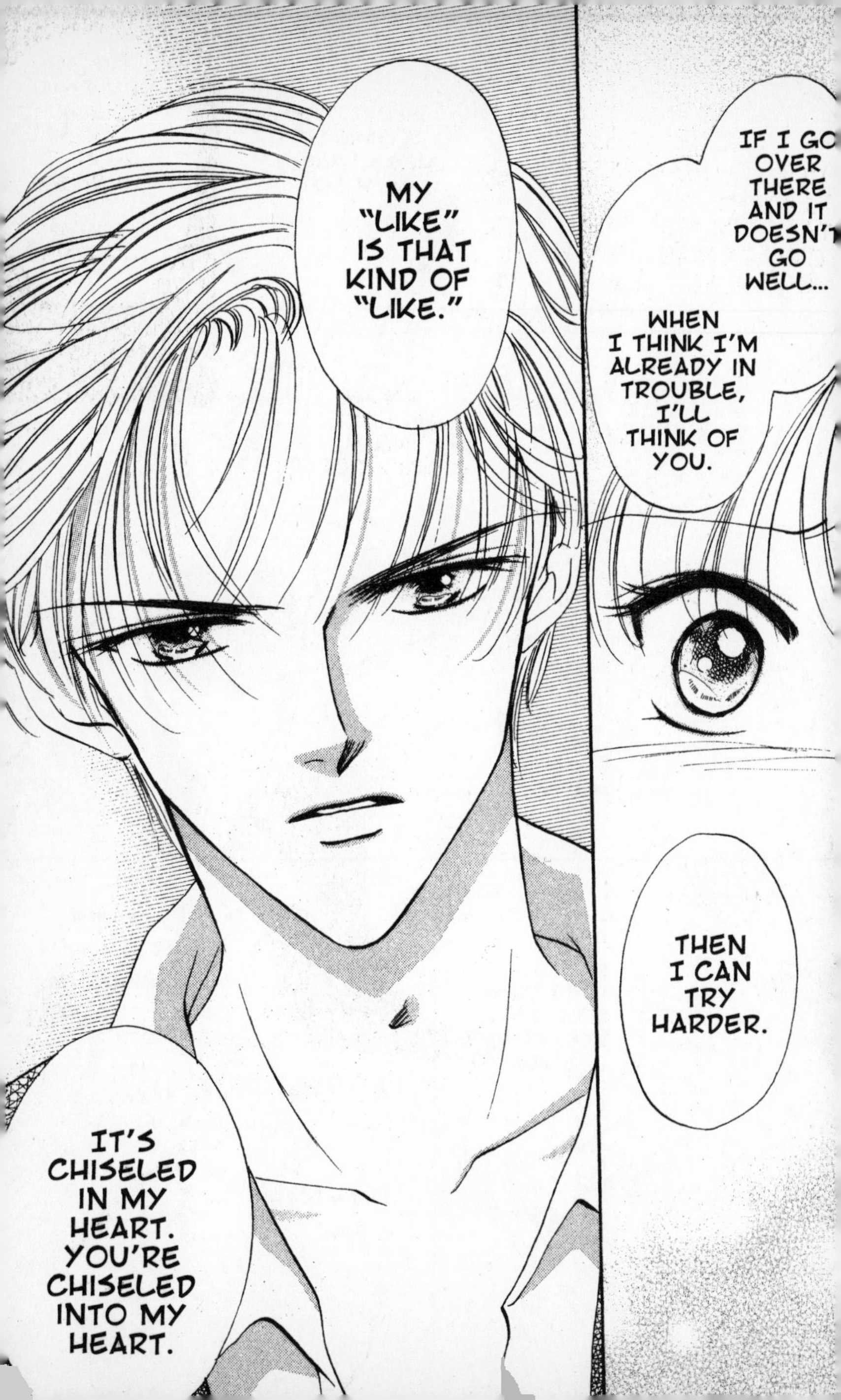
IF I GO OVER THERE AND IT DOESN'T GO WELL...
WHEN I THINK I'M ALREADY IN TROUBLE, I'LL THINK OF YOU.
THEN I CAN TRY HARDER.
MY "LIKE" IS THAT KIND OF "LIKE."
IT'S CHISELED IN MY HEART. YOU'RE CHISELED INTO MY HEART.

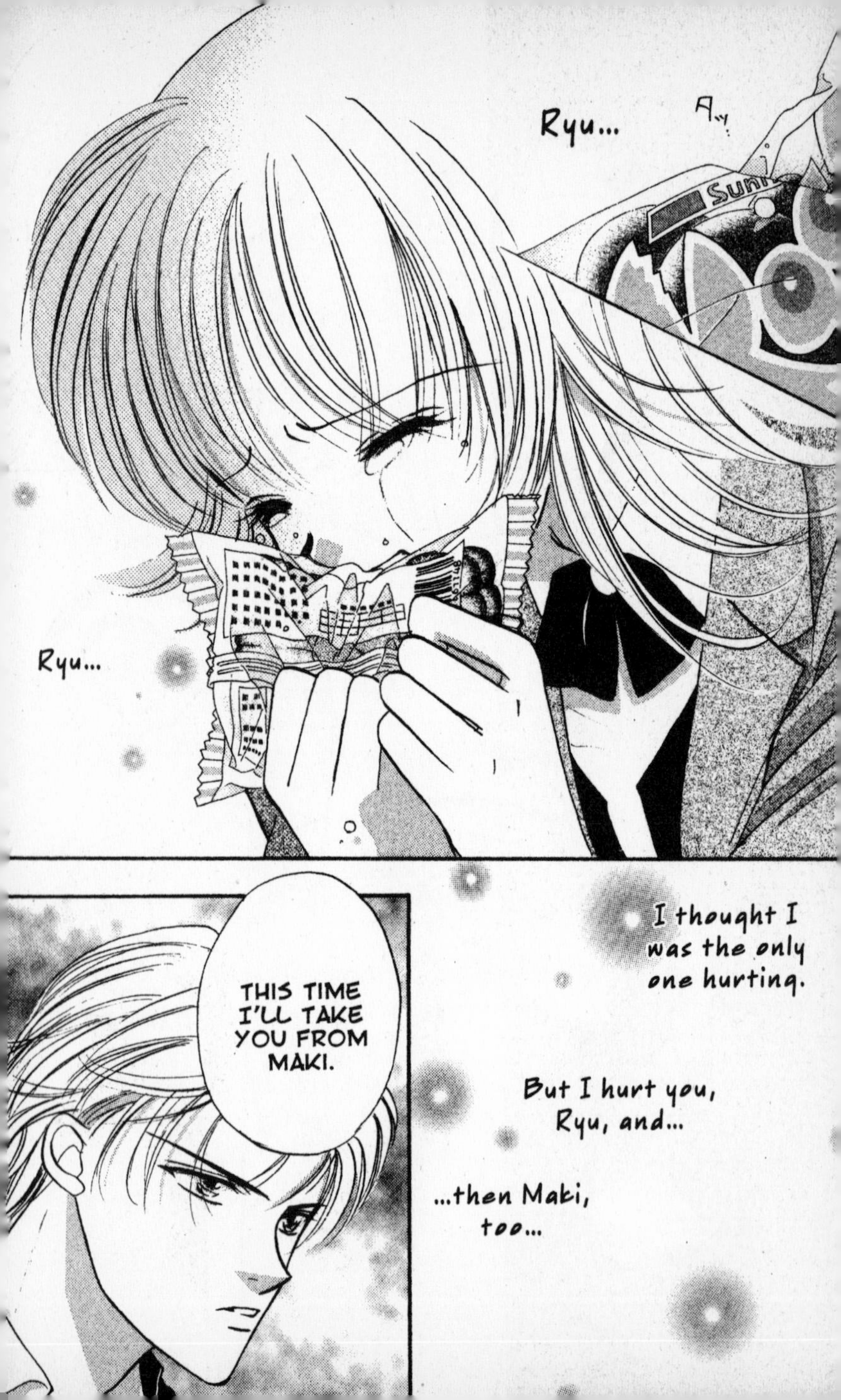

Ryu...
Ryu...
I thought I was the only one hurting.
But I hurt you, Ryu, and...
...then Maki, too...
THIS TIME I'LL TAKE YOU FROM MAKI.

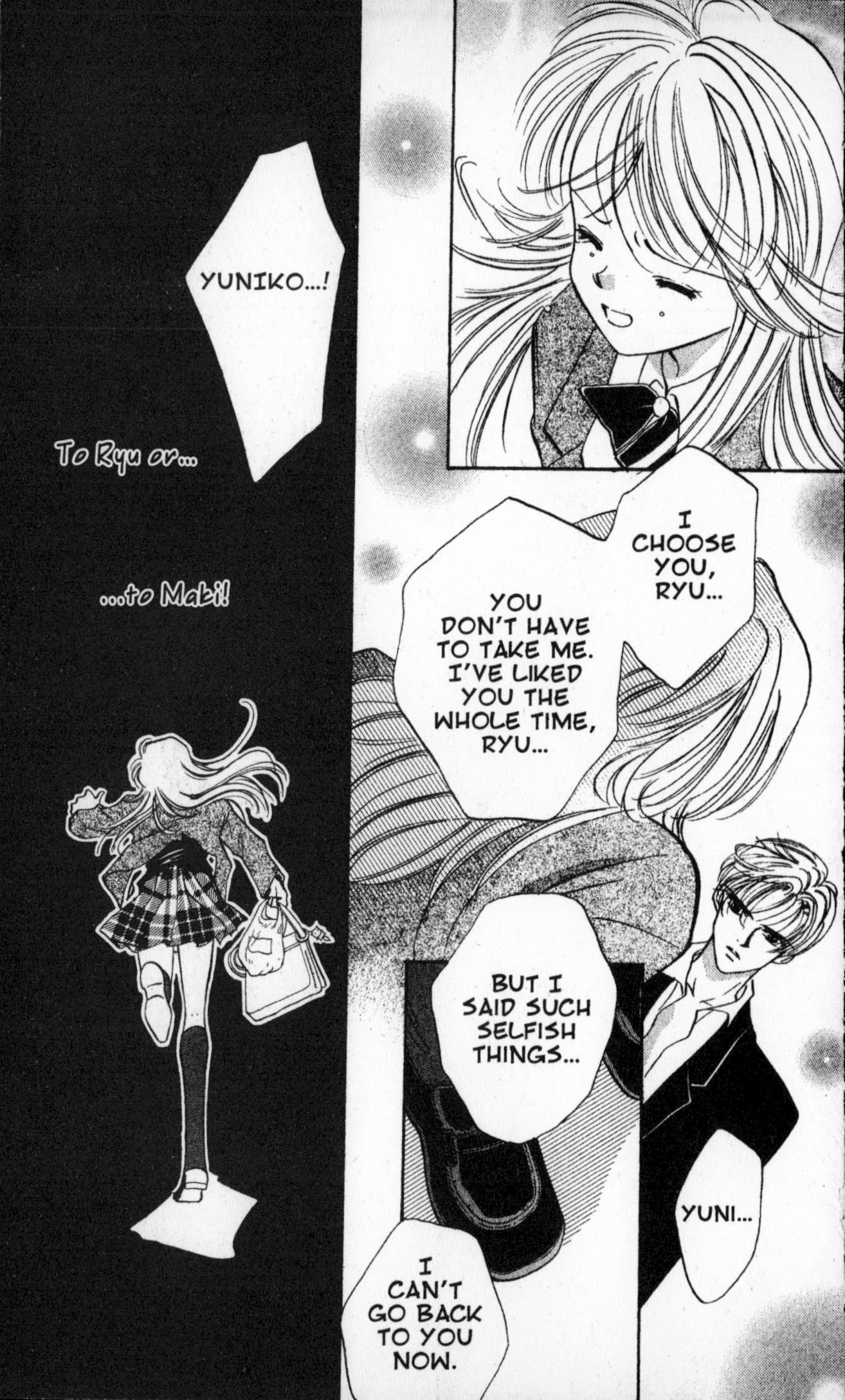
I CHOOSE YOU, RYU...
YOU DON'T HAVE TO TAKE ME. I'VE LIKED YOU THE WHOLE TIME, RYU...
BUT I SAID SUCH SELFISH THINGS...
YUNI...
I CAN'T GO BACK TO YOU NOW.
YUNIKO...!
To Ryu or...
...to Maki!

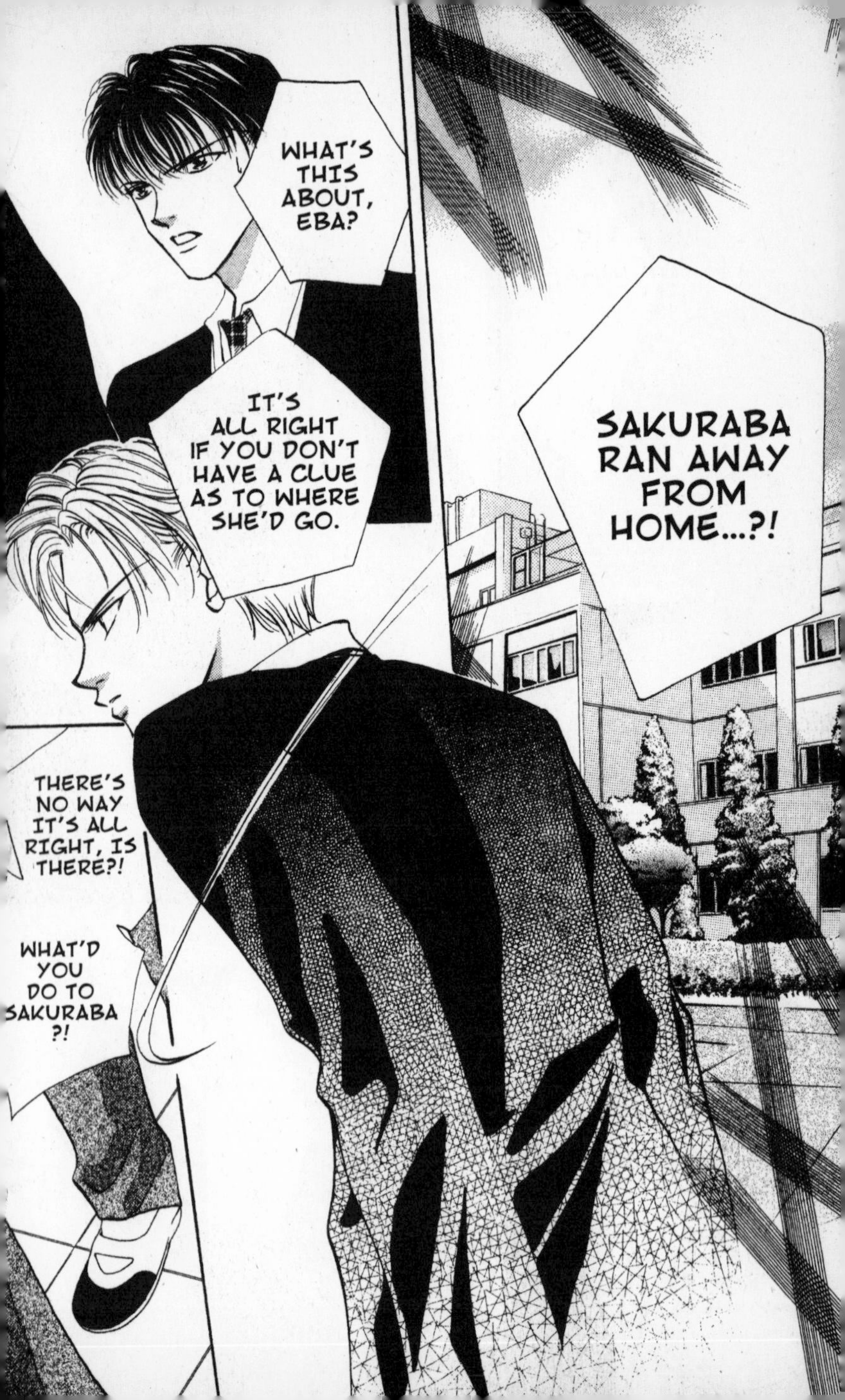
SAKURABA RAN AWAY FROM HOME...?!
WHAT'S THIS ABOUT, EBA?
IT'S ALL RIGHT IF YOU DON'T HAVE A CLUE AS TO WHERE SHE'D GO.
THERE'S NO WAY IT'S ALL RIGHT, IS THERE?!
WHAT'D YOU DO TO SAKURABA?!

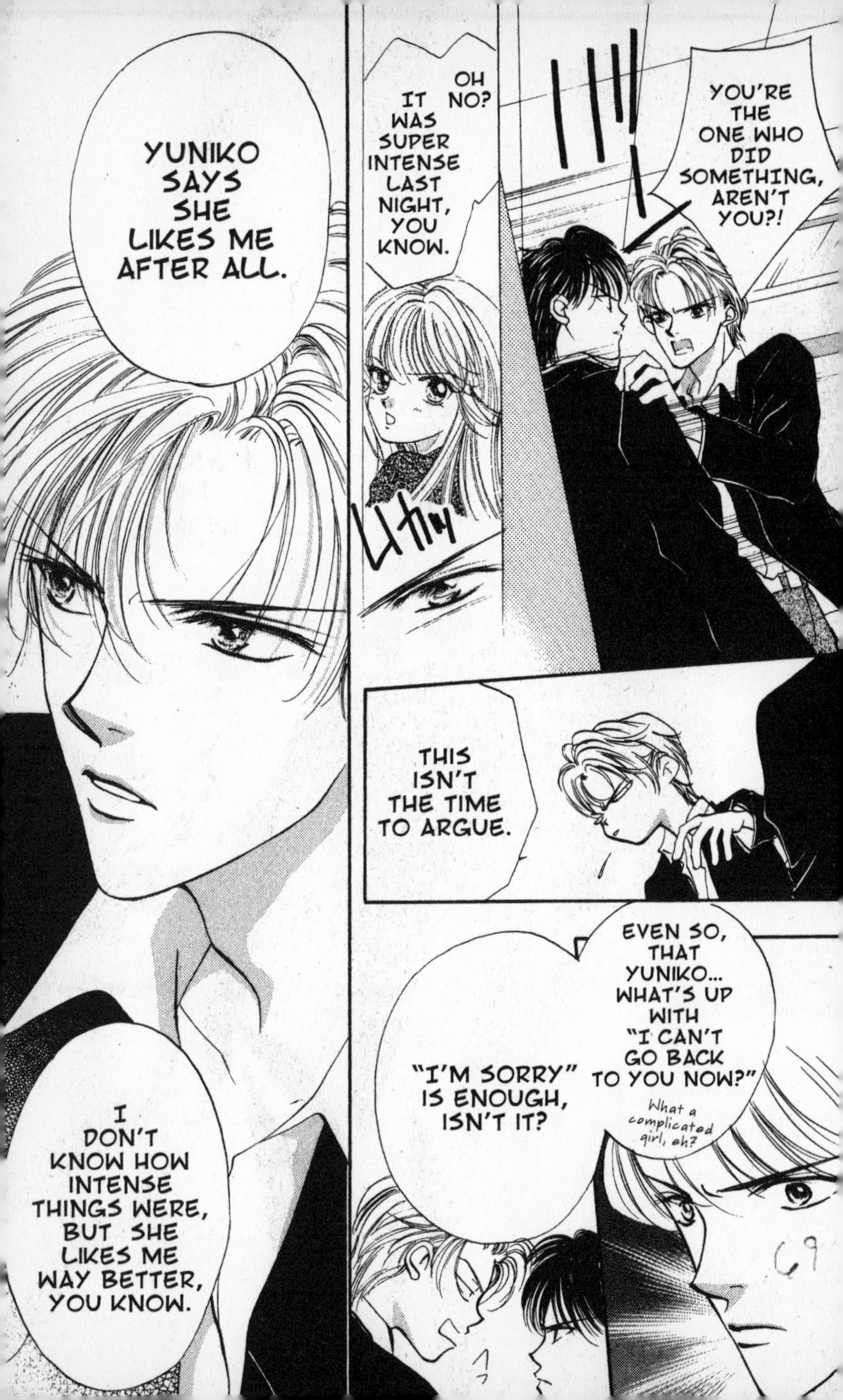
YOU'RE THE ONE WHO DID SOMETHING, AREN'T YOU?!
OH NO? IT WAS SUPER INTENSE LAST NIGHT, YOU KNOW.
THIS ISN'T THE TIME TO ARGUE.
EVEN SO, THAT YUNIKO... WHAT'S UP WITH "I CAN'T GO BACK TO YOU NOW?"
What a complicated girl, eh?
"I'M SORRY" IS ENOUGH, ISN'T IT?
YUNIKO SAYS SHE LIKES ME AFTER ALL.
I DON'T KNOW HOW INTENSE THINGS WERE, BUT SHE LIKES ME WAY BETTER, YOU KNOW.

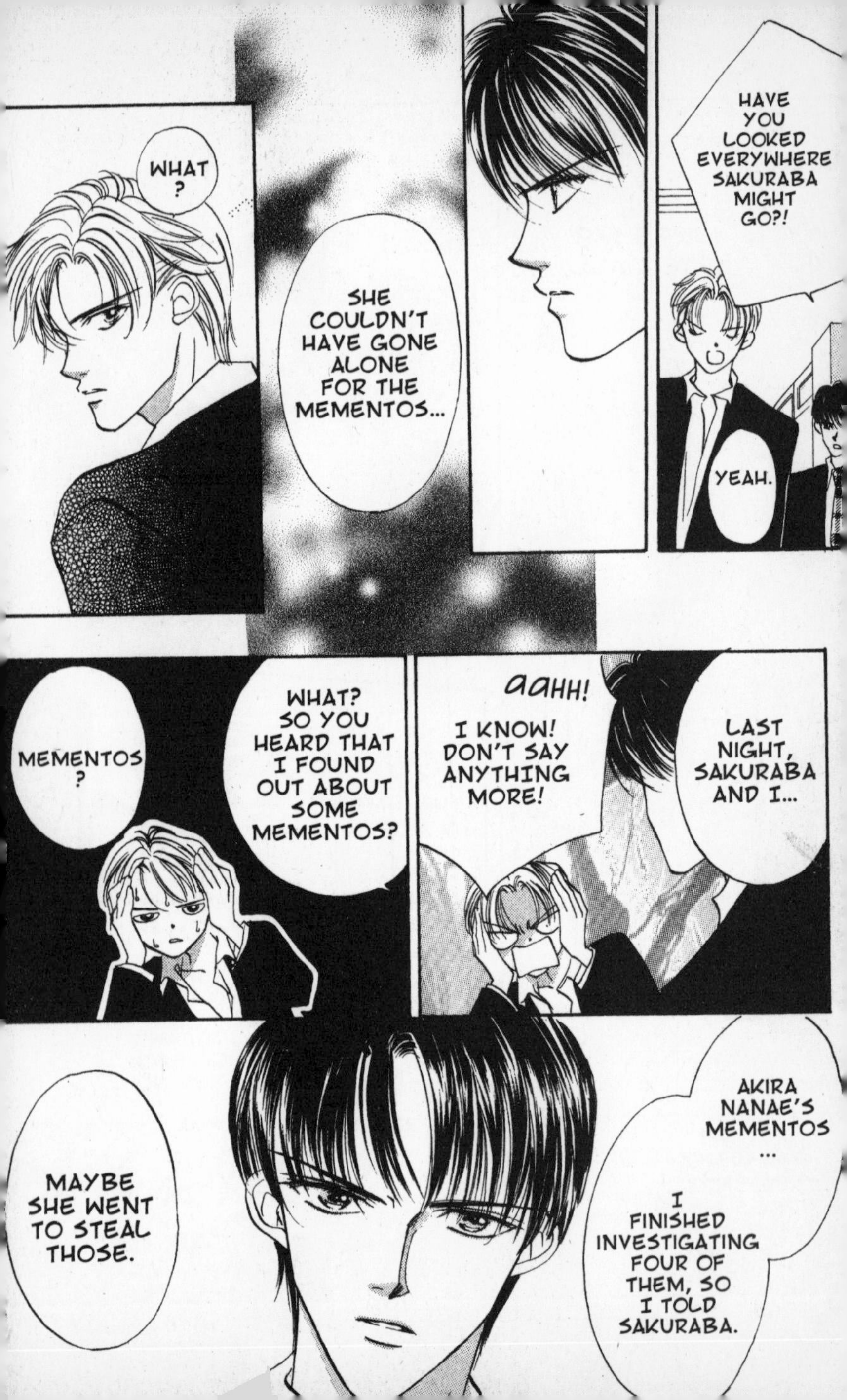

HAVE YOU LOOKED EVERYWHERE SAKURABA MIGHT GO?!
YEAH.
SHE COULDN'T HAVE GONE ALONE FOR THE MEMENTOS...
WHAT?
LAST NIGHT, SAKURABA AND I...
aahh!
I KNOW! DON'T SAY ANYTHING MORE!
WHAT? SO YOU HEARD THAT I FOUND OUT ABOUT SOME MEMENTOS?
MEMENTOS?
AKIRA NANAE'S MEMENTOS...
I FINISHED INVESTIGATING FOUR OF THEM, SO I TOLD SAKURABA.
MAYBE SHE WENT TO STEAL THOSE.

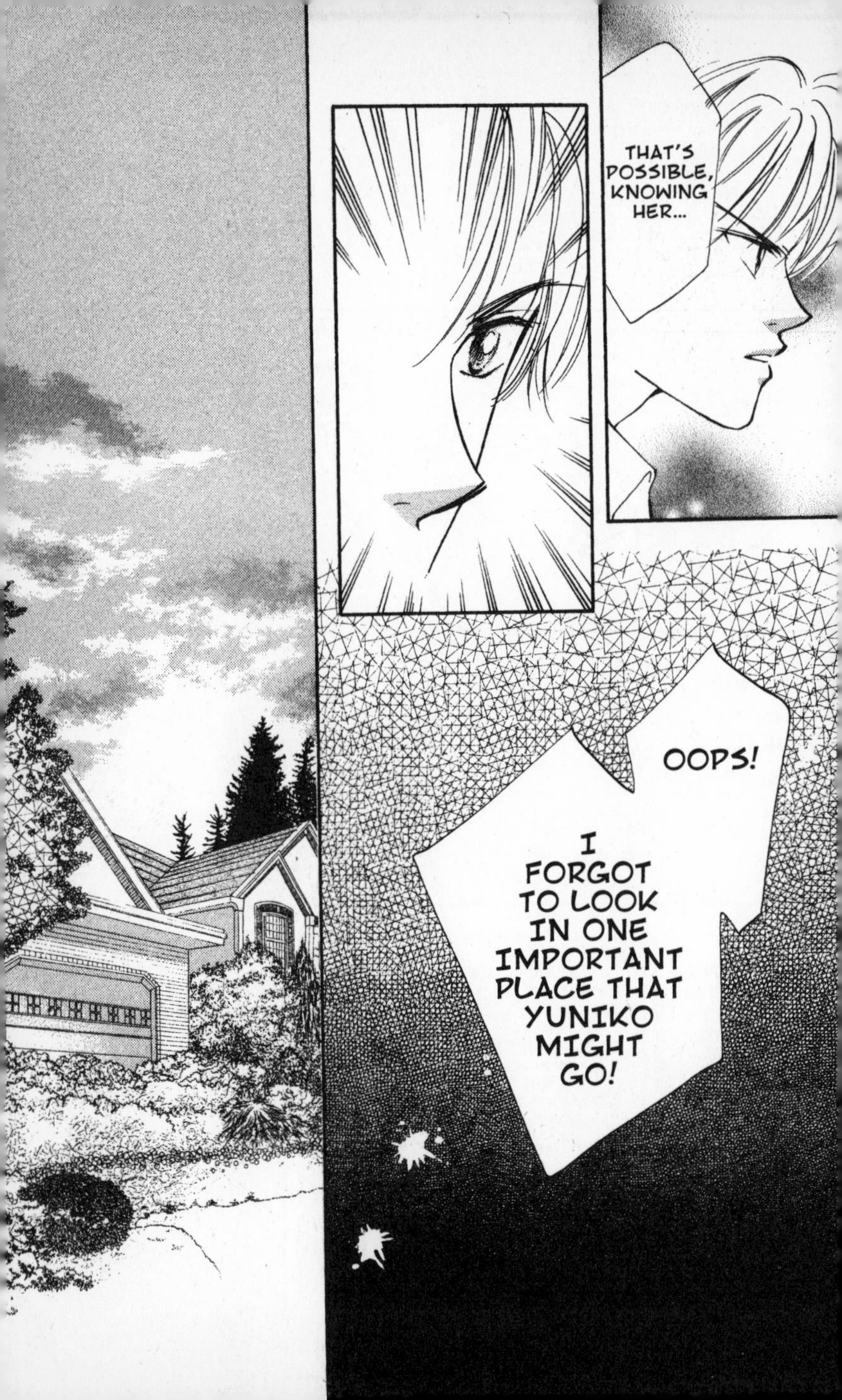
THAT'S POSSIBLE, KNOWING HER...
OOPS!
I FORGOT TO LOOK IN ONE IMPORTANT PLACE THAT YUNIKO MIGHT GO!

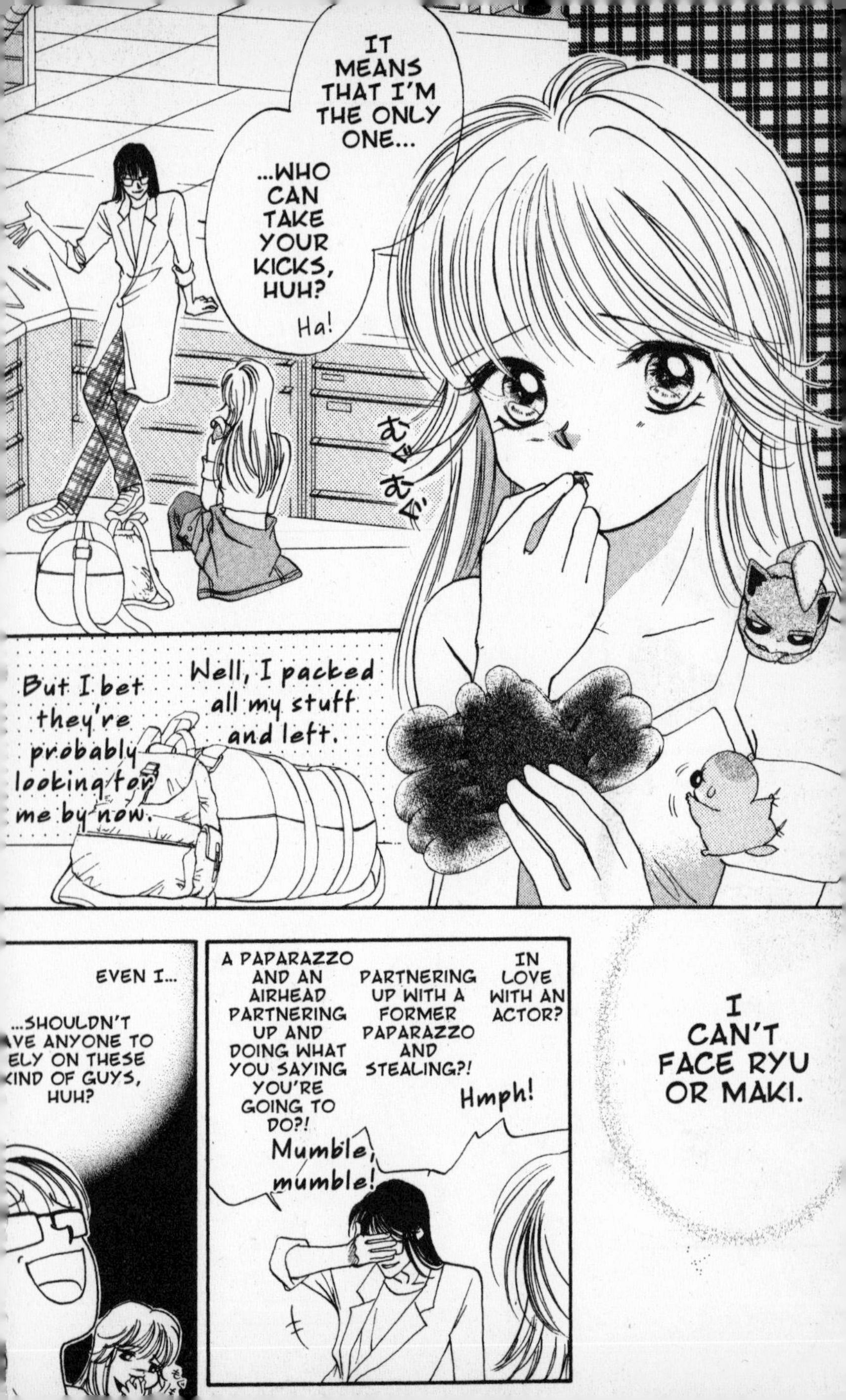
むぐ むぐ
IT MEANS THAT I'M THE ONLY ONE...
...WHO CAN TAKE YOUR KICKS, HUH?
Ha!
Well, I packed all my stuff and left.
But I bet they're probably looking for me by now.
I CAN'T FACE RYU OR MAKI.
IN LOVE WITH AN ACTOR?
PARTNERING UP WITH A FORMER PAPARAZZO AND STEALING?!
A PAPARAZZO AND AN AIRHEAD PARTNERING UP AND DOING WHAT YOU SAYING YOU'RE GOING TO DO?!
Hmph!
Mumble, mumble!
EVEN I...
...SHOULDN'T AVE ANYONE TO ELY ON THESE KIND OF GUYS, HUH?

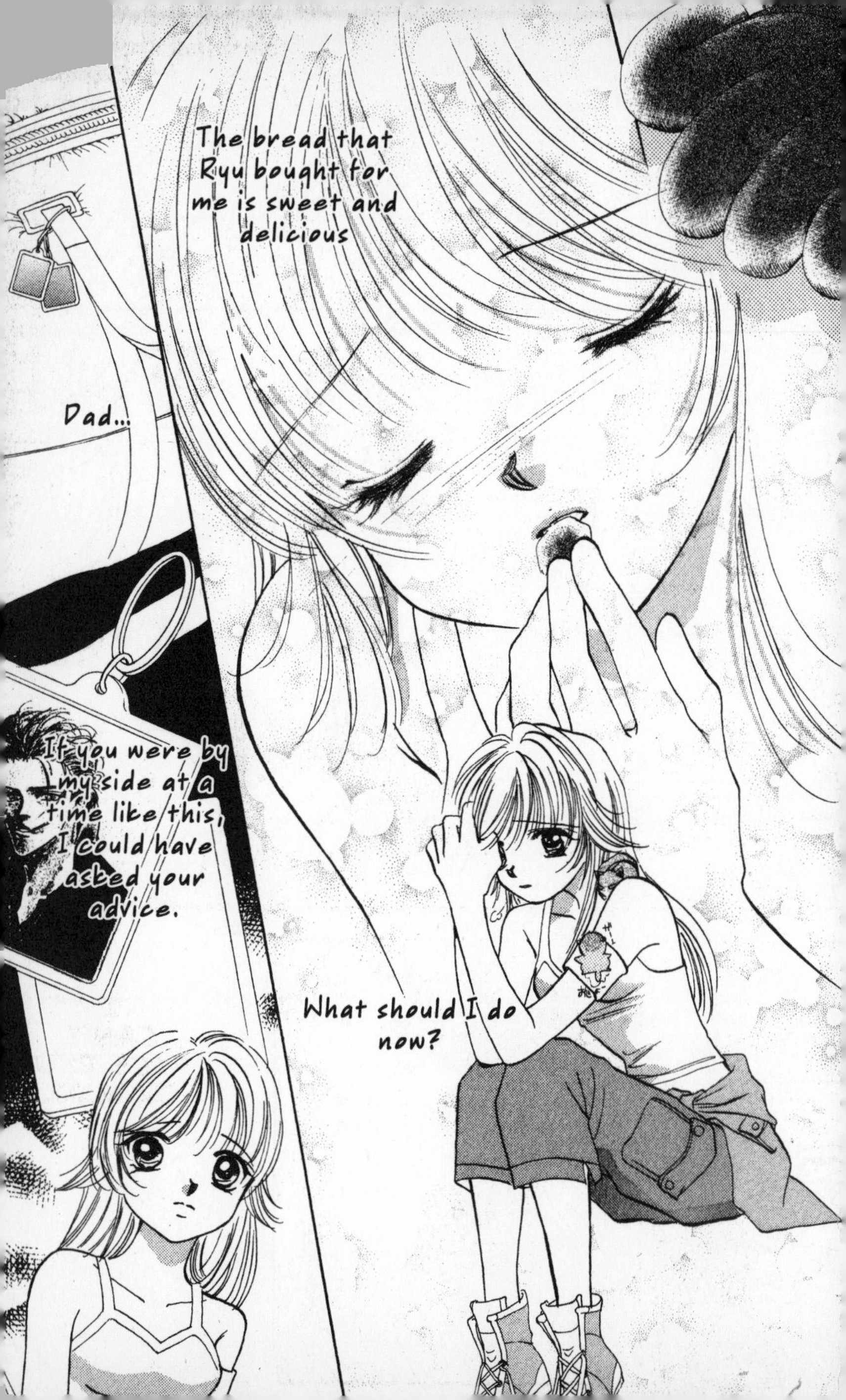
The bread that Ryu bought for me is sweet and delicious
Dad...
If you were by my side at a time like this, I could have asked your advice.
What should I do now?

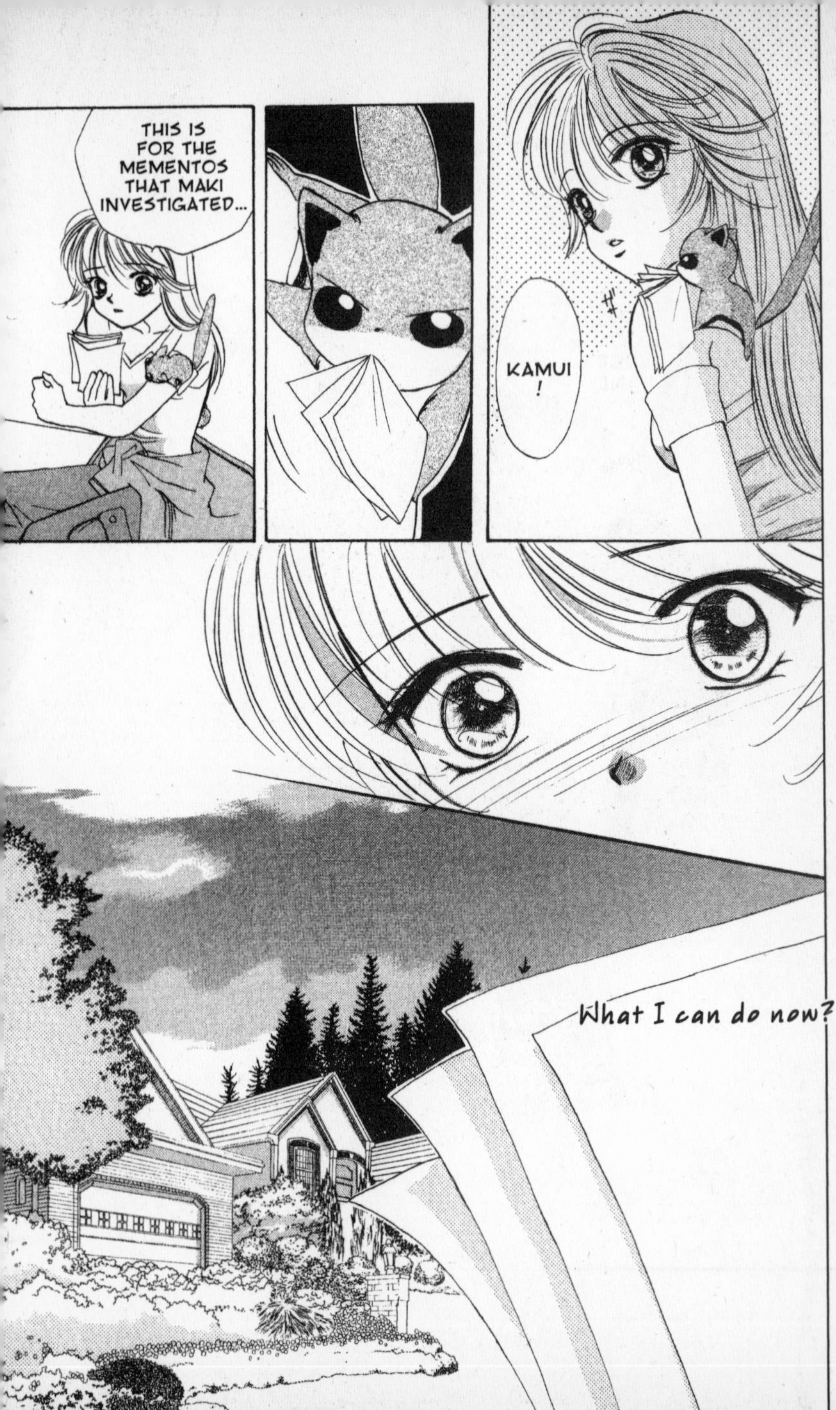
KAMUI!
THIS IS FOR THE MEMENTOS THAT MAKI INVESTIGATED...
What I can do now?

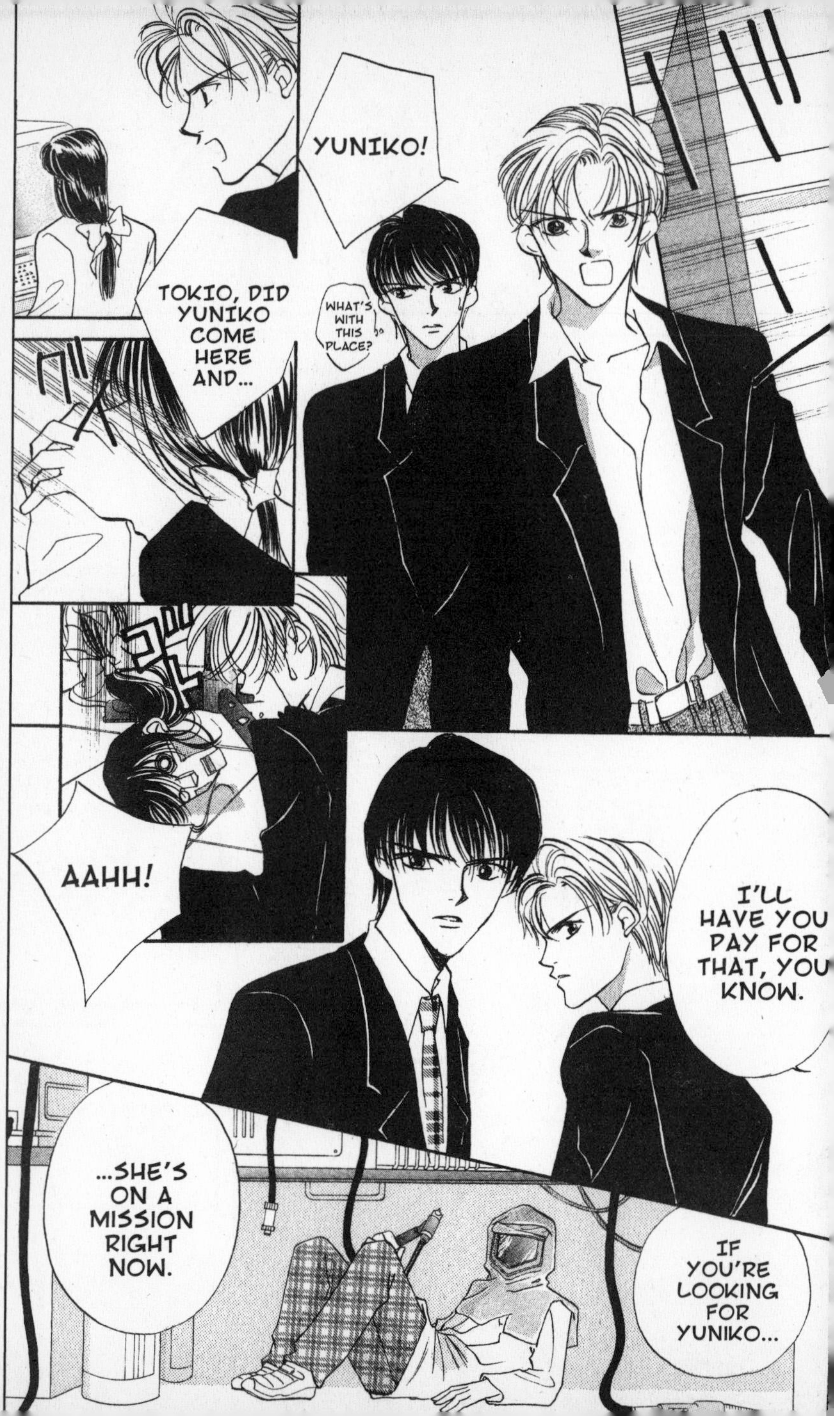
WHAT'S WITH THIS PLACE?
YUNIKO!
TOKIO, DID YUNIKO COME HERE AND...
AAHH!
I'LL HAVE YOU PAY FOR THAT, YOU KNOW.
IF YOU'RE LOOKING FOR YUNIKO...
...SHE'S ON A MISSION RIGHT NOW.

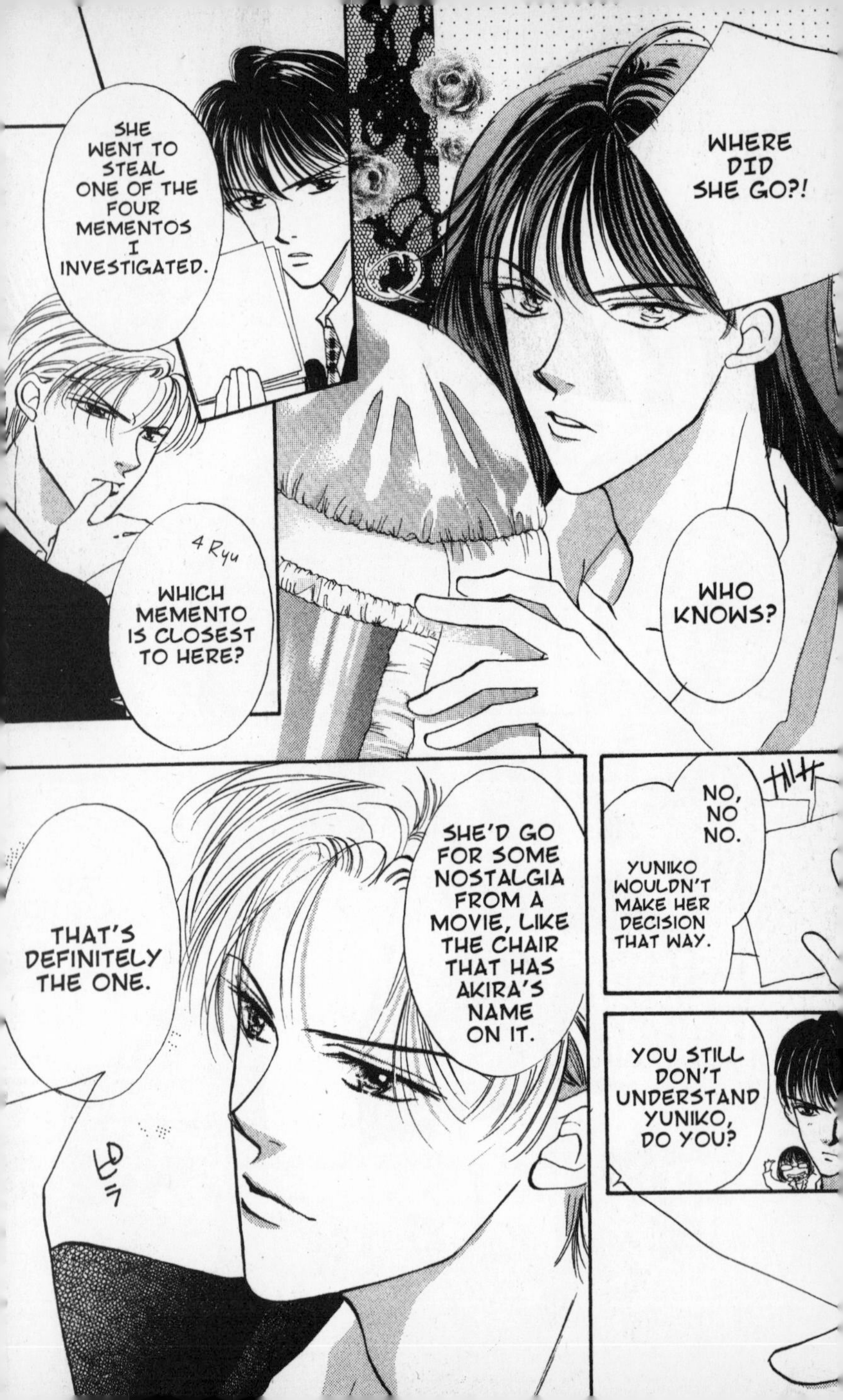
WHERE DID SHE GO?!
WHO KNOWS?
SHE WENT TO STEAL ONE OF THE FOUR MEMENTOS I INVESTIGATED.
4 Ryu
WHICH MEMENTO IS CLOSEST TO HERE?
NO, NO NO.
YUNIKO WOULDN'T MAKE HER DECISION THAT WAY.
YOU STILL DON'T UNDERSTAND YUNIKO, DO YOU?
SHE'D GO FOR SOME NOSTALGIA FROM A MOVIE, LIKE THE CHAIR THAT HAS AKIRA'S NAME ON IT.
THAT'S DEFINITELY THE ONE.

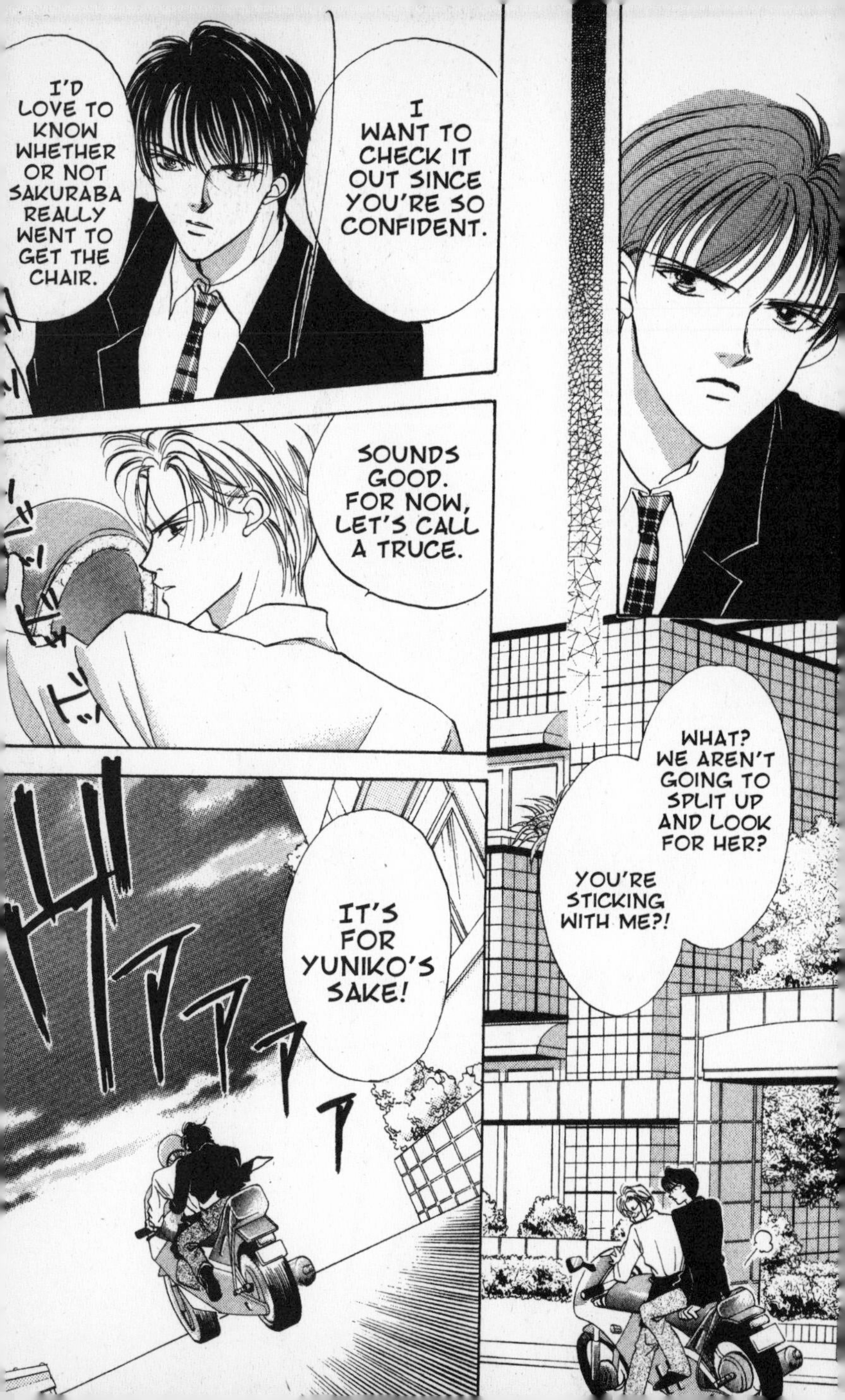
I'D LOVE TO KNOW WHETHER OR NOT SAKURABA REALLY WENT TO GET THE CHAIR.
I WANT TO CHECK IT OUT SINCE YOU'RE SO CONFIDENT.
SOUNDS GOOD. FOR NOW, LET'S CALL A TRUCE.
WHAT? WE AREN'T GOING TO SPLIT UP AND LOOK FOR HER?
YOU'RE STICKING WITH ME?!
IT'S FOR YUNIKO'S SAKE!

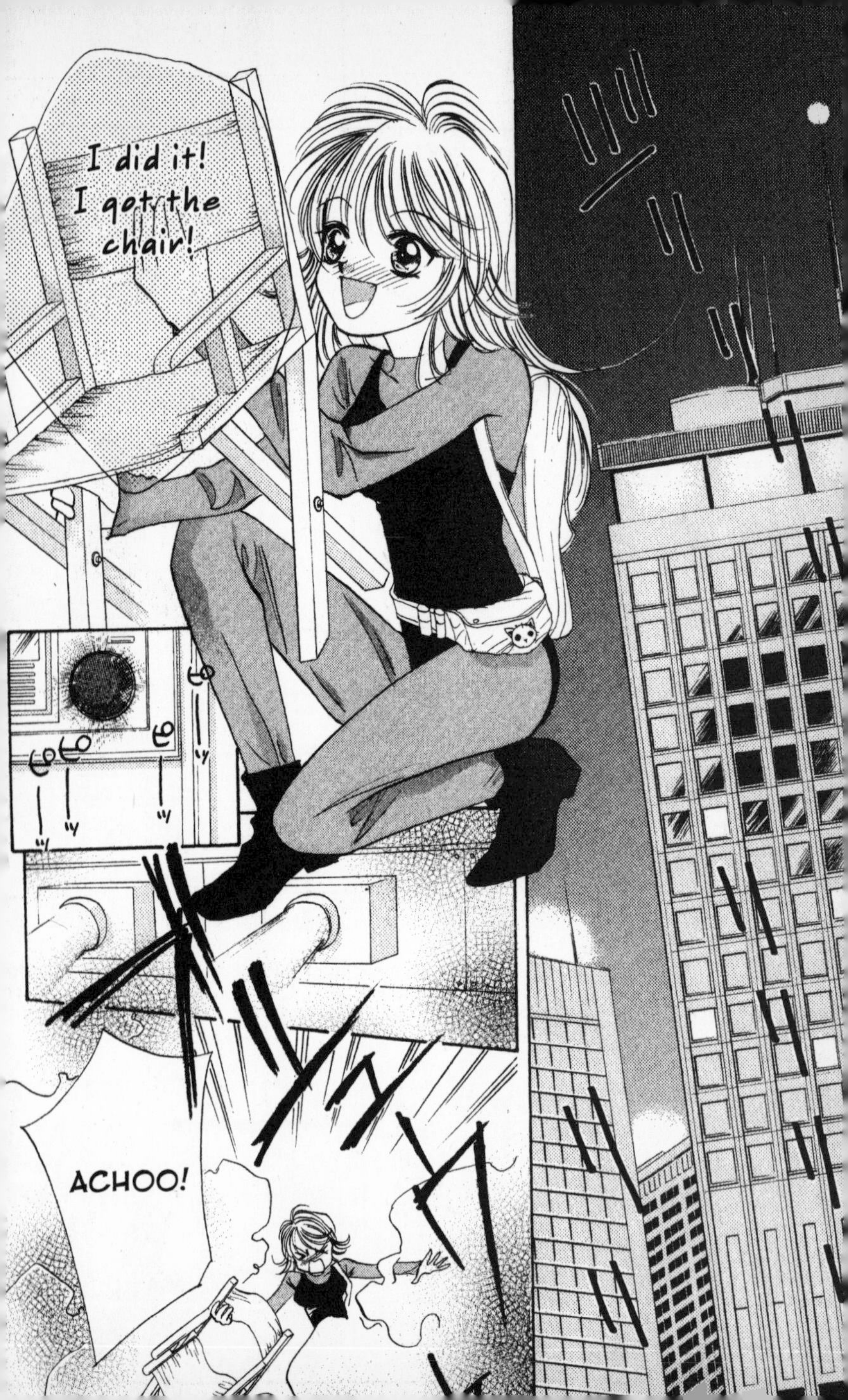
I did it! I got the chair!
ACHOO!

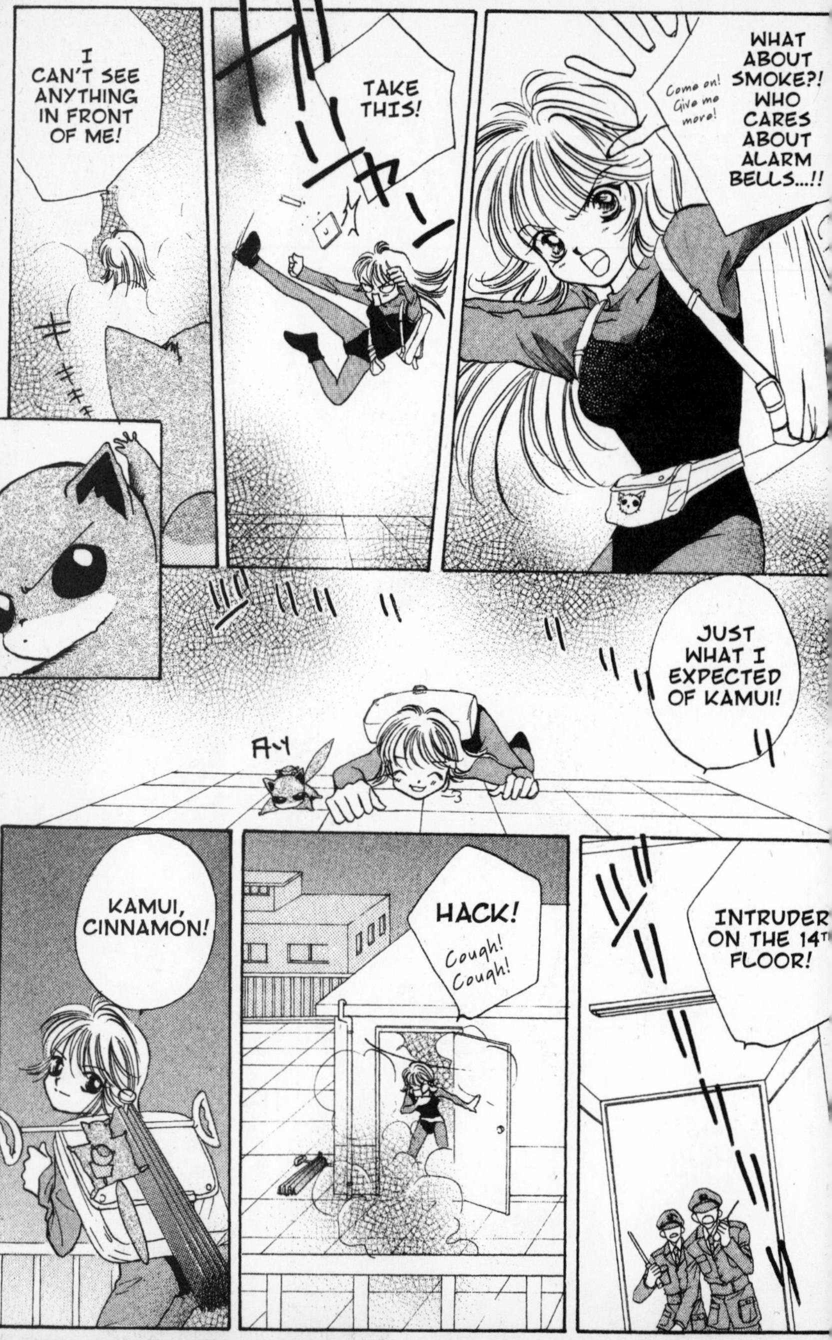

WHAT ABOUT SMOKE?! WHO CARES ABOUT ALARM BELLS...!!
Come on! Give me more!
TAKE THIS!
I CAN'T SEE ANYTHING IN FRONT OF ME!
JUST WHAT I EXPECTED OF KAMUI!
INTRUDER ON THE 14TH FLOOR!
HACK!
Cough! Cough!
KAMUI, CINNAMON!

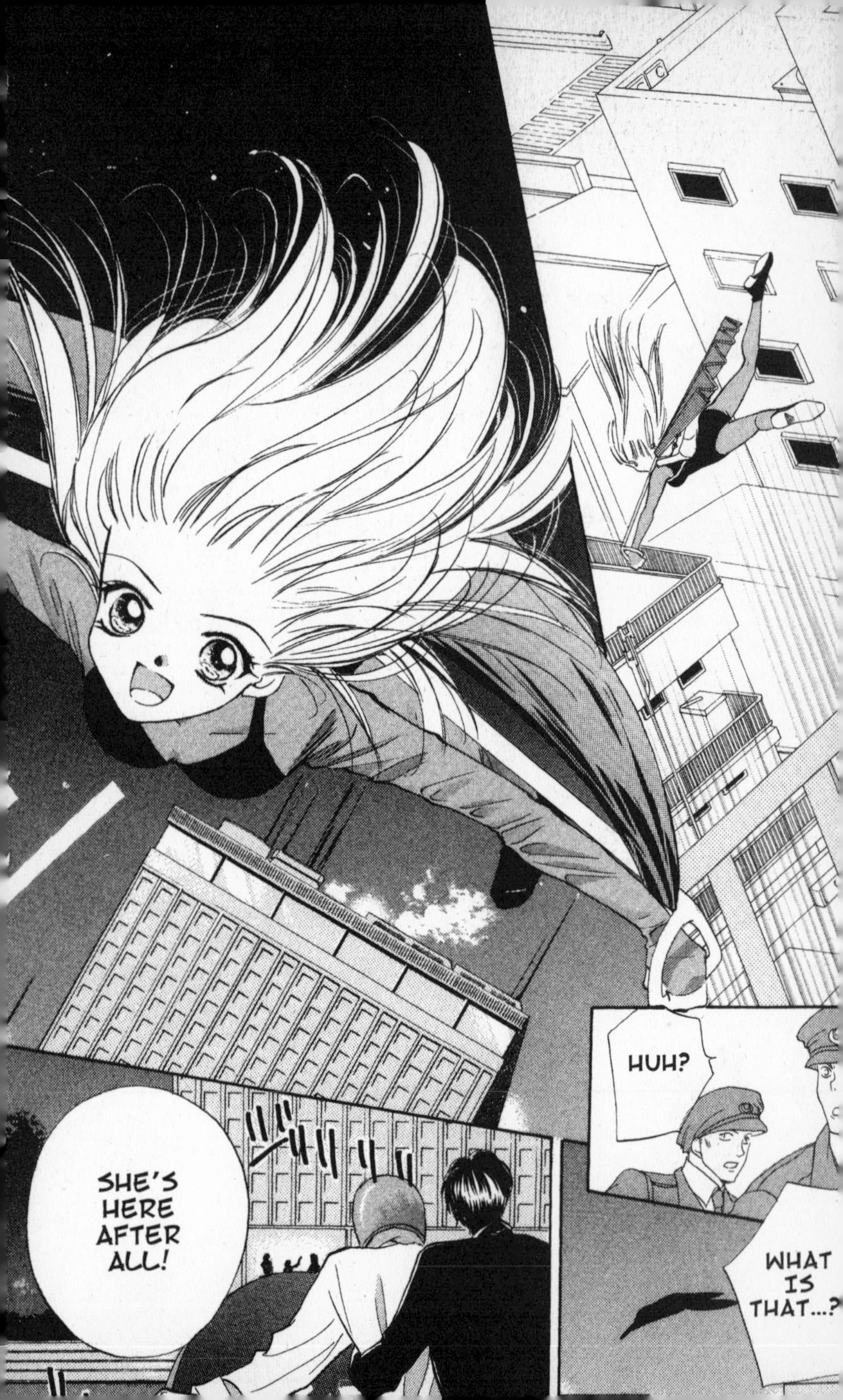
HUH?
WHAT IS THAT...?
SHE'S HERE AFTER ALL!

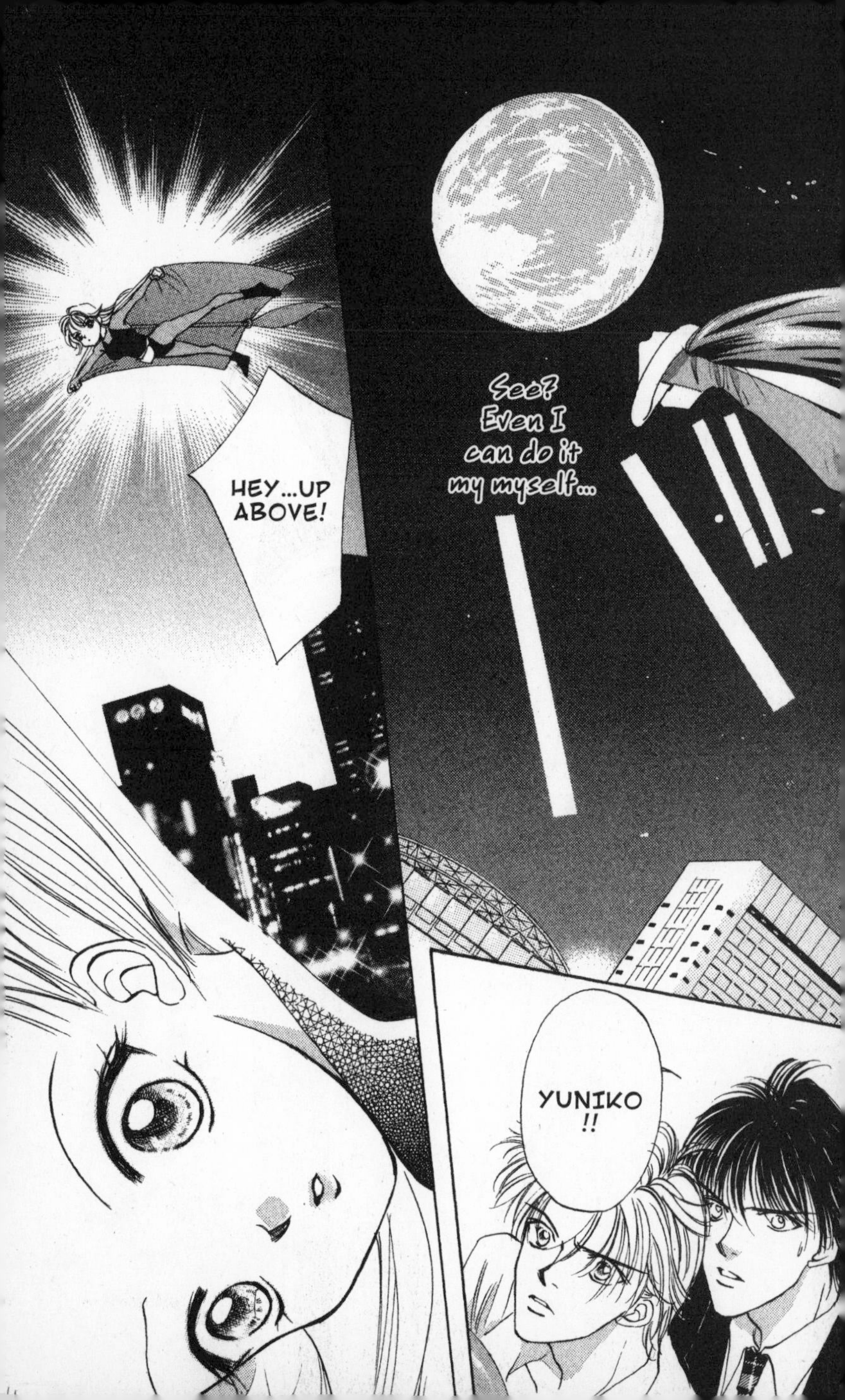
See? Even I can do it my myself...
HEY...UP ABOVE!
YUNIKO !!

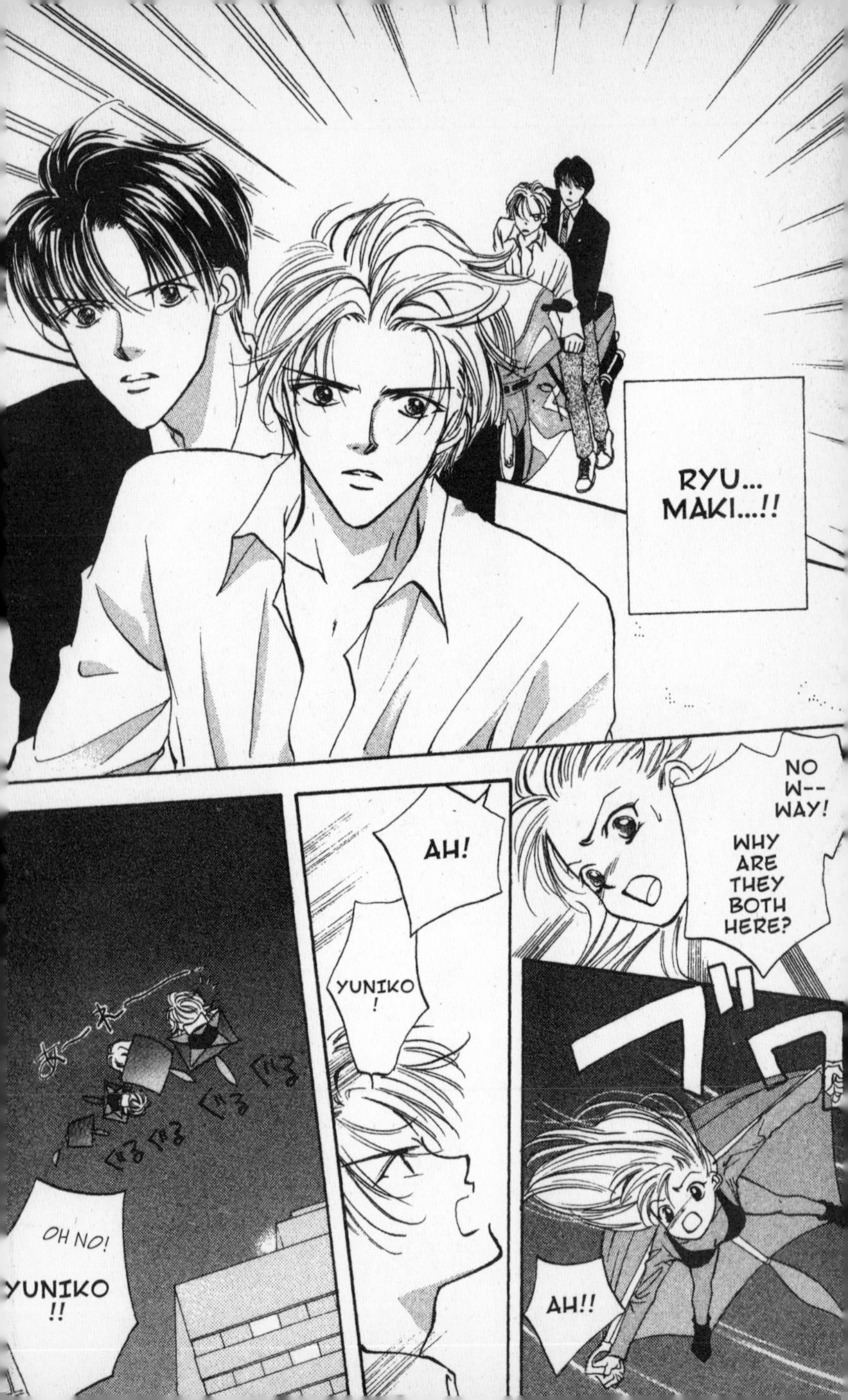
RYU... MAKI...!!
NO W-- WAY!
WHY ARE THEY BOTH HERE?
AH!!
AH!
YUNIKO!
OH NO!
YUNIKO!!

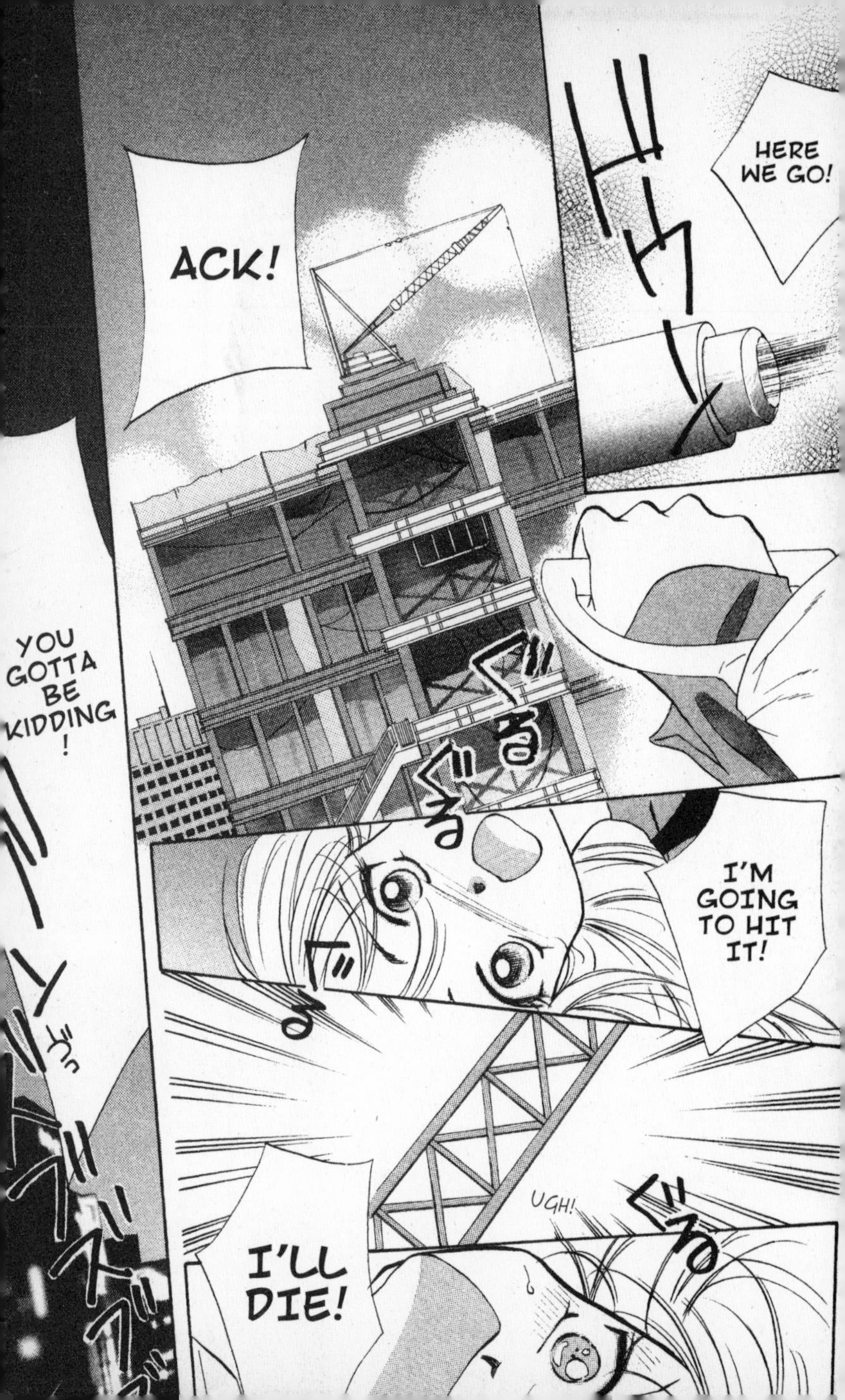
HERE WE GO!
ACK!
YOU GOTTA BE KIDDING!
I'M GOING TO HIT IT!
UGH!
I'LL DIE!

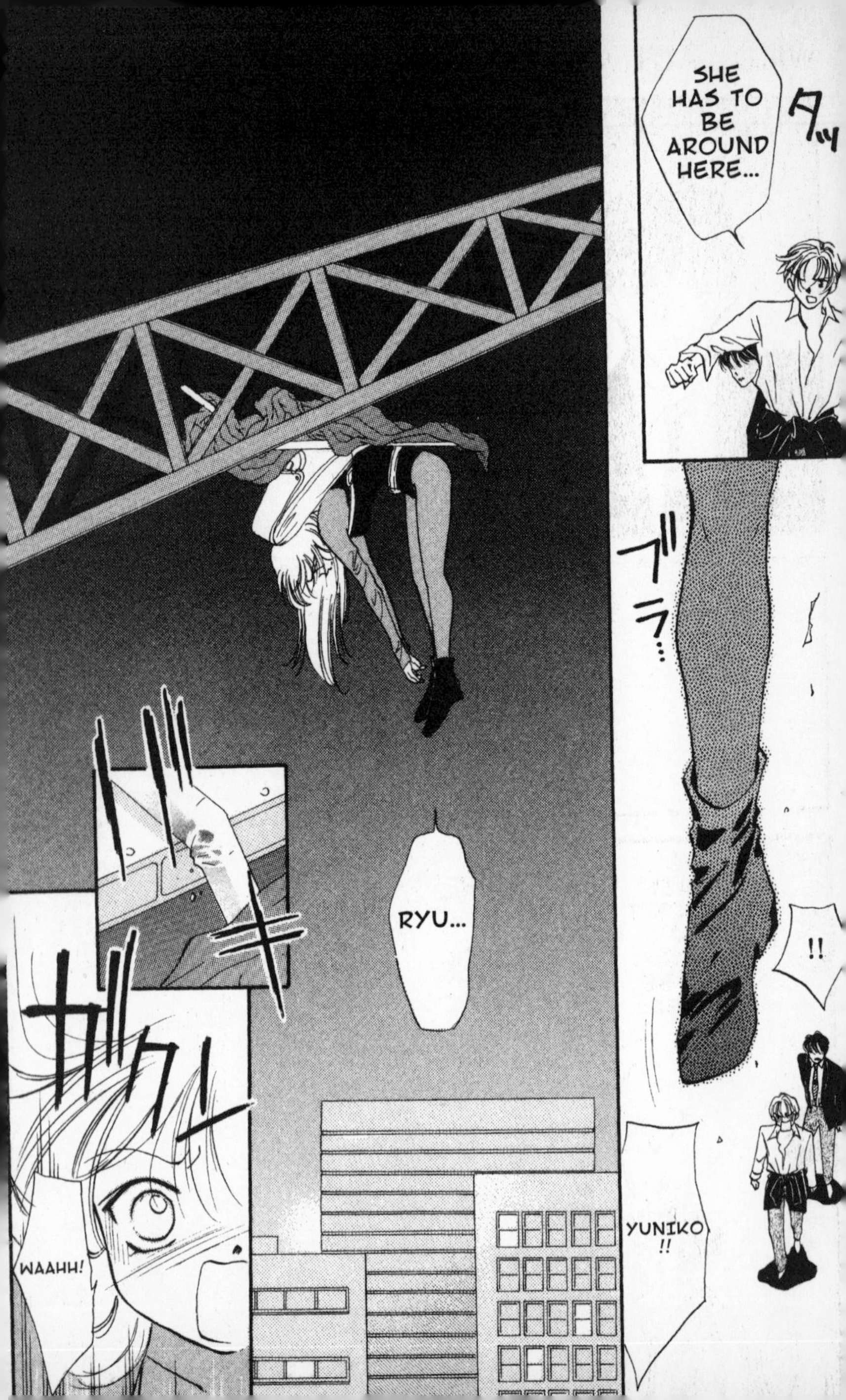
SHE HAS TO BE AROUND HERE...
タッ
ブラ…
!!
YUNIKO!!
RYU...
WAAHH!

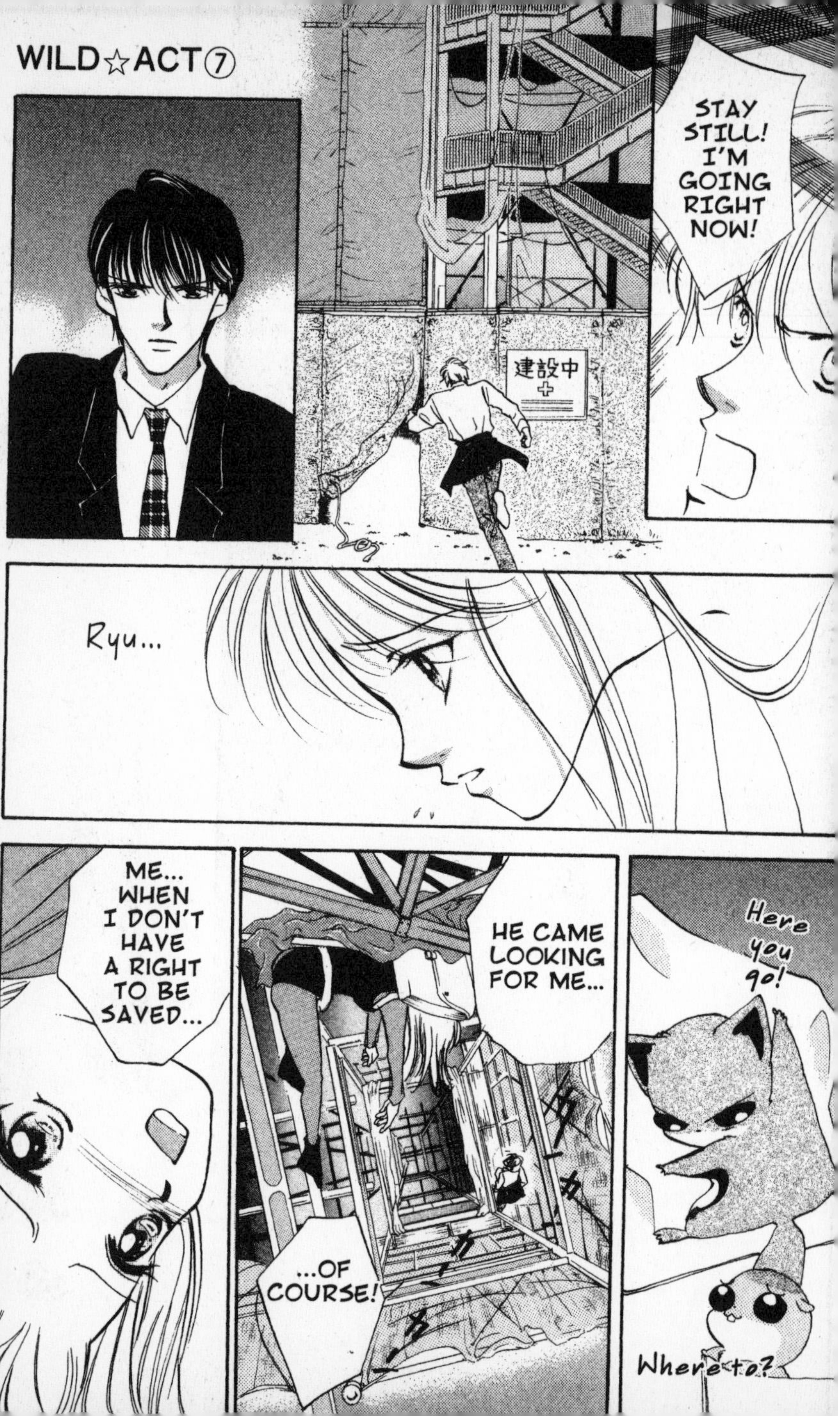
STAY STILL! I'M GOING RIGHT NOW!
建設中
Ryu...
Here you go!
Where to?
HE CAME LOOKING FOR ME...
...OF COURSE!
ME... WHEN I DON'T HAVE A RIGHT TO BE SAVED...

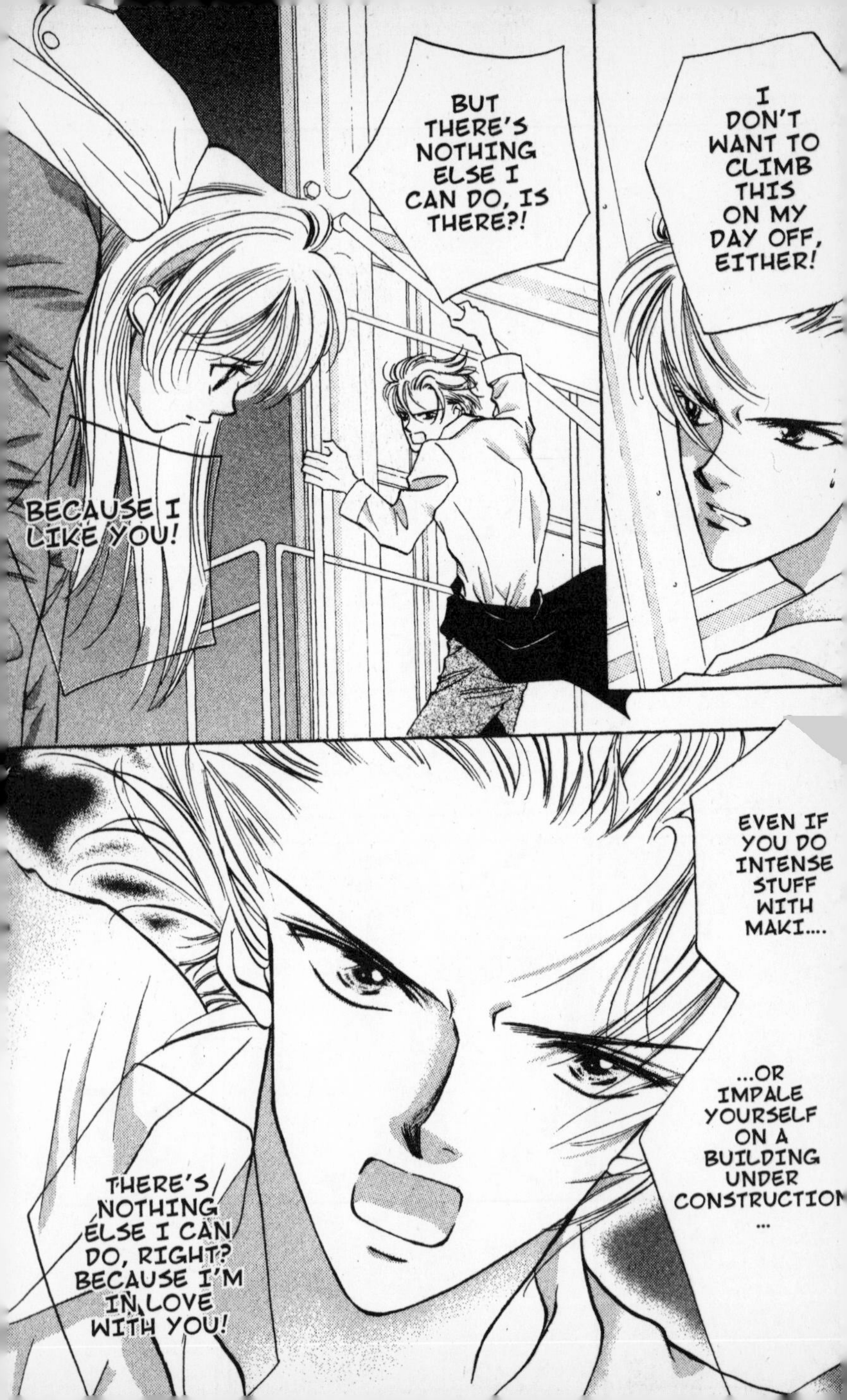
I DON'T WANT TO CLIMB THIS ON MY DAY OFF, EITHER!
BUT THERE'S NOTHING ELSE I CAN DO, IS THERE?!
BECAUSE I LIKE YOU!
EVEN IF YOU DO INTENSE STUFF WITH MAKI....
...OR IMPALE YOURSELF ON A BUILDING UNDER CONSTRUCTION...
THERE'S NOTHING ELSE I CAN DO, RIGHT? BECAUSE I'M IN LOVE WITH YOU!

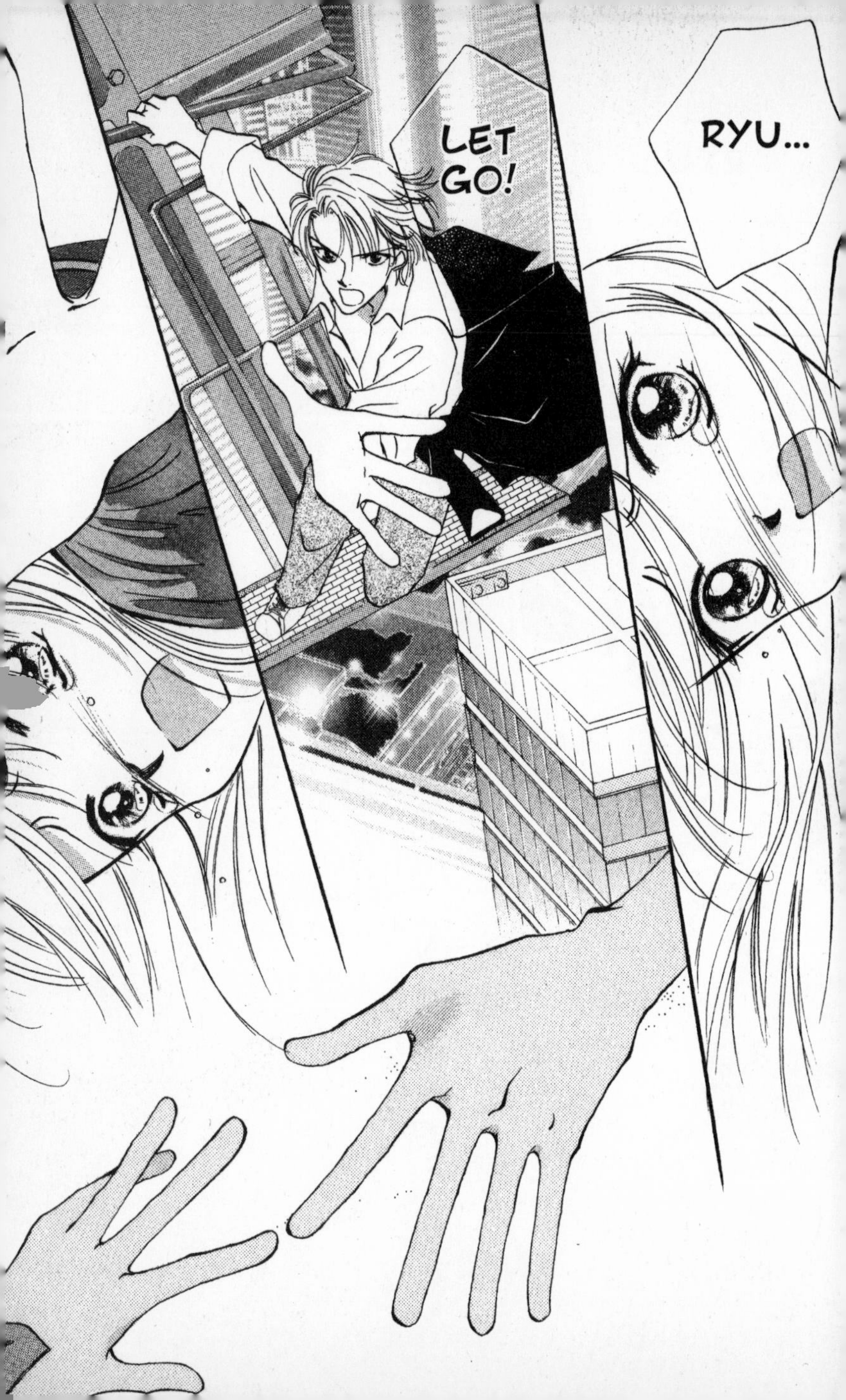
RYU...
LET GO!

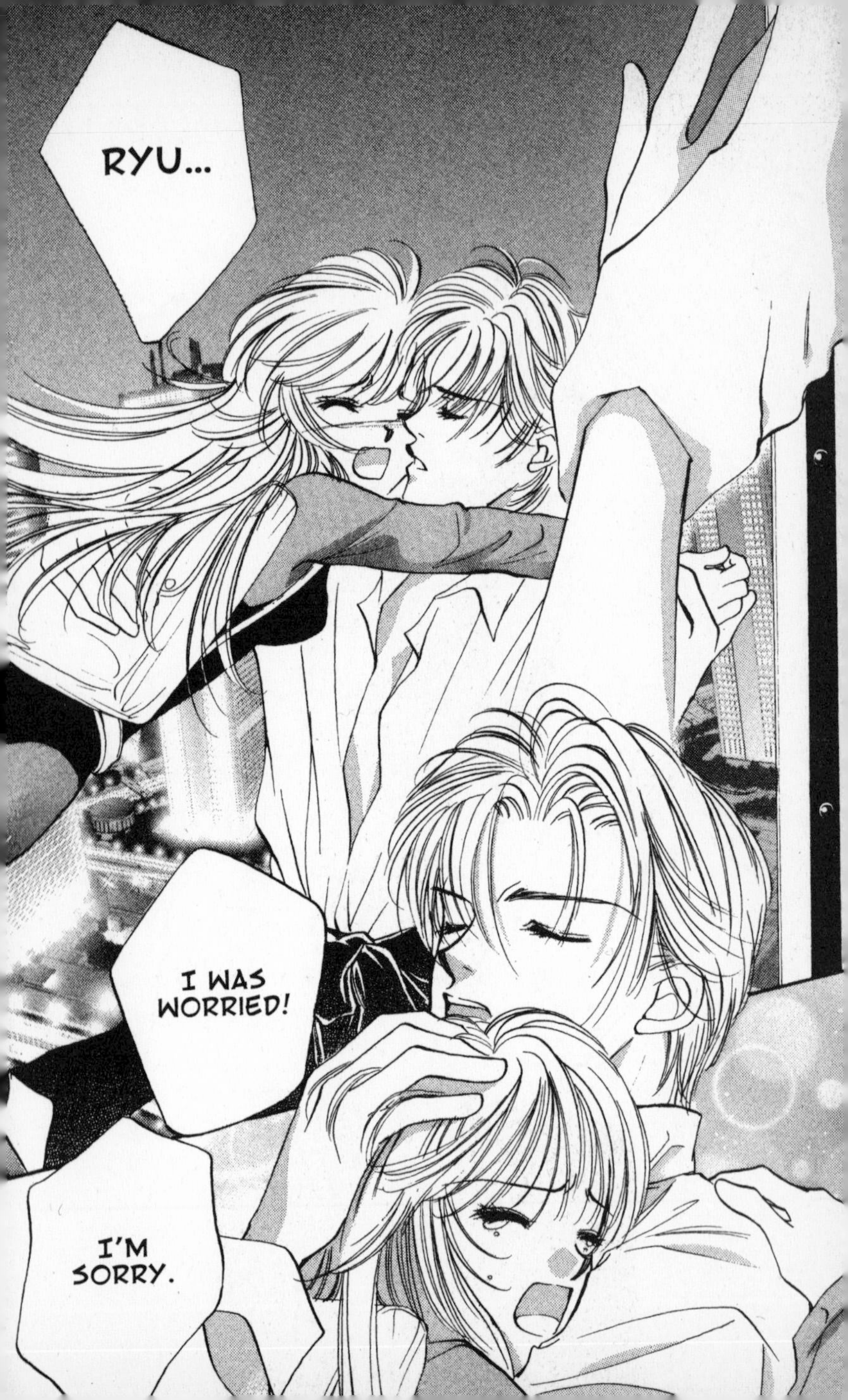
RYU...
I WAS WORRIED!
I'M SORRY.

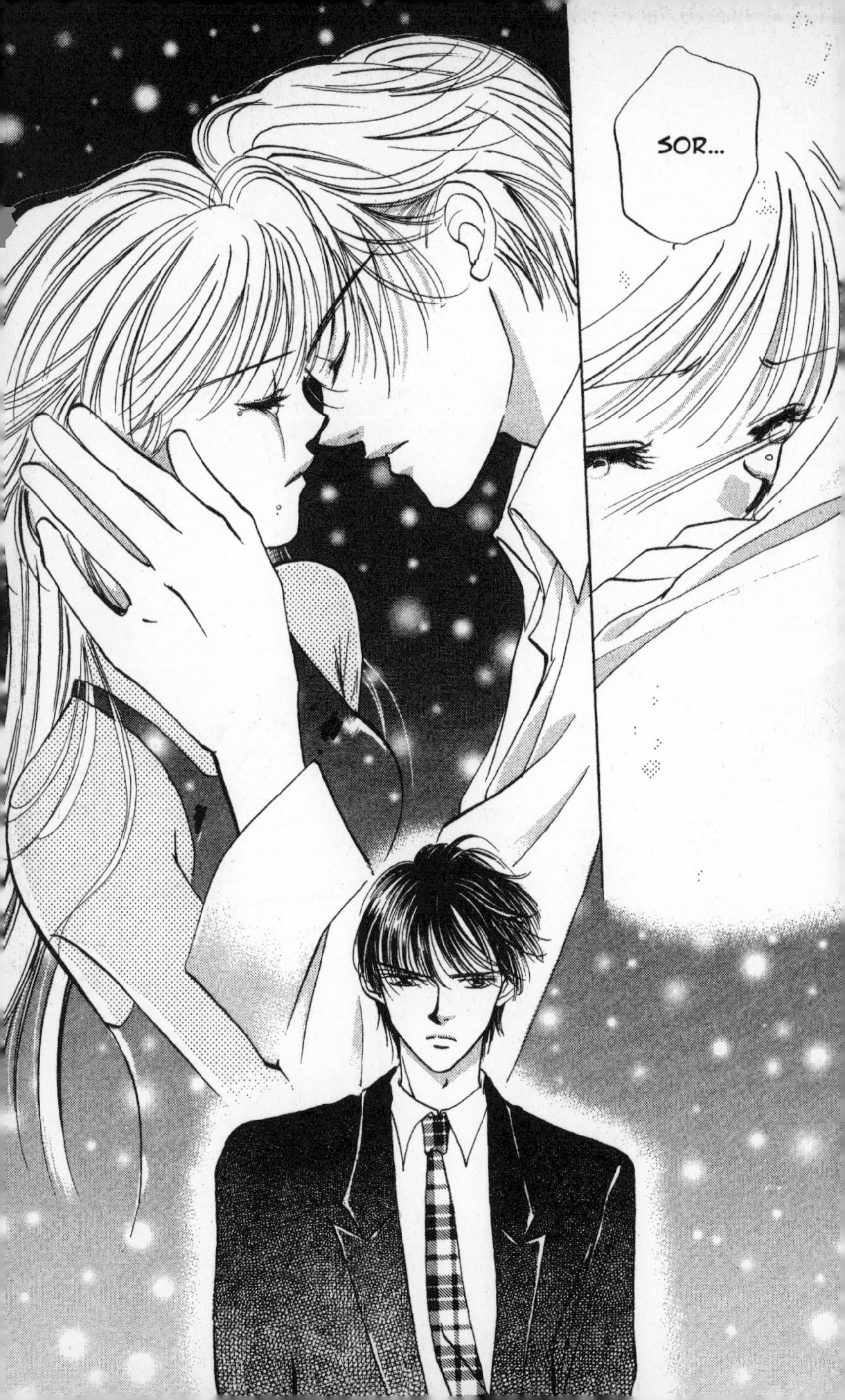
SOR...

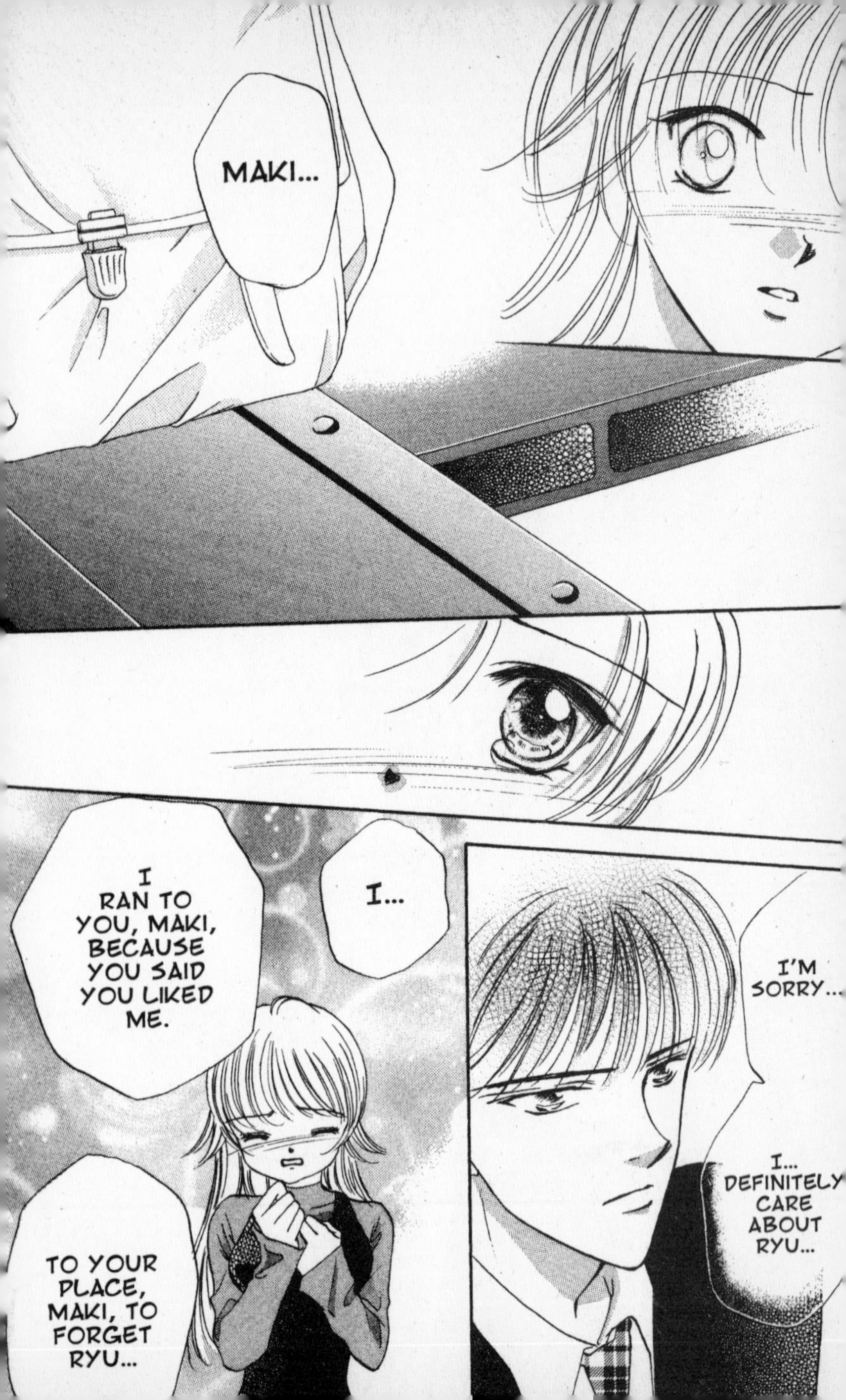
MAKI...
I'M SORRY...
I... DEFINITELY CARE ABOUT RYU...
I...
I RAN TO YOU, MAKI, BECAUSE YOU SAID YOU LIKED ME.
TO YOUR PLACE, MAKI, TO FORGET RYU...

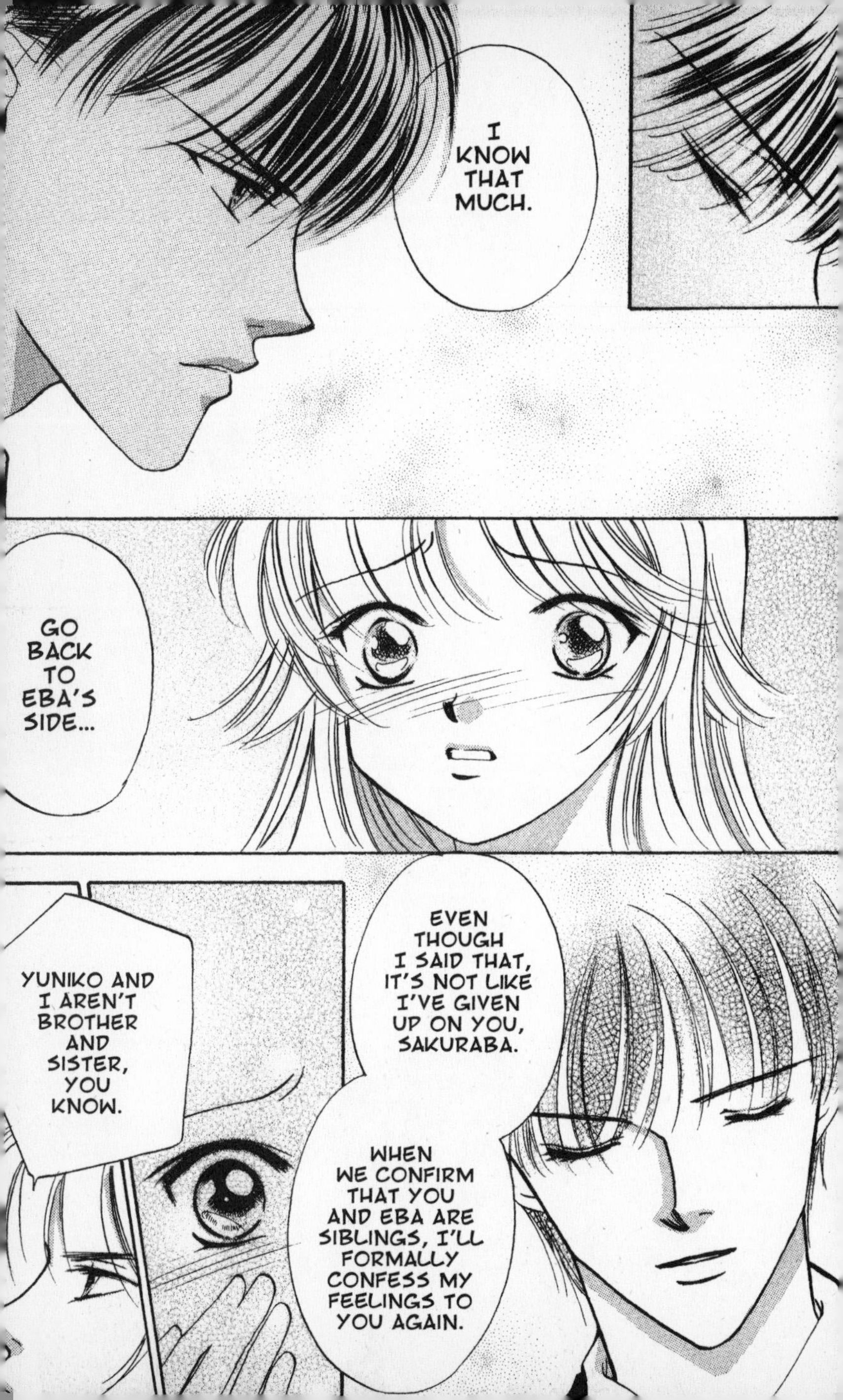

I KNOW THAT MUCH.
GO BACK TO EBA'S SIDE...
EVEN THOUGH I SAID THAT, IT'S NOT LIKE I'VE GIVEN UP ON YOU, SAKURABA.
WHEN WE CONFIRM THAT YOU AND EBA ARE SIBLINGS, I'LL FORMALLY CONFESS MY FEELINGS TO YOU AGAIN.
YUNIKO AND I AREN'T BROTHER AND SISTER, YOU KNOW.

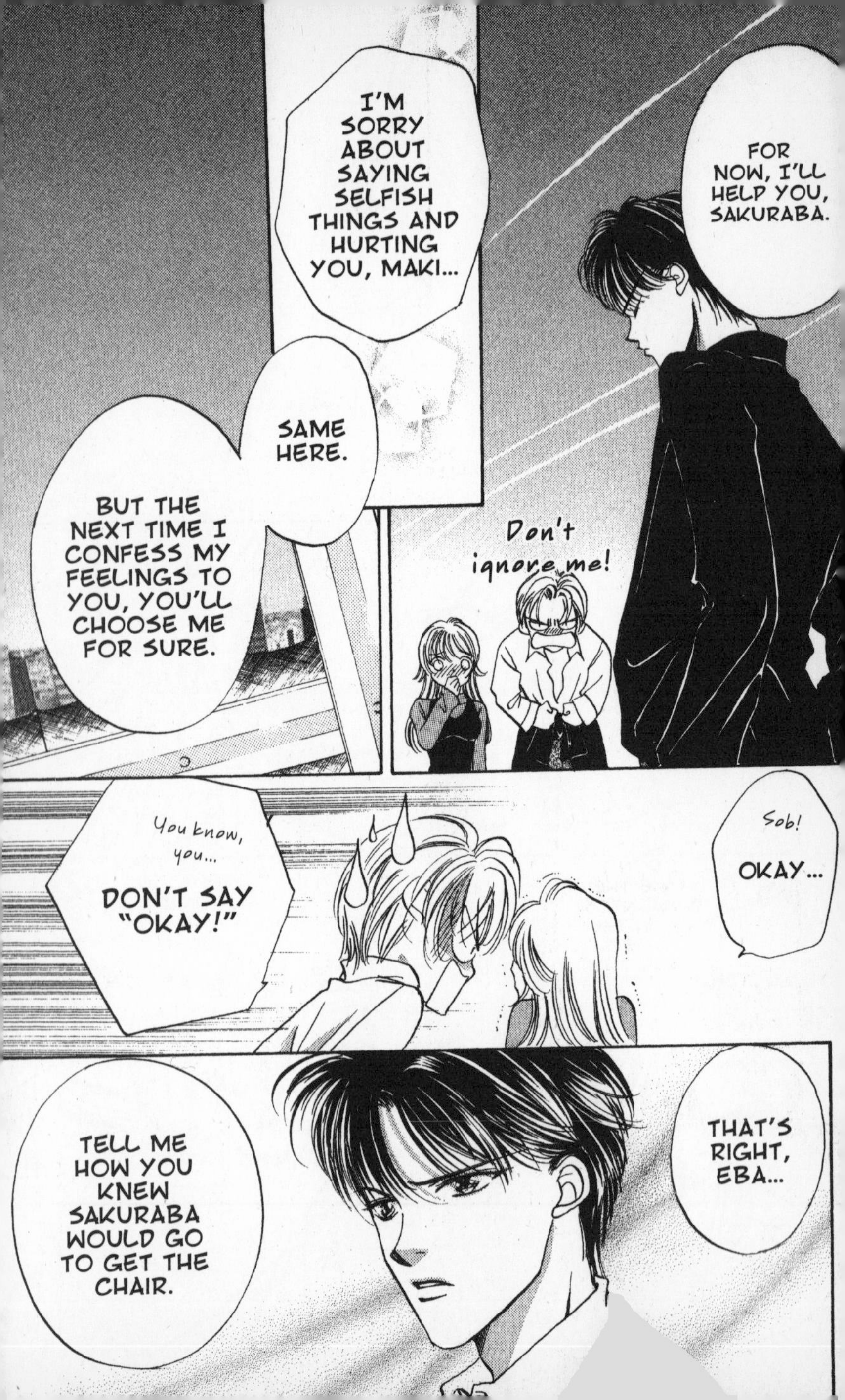
FOR NOW, I'LL HELP YOU, SAKURABA.
Don't ignore me!
I'M SORRY ABOUT SAYING SELFISH THINGS AND HURTING YOU, MAKI...
SAME HERE.
BUT THE NEXT TIME I CONFESS MY FEELINGS TO YOU, YOU'LL CHOOSE ME FOR SURE.
Sob!
OKAY...
You know, you...
DON'T SAY "OKAY!"
THAT'S RIGHT, EBA...
TELL ME HOW YOU KNEW SAKURABA WOULD GO TO GET THE CHAIR.

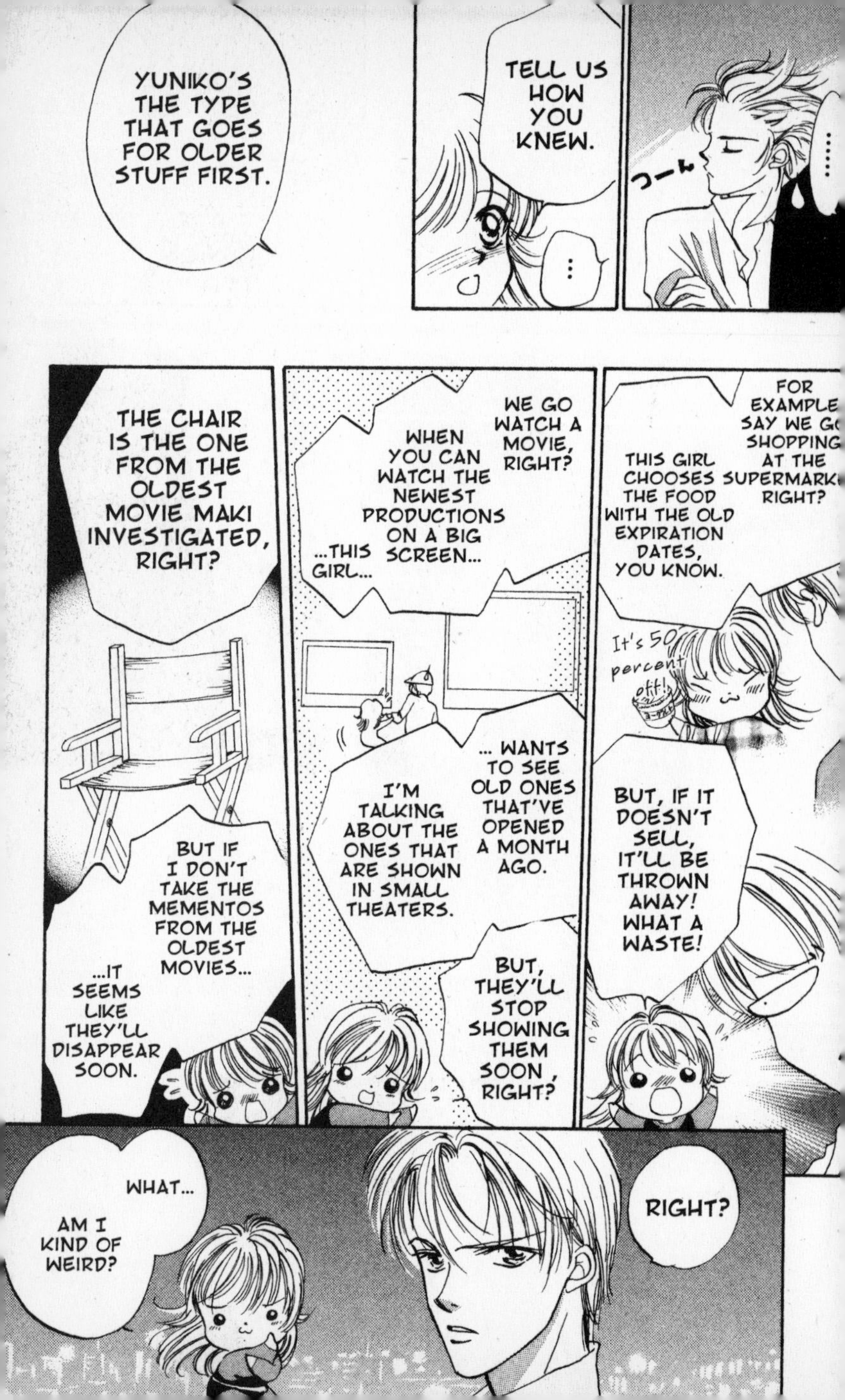
......
TELL US HOW YOU KNEW.
...
YUNIKO'S THE TYPE THAT GOES FOR OLDER STUFF FIRST.
FOR EXAMPLE SAY WE G SHOPPING AT THE SUPERMARK RIGHT?
THIS GIRL CHOOSES THE FOOD WITH THE OLD EXPIRATION DATES, YOU KNOW.
It's 50 percent off!
BUT, IF IT DOESN'T SELL, IT'LL BE THROWN AWAY! WHAT A WASTE!
WE GO WATCH A MOVIE, RIGHT?
WHEN YOU CAN WATCH THE NEWEST PRODUCTIONS ON A BIG SCREEN...
...THIS GIRL...
... WANTS TO SEE OLD ONES THAT'VE OPENED A MONTH AGO.
I'M TALKING ABOUT THE ONES THAT ARE SHOWN IN SMALL THEATERS.
BUT, THEY'LL STOP SHOWING THEM SOON, RIGHT?
THE CHAIR IS THE ONE FROM THE OLDEST MOVIE MAKI INVESTIGATED, RIGHT?
BUT IF I DON'T TAKE THE MEMENTOS FROM THE OLDEST MOVIES...
...IT SEEMS LIKE THEY'LL DISAPPEAR SOON.
RIGHT?
WHAT...
AM I KIND OF WEIRD?

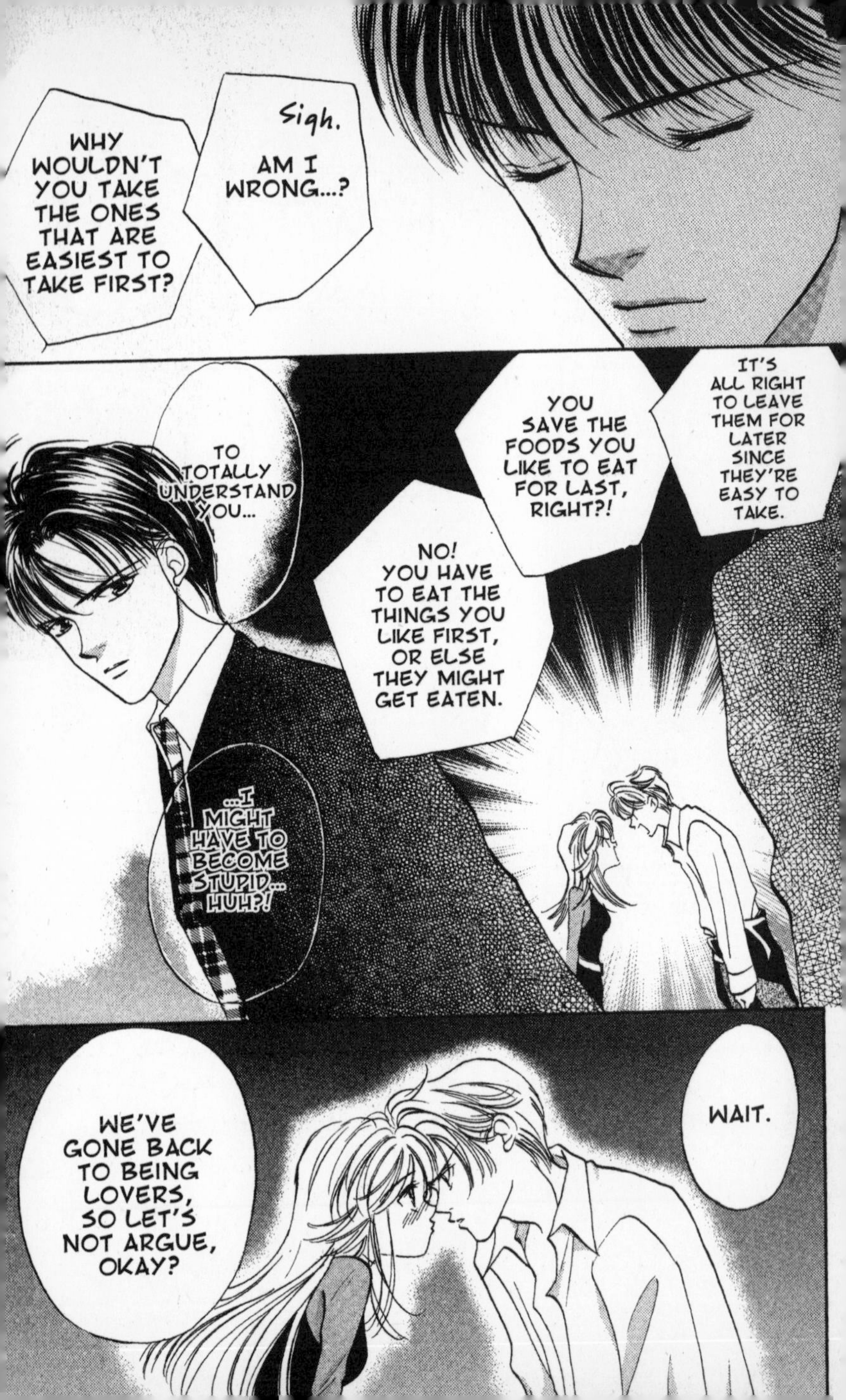
Sigh.
AM I WRONG...?
WHY WOULDN'T YOU TAKE THE ONES THAT ARE EASIEST TO TAKE FIRST?
IT'S ALL RIGHT TO LEAVE THEM FOR LATER SINCE THEY'RE EASY TO TAKE.
YOU SAVE THE FOODS YOU LIKE TO EAT FOR LAST, RIGHT?!
NO! YOU HAVE TO EAT THE THINGS YOU LIKE FIRST, OR ELSE THEY MIGHT GET EATEN.
TO TOTALLY UNDERSTAND YOU...
...I MIGHT HAVE TO BECOME STUPID... HUH?!
WAIT.
WE'VE GONE BACK TO BEING LOVERS, SO LET'S NOT ARGUE, OKAY?

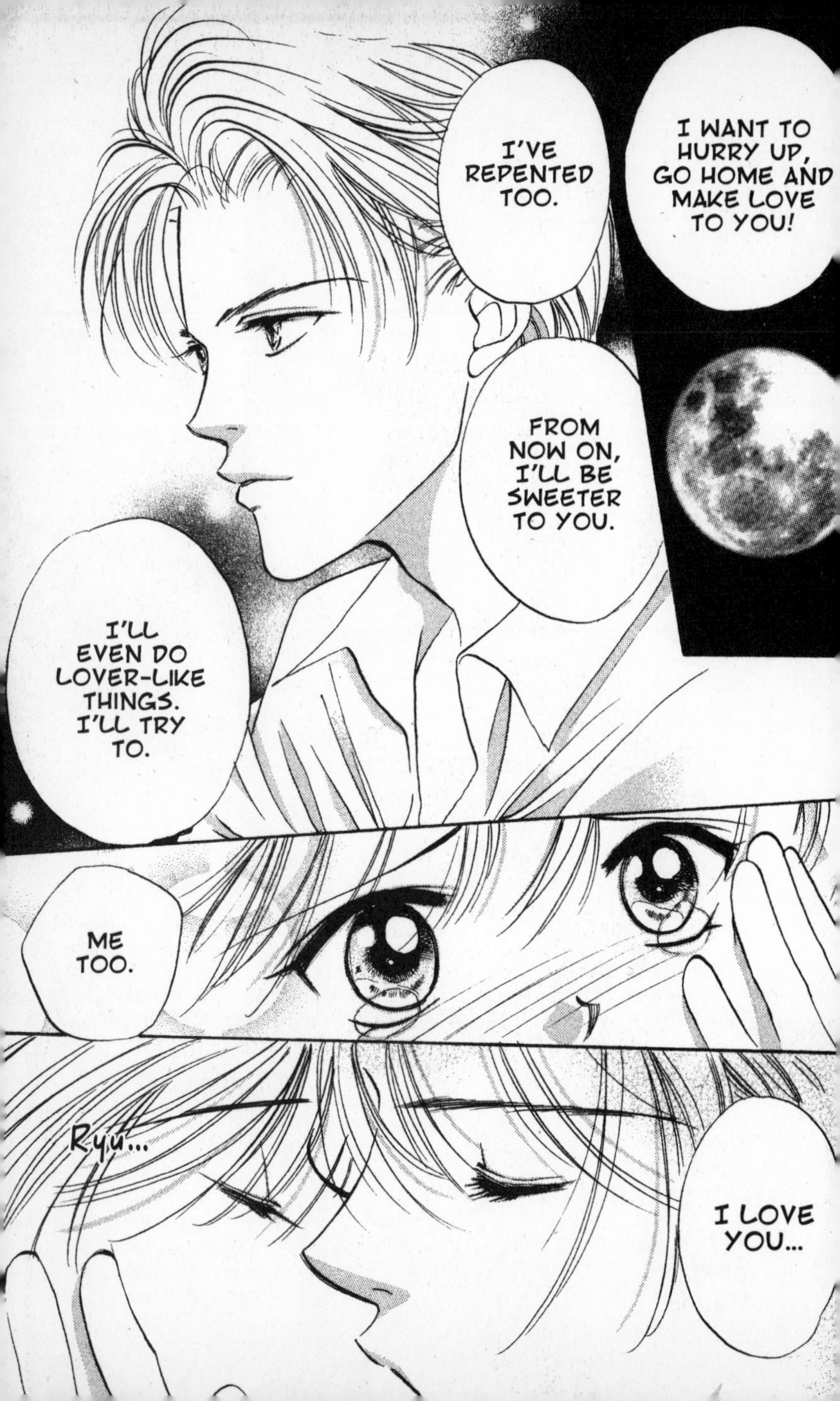
I WANT TO HURRY UP, GO HOME AND MAKE LOVE TO YOU!
I'VE REPENTED TOO.
FROM NOW ON, I'LL BE SWEETER TO YOU.
I'LL EVEN DO LOVER-LIKE THINGS. I'LL TRY TO.
ME TOO.
I LOVE YOU...
Ryu...

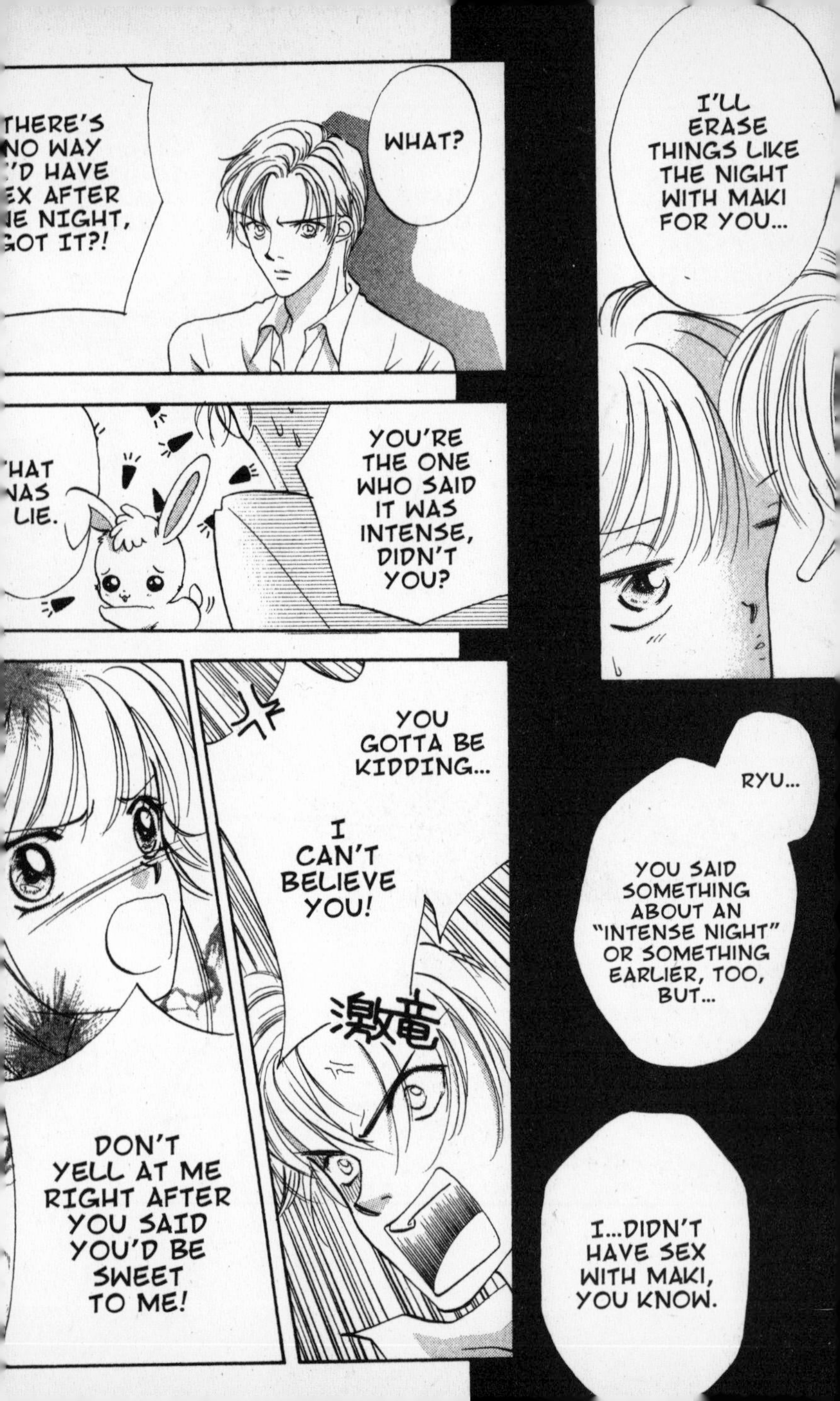
I'LL ERASE THINGS LIKE THE NIGHT WITH MAKI FOR YOU...
RYU...
YOU SAID SOMETHING ABOUT AN "INTENSE NIGHT" OR SOMETHING EARLIER, TOO, BUT...
I...DIDN'T HAVE SEX WITH MAKI, YOU KNOW.
WHAT?
THERE'S NO WAY 'D HAVE EX AFTER E NIGHT, GOT IT?!
YOU'RE THE ONE WHO SAID IT WAS INTENSE, DIDN'T YOU?
HAT VAS LIE.
YOU GOTTA BE KIDDING...
I CAN'T BELIEVE YOU!
激竜
DON'T YELL AT ME RIGHT AFTER YOU SAID YOU'D BE SWEET TO ME!

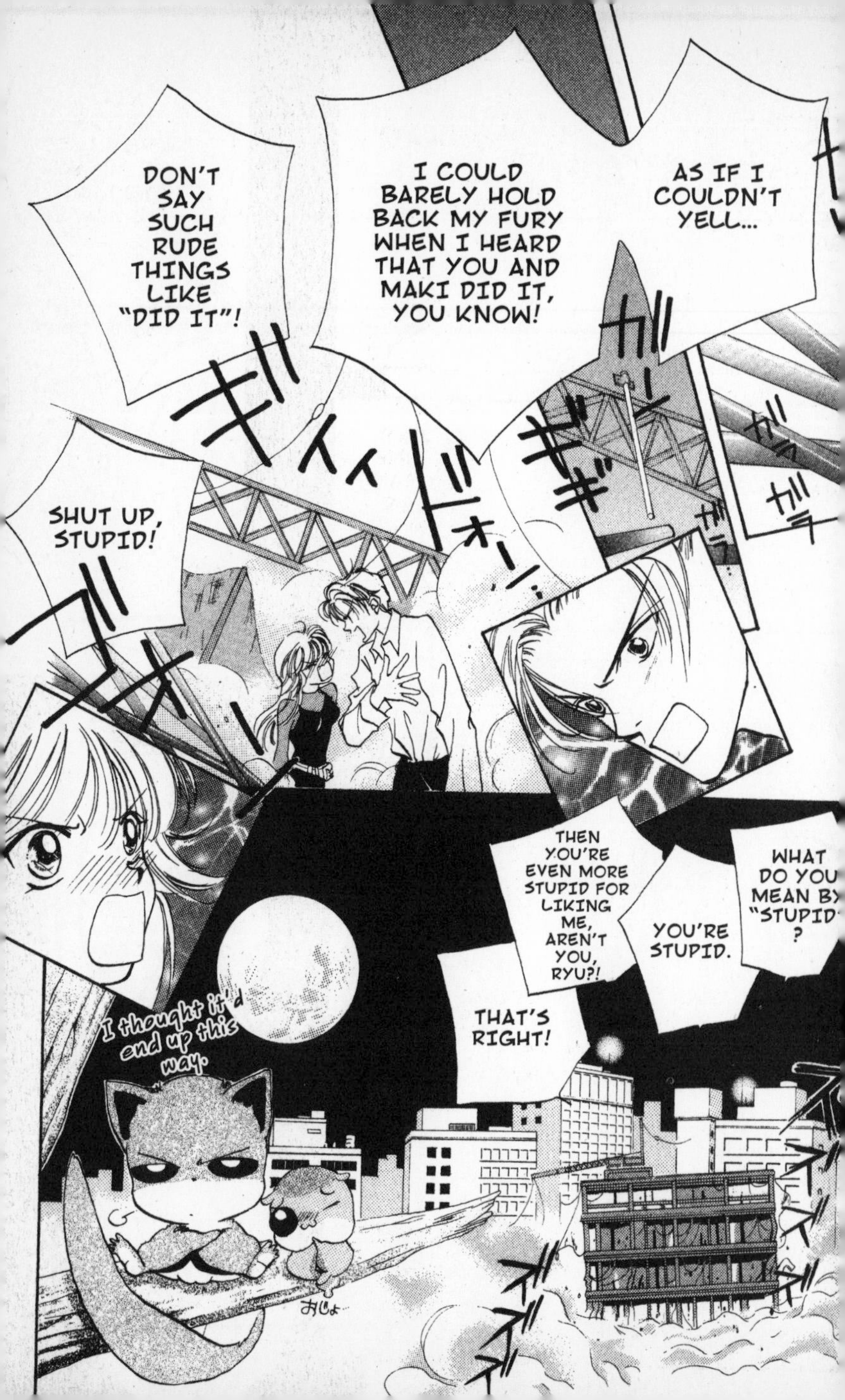
AS IF I COULDN'T YELL...
I COULD BARELY HOLD BACK MY FURY WHEN I HEARD THAT YOU AND MAKI DID IT, YOU KNOW!
DON'T SAY SUCH RUDE THINGS LIKE "DID IT"!
SHUT UP, STUPID!
WHAT DO YOU MEAN BY "STUPID"?
YOU'RE STUPID.
THEN YOU'RE EVEN MORE STUPID FOR LIKING ME, AREN'T YOU, RYU?!
THAT'S RIGHT!
I thought it'd end up this way.

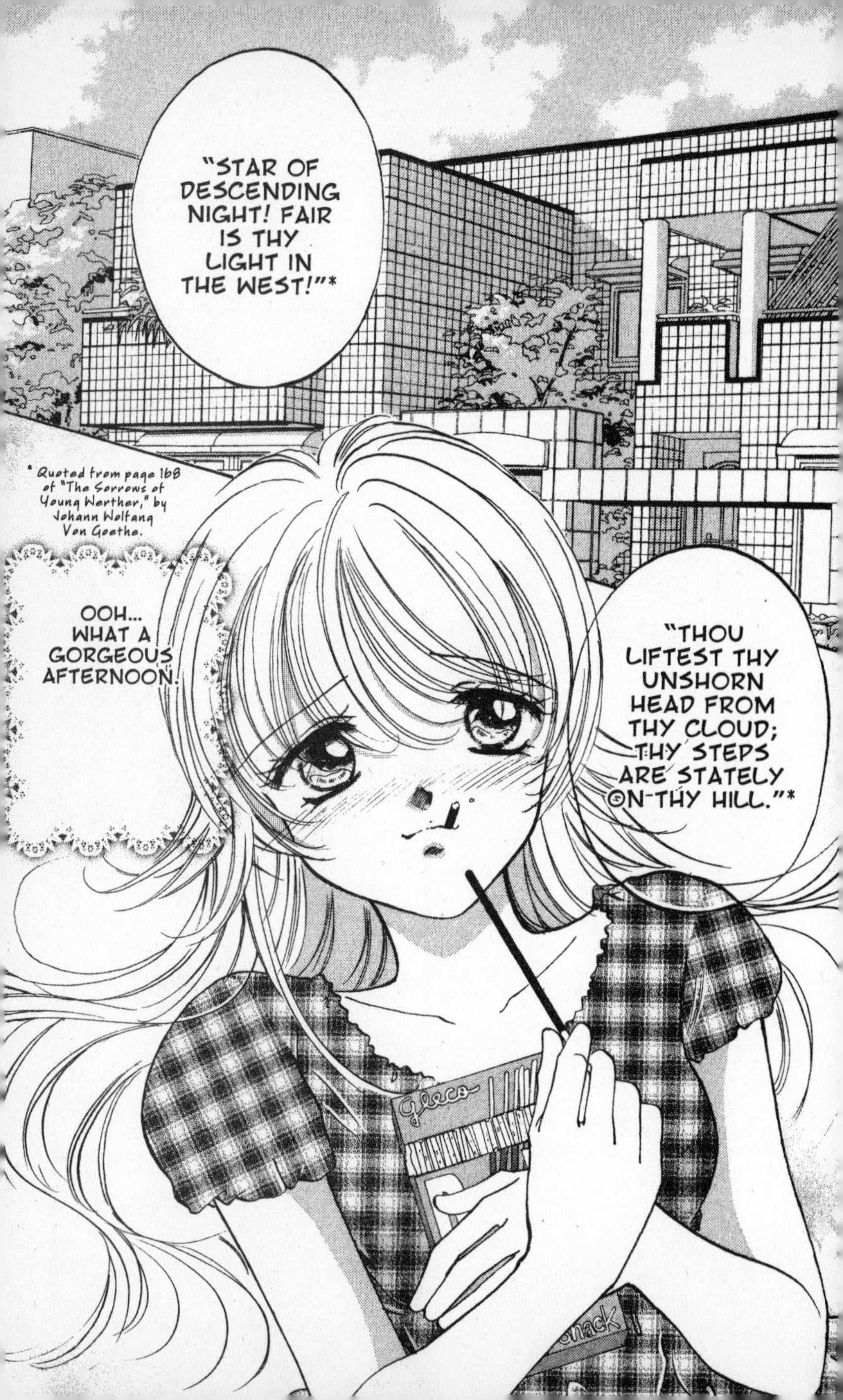
"STAR OF DESCENDING NIGHT! FAIR IS THY LIGHT IN THE WEST!"*
"THOU LIFTEST THY UNSHORN HEAD FROM THY CLOUD; THY STEPS ARE STATELY ON THY HILL."*
OOH... WHAT A GORGEOUS AFTERNOON.
* Quoted from page 168 of "The Sorrows of Young Werther," by Johann Wolfang Von Goethe.

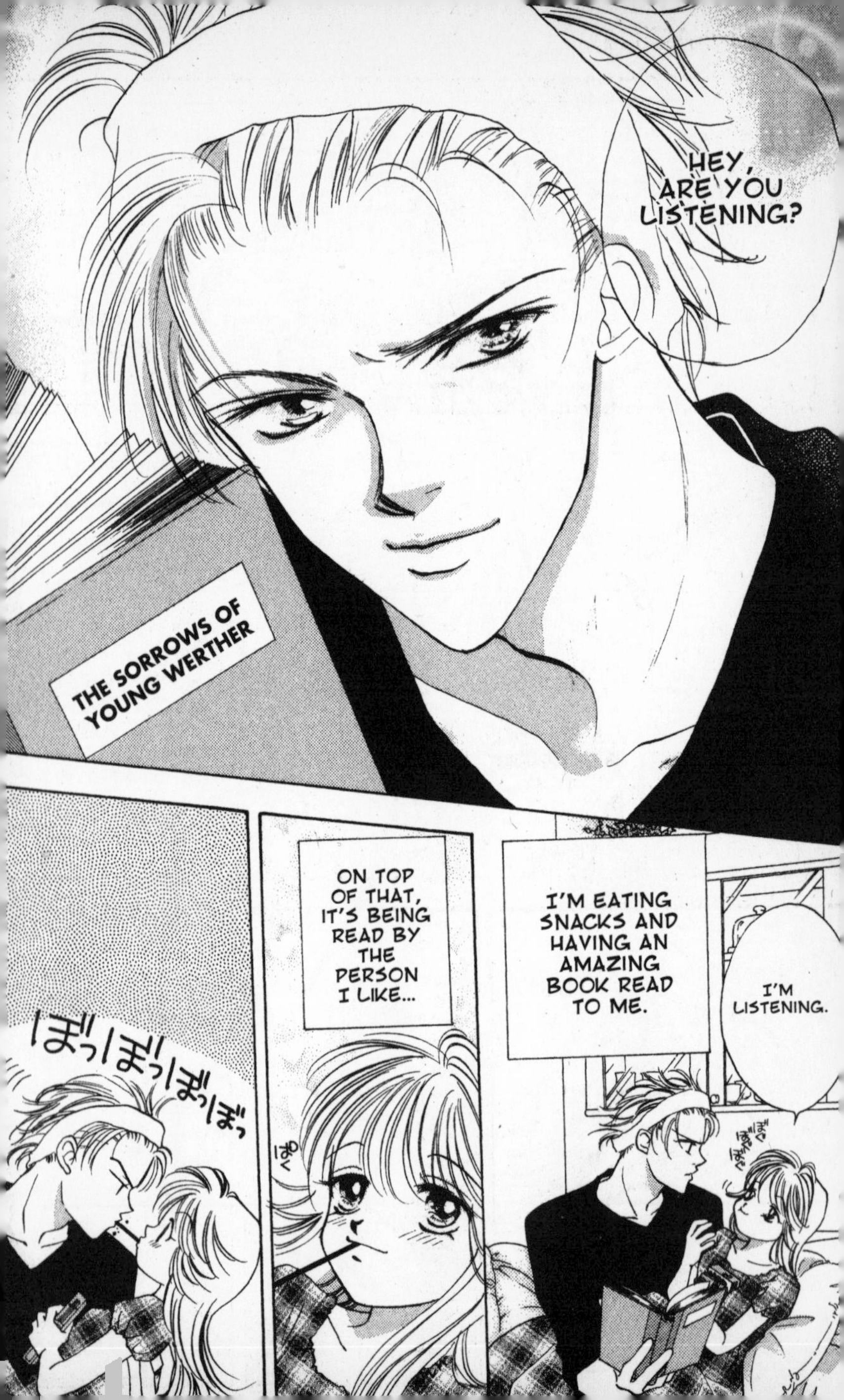
HEY, ARE YOU LISTENING?
THE SORROWS OF YOUNG WERTHER
I'M LISTENING.
I'M EATING SNACKS AND HAVING AN AMAZING BOOK READ TO ME.
ON TOP OF THAT, IT'S BEING READ BY THE PERSON I LIKE...
ぽっぽっぽっぽっ

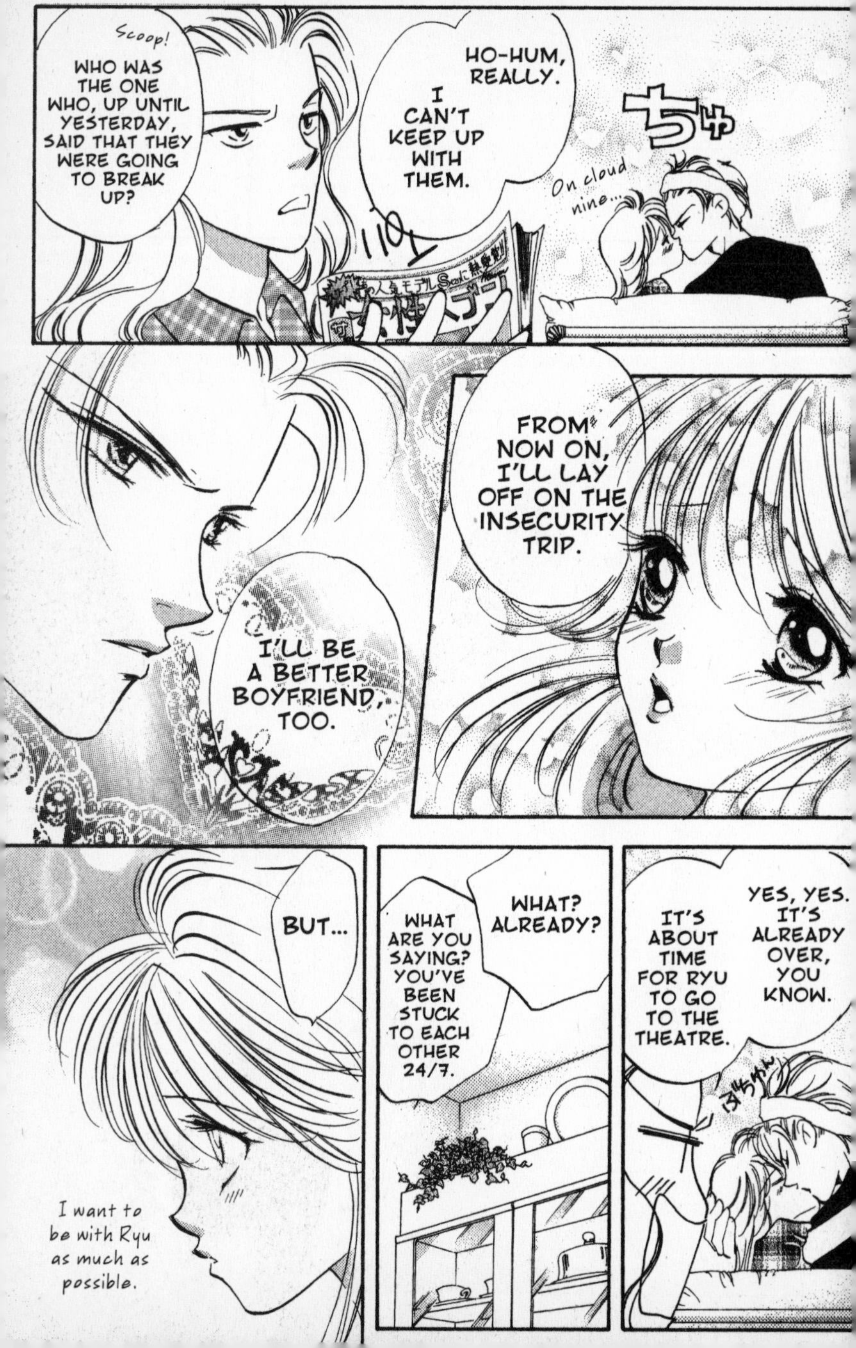
ちゅ
On cloud nine...
HO-HUM, REALLY.
I CAN'T KEEP UP WITH THEM.
Scoop!
WHO WAS THE ONE WHO, UP UNTIL YESTERDAY, SAID THAT THEY WERE GOING TO BREAK UP?
FROM NOW ON, I'LL LAY OFF ON THE INSECURITY TRIP.
I'LL BE A BETTER BOYFRIEND, TOO.
YES, YES. IT'S ALREADY OVER, YOU KNOW.
IT'S ABOUT TIME FOR RYU TO GO TO THE THEATRE.
WHAT? ALREADY?
WHAT ARE YOU SAYING? YOU'VE BEEN STUCK TO EACH OTHER 24/7.
BUT...
I want to be with Ryu as much as possible.

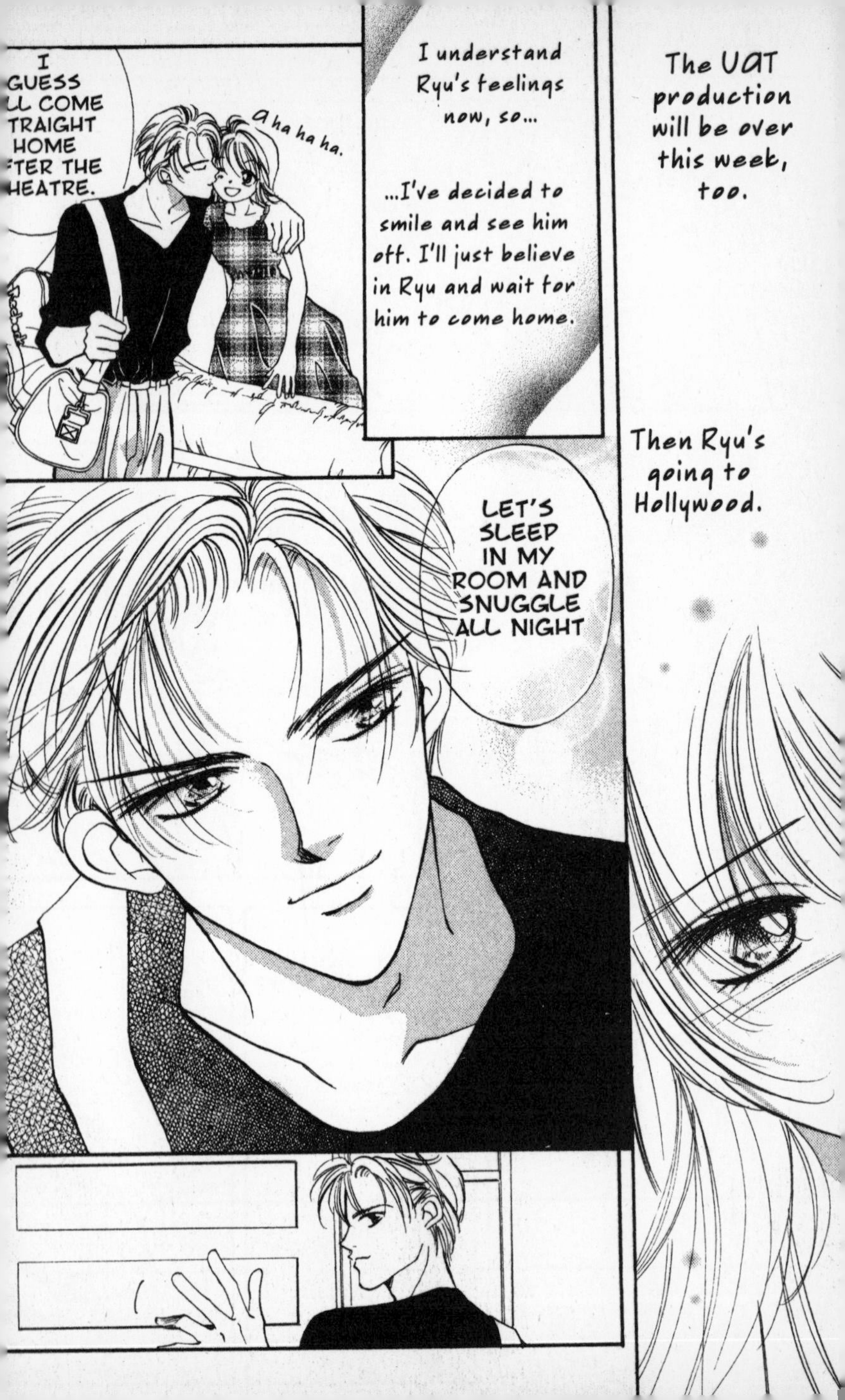
The UAT production will be over this week, too.
Then Ryu's going to Hollywood.
I understand Ryu's feelings now, so...
...I've decided to smile and see him off. I'll just believe in Ryu and wait for him to come home.
I GUESS LL COME TRAIGHT HOME FTER THE HEATRE.
a ha ha ha.
LET'S SLEEP IN MY ROOM AND SNUGGLE ALL NIGHT

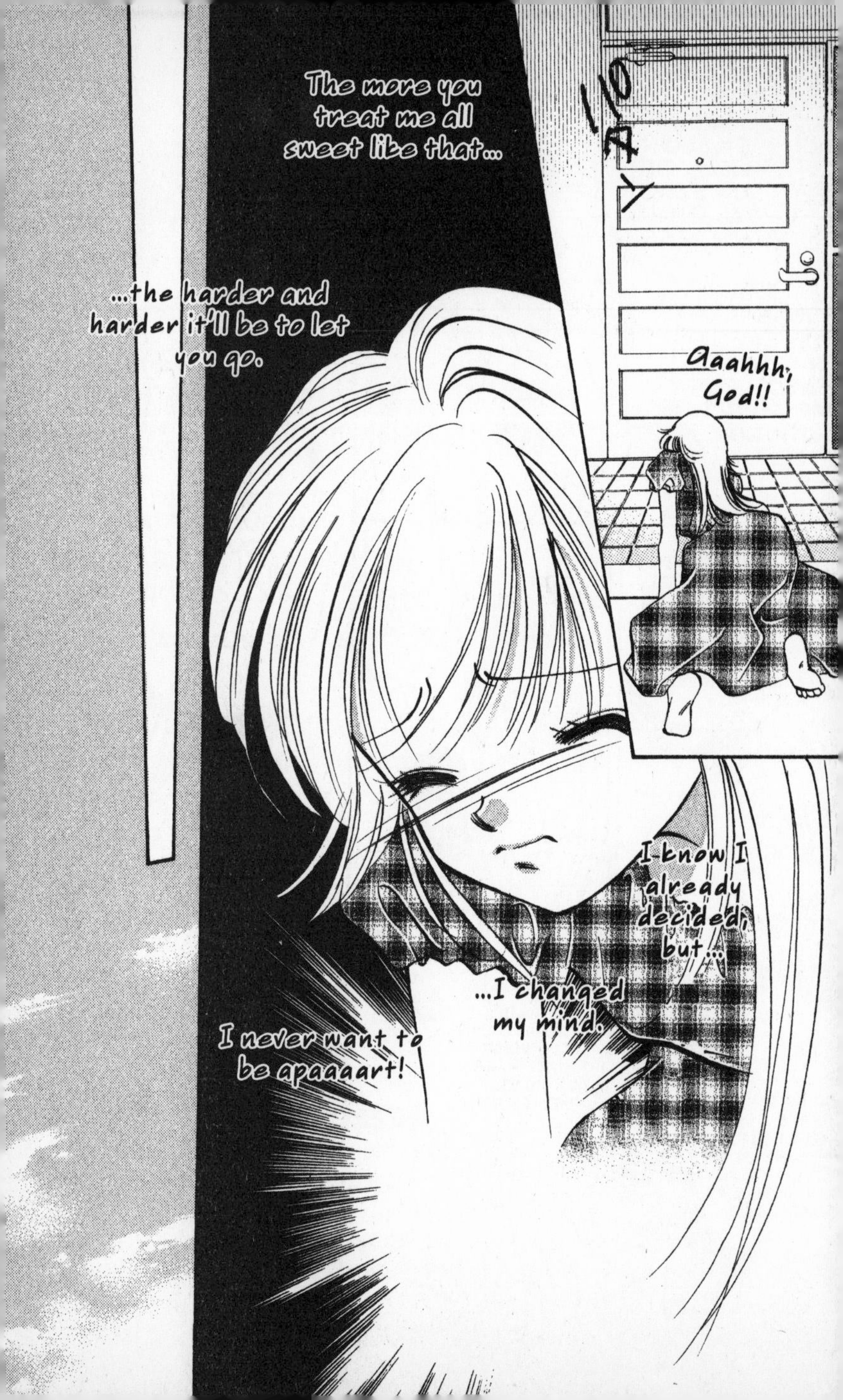
Aaahhh, God!!
The more you treat me all sweet like that...
...the harder and harder it'll be to let you go.
I know I already decided, but...
...I changed my mind.
I never want to be apaaaart!

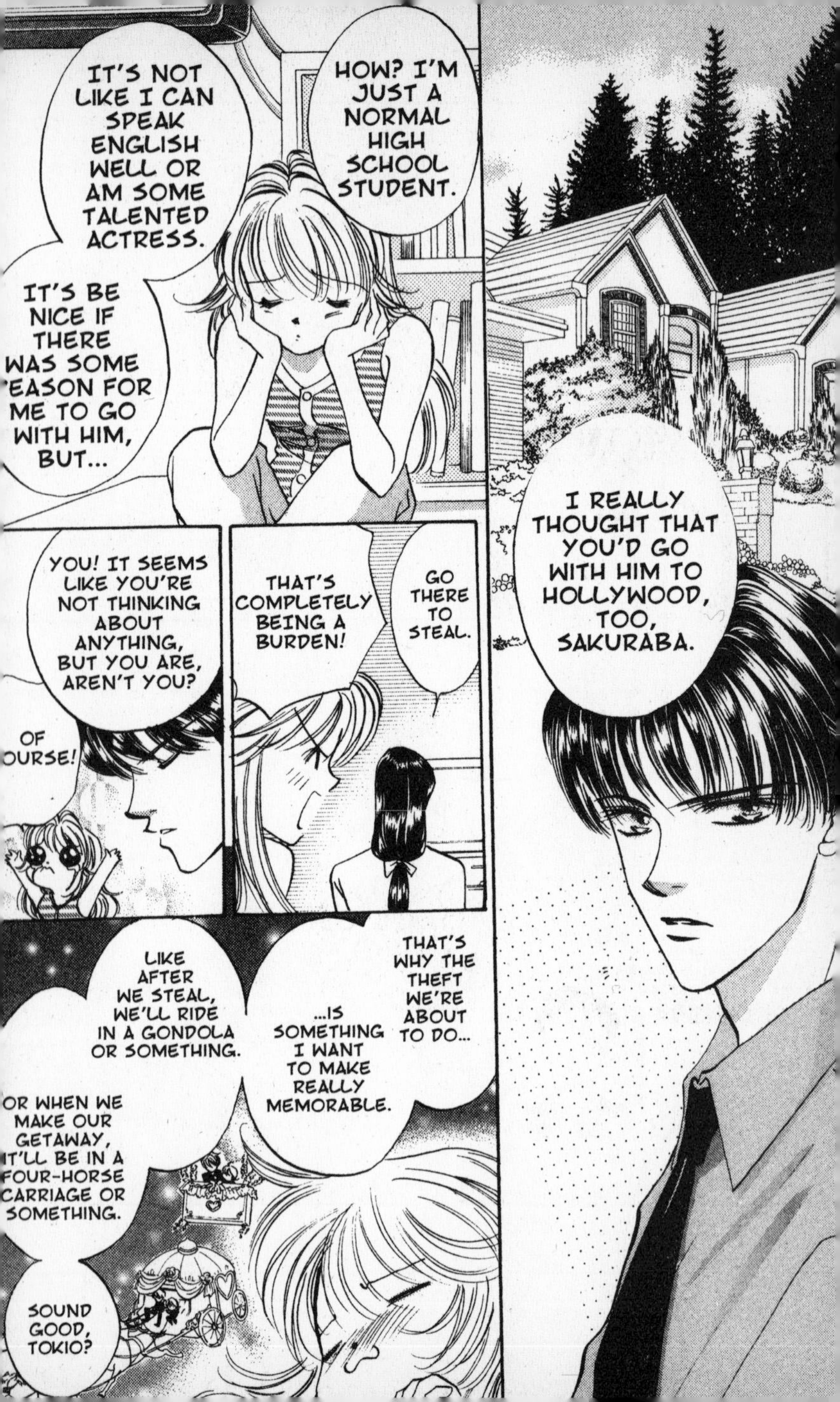
I REALLY THOUGHT THAT YOU'D GO WITH HIM TO HOLLYWOOD, TOO, SAKURABA.
HOW? I'M JUST A NORMAL HIGH SCHOOL STUDENT.
IT'S NOT LIKE I CAN SPEAK ENGLISH WELL OR AM SOME TALENTED ACTRESS.
IT'S BE NICE IF THERE WAS SOME EASON FOR ME TO GO WITH HIM, BUT...
GO THERE TO STEAL.
THAT'S COMPLETELY BEING A BURDEN!
YOU! IT SEEMS LIKE YOU'RE NOT THINKING ABOUT ANYTHING, BUT YOU ARE, AREN'T YOU?
OF OURSE!
THAT'S WHY THE THEFT WE'RE ABOUT TO DO...
...IS SOMETHING I WANT TO MAKE REALLY MEMORABLE.
LIKE AFTER WE STEAL, WE'LL RIDE IN A GONDOLA OR SOMETHING.
OR WHEN WE MAKE OUR GETAWAY, IT'LL BE IN A FOUR-HORSE CARRIAGE OR SOMETHING.
SOUND GOOD, TOKIO?

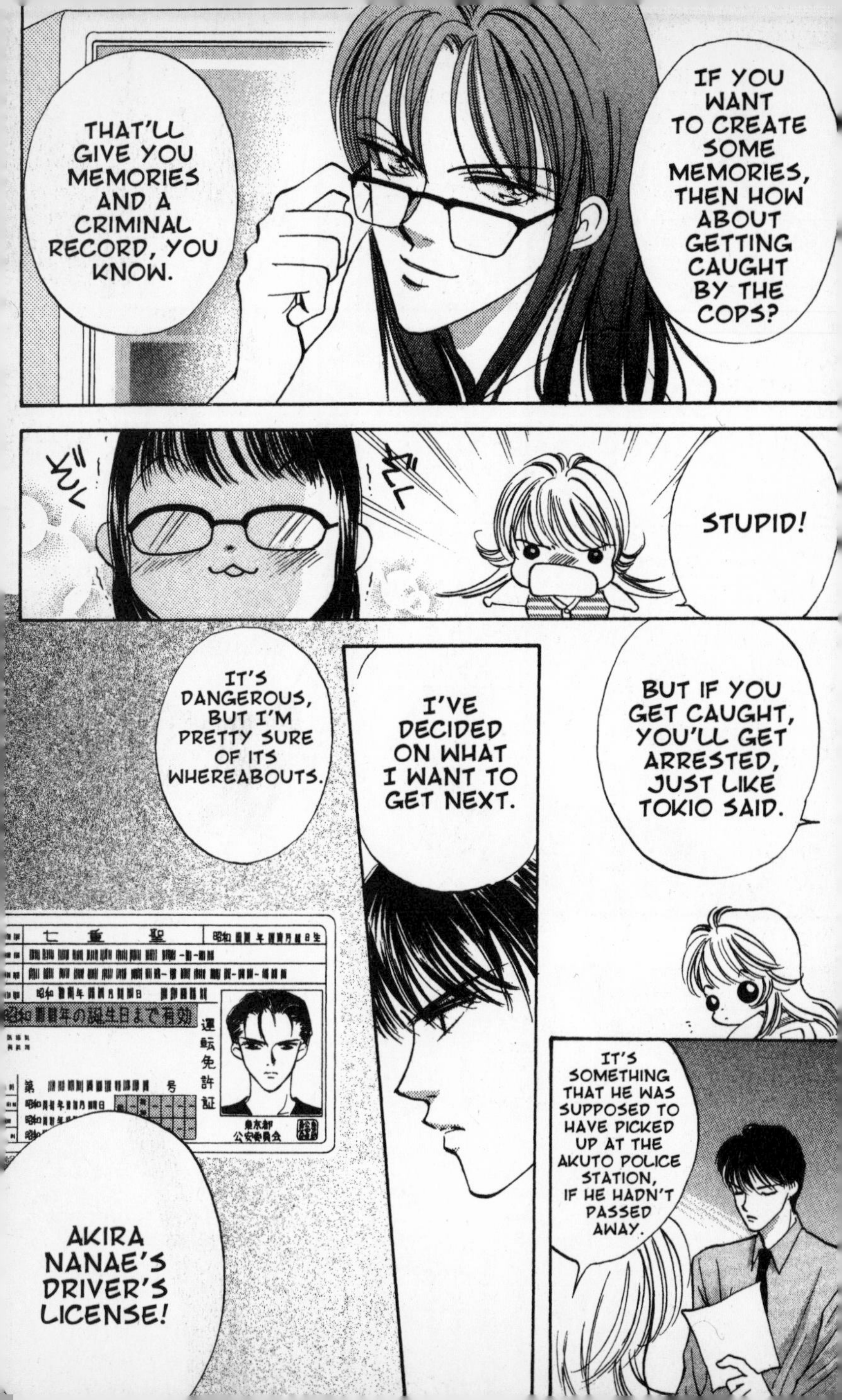
IF YOU WANT TO CREATE SOME MEMORIES, THEN HOW ABOUT GETTING CAUGHT BY THE COPS?
THAT'LL GIVE YOU MEMORIES AND A CRIMINAL RECORD, YOU KNOW.
STUPID!
BUT IF YOU GET CAUGHT, YOU'LL GET ARRESTED, JUST LIKE TOKIO SAID.
IT'S SOMETHING THAT HE WAS SUPPOSED TO HAVE PICKED UP AT THE AKUTO POLICE STATION, IF HE HADN'T PASSED AWAY.
I'VE DECIDED ON WHAT I WANT TO GET NEXT.
IT'S DANGEROUS, BUT I'M PRETTY SURE OF ITS WHEREABOUTS.
七重 聖
運転免許証
東京都 公安委員会
AKIRA NANAE'S DRIVER'S LICENSE!

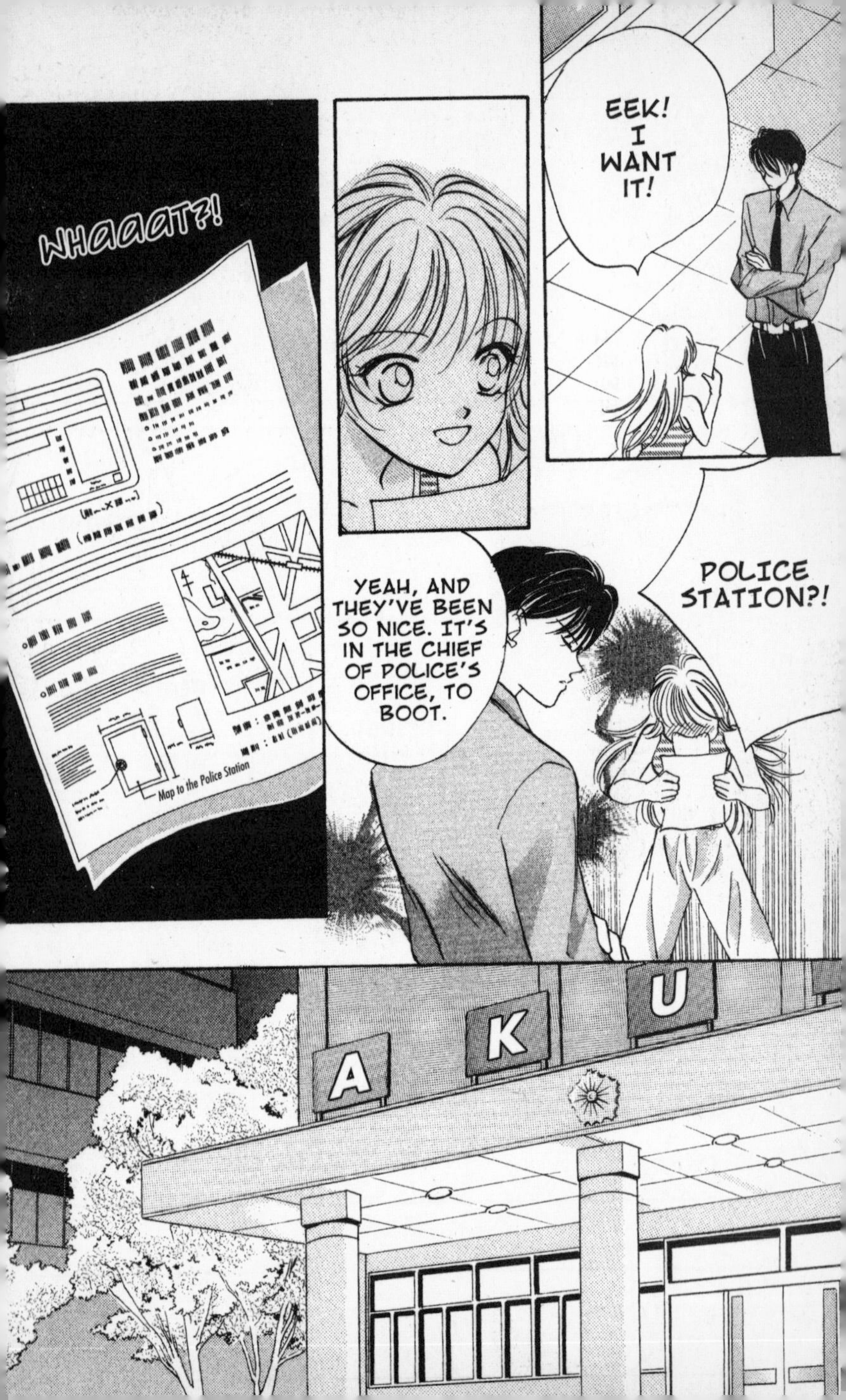
EEK! I WANT IT!
POLICE STATION?!
YEAH, AND THEY'VE BEEN SO NICE. IT'S IN THE CHIEF OF POLICE'S OFFICE, TO BOOT.
WHAAAT?!
Map to the Police Station
A K U

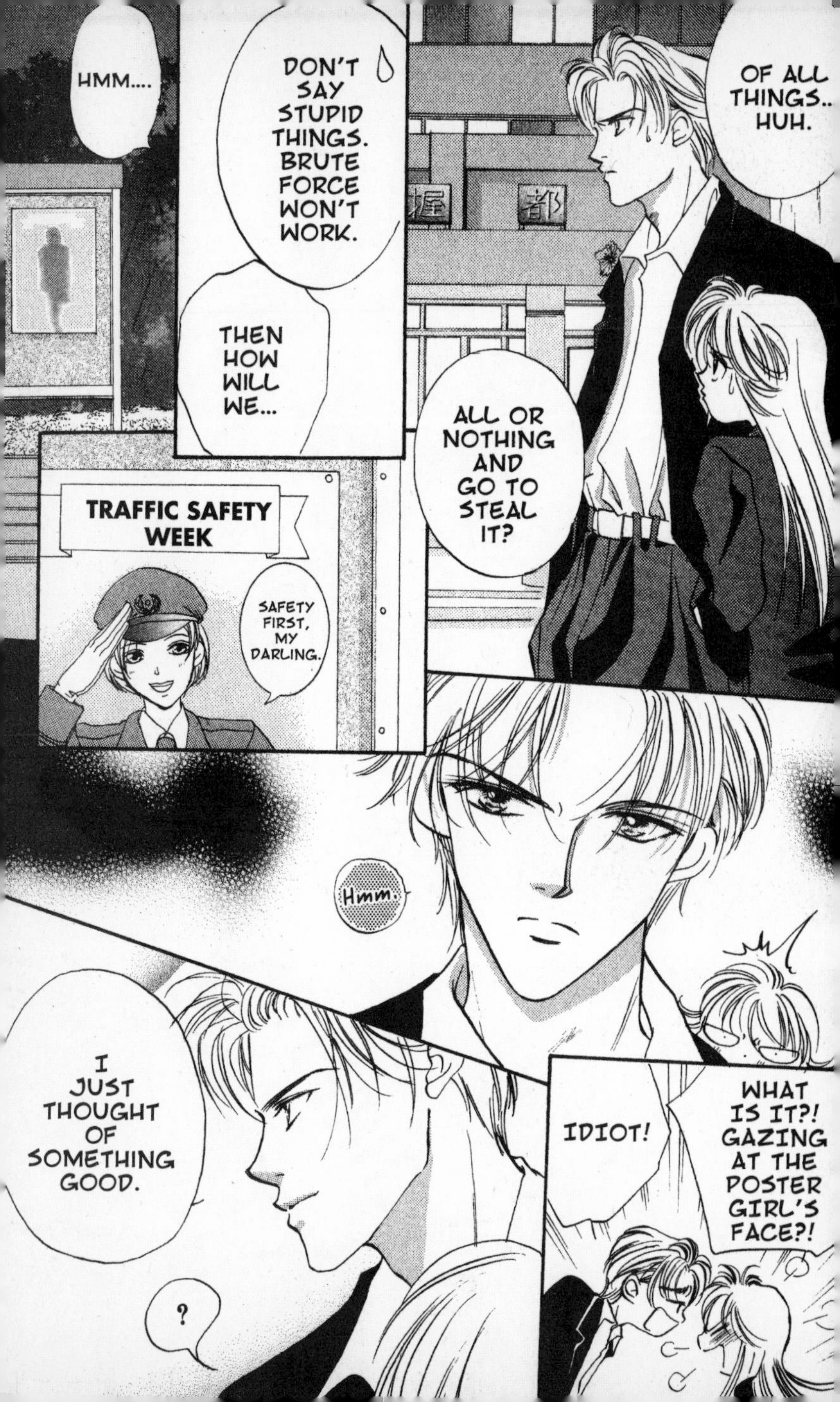
OF ALL THINGS.. HUH.
DON'T SAY STUPID THINGS. BRUTE FORCE WON'T WORK.
THEN HOW WILL WE...
ALL OR NOTHING AND GO TO STEAL IT?
HMM....
TRAFFIC SAFETY WEEK
SAFETY FIRST, MY DARLING.
Hmm.
WHAT IS IT?! GAZING AT THE POSTER GIRL'S FACE?!
IDIOT!
I JUST THOUGHT OF SOMETHING GOOD.
?

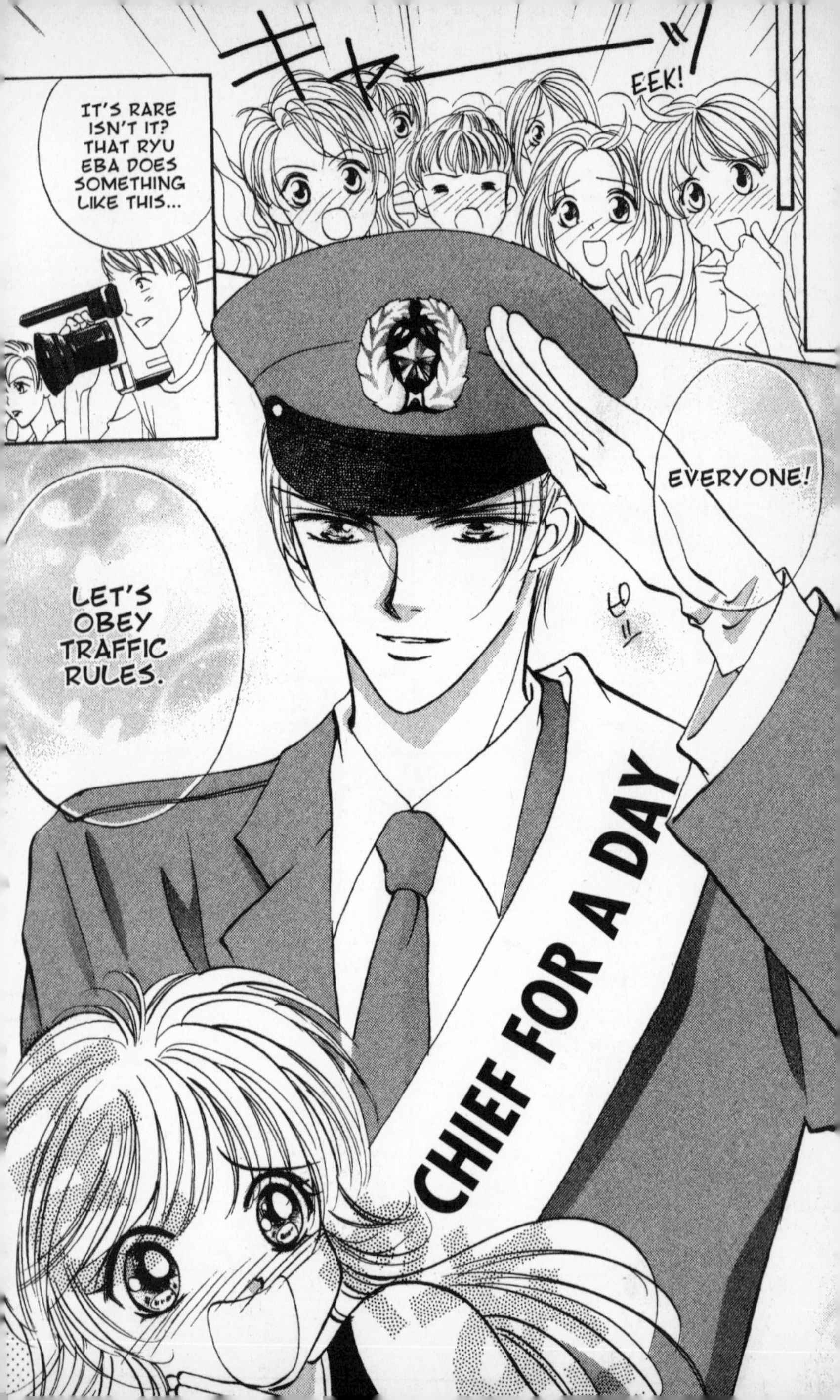

EEK!
IT'S RARE ISN'T IT? THAT RYU EBA DOES SOMETHING LIKE THIS...
EVERYONE!
LET'S OBEY TRAFFIC RULES.
CHIEF FOR A DAY

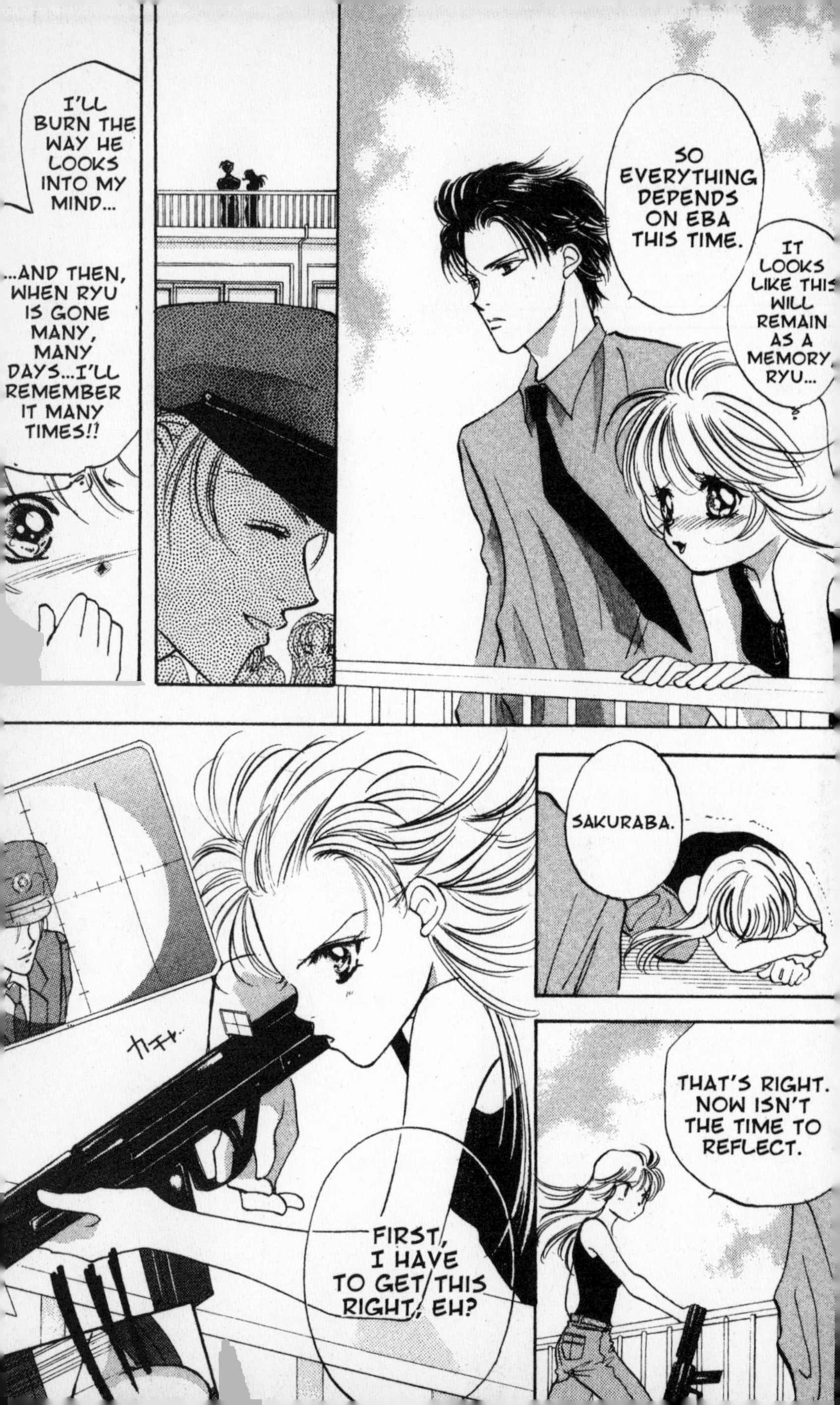
SO EVERYTHING DEPENDS ON EBA THIS TIME.
IT LOOKS LIKE THIS WILL REMAIN AS A MEMORY, RYU...
I'LL BURN THE WAY HE LOOKS INTO MY MIND...
...AND THEN, WHEN RYU IS GONE MANY, MANY DAYS...I'LL REMEMBER IT MANY TIMES!!
SAKURABA.
THAT'S RIGHT. NOW ISN'T THE TIME TO REFLECT.
カチャ…
FIRST, I HAVE TO GET THIS RIGHT, EH?

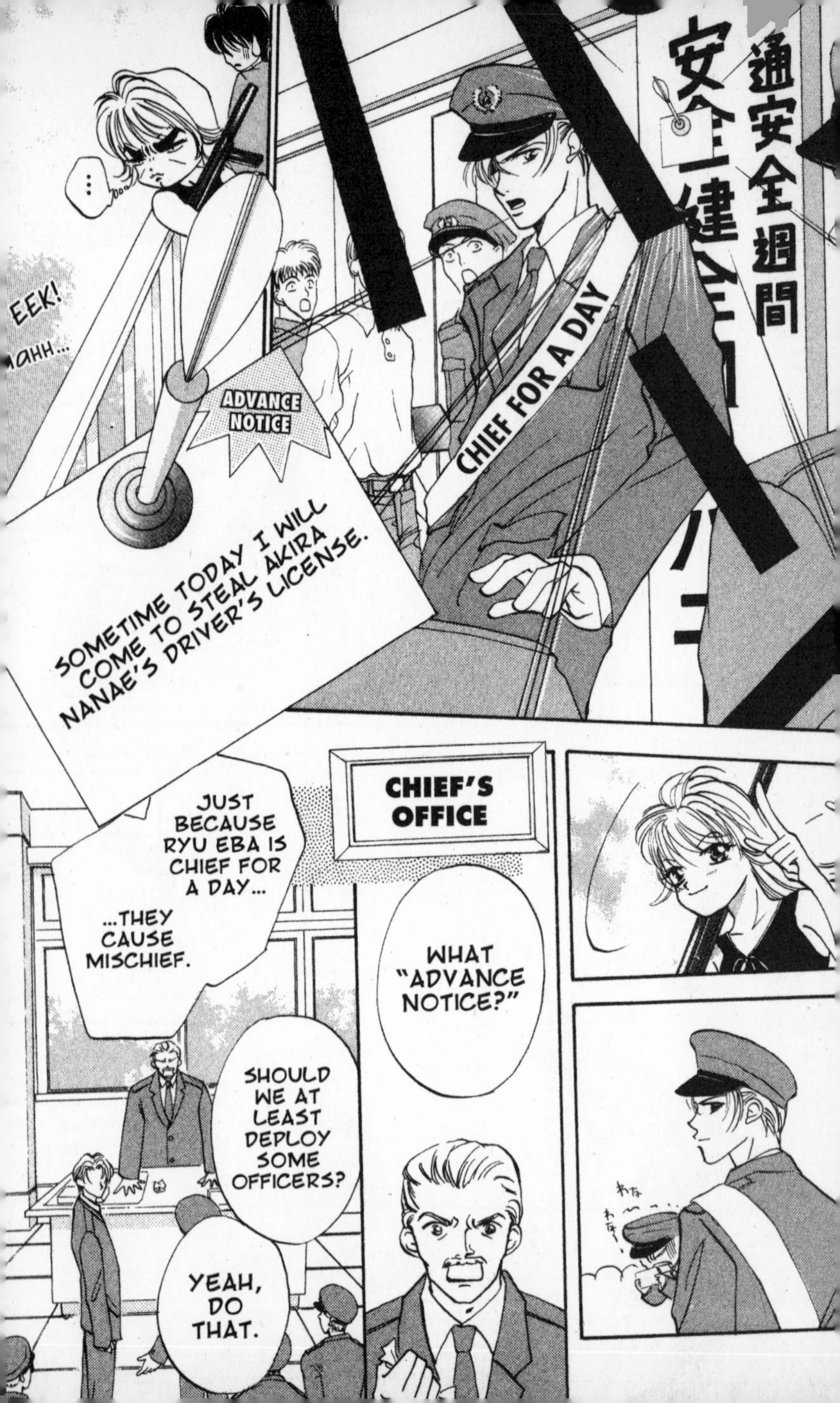

通安全週間
CHIEF FOR A DAY
ADVANCE NOTICE
SOMETIME TODAY I WILL COME TO STEAL AKIRA NANAE'S DRIVER'S LICENSE.
...
EEK!
AAHH...
CHIEF'S OFFICE
WHAT "ADVANCE NOTICE?"
JUST BECAUSE RYU EBA IS CHIEF FOR A DAY...
...THEY CAUSE MISCHIEF.
SHOULD WE AT LEAST DEPLOY SOME OFFICERS?
YEAH, DO THAT.

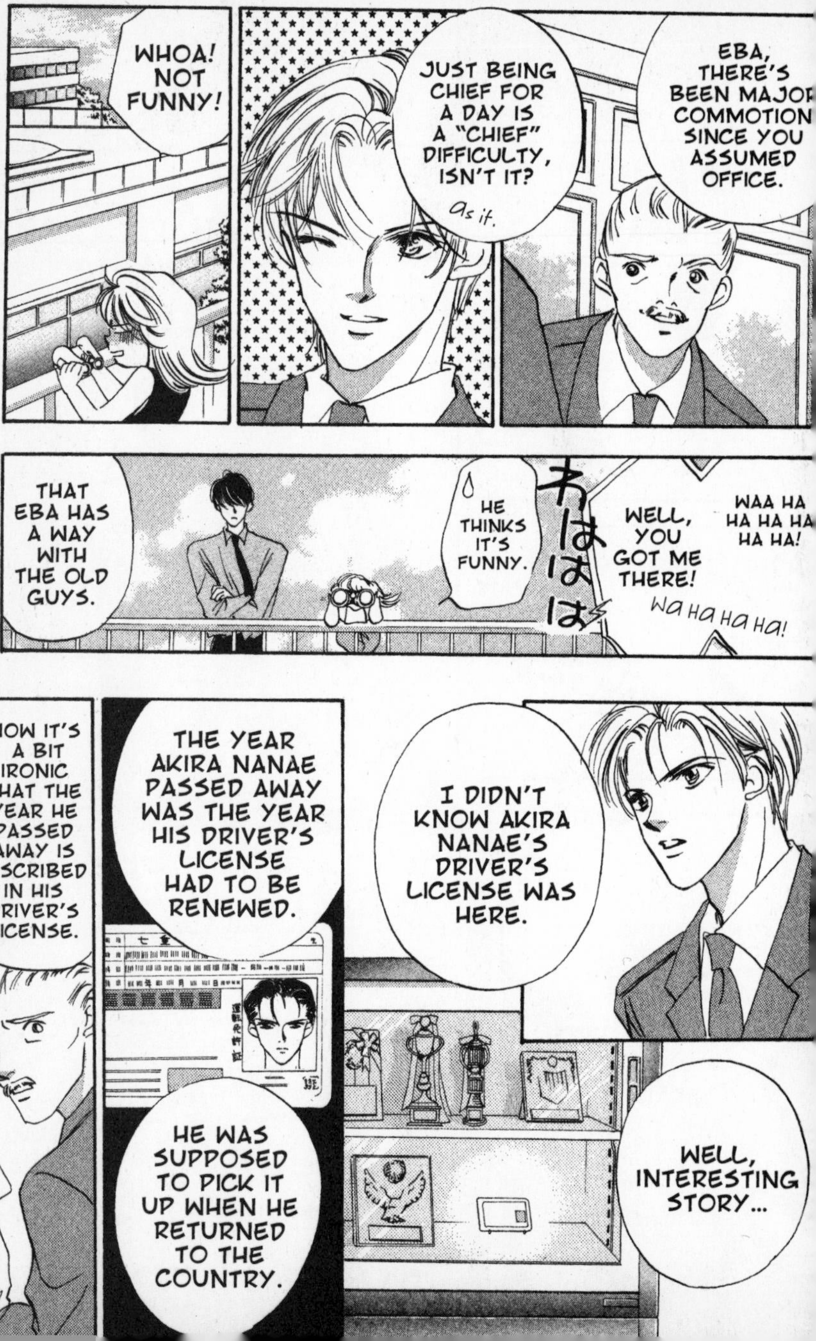
EBA, THERE'S BEEN MAJOR COMMOTION SINCE YOU ASSUMED OFFICE.
JUST BEING CHIEF FOR A DAY IS A "CHIEF" DIFFICULTY, ISN'T IT?
as if.
WHOA! NOT FUNNY!
WAA HA HA HA HA HA HA!
WELL, YOU GOT ME THERE!
Wa ha ha ha!
わははは
HE THINKS IT'S FUNNY.
THAT EBA HAS A WAY WITH THE OLD GUYS.
I DIDN'T KNOW AKIRA NANAE'S DRIVER'S LICENSE WAS HERE.
WELL, INTERESTING STORY...
THE YEAR AKIRA NANAE PASSED AWAY WAS THE YEAR HIS DRIVER'S LICENSE HAD TO BE RENEWED.
HE WAS SUPPOSED TO PICK IT UP WHEN HE RETURNED TO THE COUNTRY.
NOW IT'S A BIT IRONIC THAT THE YEAR HE PASSED AWAY IS INSCRIBED IN HIS DRIVER'S LICENSE.

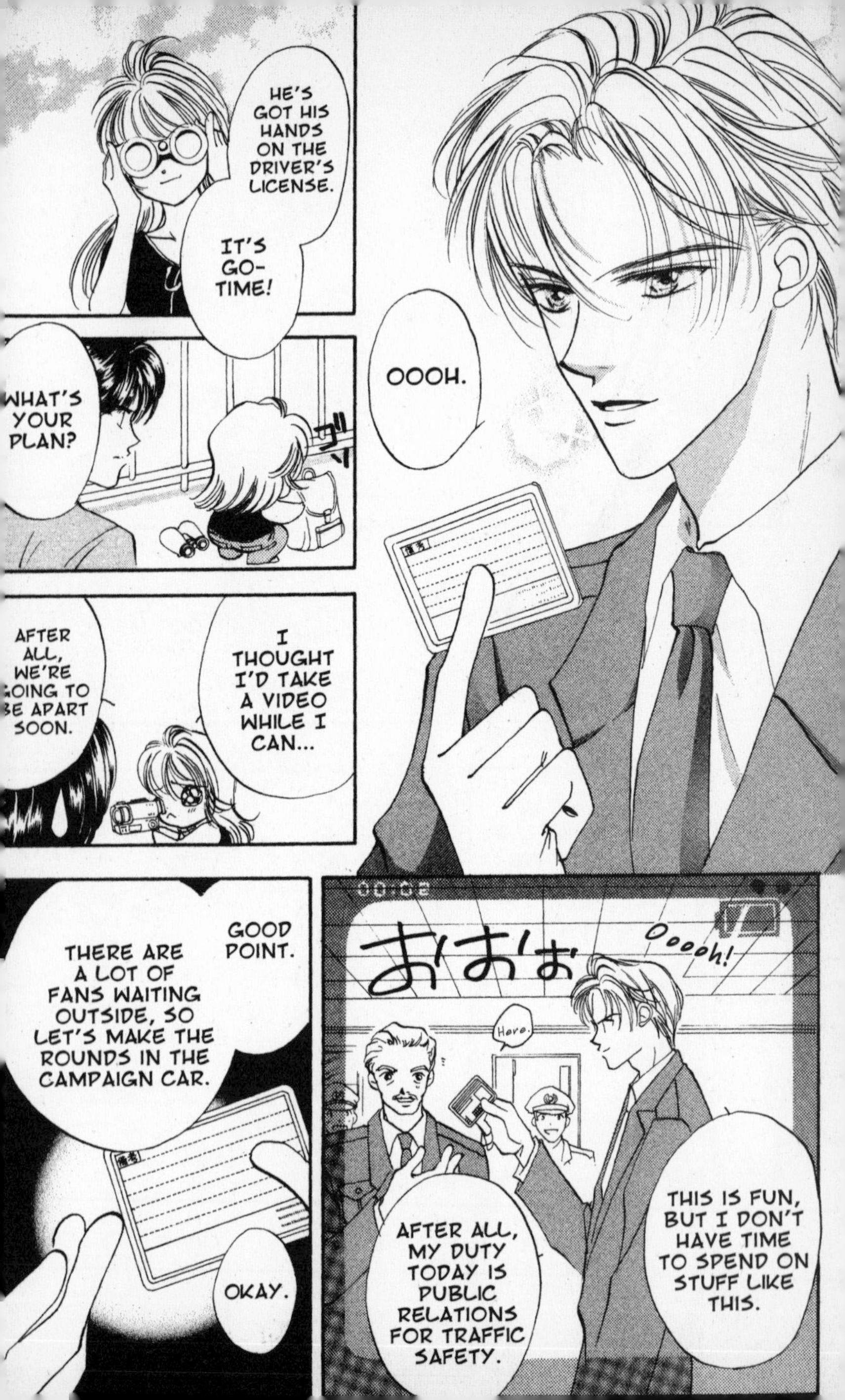
OOOH.
HE'S GOT HIS HANDS ON THE DRIVER'S LICENSE.
IT'S GO-TIME!
WHAT'S YOUR PLAN?
I THOUGHT I'D TAKE A VIDEO WHILE I CAN...
AFTER ALL, WE'RE GOING TO BE APART SOON.
おおぉ
Ooooh!
Here.
THIS IS FUN, BUT I DON'T HAVE TIME TO SPEND ON STUFF LIKE THIS.
AFTER ALL, MY DUTY TODAY IS PUBLIC RELATIONS FOR TRAFFIC SAFETY.
GOOD POINT.
THERE ARE A LOT OF FANS WAITING OUTSIDE, SO LET'S MAKE THE ROUNDS IN THE CAMPAIGN CAR.
OKAY.

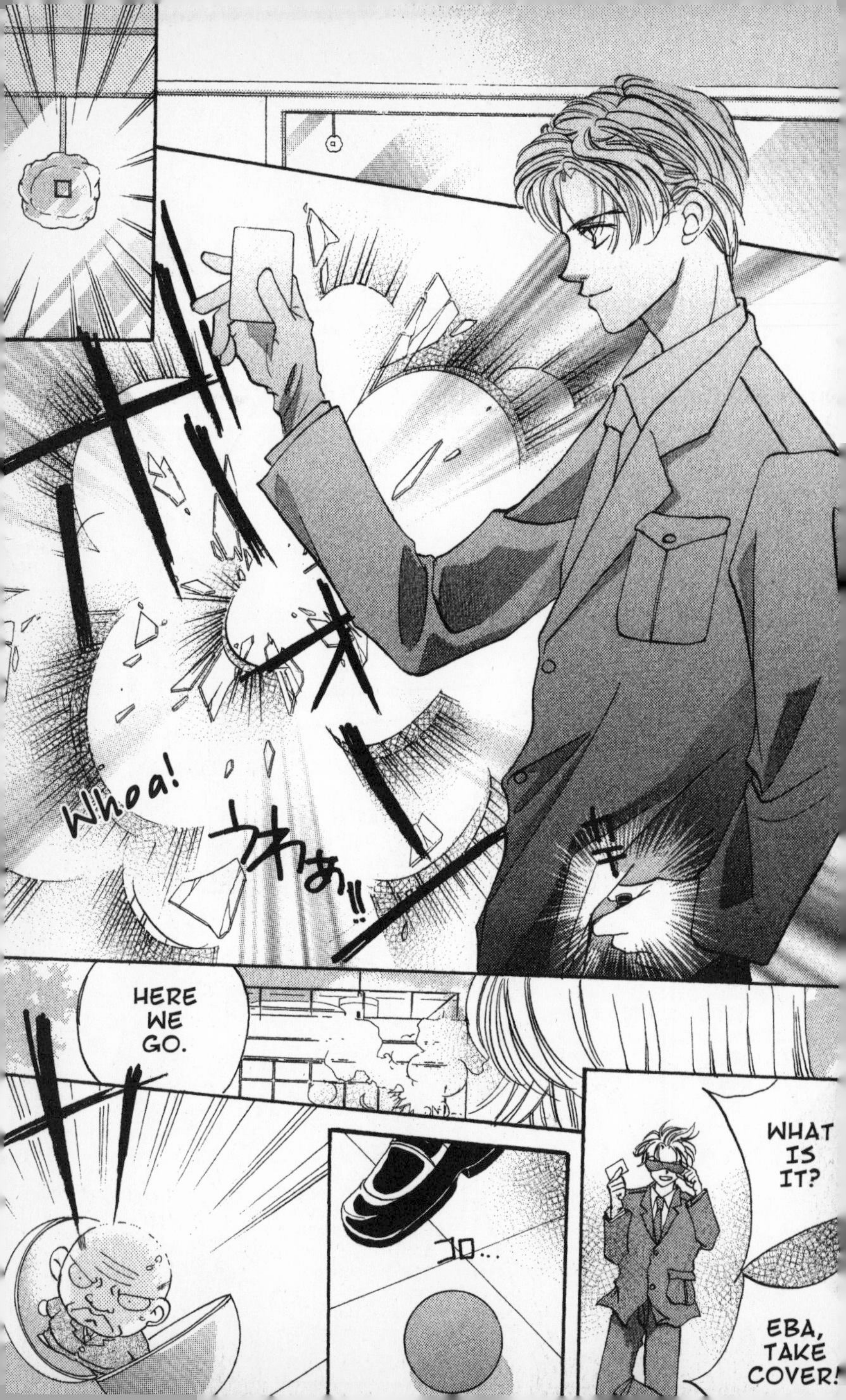
キ
Whoa!
うわぁ!!
HERE WE GO.
WHAT IS IT?
EBA, TAKE COVER!
コロ...

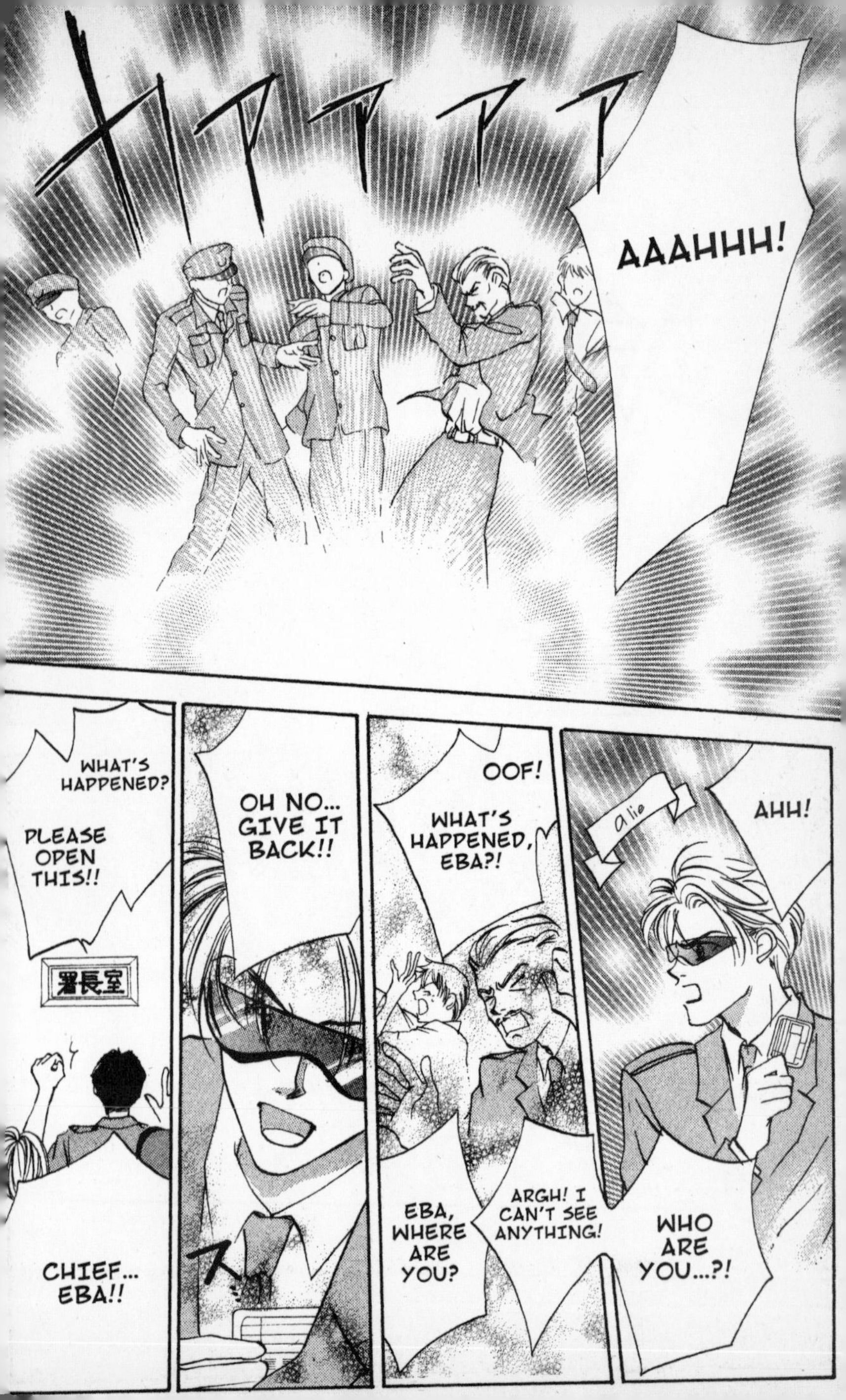
AAAHHH!
a lie
AHH!
WHO ARE YOU...?!
OOF!
WHAT'S HAPPENED, EBA?!
ARGH! I CAN'T SEE ANYTHING!
EBA, WHERE ARE YOU?
OH NO... GIVE IT BACK!!
WHAT'S HAPPENED?
PLEASE OPEN THIS!!
署長室
CHIEF... EBA!!

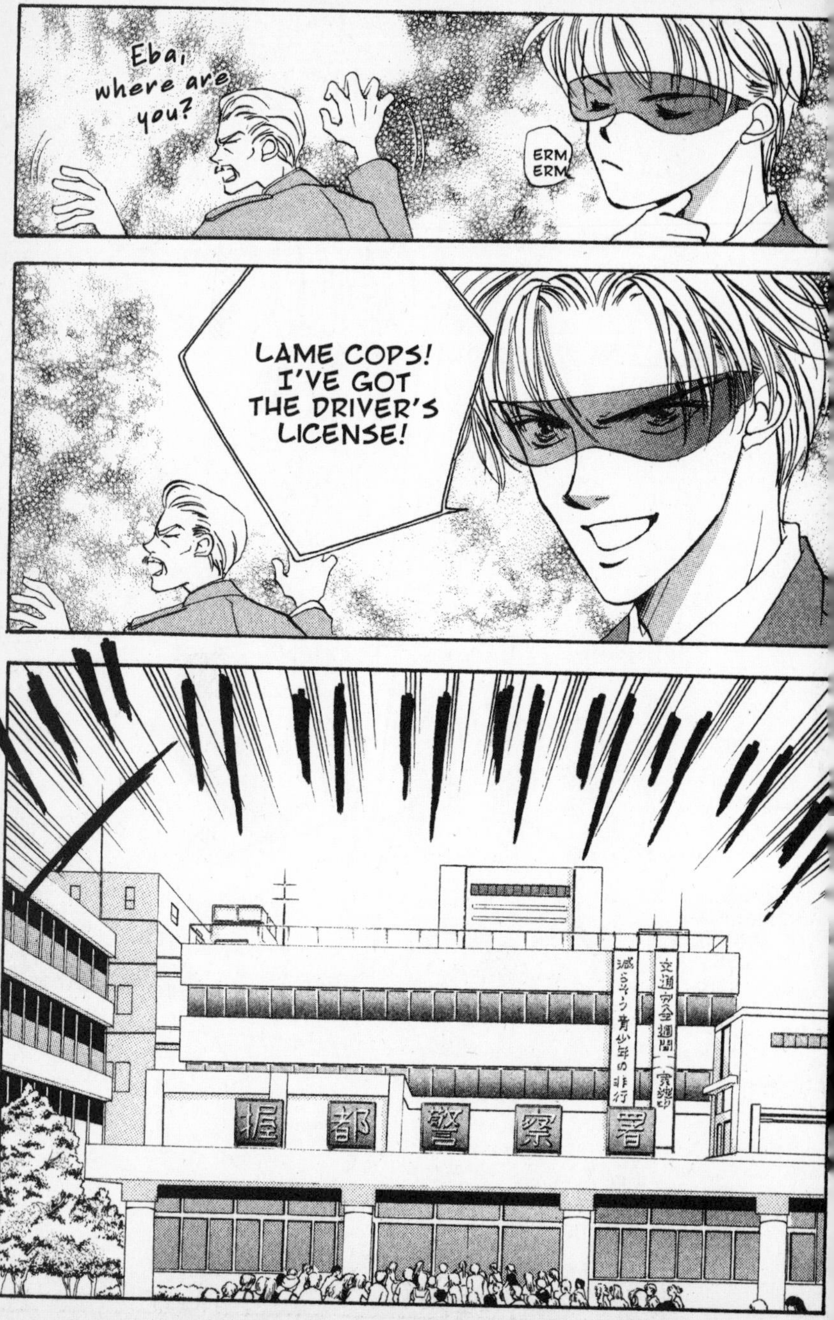
ERM ERM
Eba, where are you?
LAME COPS! I'VE GOT THE DRIVER'S LICENSE!
交通安全週間 実施中
減らそう青少年の非行
堀都警察署

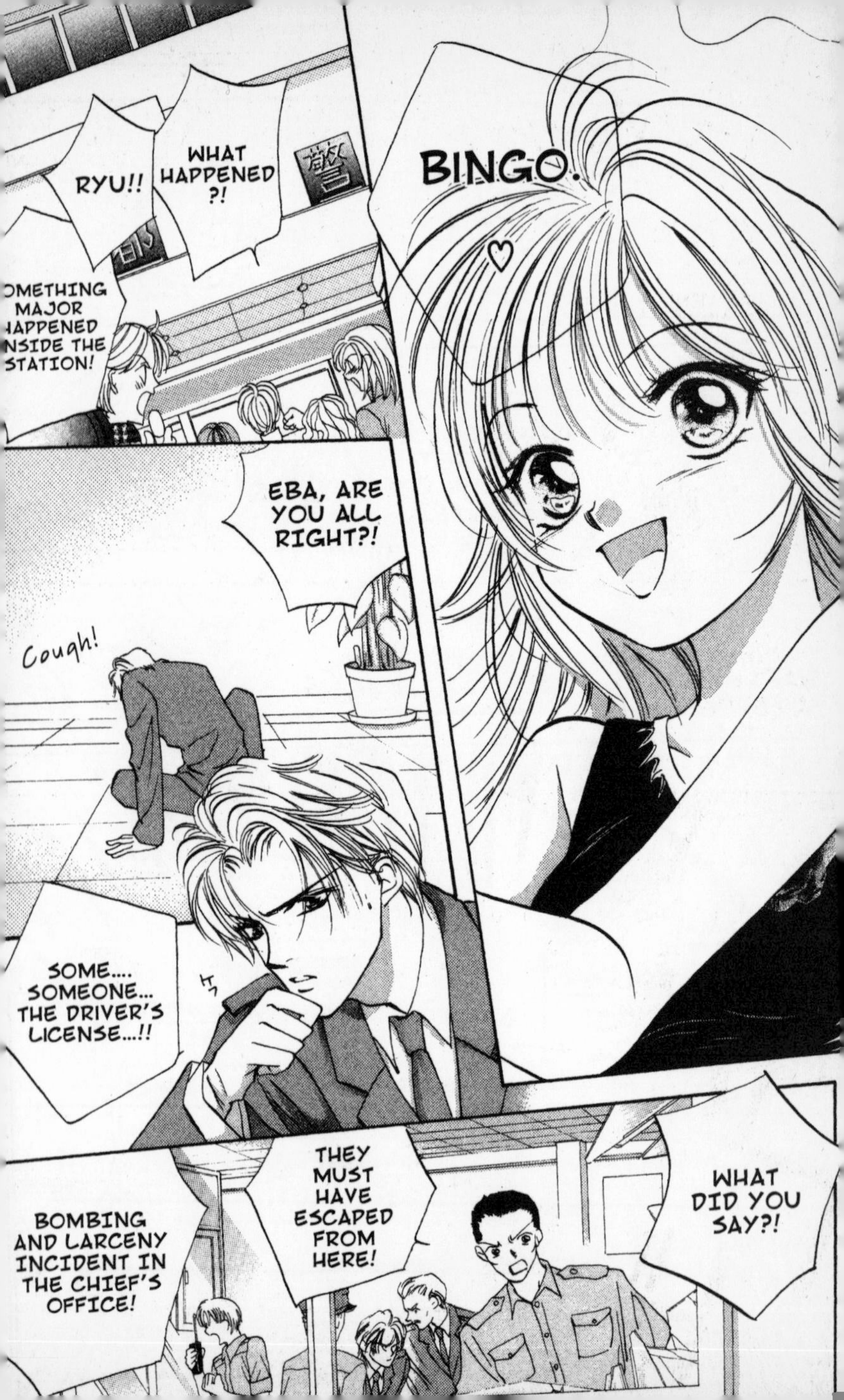
BINGO.
WHAT HAPPENED ?!
RYU!!
OMETHING MAJOR HAPPENED NSIDE THE STATION!
EBA, ARE YOU ALL RIGHT?!
Cough!
SOME.... SOMEONE... THE DRIVER'S LICENSE...!!
WHAT DID YOU SAY?!
THEY MUST HAVE ESCAPED FROM HERE!
BOMBING AND LARCENY INCIDENT IN THE CHIEF'S OFFICE!

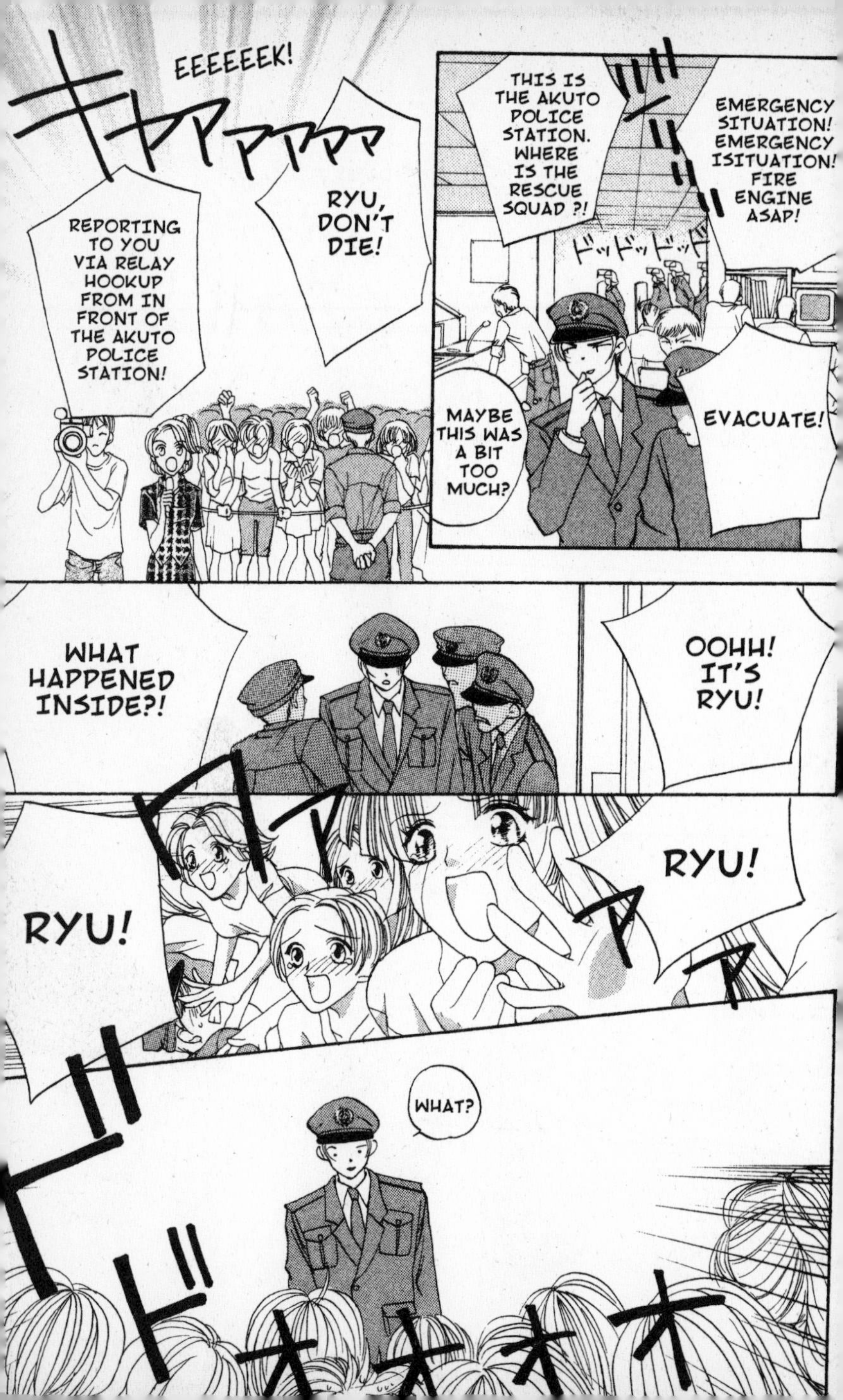

EMERGENCY SITUATION! EMERGENCY ISITUATION! FIRE ENGINE ASAP!
THIS IS THE AKUTO POLICE STATION. WHERE IS THE RESCUE SQUAD ?!
ドッドッドッド
EVACUATE!
MAYBE THIS WAS A BIT TOO MUCH?
EEEEEEK!
RYU, DON'T DIE!
REPORTING TO YOU VIA RELAY HOOKUP FROM IN FRONT OF THE AKUTO POLICE STATION!
OOHH! IT'S RYU!
WHAT HAPPENED INSIDE?!
RYU!
RYU!
WHAT?

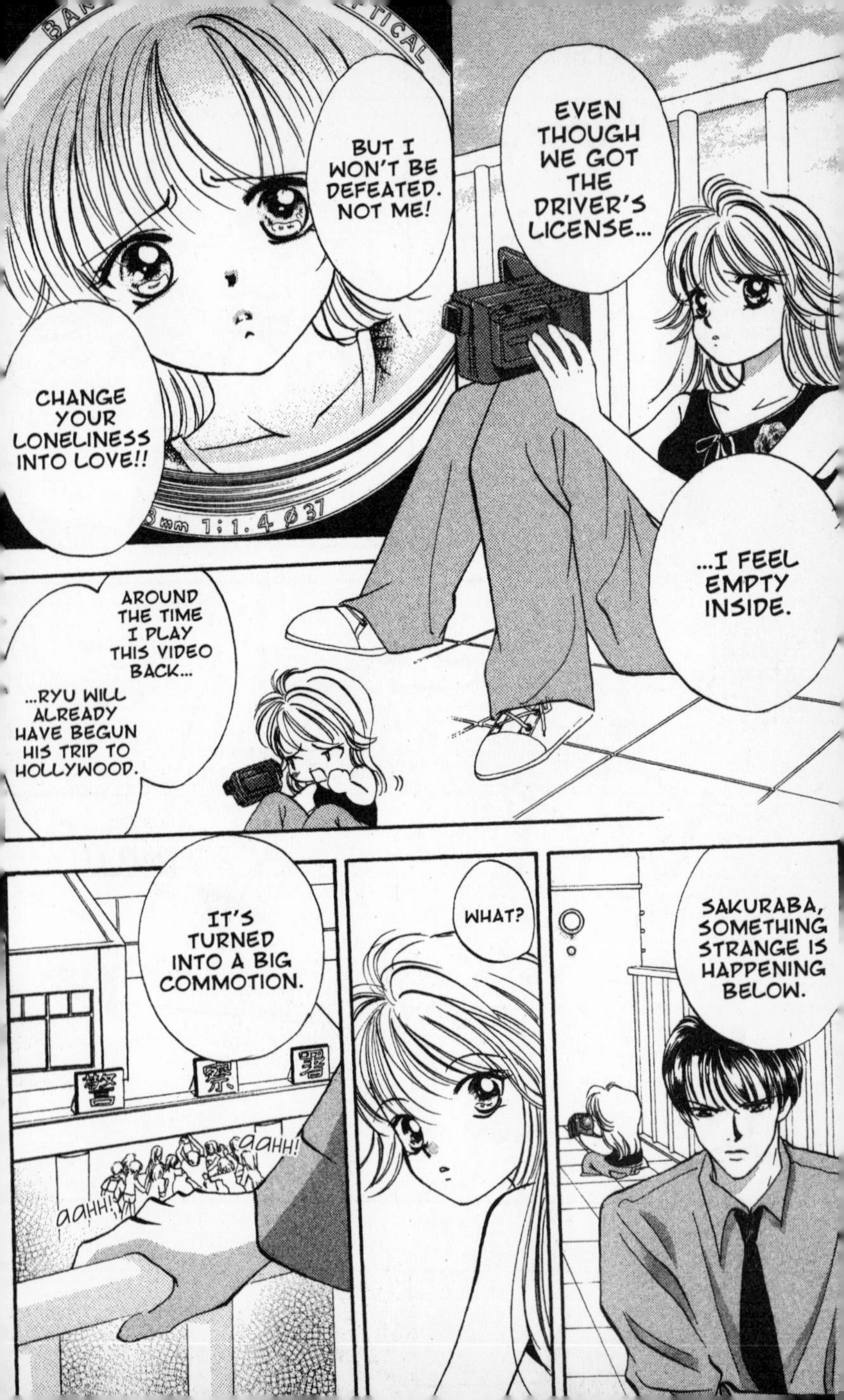
EVEN THOUGH WE GOT THE DRIVER'S LICENSE...
...I FEEL EMPTY INSIDE.
BUT I WON'T BE DEFEATED. NOT ME!
CHANGE YOUR LONELINESS INTO LOVE!!
AROUND THE TIME I PLAY THIS VIDEO BACK...
...RYU WILL ALREADY HAVE BEGUN HIS TRIP TO HOLLYWOOD.
SAKURABA, SOMETHING STRANGE IS HAPPENING BELOW.
WHAT?
IT'S TURNED INTO A BIG COMMOTION.
警察署
aahh!
aahh!

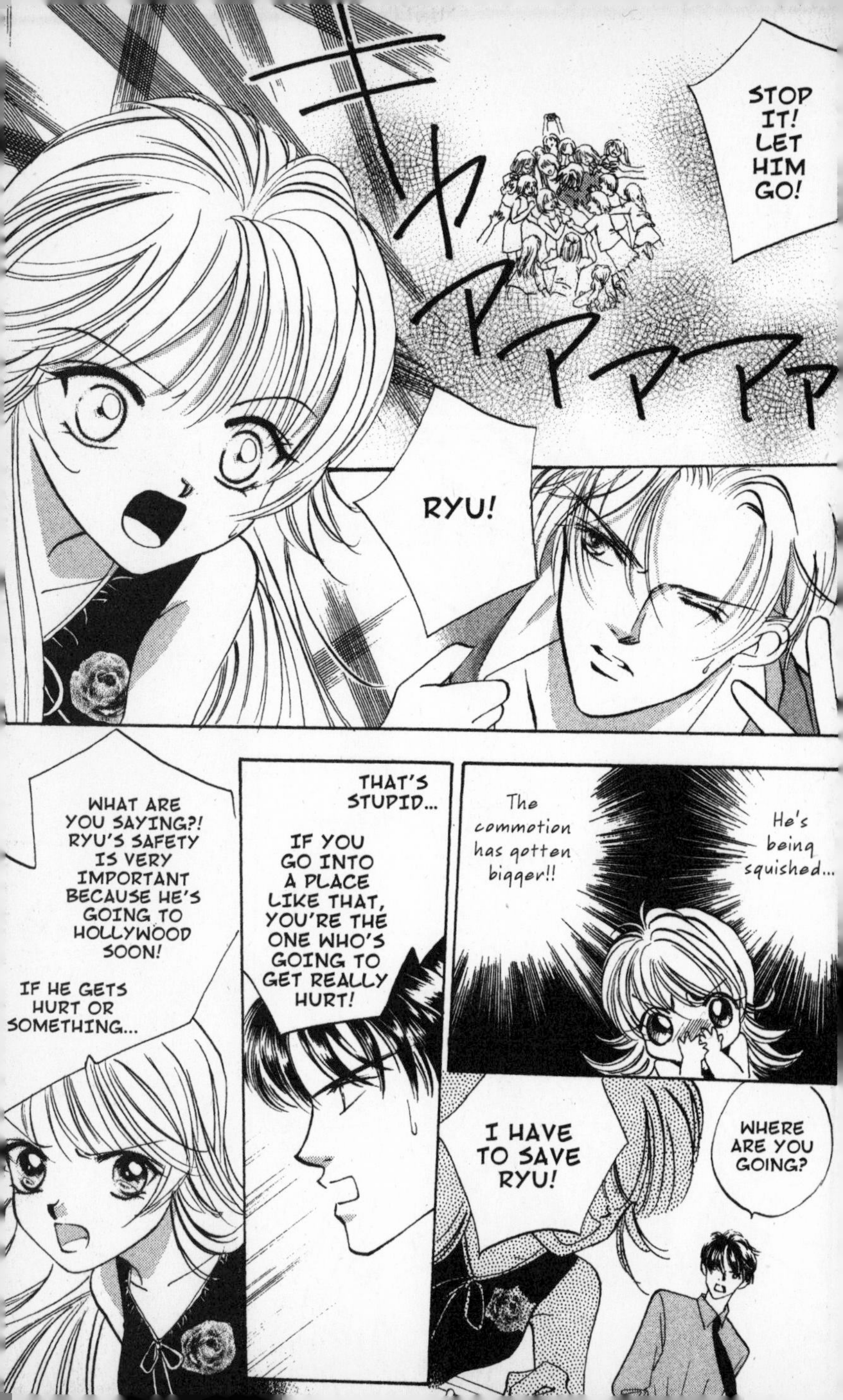

STOP IT! LET HIM GO!
キャアアアア
RYU!
He's being squished...
The commotion has gotten bigger!!
WHERE ARE YOU GOING?
I HAVE TO SAVE RYU!
THAT'S STUPID...
IF YOU GO INTO A PLACE LIKE THAT, YOU'RE THE ONE WHO'S GOING TO GET REALLY HURT!
WHAT ARE YOU SAYING?! RYU'S SAFETY IS VERY IMPORTANT BECAUSE HE'S GOING TO HOLLYWOOD SOON!
IF HE GETS HURT OR SOMETHING...

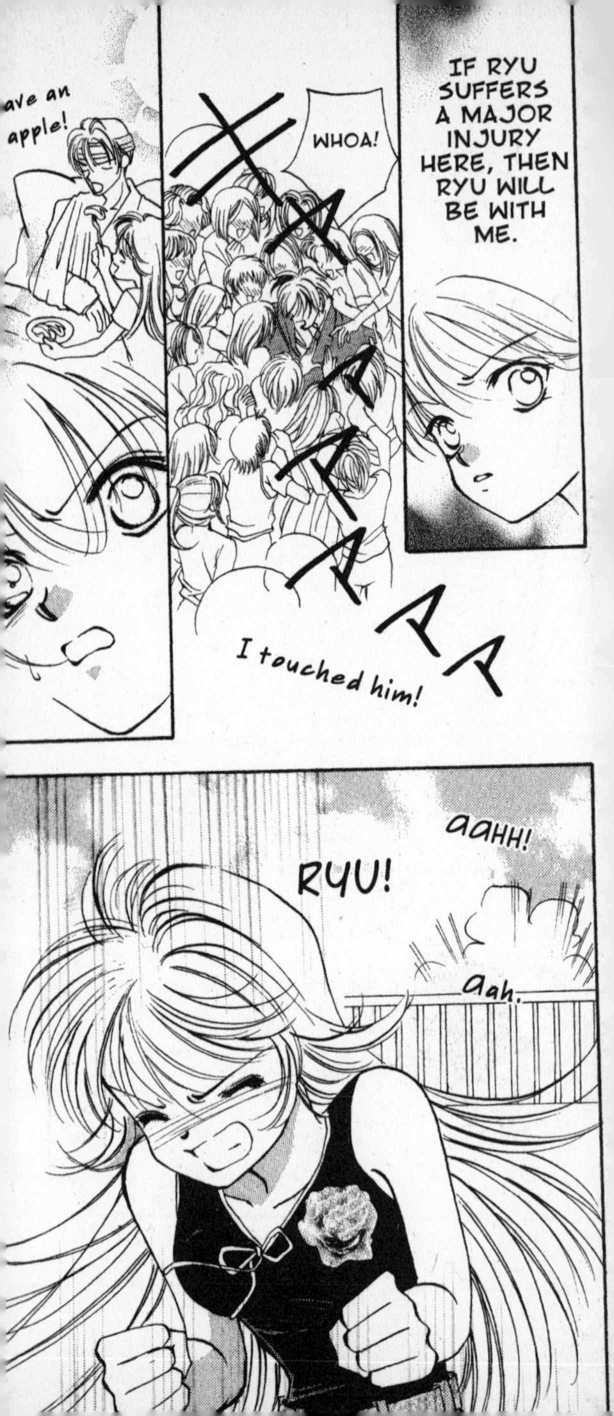
IF RYU SUFFERS A MAJOR INJURY HERE, THEN RYU WILL BE WITH ME.
WHOA!
I touched him!
ave an apple!
aahh!
RYU!
aah.

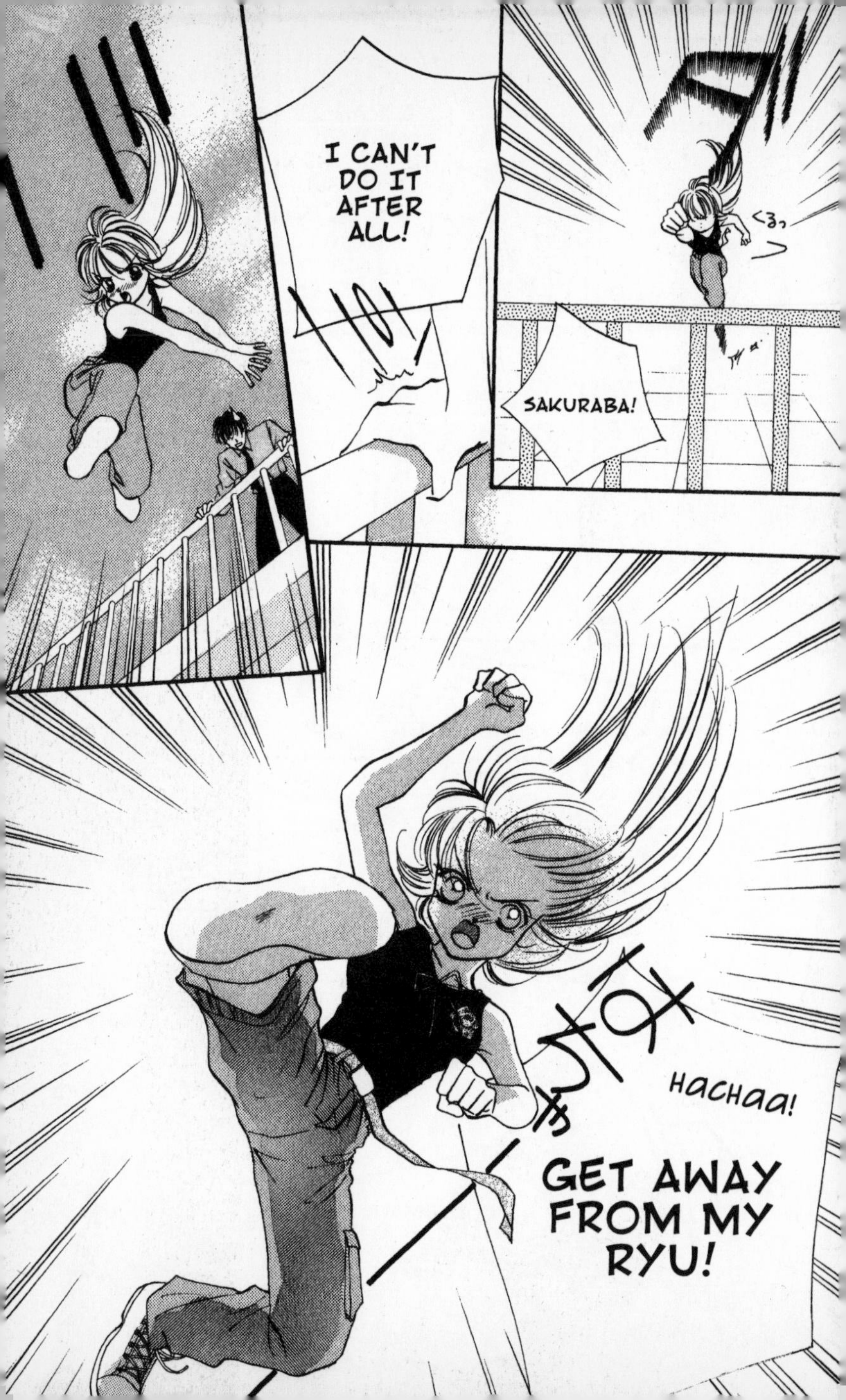
くるっ
SAKURABA!
I CAN'T DO IT AFTER ALL!
HACHAA!
GET AWAY FROM MY RYU!

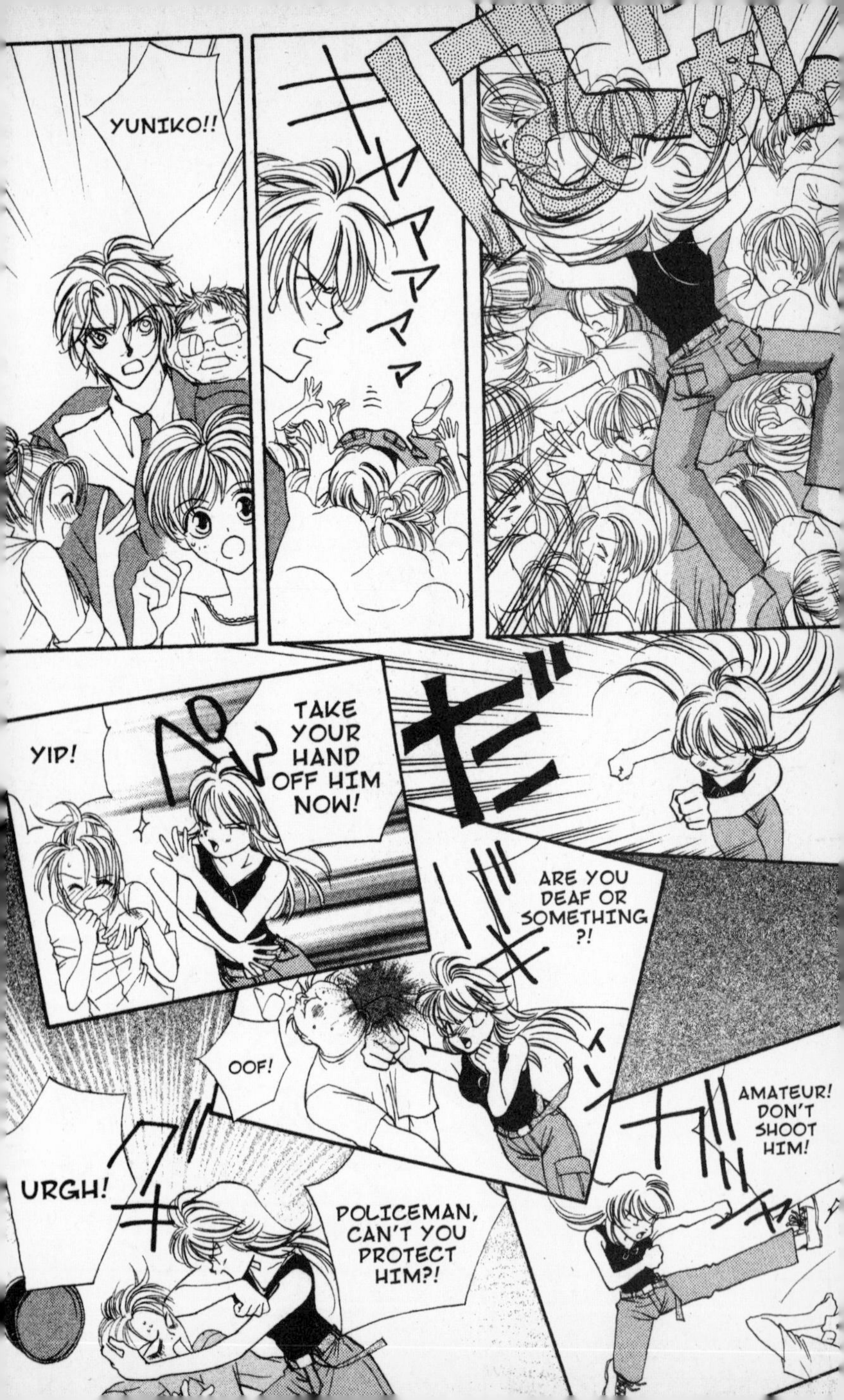
YUNIKO!!
TAKE YOUR HAND OFF HIM NOW!
YIP!
ARE YOU DEAF OR SOMETHING?!
OOF!
AMATEUR! DON'T SHOOT HIM!
POLICEMAN, CAN'T YOU PROTECT HIM?!
URGH!

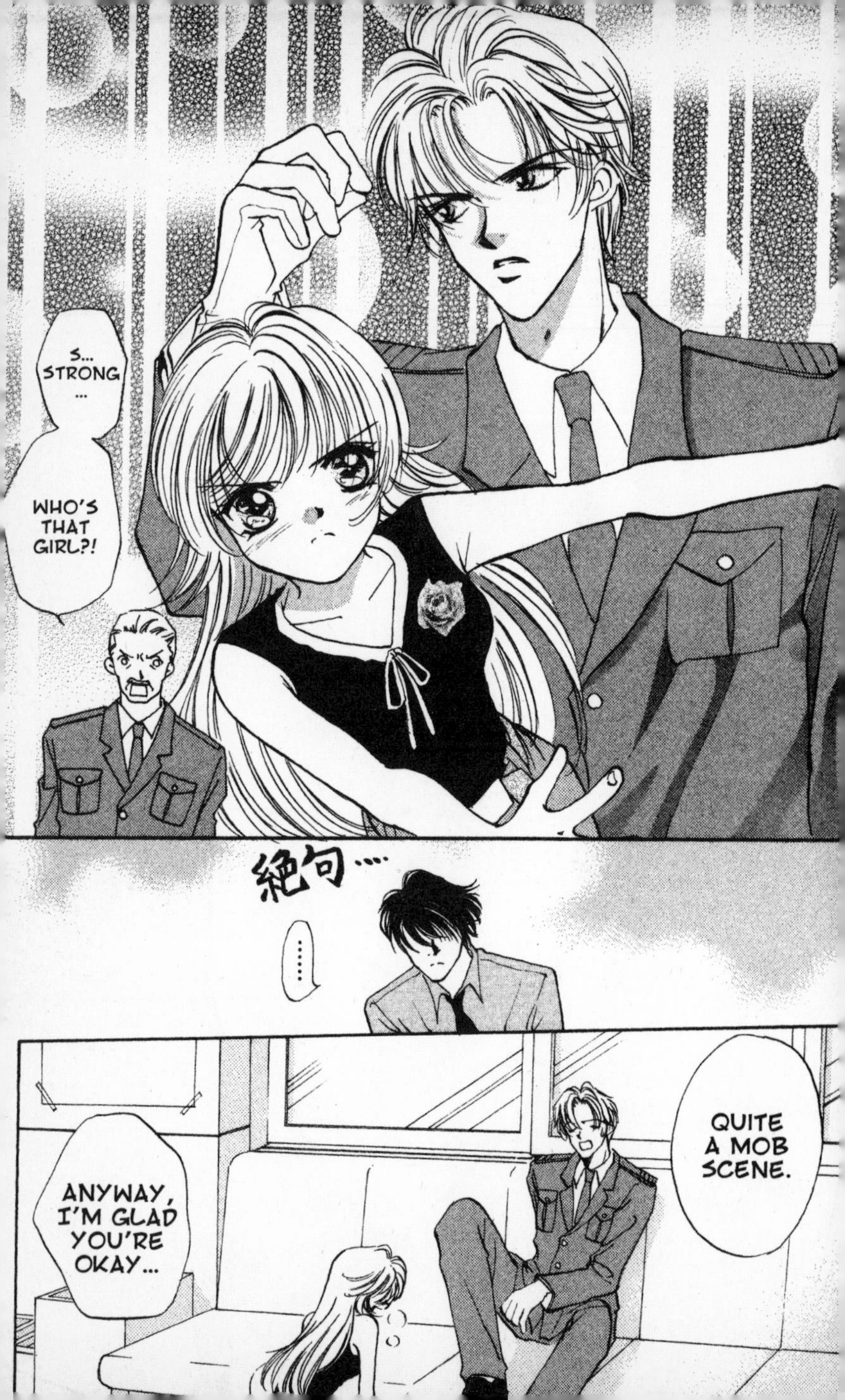
S... STRONG ...
WHO'S THAT GIRL?!
絶句....
......
QUITE A MOB SCENE.
ANYWAY, I'M GLAD YOU'RE OKAY...

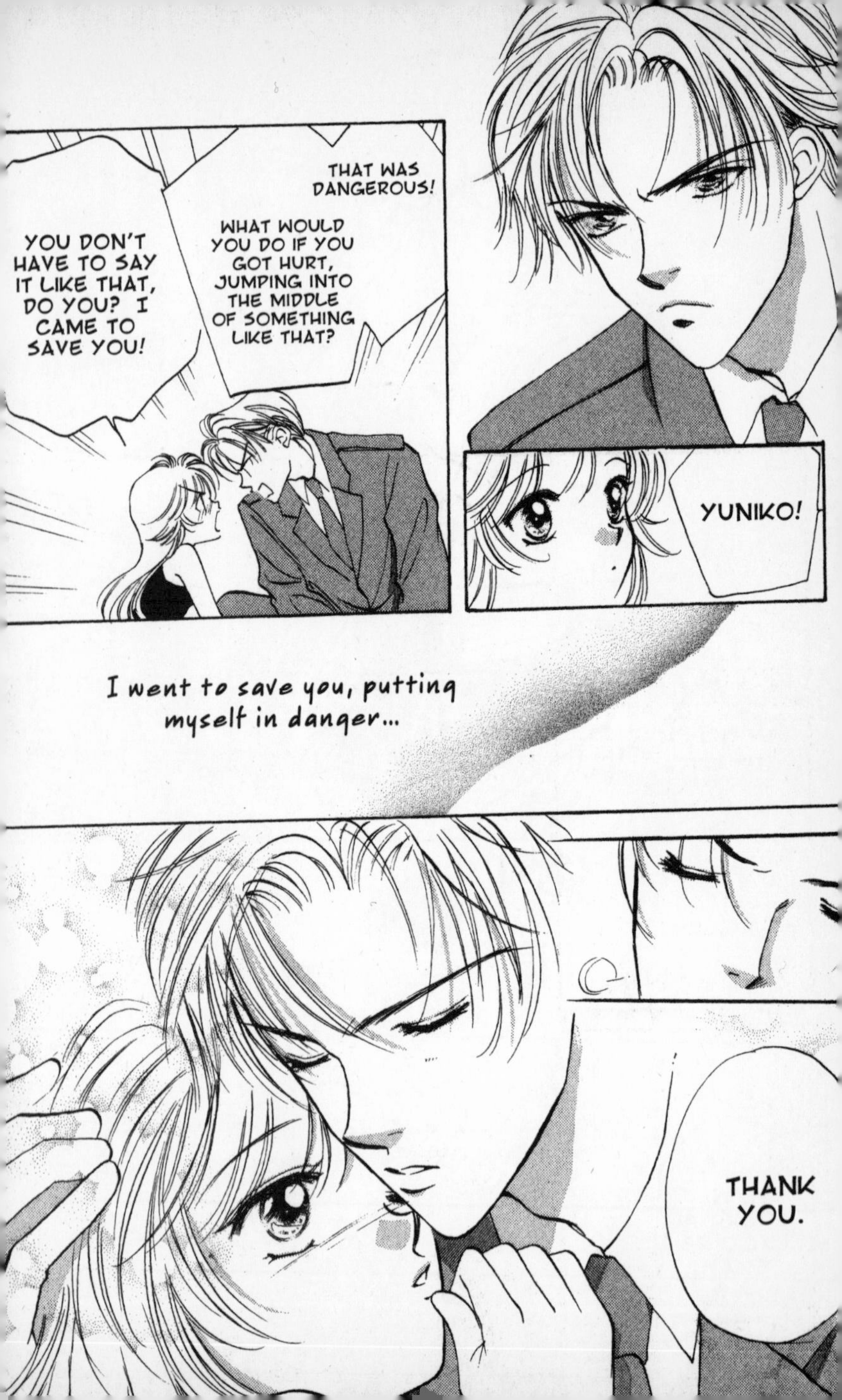
YUNIKO!
THAT WAS DANGEROUS!
WHAT WOULD YOU DO IF YOU GOT HURT, JUMPING INTO THE MIDDLE OF SOMETHING LIKE THAT?
YOU DON'T HAVE TO SAY IT LIKE THAT, DO YOU? I CAME TO SAVE YOU!
I went to save you, putting myself in danger...
THANK YOU.

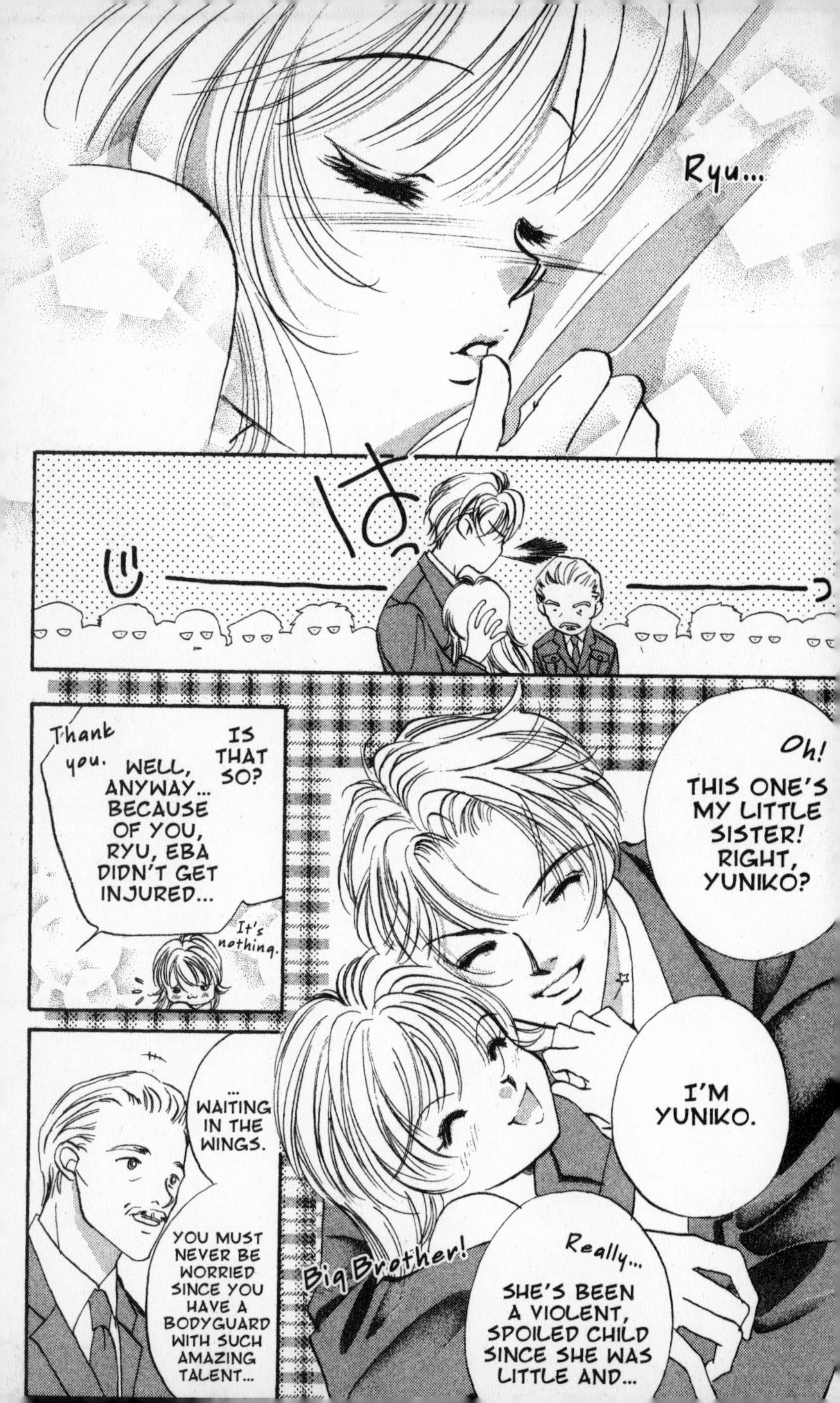
Ryu...
はっ
じ——っ
Oh!
THIS ONE'S MY LITTLE SISTER! RIGHT, YUNIKO?
IS THAT SO?
WELL, ANYWAY... BECAUSE OF YOU, RYU, EBA DIDN'T GET INJURED...
Thank you.
It's nothing.
I'M YUNIKO.
Big Brother!
Really...
SHE'S BEEN A VIOLENT, SPOILED CHILD SINCE SHE WAS LITTLE AND...
... WAITING IN THE WINGS.
YOU MUST NEVER BE WORRIED SINCE YOU HAVE A BODYGUARD WITH SUCH AMAZING TALENT...

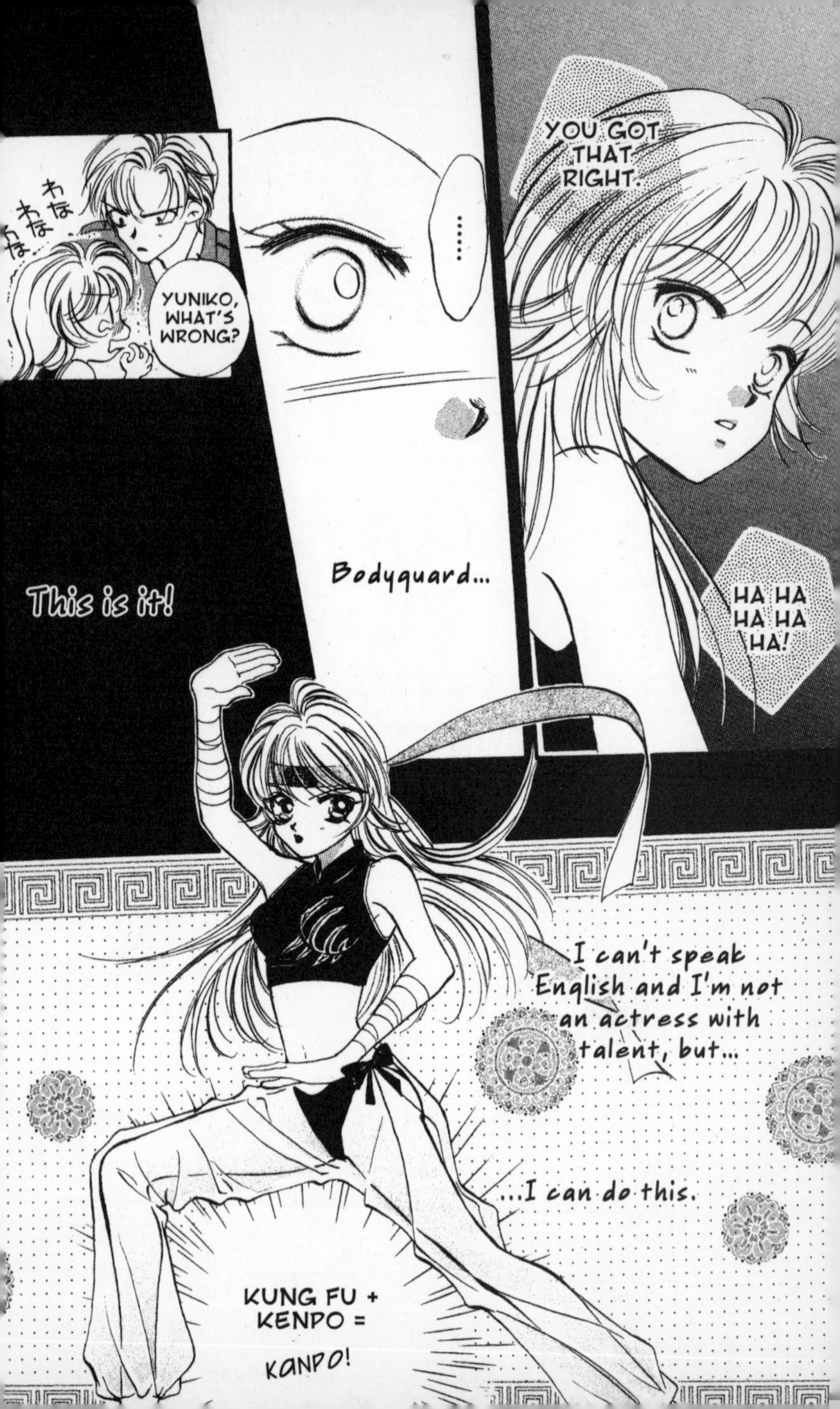
YOU GOT THAT RIGHT.
HA HA HA HA HA!
......
Bodyguard...
わなわなわな
YUNIKO, WHAT'S WRONG?
This is it!
I can't speak English and I'm not an actress with talent, but...
...I can do this.
KUNG FU + KENPO = KANPO!

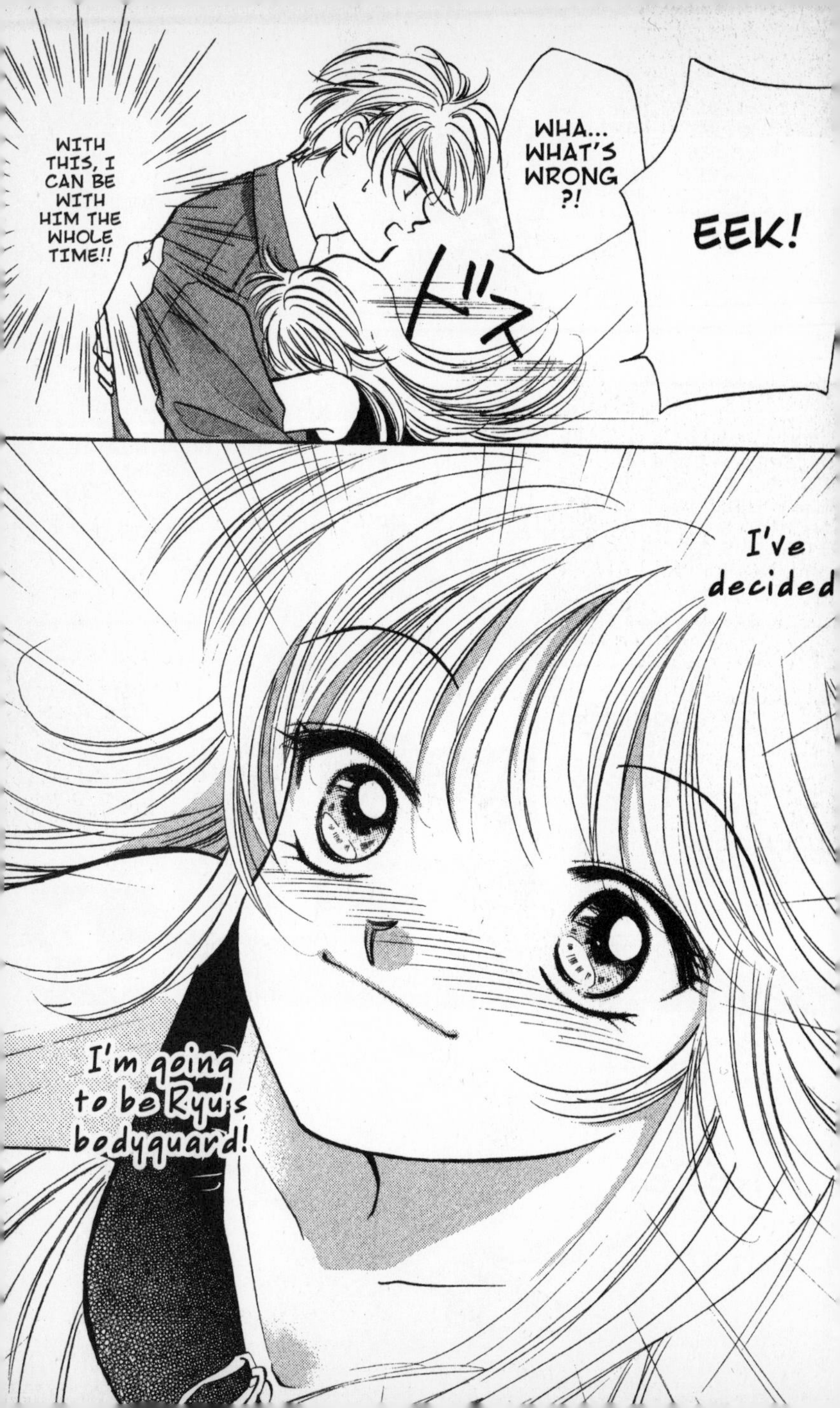
EEK!
WHA... WHAT'S WRONG ?!
ドス
WITH THIS, I CAN BE WITH HIM THE WHOLE TIME!!
I've decided
I'm going to be Ryu's bodyguard!

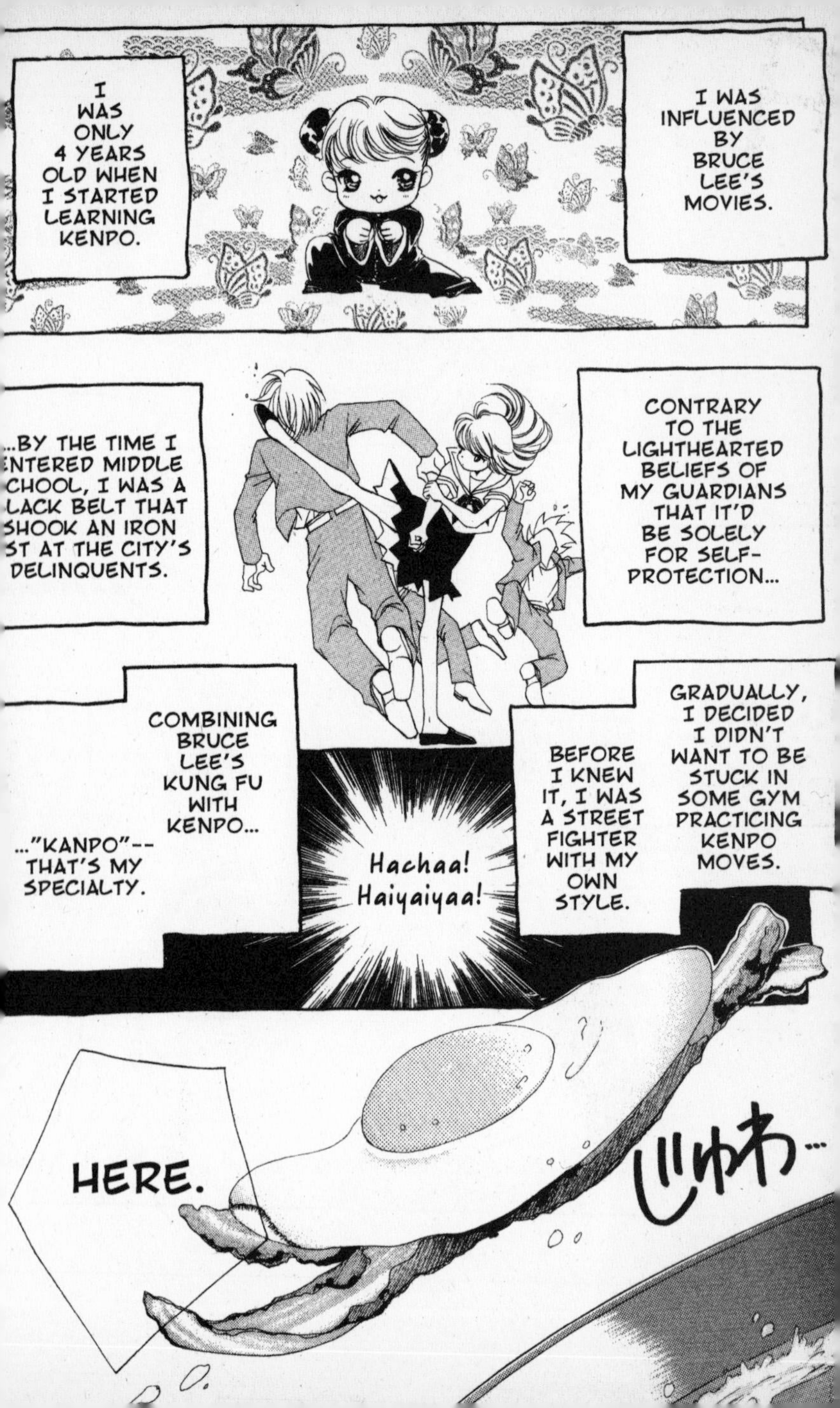
I WAS INFLUENCED BY BRUCE LEE'S MOVIES.
I WAS ONLY 4 YEARS OLD WHEN I STARTED LEARNING KENPO.
CONTRARY TO THE LIGHTHEARTED BELIEFS OF MY GUARDIANS THAT IT'D BE SOLELY FOR SELF-PROTECTION...
...BY THE TIME I NTERED MIDDLE CHOOL, I WAS A LACK BELT THAT SHOOK AN IRON ST AT THE CITY'S DELINQUENTS.
GRADUALLY, I DECIDED I DIDN'T WANT TO BE STUCK IN SOME GYM PRACTICING KENPO MOVES.
BEFORE I KNEW IT, I WAS A STREET FIGHTER WITH MY OWN STYLE.
Hachaa! Haiyaiyaa!
COMBINING BRUCE LEE'S KUNG FU WITH KENPO...
..."KANPO"-- THAT'S MY SPECIALTY.
じゅわ…
HERE.

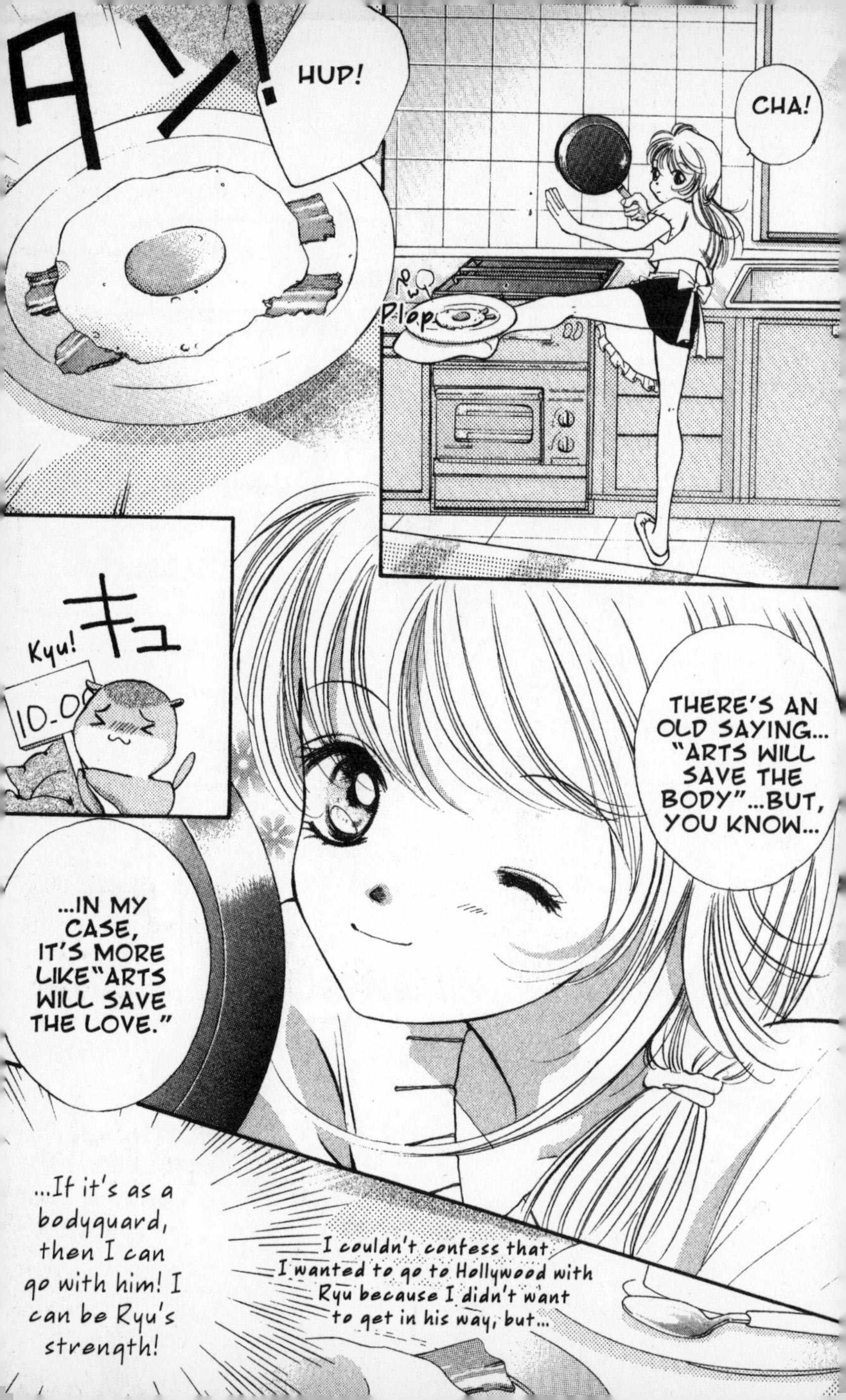
CHA!
Plop
タン!
HUP!
THERE'S AN OLD SAYING... "ARTS WILL SAVE THE BODY"...BUT, YOU KNOW...
...IN MY CASE, IT'S MORE LIKE "ARTS WILL SAVE THE LOVE."
Kyu! キュ
I couldn't confess that I wanted to go to Hollywood with Ryu because I didn't want to get in his way, but...
...If it's as a bodyguard, then I can go with him! I can be Ryu's strength!

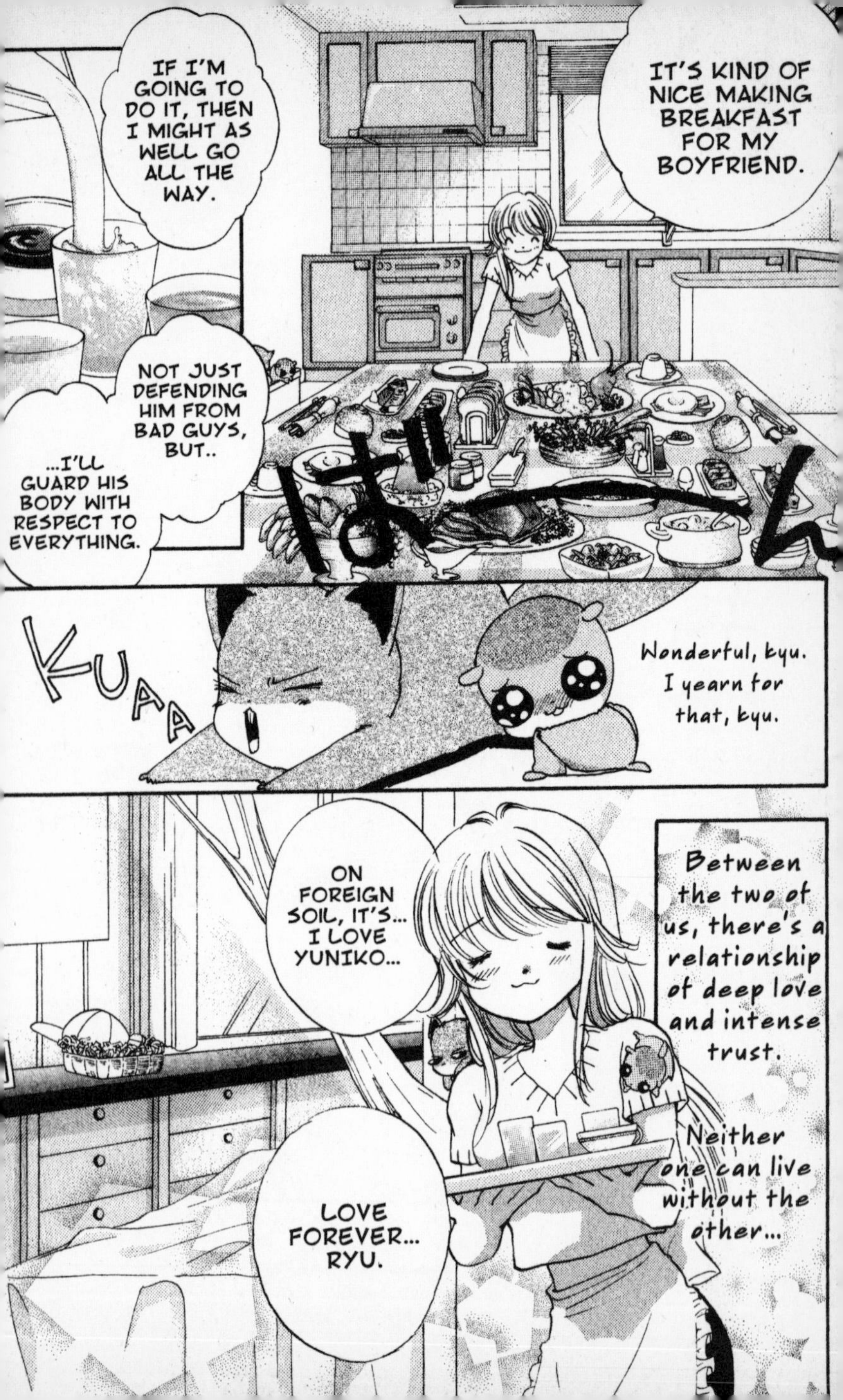
IT'S KIND OF NICE MAKING BREAKFAST FOR MY BOYFRIEND.
IF I'M GOING TO DO IT, THEN I MIGHT AS WELL GO ALL THE WAY.
NOT JUST DEFENDING HIM FROM BAD GUYS, BUT..
...I'LL GUARD HIS BODY WITH RESPECT TO EVERYTHING.
Wonderful, kyu. I yearn for that, kyu.
KUAA
Between the two of us, there's a relationship of deep love and intense trust.
Neither one can live without the other...
ON FOREIGN SOIL, IT'S... I LOVE YUNIKO...
LOVE FOREVER... RYU.

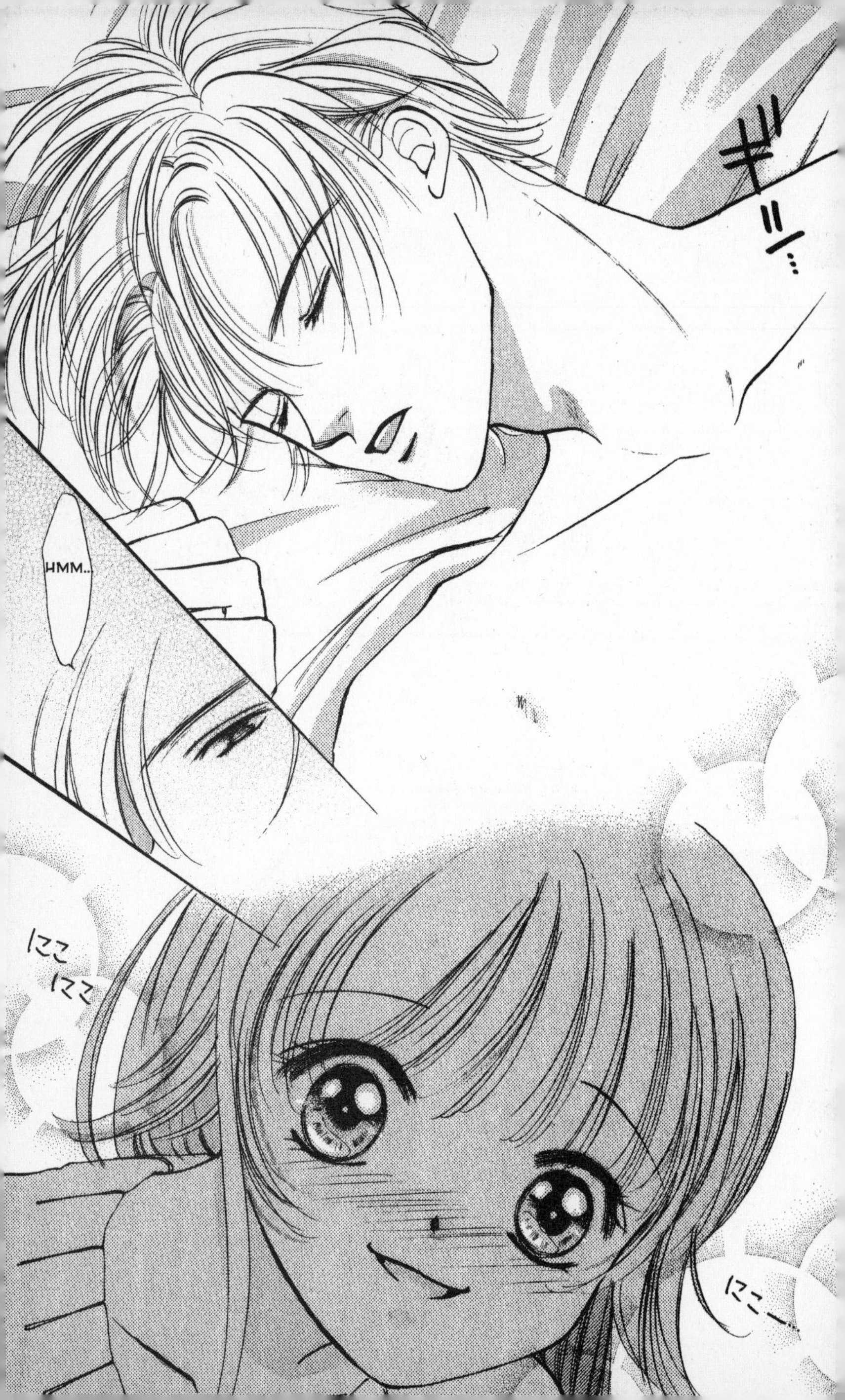
ギュー…
HMM...
にこにこ
にこー…

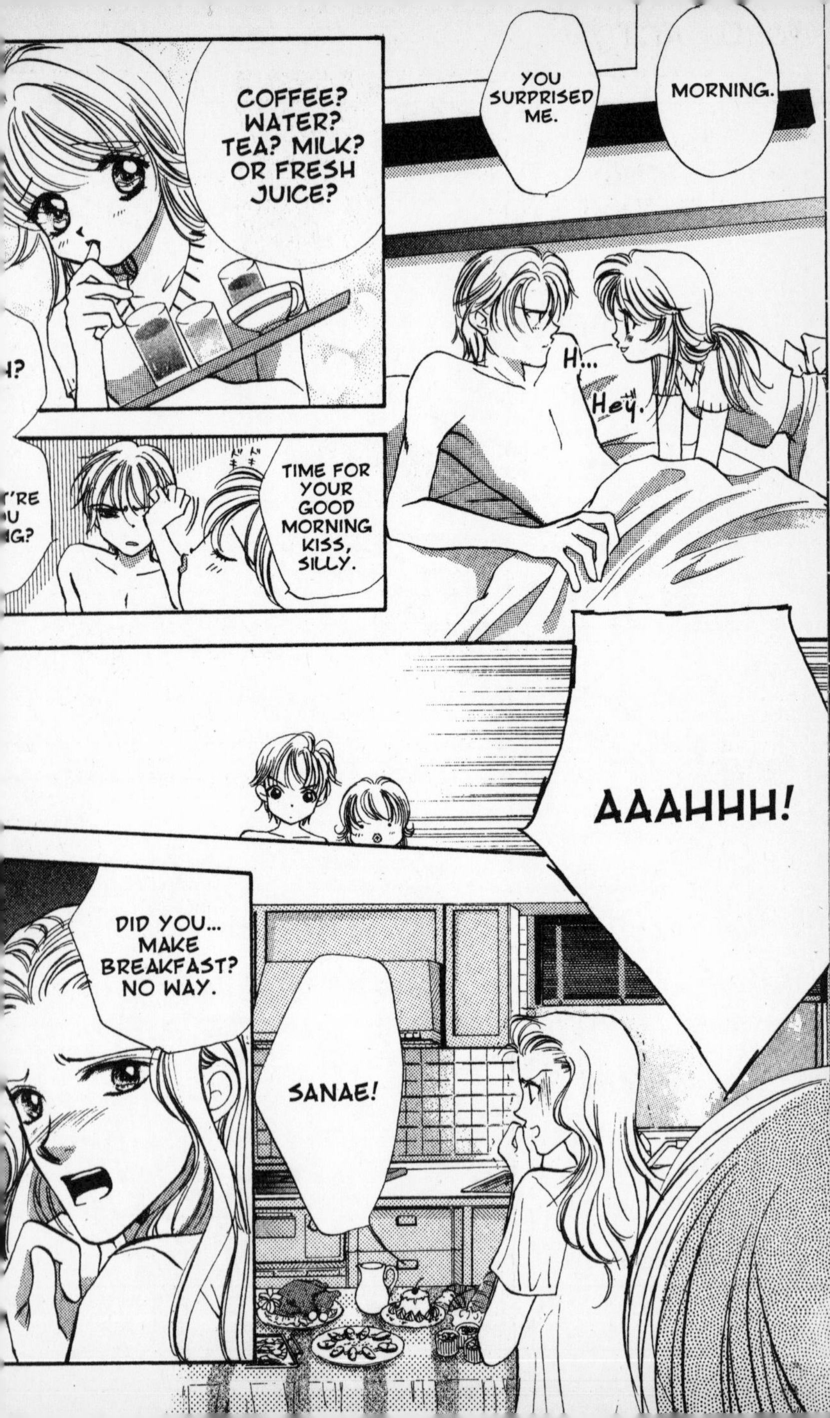
MORNING.
YOU SURPRISED ME.
H...
Hey.
COFFEE? WATER? TEA? MILK? OR FRESH JUICE?
ドキドキ
TIME FOR YOUR GOOD MORNING KISS, SILLY.
AAAHHH!
SANAE!
DID YOU... MAKE BREAKFAST? NO WAY.

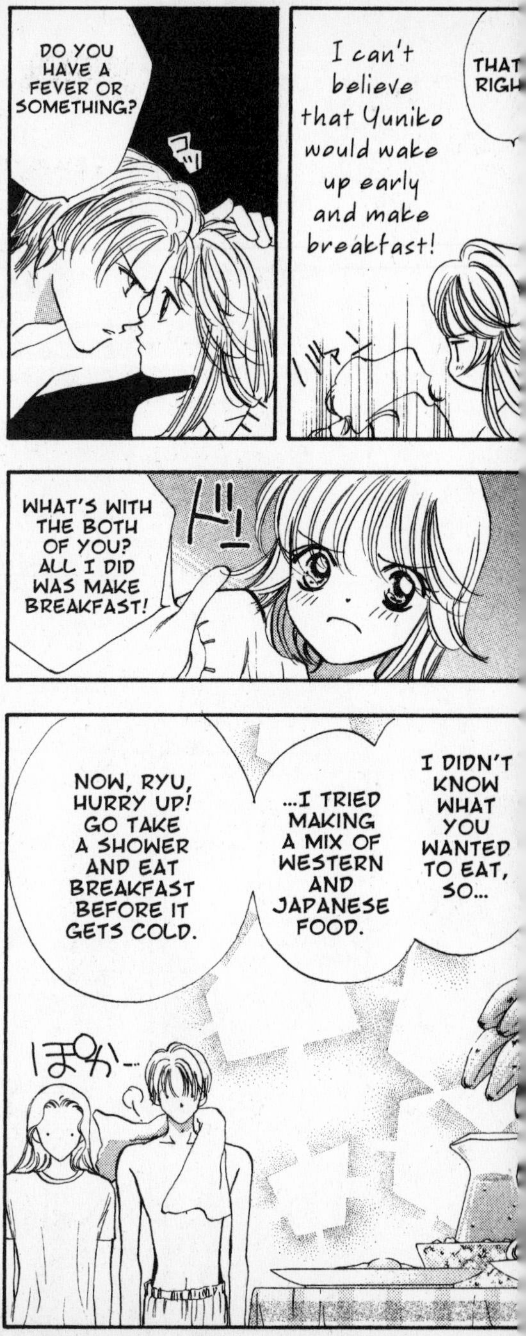
THAT RIGH
I can't believe that Yuniko would wake up early and make breakfast!
DO YOU HAVE A FEVER OR SOMETHING?
WHAT'S WITH THE BOTH OF YOU? ALL I DID WAS MAKE BREAKFAST!
I DIDN'T KNOW WHAT YOU WANTED TO EAT, SO...
...I TRIED MAKING A MIX OF WESTERN AND JAPANESE FOOD.
NOW, RYU, HURRY UP! GO TAKE A SHOWER AND EAT BREAKFAST BEFORE IT GETS COLD.
ぽか～…

The Thing I Like Best About Myself

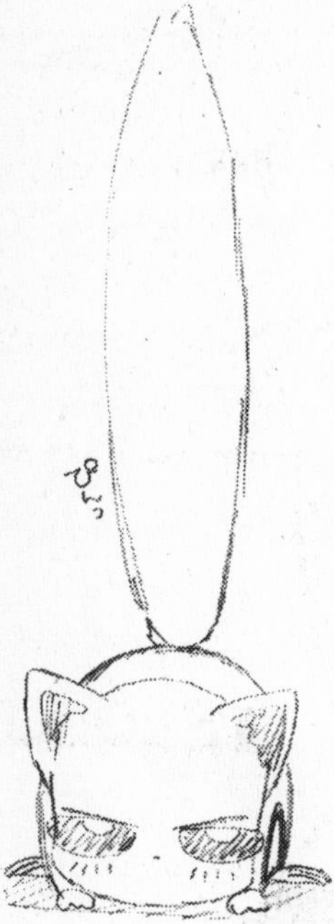

My straight tail

by Kamui

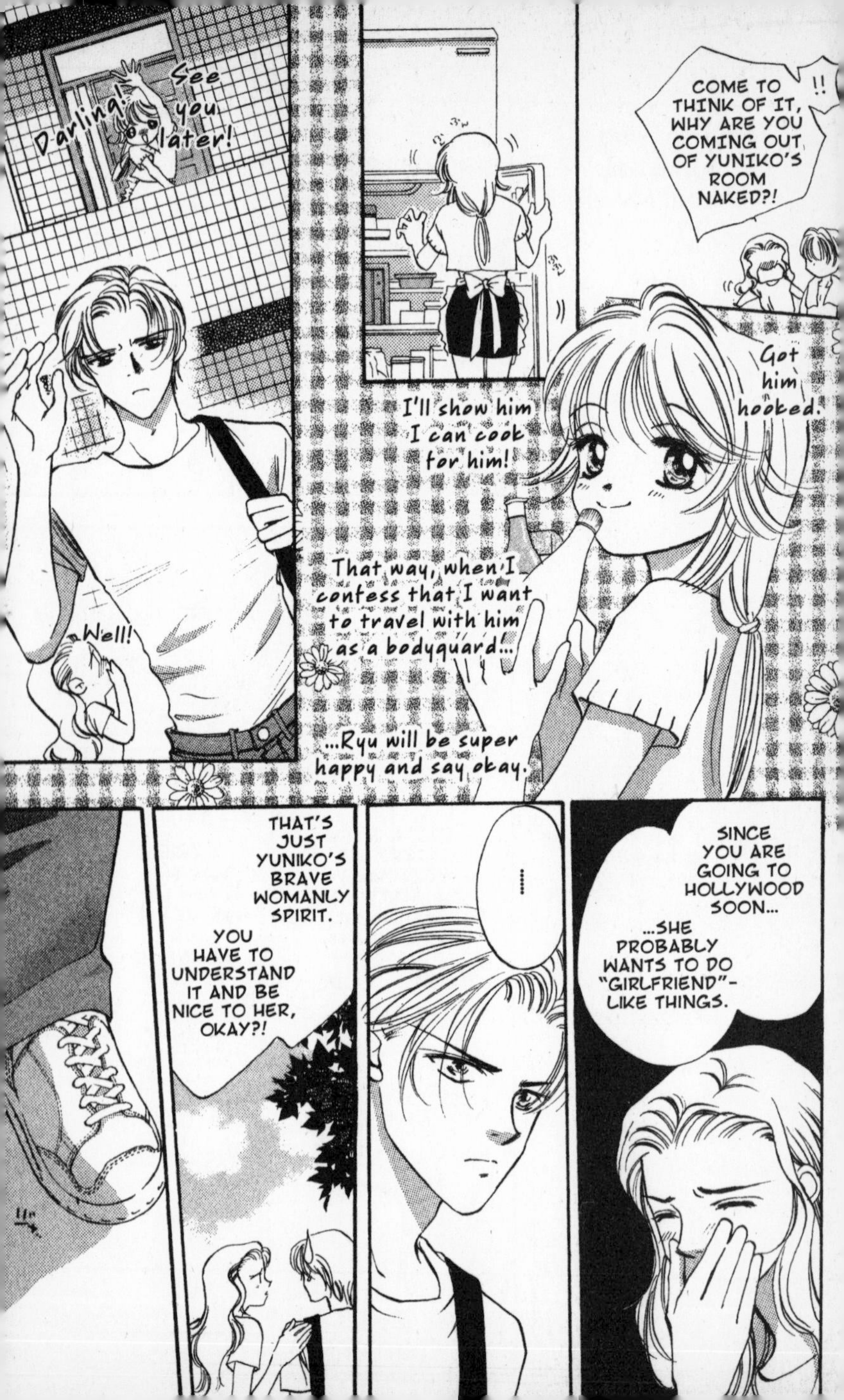

!!
COME TO THINK OF IT, WHY ARE YOU COMING OUT OF YUNIKO'S ROOM NAKED?!
Got him hooked.
I'll show him I can cook for him!
That way, when I confess that I want to travel with him as a bodyguard...
...Ryu will be super happy and say okay.
Darling! See you later!
Well!
SINCE YOU ARE GOING TO HOLLYWOOD SOON...
...SHE PROBABLY WANTS TO DO "GIRLFRIEND"-LIKE THINGS.
......
THAT'S JUST YUNIKO'S BRAVE WOMANLY SPIRIT.
YOU HAVE TO UNDERSTAND IT AND BE NICE TO HER, OKAY?!

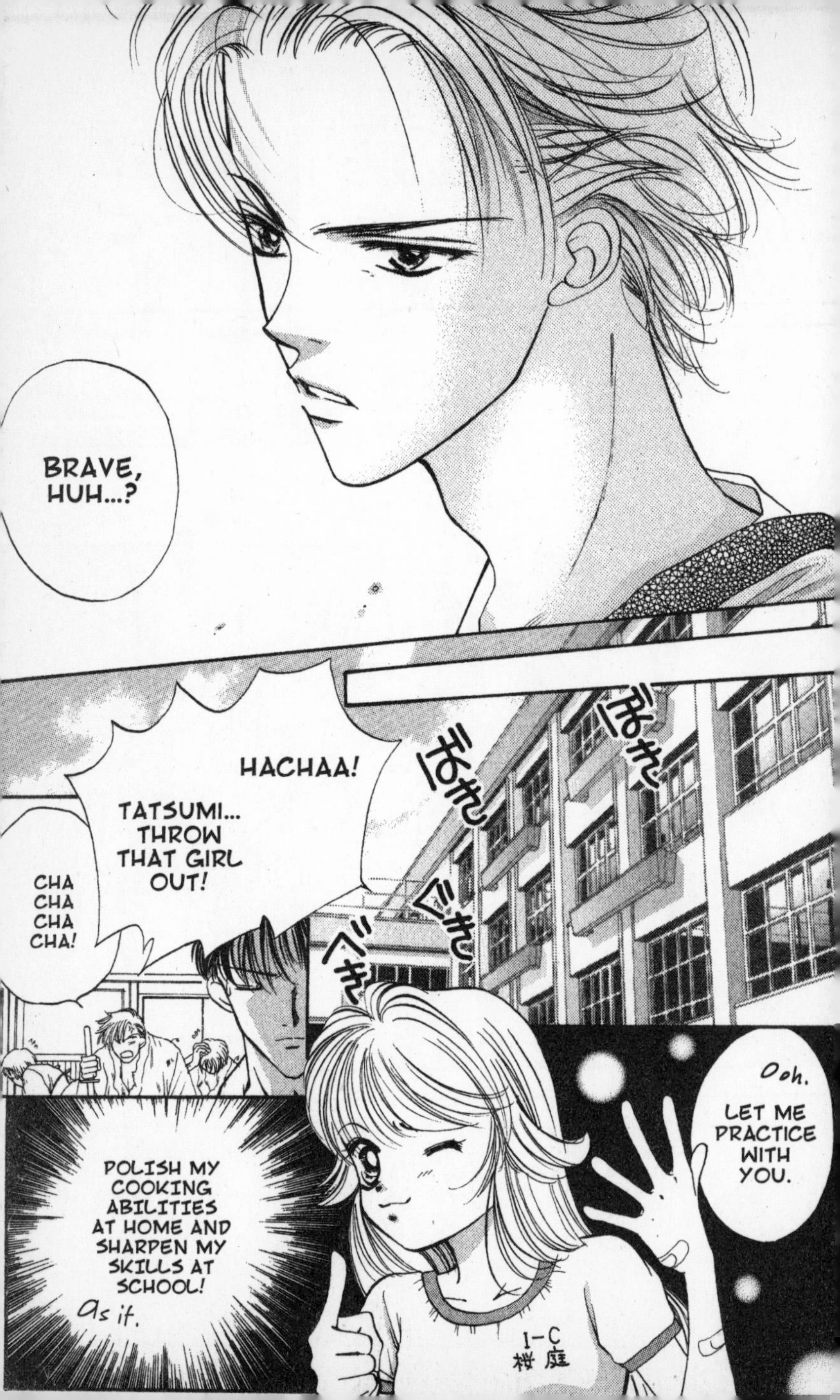
BRAVE, HUH...?
ぽき
ぼき
ぐき
べき
HACHAA!
TATSUMI... THROW THAT GIRL OUT!
CHA CHA CHA CHA!
Ooh.
LET ME PRACTICE WITH YOU.
POLISH MY COOKING ABILITIES AT HOME AND SHARPEN MY SKILLS AT SCHOOL!
As if.
I-C
桜庭

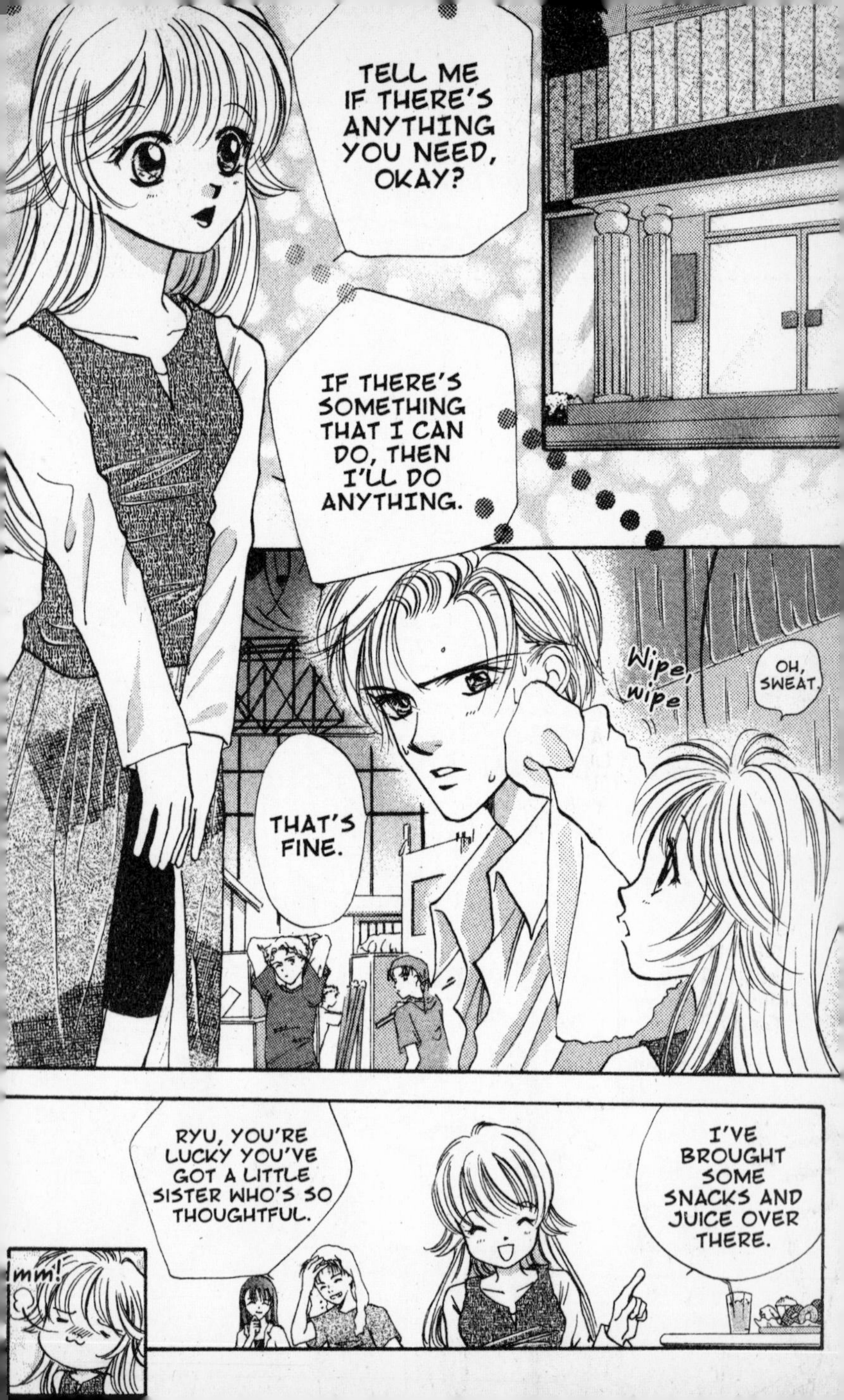
TELL ME IF THERE'S ANYTHING YOU NEED, OKAY?
IF THERE'S SOMETHING THAT I CAN DO, THEN I'LL DO ANYTHING.
OH, SWEAT.
Wipe, wipe
THAT'S FINE.
I'VE BROUGHT SOME SNACKS AND JUICE OVER THERE.
RYU, YOU'RE LUCKY YOU'VE GOT A LITTLE SISTER WHO'S SO THOUGHTFUL.
mm!

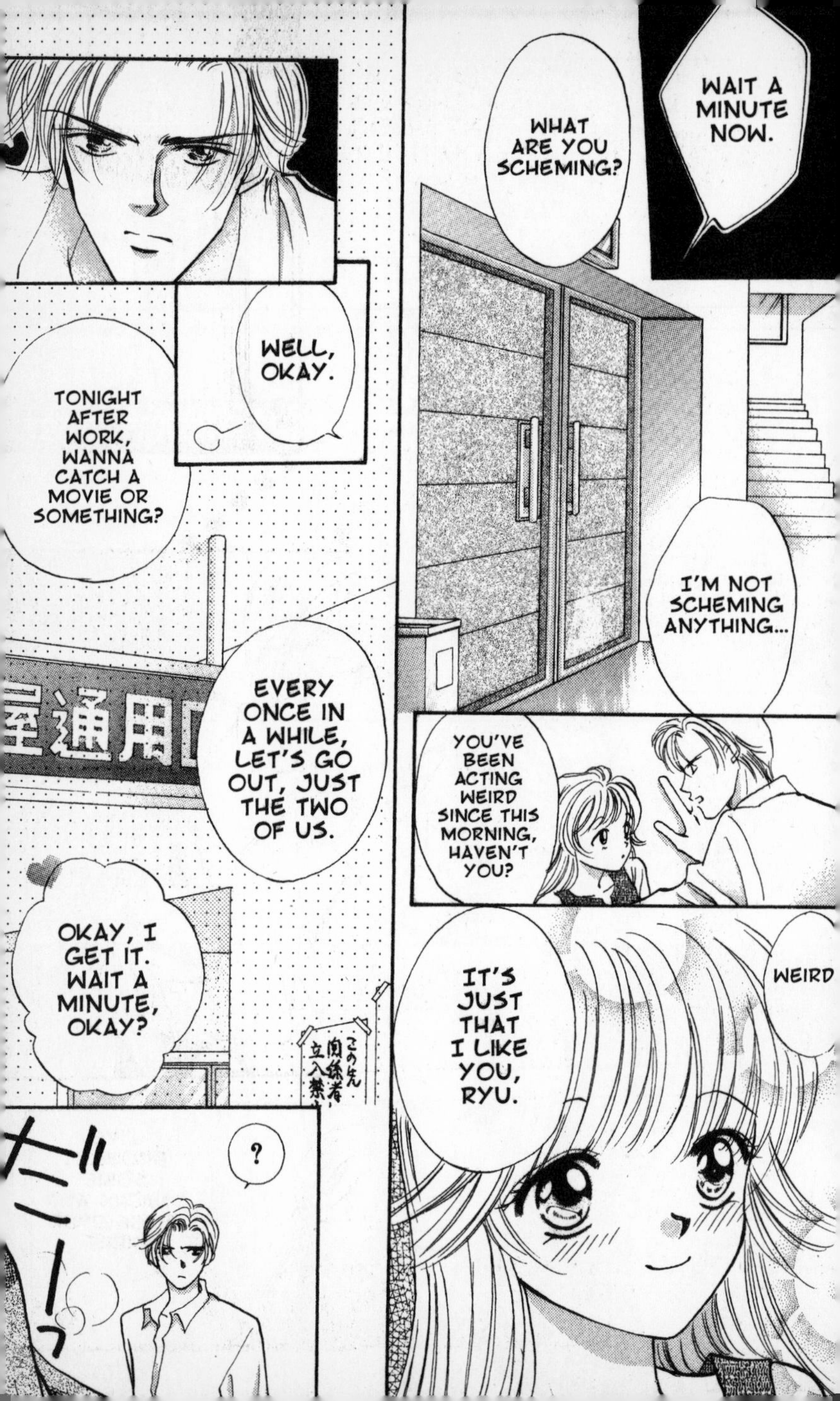
WAIT A MINUTE NOW.
WHAT ARE YOU SCHEMING?
I'M NOT SCHEMING ANYTHING...
YOU'VE BEEN ACTING WEIRD SINCE THIS MORNING, HAVEN'T YOU?
WEIRD
IT'S JUST THAT I LIKE YOU, RYU.
WELL, OKAY.
TONIGHT AFTER WORK, WANNA CATCH A MOVIE OR SOMETHING?
屋通用
EVERY ONCE IN A WHILE, LET'S GO OUT, JUST THE TWO OF US.
OKAY, I GET IT. WAIT A MINUTE, OKAY?
この先 関係者 立入禁
?
だーっ

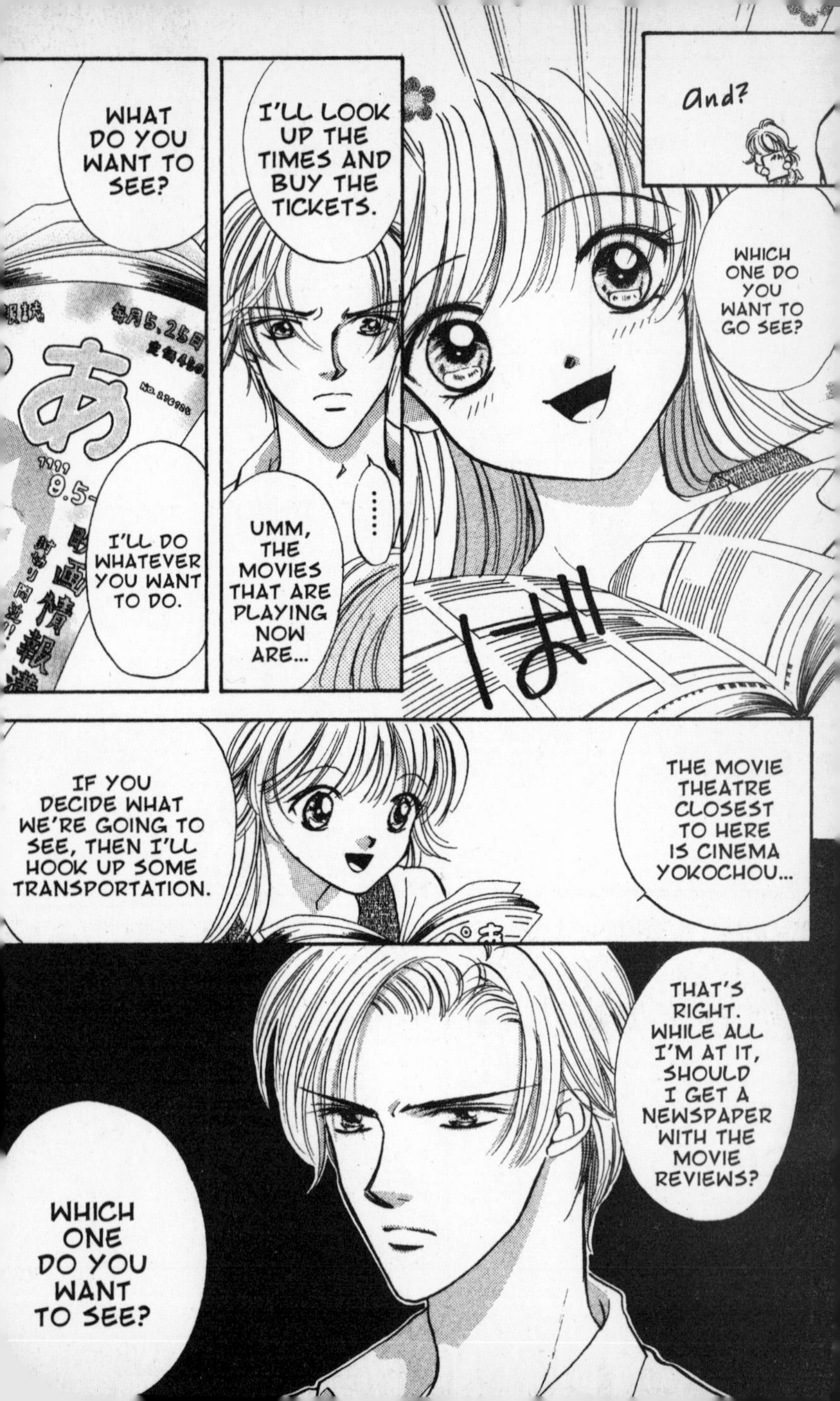
And?
WHICH ONE DO YOU WANT TO GO SEE?
I'LL LOOK UP THE TIMES AND BUY THE TICKETS.
......
UMM, THE MOVIES THAT ARE PLAYING NOW ARE...
WHAT DO YOU WANT TO SEE?
I'LL DO WHATEVER YOU WANT TO DO.
THE MOVIE THEATRE CLOSEST TO HERE IS CINEMA YOKOCHOU...
IF YOU DECIDE WHAT WE'RE GOING TO SEE, THEN I'LL HOOK UP SOME TRANSPORTATION.
THAT'S RIGHT. WHILE ALL I'M AT IT, SHOULD I GET A NEWSPAPER WITH THE MOVIE REVIEWS?
WHICH ONE DO YOU WANT TO SEE?

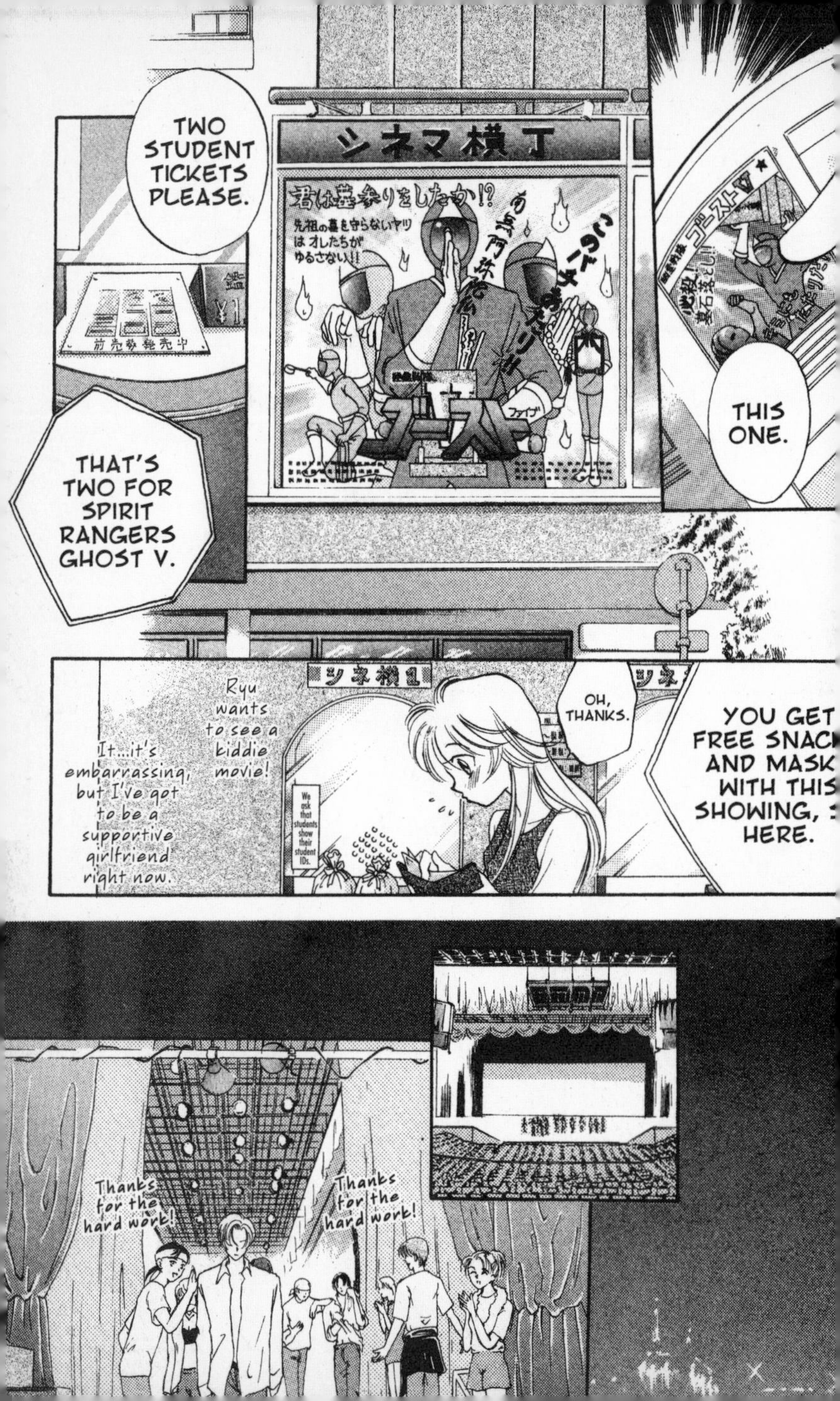

THIS ONE.
TWO STUDENT TICKETS PLEASE.
シネマ横丁
君は墓参りをしたか!?
先祖の墓を守らないヤツは オレたちが ゆるさない!!
前売券発売中
THAT'S TWO FOR SPIRIT RANGERS GHOST V.
YOU GET FREE SNAC AND MASK WITH THIS SHOWING, HERE.
OH, THANKS.
シネ横1
Ryu wants to see a kiddie movie!
It...it's embarrassing, but I've got to be a supportive girlfriend right now.
We ask that students show their student IDs.
Thanks for the hard work!
Thanks for the hard work!

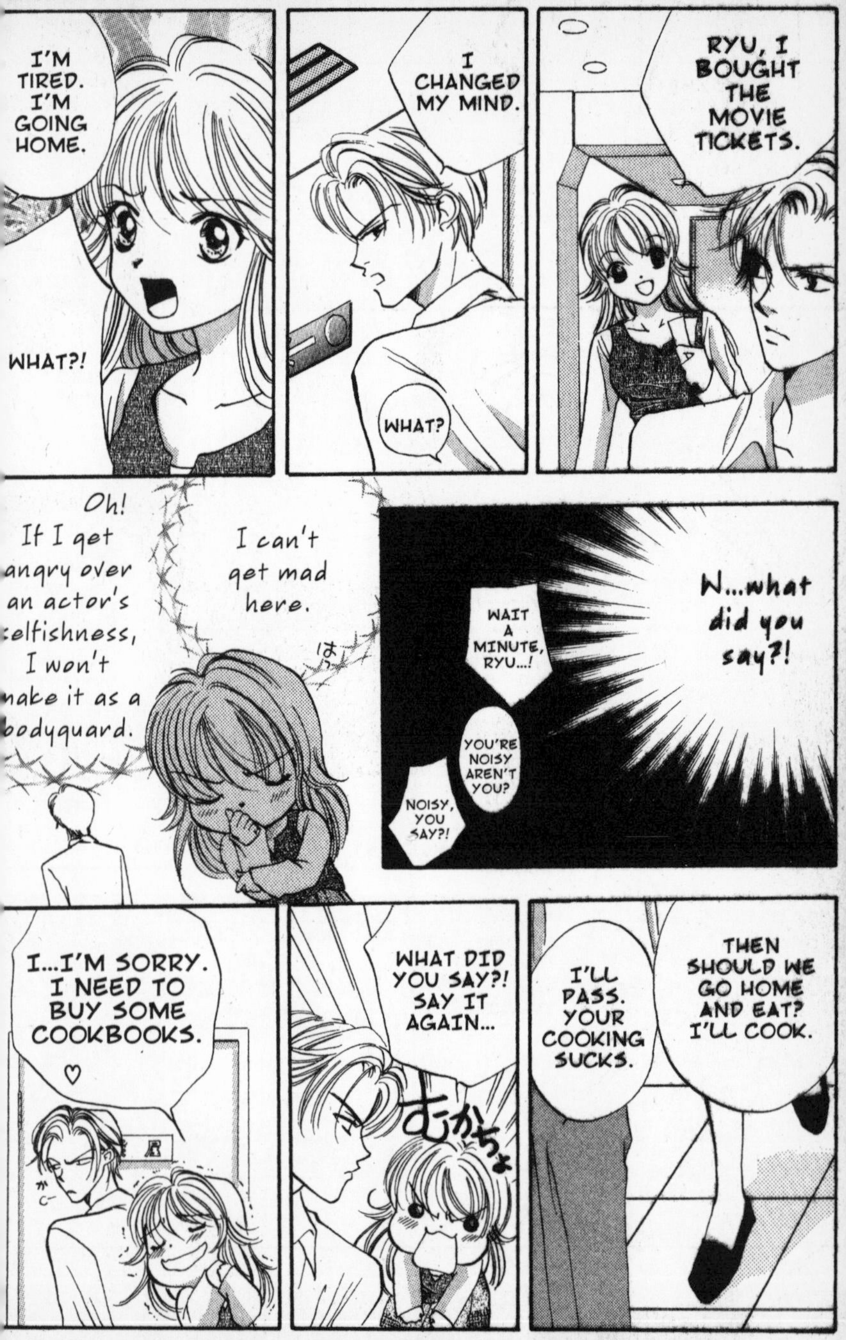
RYU, I BOUGHT THE MOVIE TICKETS.
I CHANGED MY MIND.
WHAT?
I'M TIRED. I'M GOING HOME.
WHAT?!
W...what did you say?!
WAIT A MINUTE, RYU...!
YOU'RE NOISY AREN'T YOU?
NOISY, YOU SAY?!
I can't get mad here.
はっ
Oh! If I get angry over an actor's elfishness, I won't ake it as a bodyguard.
THEN SHOULD WE GO HOME AND EAT? I'LL COOK.
I'LL PASS. YOUR COOKING SUCKS.
WHAT DID YOU SAY?! SAY IT AGAIN...
むかちょ
I...I'M SORRY. I NEED TO BUY SOME COOKBOOKS. ♡
かー

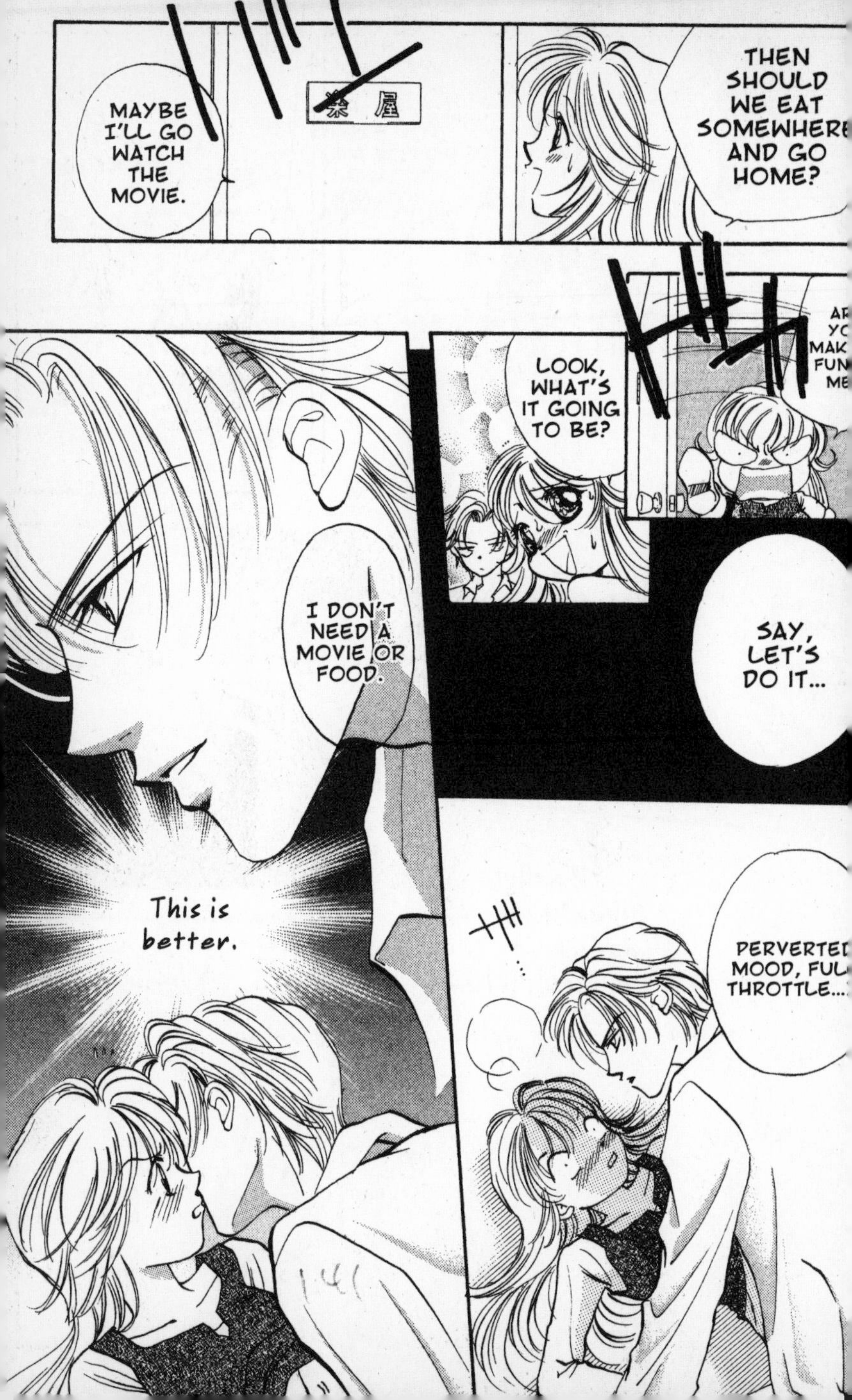

THEN SHOULD WE EAT SOMEWHERE AND GO HOME?
MAYBE I'LL GO WATCH THE MOVIE.
LOOK, WHAT'S IT GOING TO BE?
SAY, LET'S DO IT...
PERVERTED MOOD, FUL THROTTLE...
I DON'T NEED A MOVIE OR FOOD.
This is better.

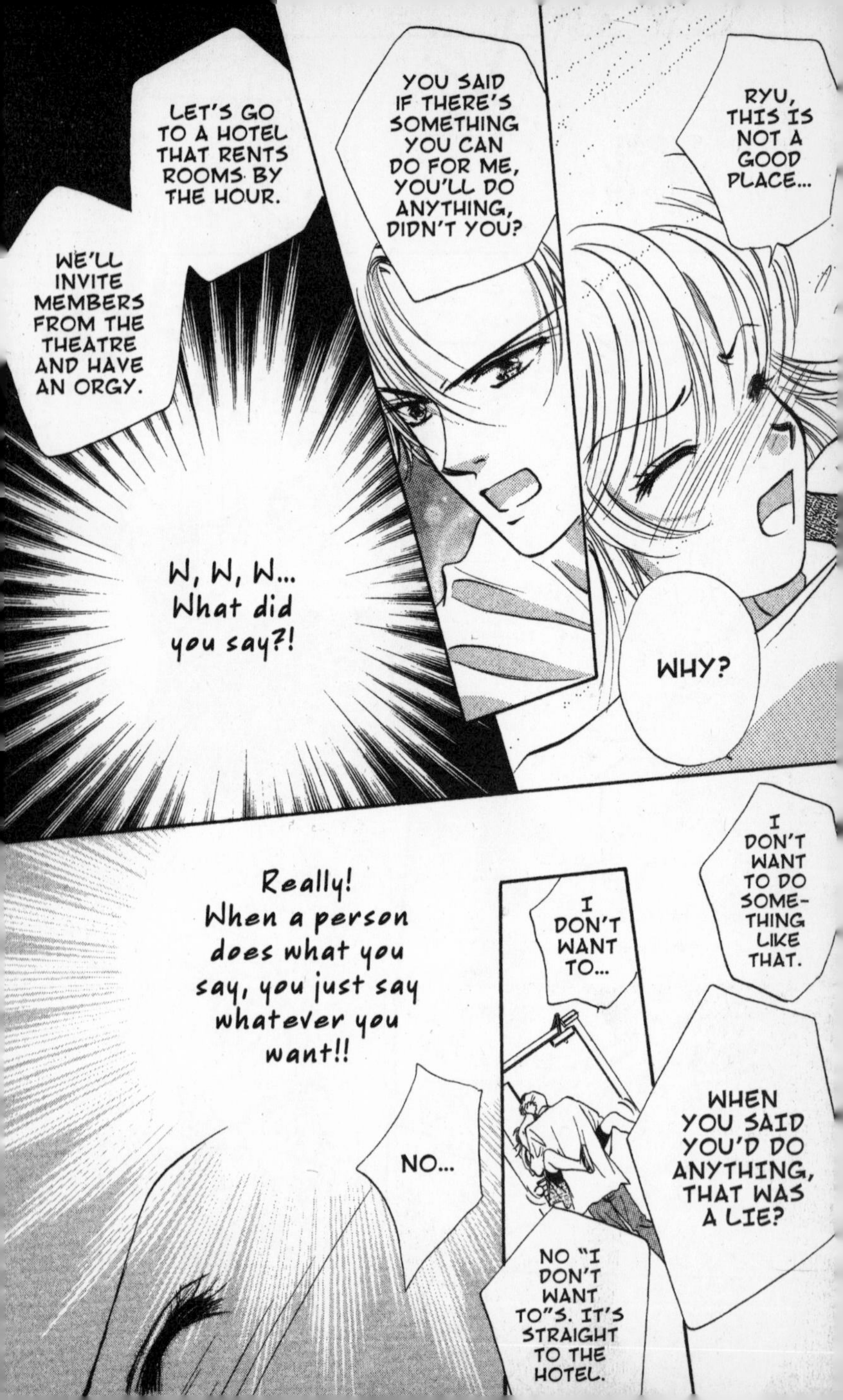
RYU, THIS IS NOT A GOOD PLACE...
WHY?
YOU SAID IF THERE'S SOMETHING YOU CAN DO FOR ME, YOU'LL DO ANYTHING, DIDN'T YOU?
LET'S GO TO A HOTEL THAT RENTS ROOMS BY THE HOUR.
WE'LL INVITE MEMBERS FROM THE THEATRE AND HAVE AN ORGY.
W, W, W... What did you say?!
I DON'T WANT TO DO SOME-THING LIKE THAT.
WHEN YOU SAID YOU'D DO ANYTHING, THAT WAS A LIE?
I DON'T WANT TO...
NO "I DON'T WANT TO"S. IT'S STRAIGHT TO THE HOTEL.
NO...
Really! When a person does what you say, you just say whatever you want!!

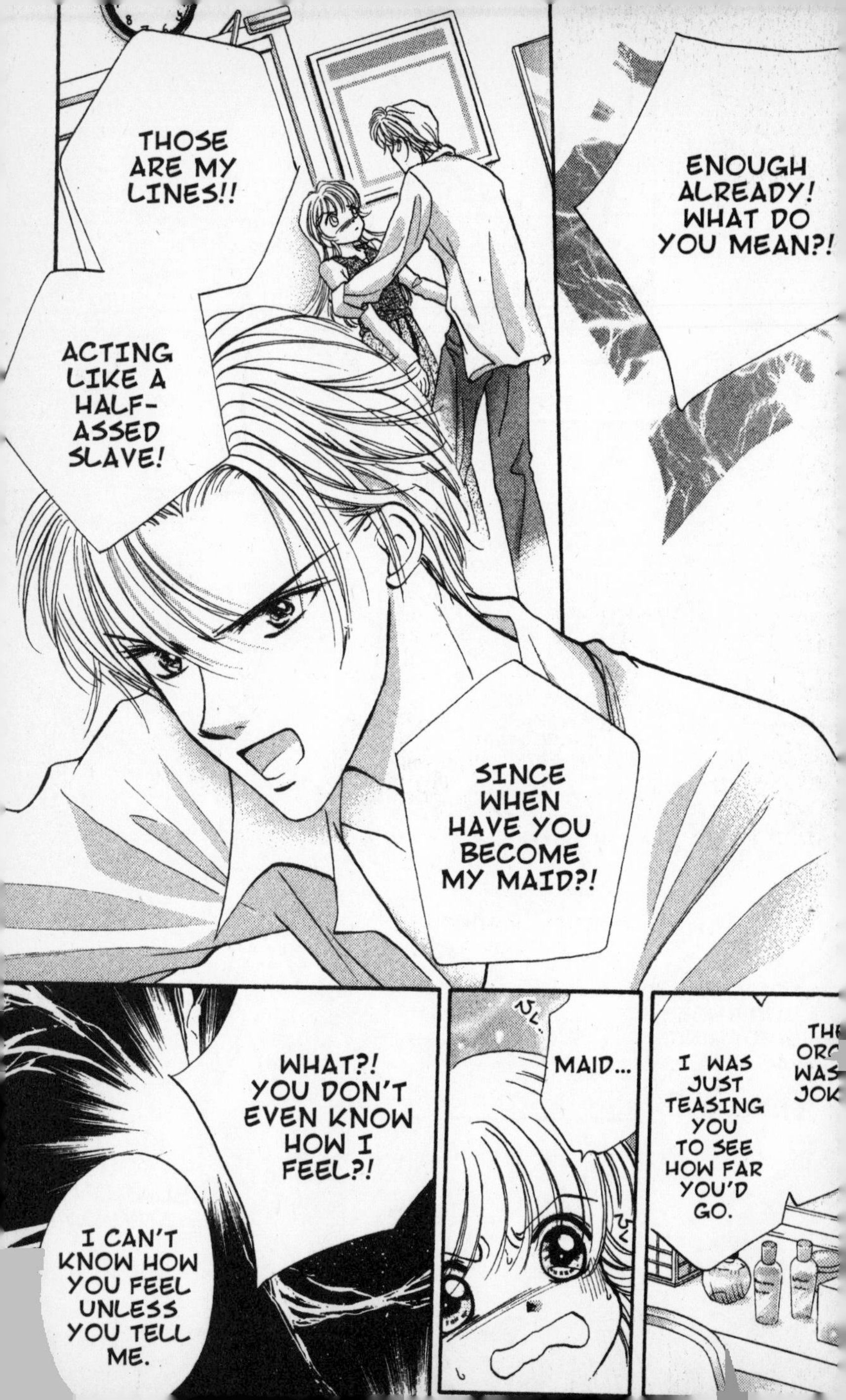
ENOUGH ALREADY! WHAT DO YOU MEAN?!
THOSE ARE MY LINES!!
ACTING LIKE A HALF-ASSED SLAVE!
SINCE WHEN HAVE YOU BECOME MY MAID?!
I WAS JUST TEASING YOU TO SEE HOW FAR YOU'D GO.
MAID...
WHAT?! YOU DON'T EVEN KNOW HOW I FEEL?!
I CAN'T KNOW HOW YOU FEEL UNLESS YOU TELL ME.

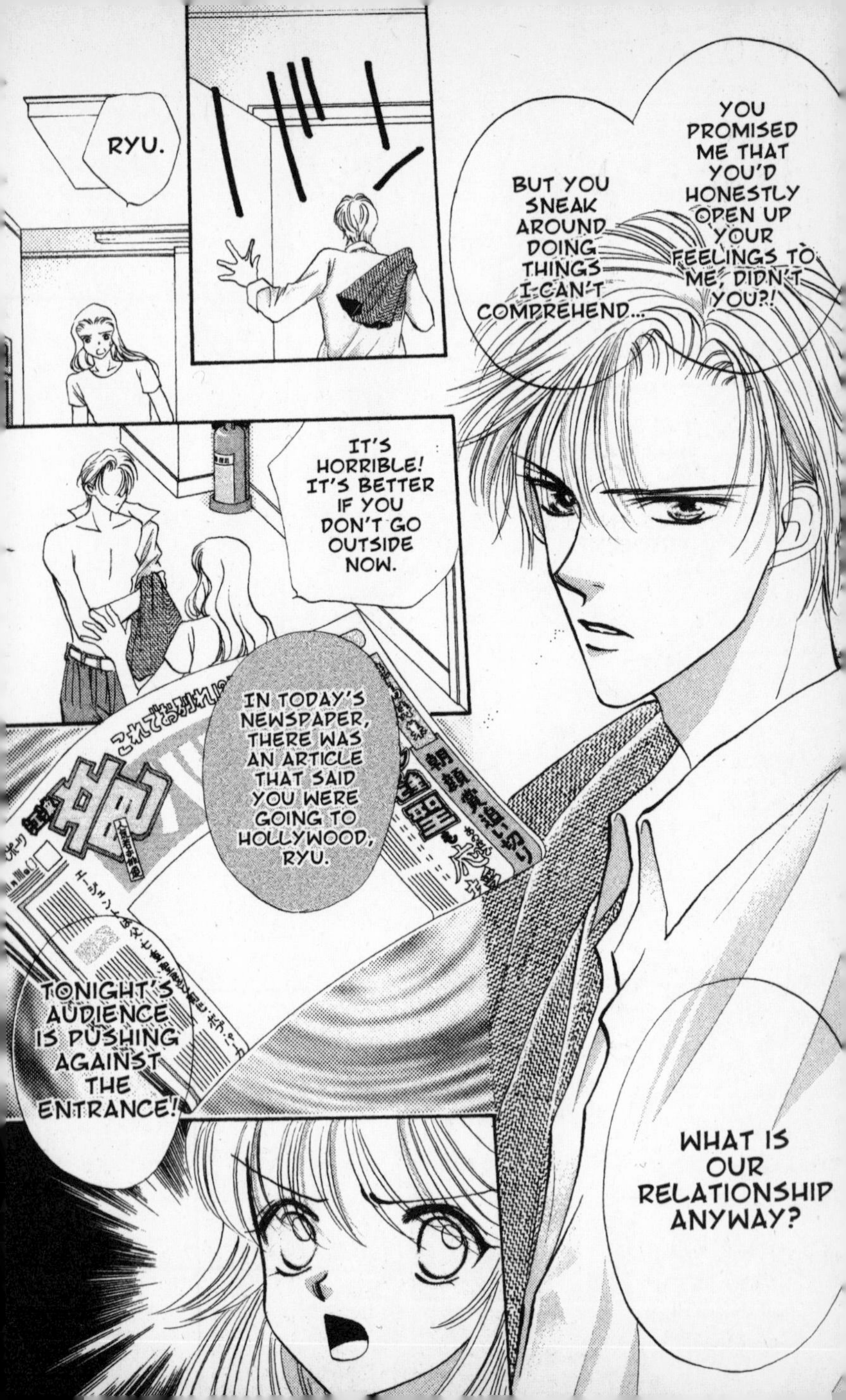
YOU PROMISED ME THAT YOU'D HONESTLY OPEN UP YOUR FEELINGS TO ME, DIDN'T YOU?!
BUT YOU SNEAK AROUND DOING THINGS I CAN'T COMPREHEND...
WHAT IS OUR RELATIONSHIP ANYWAY?
RYU.
IT'S HORRIBLE! IT'S BETTER IF YOU DON'T GO OUTSIDE NOW.
IN TODAY'S NEWSPAPER, THERE WAS AN ARTICLE THAT SAID YOU WERE GOING TO HOLLYWOOD, RYU.
TONIGHT'S AUDIENCE IS PUSHING AGAINST THE ENTRANCE!

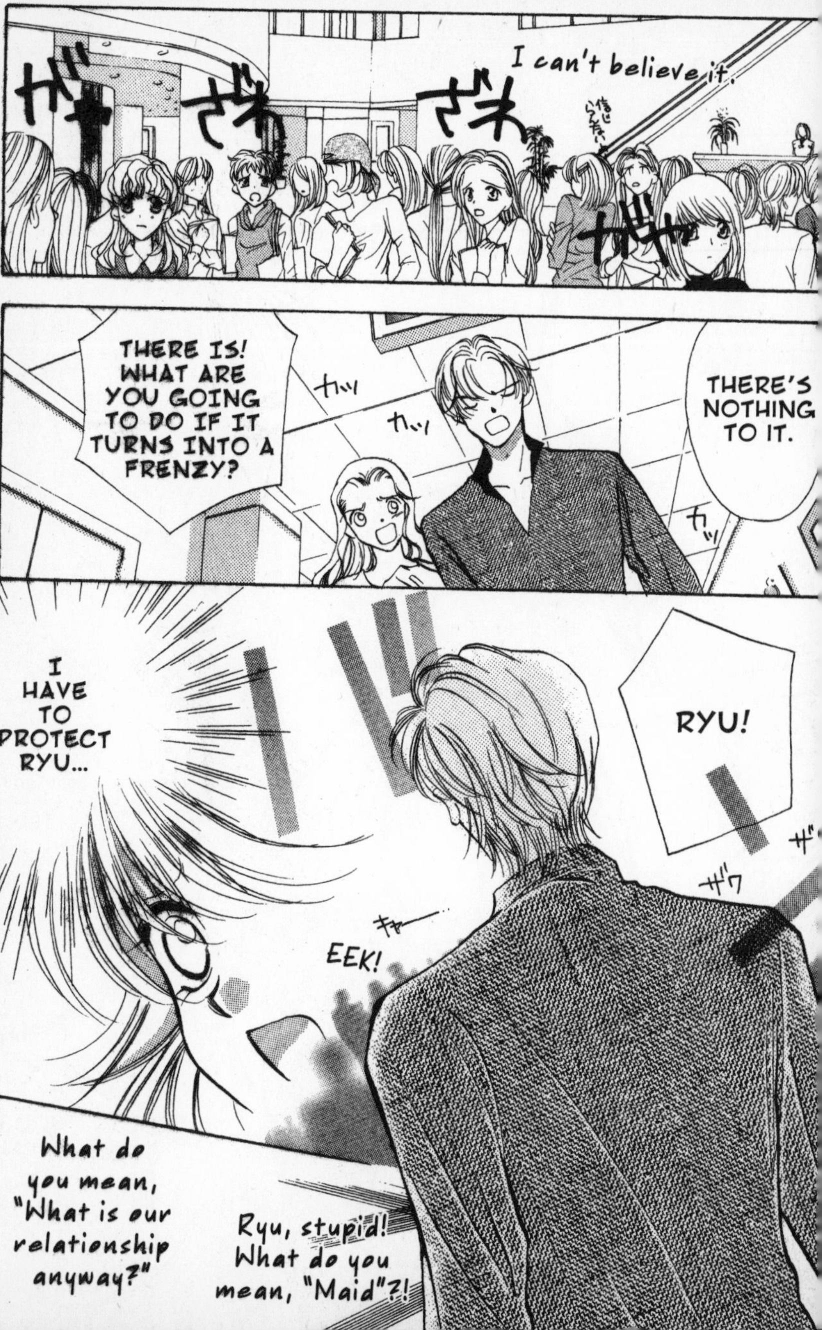
ざわ
ざわ
I can't believe it.
THERE'S NOTHING TO IT.
THERE IS! WHAT ARE YOU GOING TO DO IF IT TURNS INTO A FRENZY?
RYU!
I HAVE TO PROTECT RYU...
EEK!
Ryu, stupid! What do you mean, "Maid"?!
What do you mean, "What is our relationship anyway?"

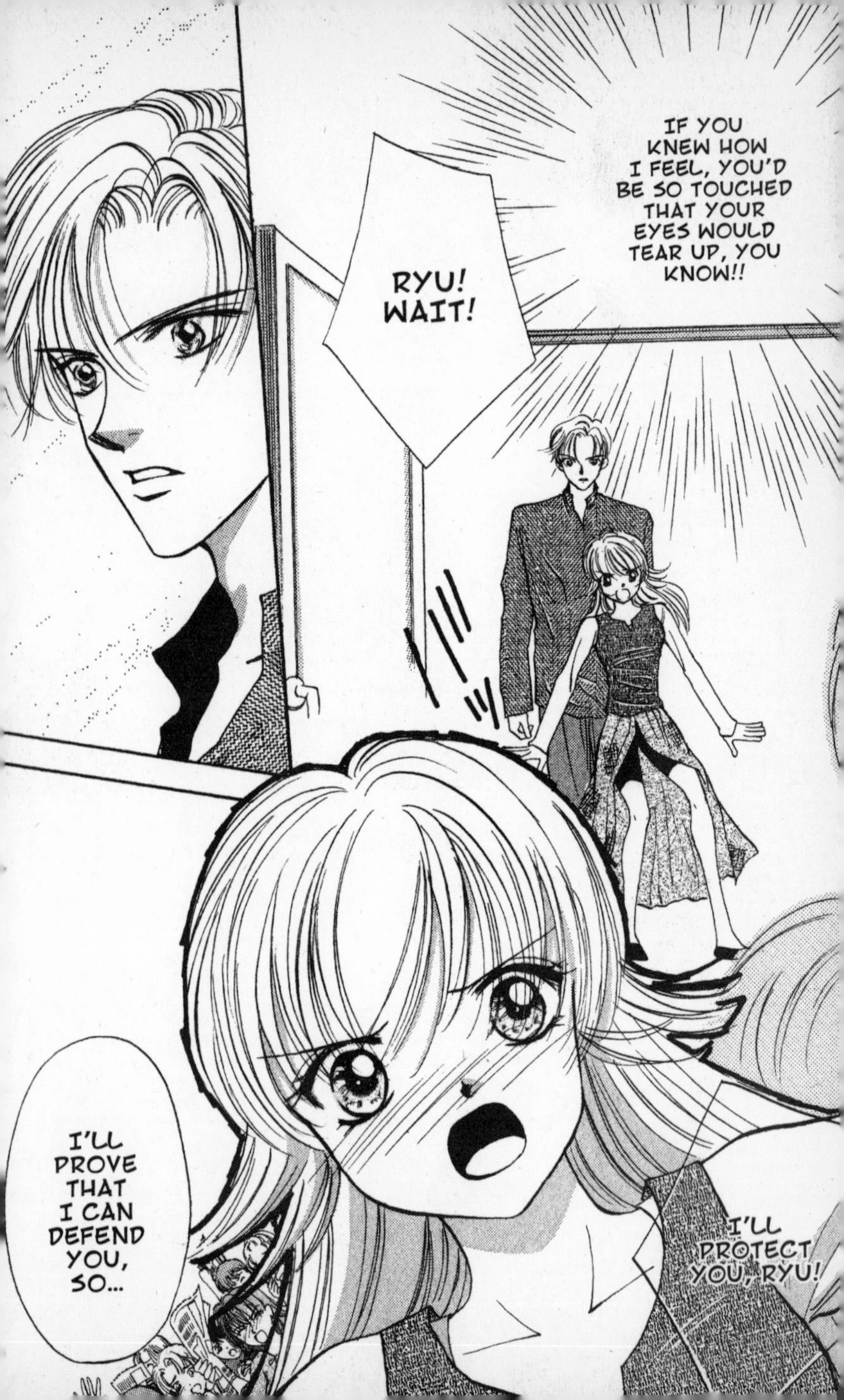
IF YOU KNEW HOW I FEEL, YOU'D BE SO TOUCHED THAT YOUR EYES WOULD TEAR UP, YOU KNOW!!
RYU! WAIT!
I'LL PROTECT YOU, RYU!
I'LL PROVE THAT I CAN DEFEND YOU, SO...

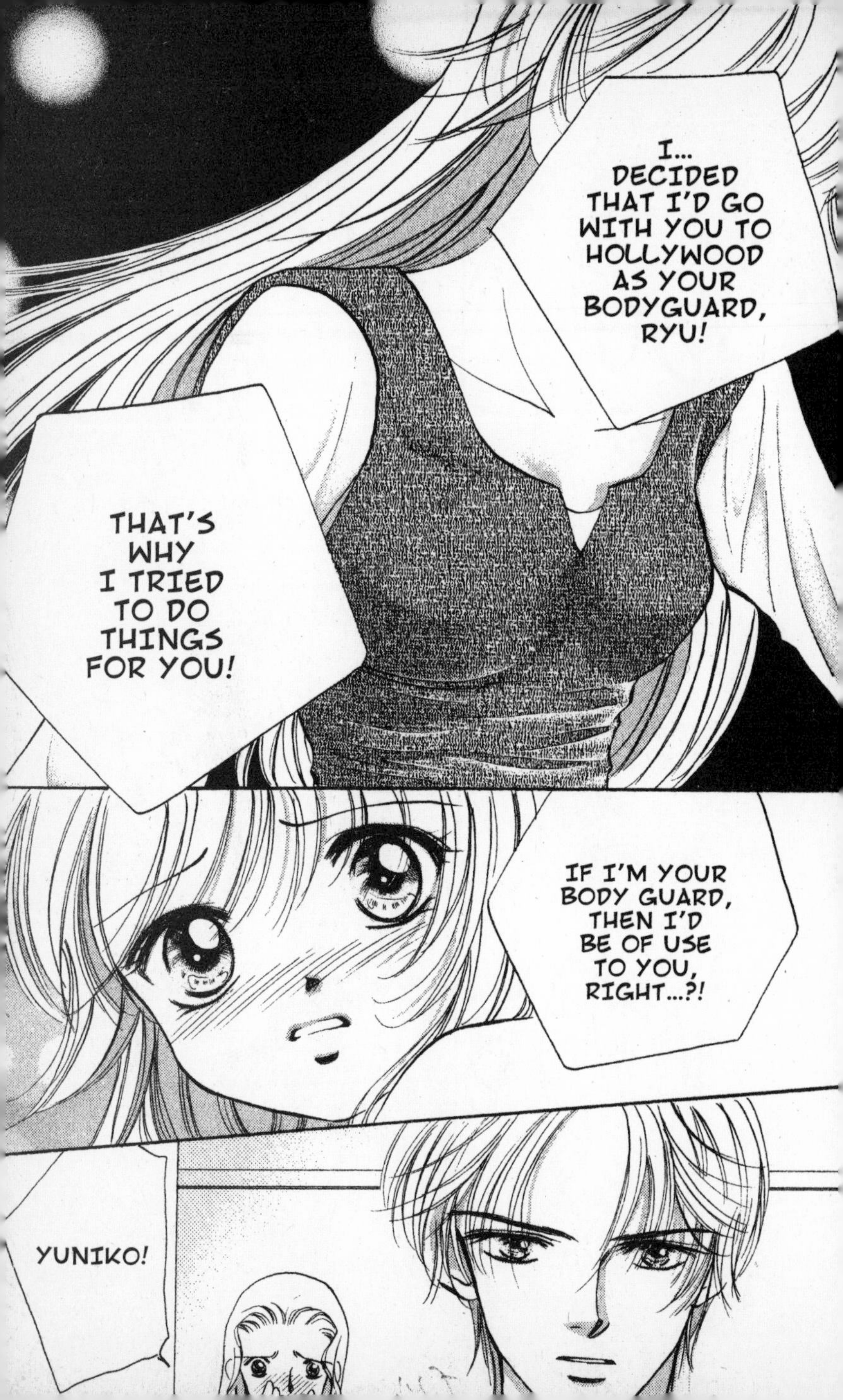
I... DECIDED THAT I'D GO WITH YOU TO HOLLYWOOD AS YOUR BODYGUARD, RYU!
THAT'S WHY I TRIED TO DO THINGS FOR YOU!
IF I'M YOUR BODY GUARD, THEN I'D BE OF USE TO YOU, RIGHT...?!
YUNIKO!

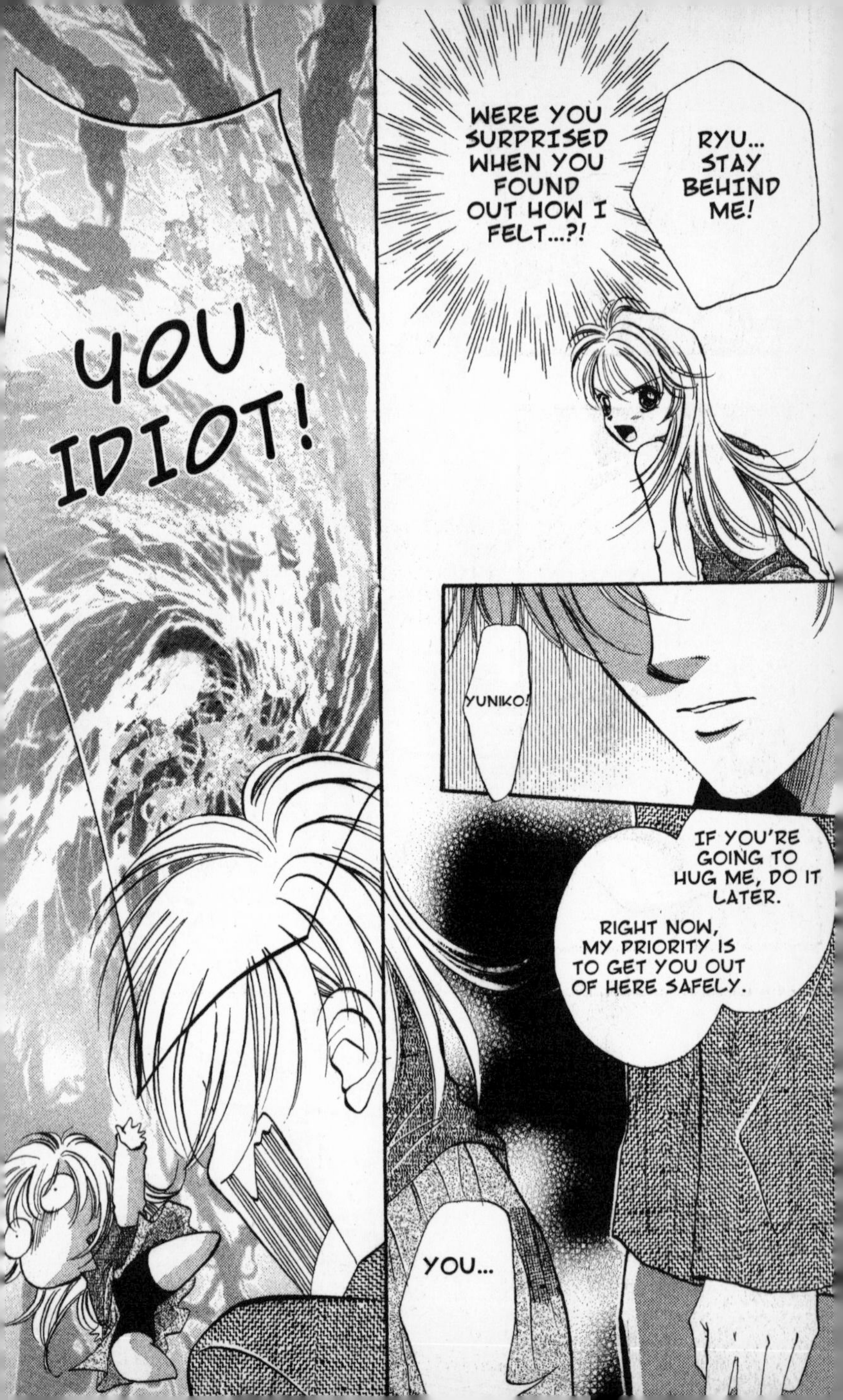
RYU... STAY BEHIND ME!
WERE YOU SURPRISED WHEN YOU FOUND OUT HOW I FELT...?!
YUNIKO!
IF YOU'RE GOING TO HUG ME, DO IT LATER.
RIGHT NOW, MY PRIORITY IS TO GET YOU OUT OF HERE SAFELY.
YOU...
YOU IDIOT!

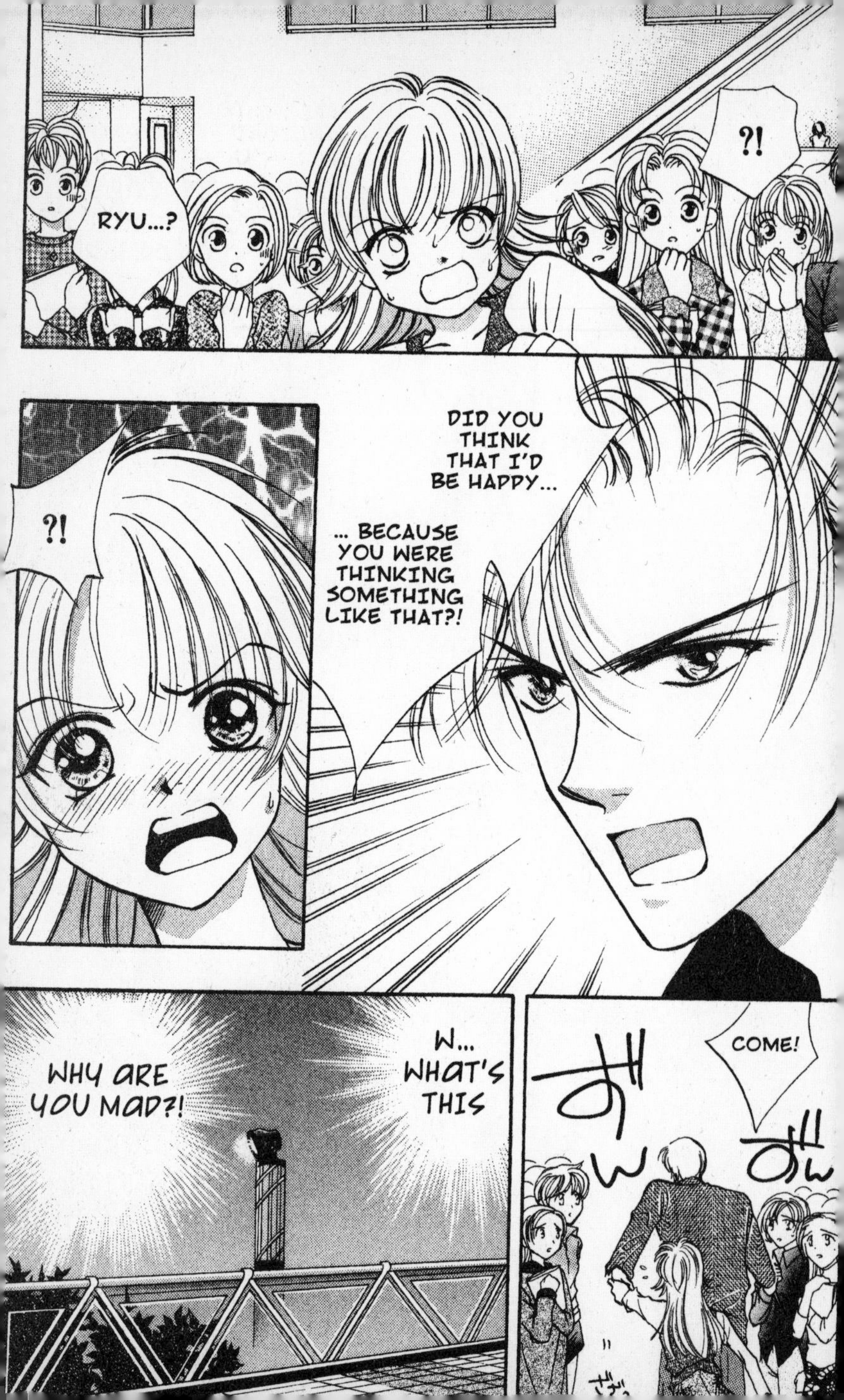
?!
RYU...?
DID YOU THINK THAT I'D BE HAPPY...
... BECAUSE YOU WERE THINKING SOMETHING LIKE THAT?!
?!
COME!
W... WHAT'S THIS
WHY ARE YOU MAD?!

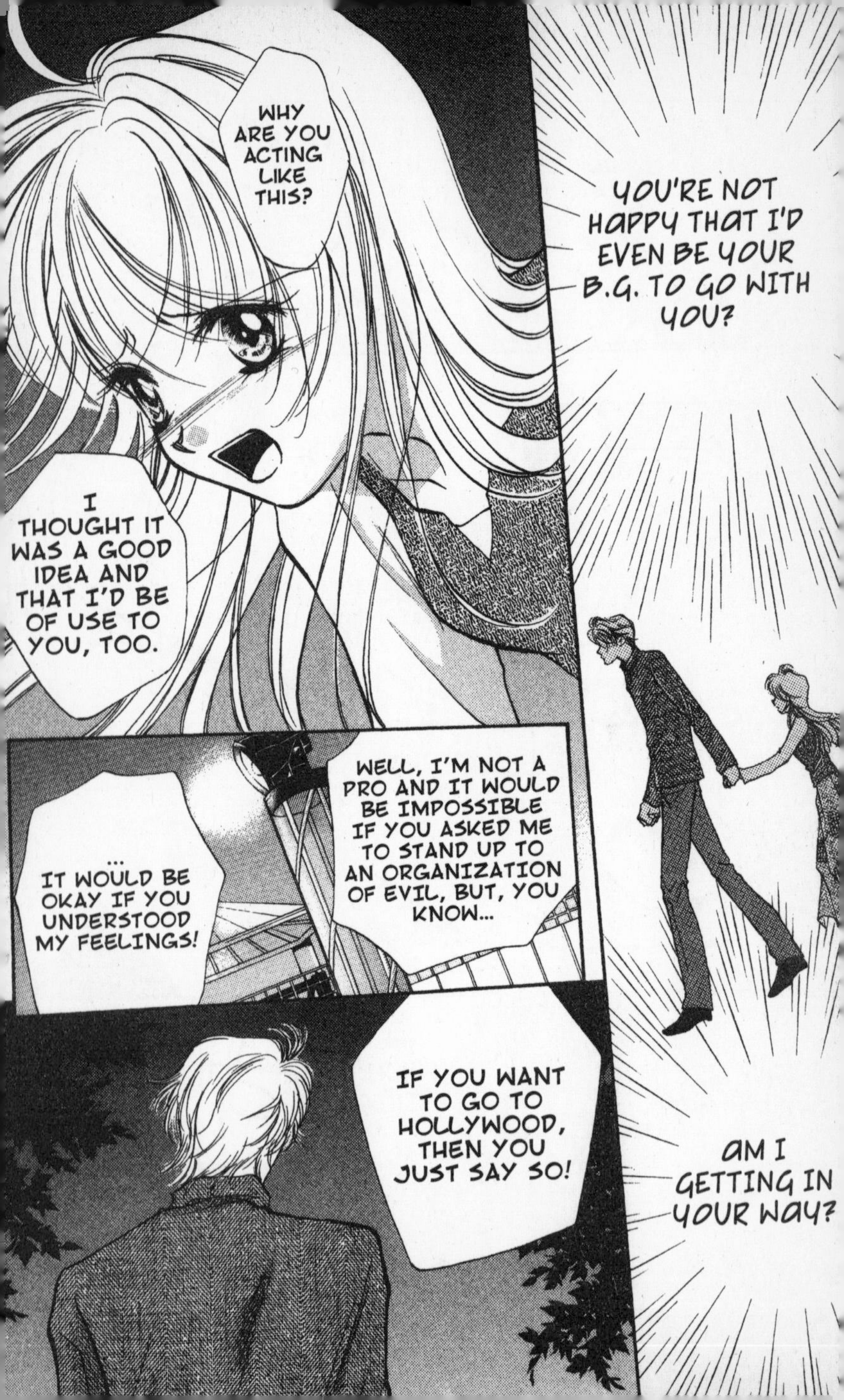
YOU'RE NOT HAPPY THAT I'D EVEN BE YOUR B.G. TO GO WITH YOU?
AM I GETTING IN YOUR WAY?
WHY ARE YOU ACTING LIKE THIS?
I THOUGHT IT WAS A GOOD IDEA AND THAT I'D BE OF USE TO YOU, TOO.
WELL, I'M NOT A PRO AND IT WOULD BE IMPOSSIBLE IF YOU ASKED ME TO STAND UP TO AN ORGANIZATION OF EVIL, BUT, YOU KNOW...
... IT WOULD BE OKAY IF YOU UNDERSTOOD MY FEELINGS!
IF YOU WANT TO GO TO HOLLYWOOD, THEN YOU JUST SAY SO!

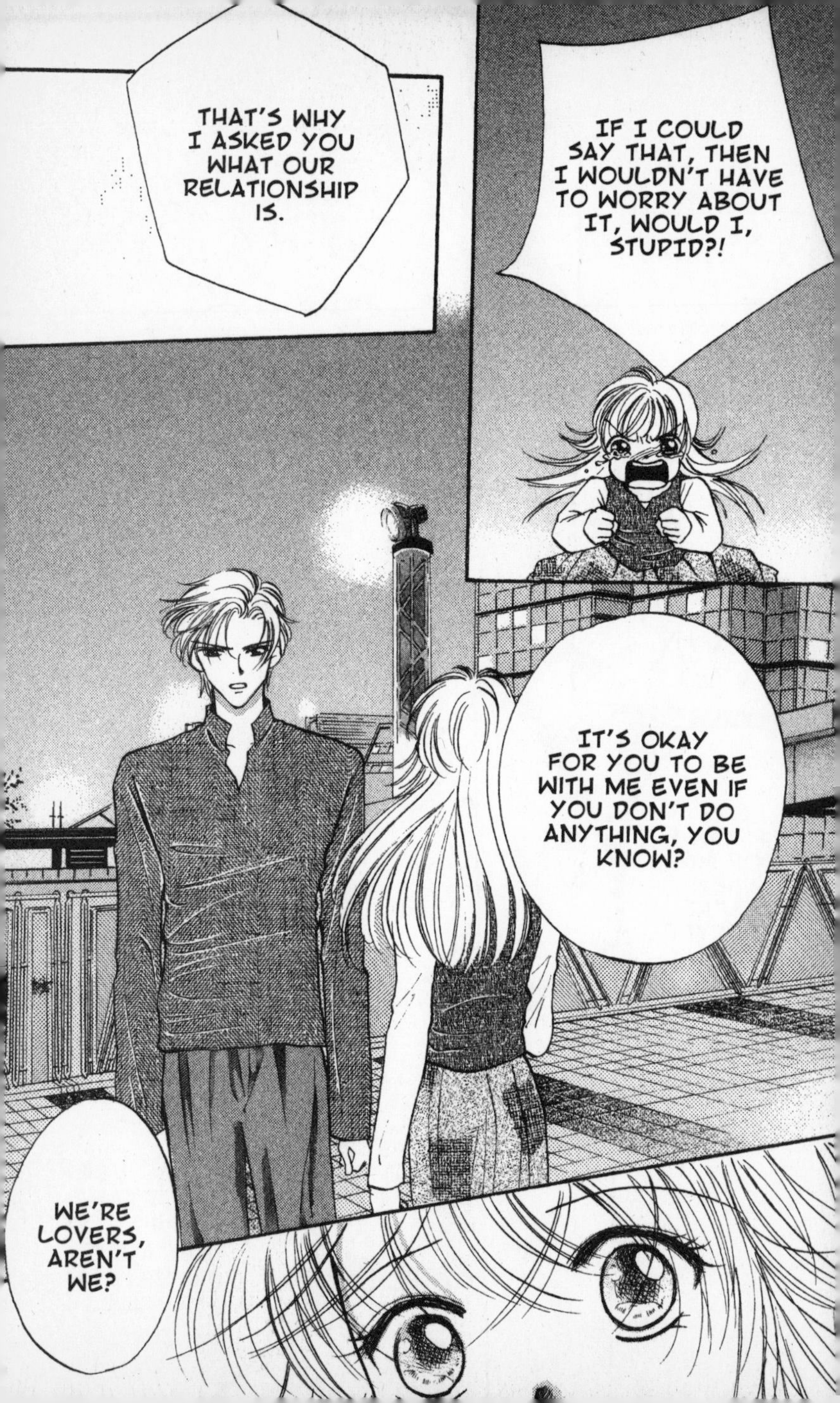
IF I COULD SAY THAT, THEN I WOULDN'T HAVE TO WORRY ABOUT IT, WOULD I, STUPID?!
THAT'S WHY I ASKED YOU WHAT OUR RELATIONSHIP IS.
IT'S OKAY FOR YOU TO BE WITH ME EVEN IF YOU DON'T DO ANYTHING, YOU KNOW?
WE'RE LOVERS, AREN'T WE?

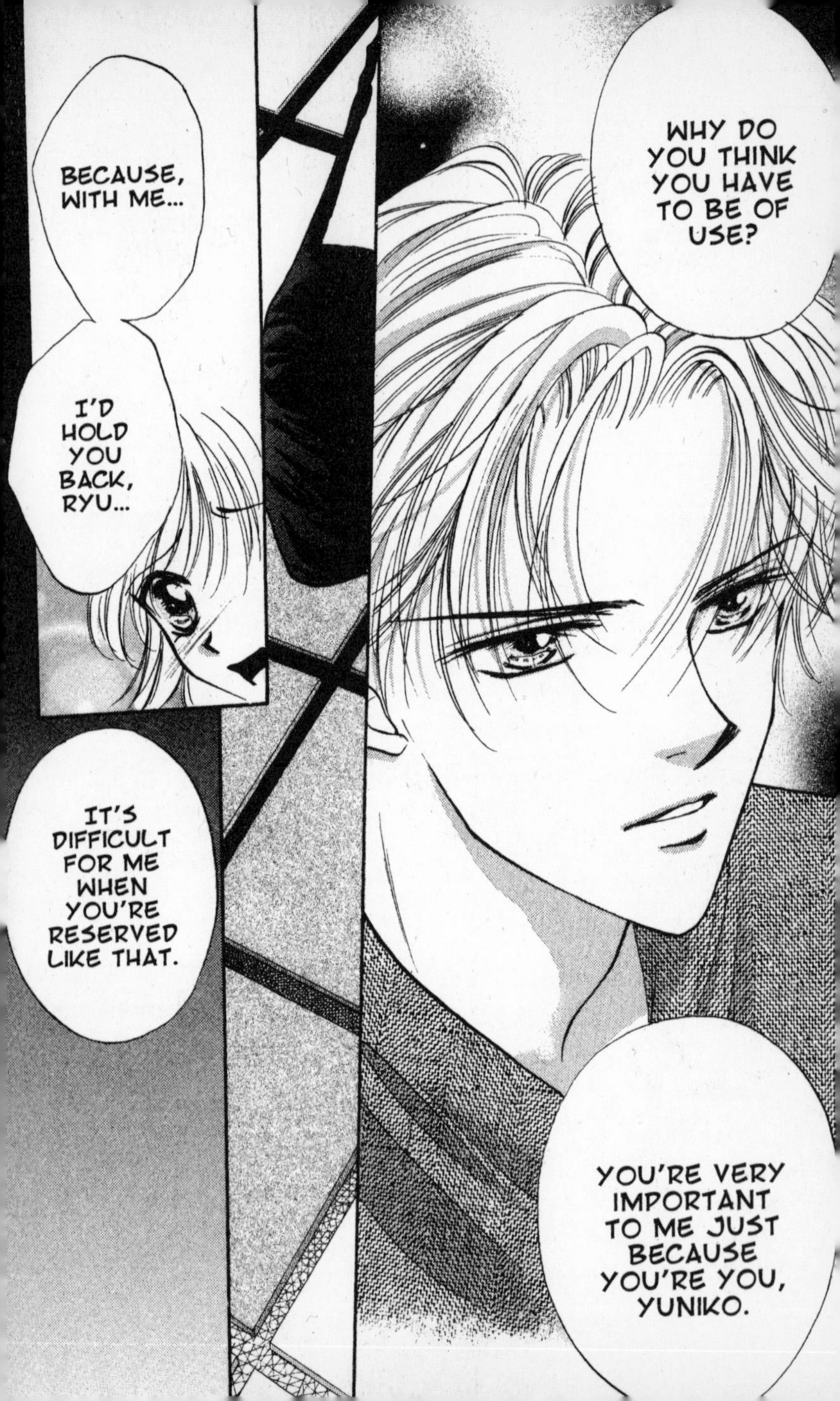
WHY DO YOU THINK YOU HAVE TO BE OF USE?
BECAUSE, WITH ME...
I'D HOLD YOU BACK, RYU...
IT'S DIFFICULT FOR ME WHEN YOU'RE RESERVED LIKE THAT.
YOU'RE VERY IMPORTANT TO ME JUST BECAUSE YOU'RE YOU, YUNIKO.

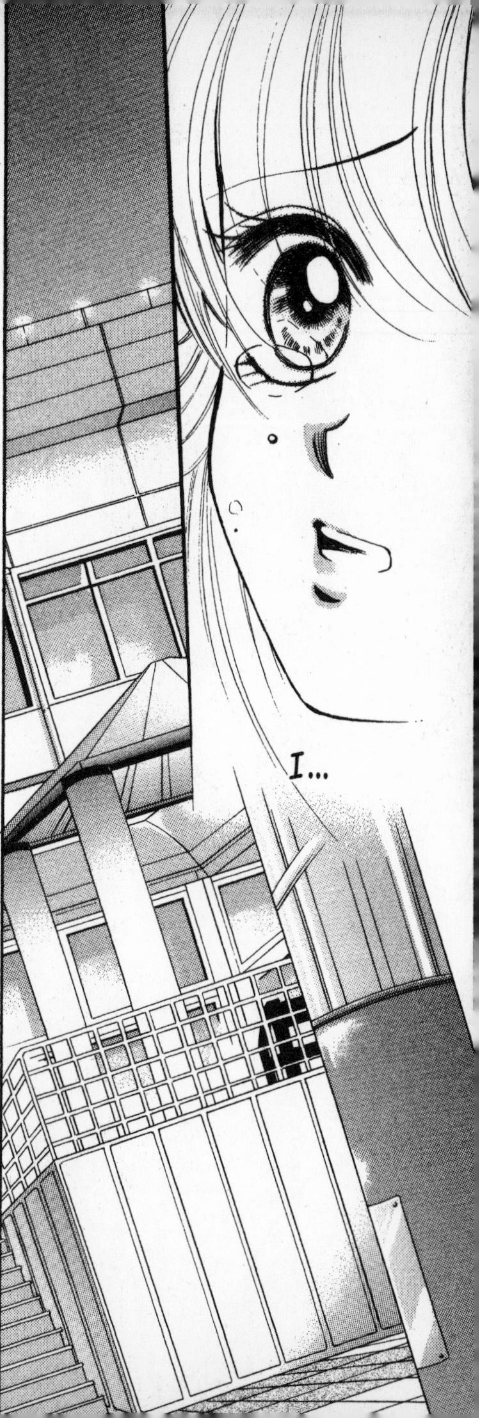
I...
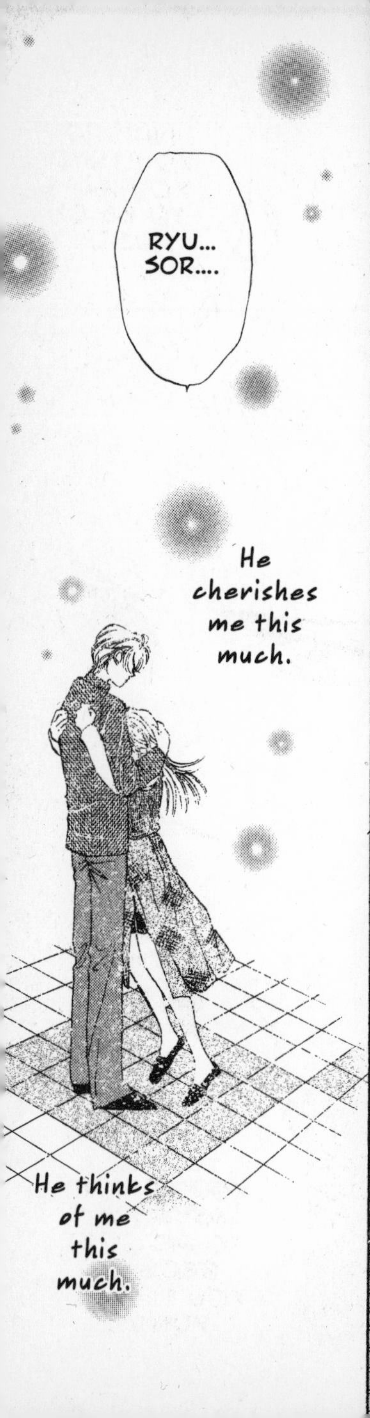
RYU... SOR....
He cherishes me this much.
He thinks of me this much.

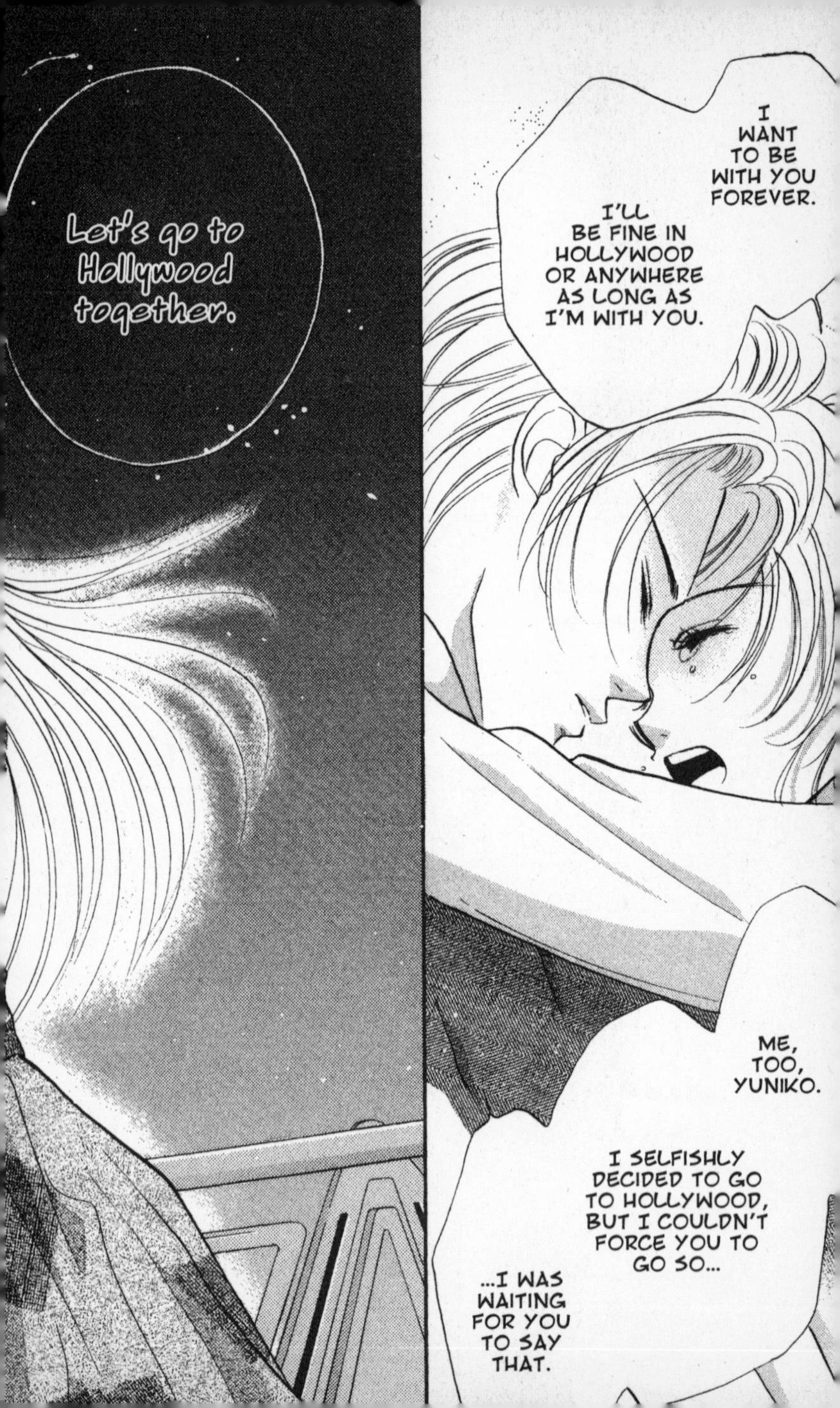
I WANT TO BE WITH YOU FOREVER.
I'LL BE FINE IN HOLLYWOOD OR ANYWHERE AS LONG AS I'M WITH YOU.
ME, TOO, YUNIKO.
I SELFISHLY DECIDED TO GO TO HOLLYWOOD, BUT I COULDN'T FORCE YOU TO GO SO...
...I WAS WAITING FOR YOU TO SAY THAT.
Let's go to Hollywood together.

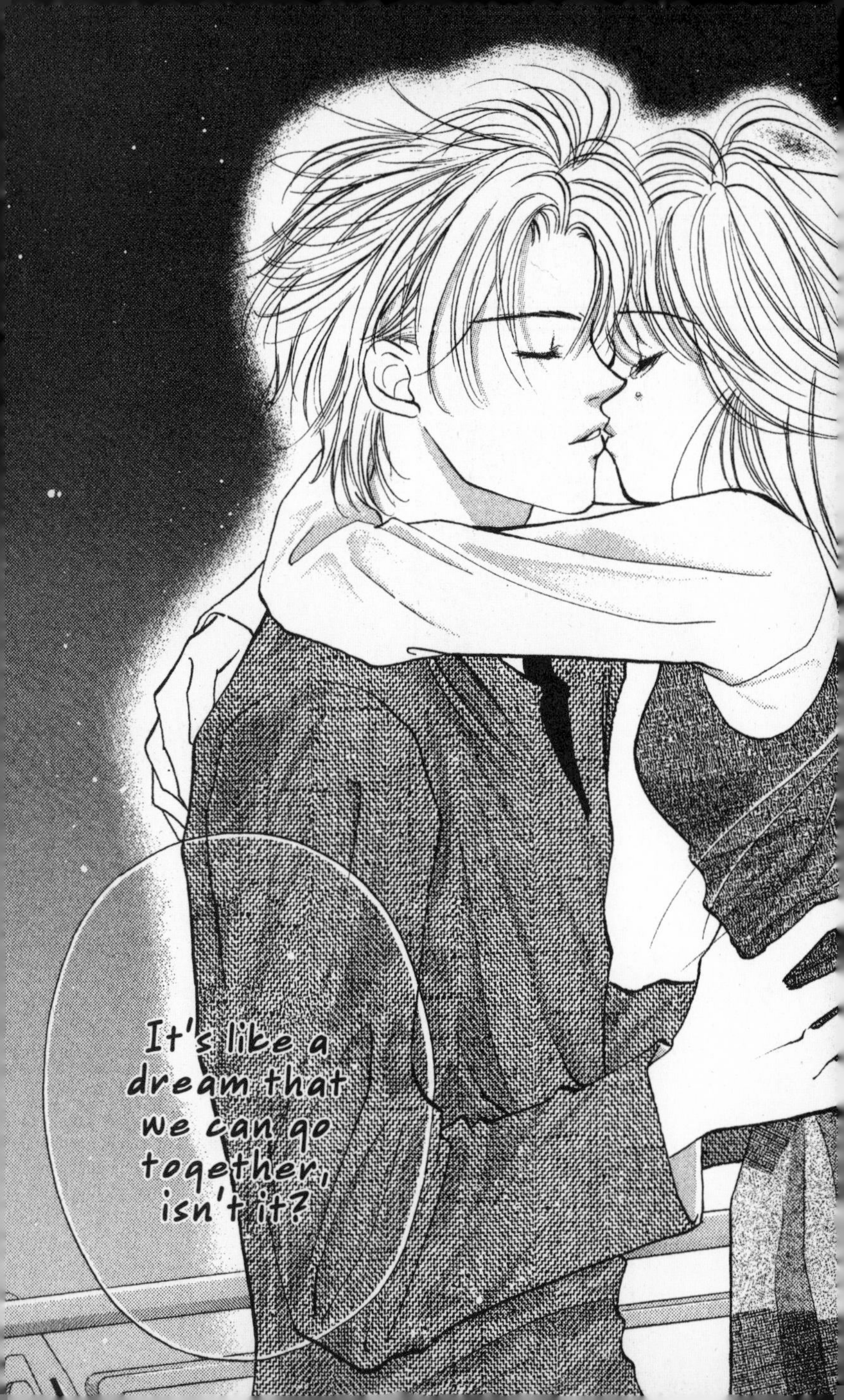
It's like a dream that we can go together, isn't it?

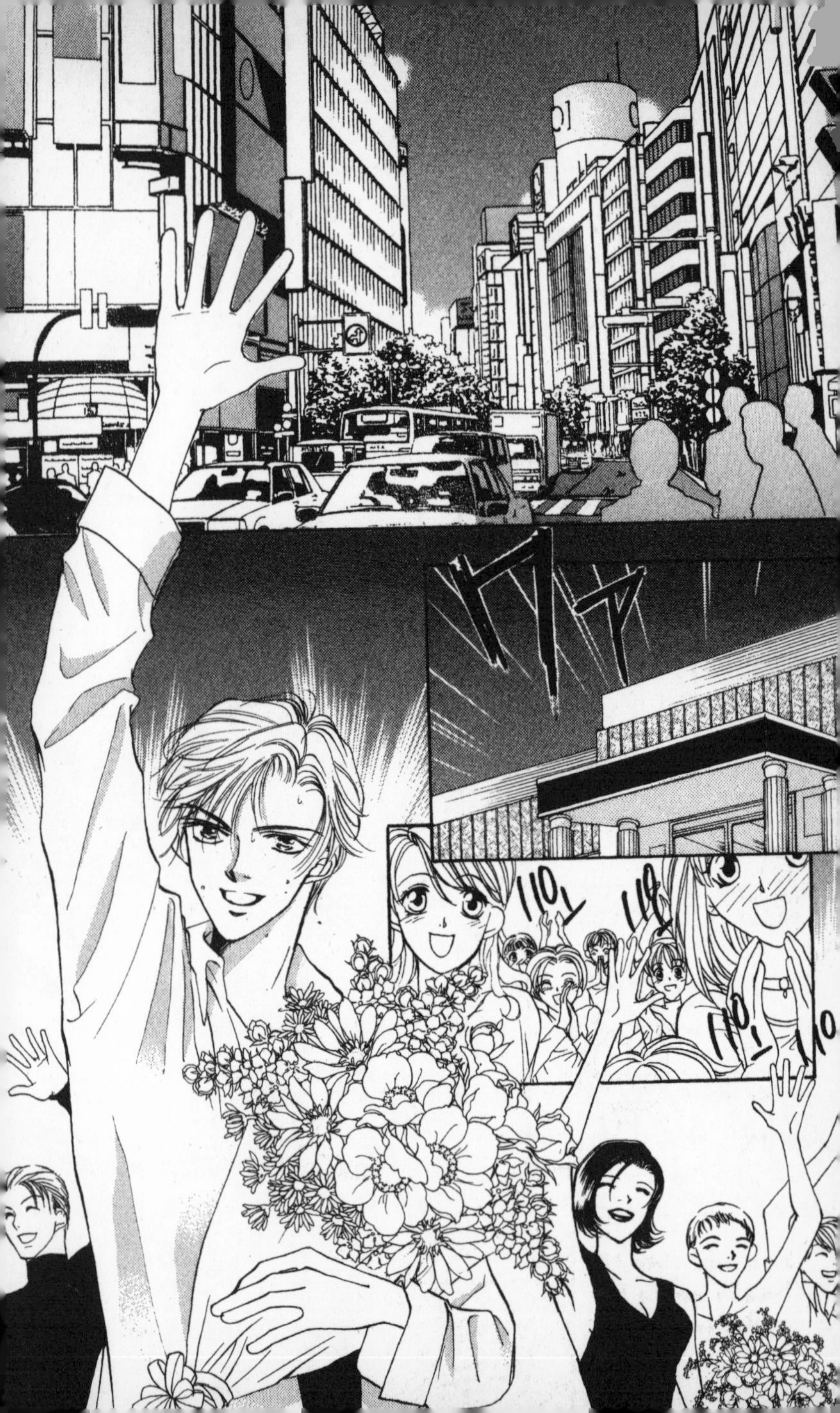
ワァ

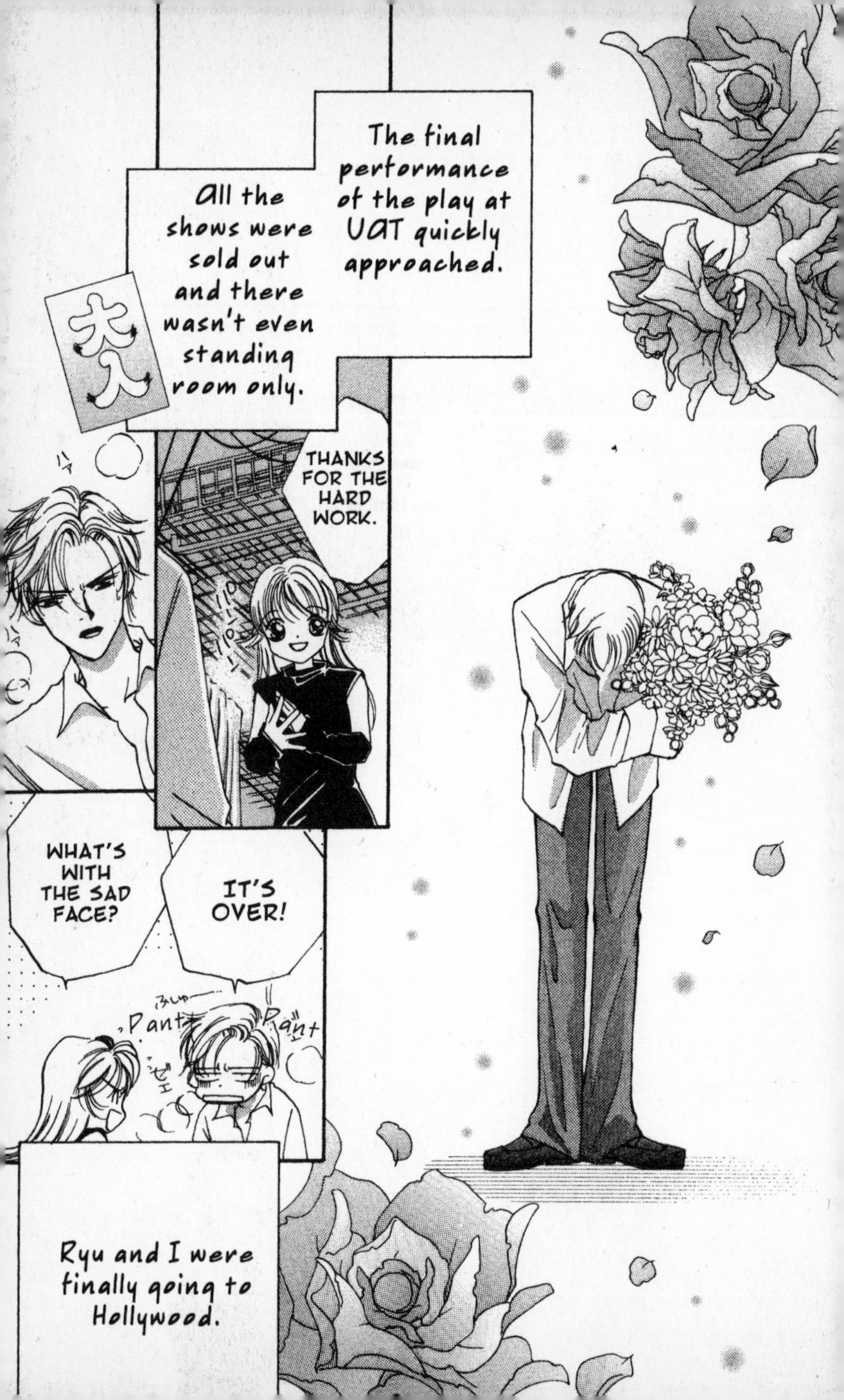

The final performance of the play at UAT quickly approached.
All the shows were sold out and there wasn't even standing room only.
大入
THANKS FOR THE HARD WORK.
IT'S OVER!
WHAT'S WITH THE SAD FACE?
Pant
Pant
Ryu and I were finally going to Hollywood.

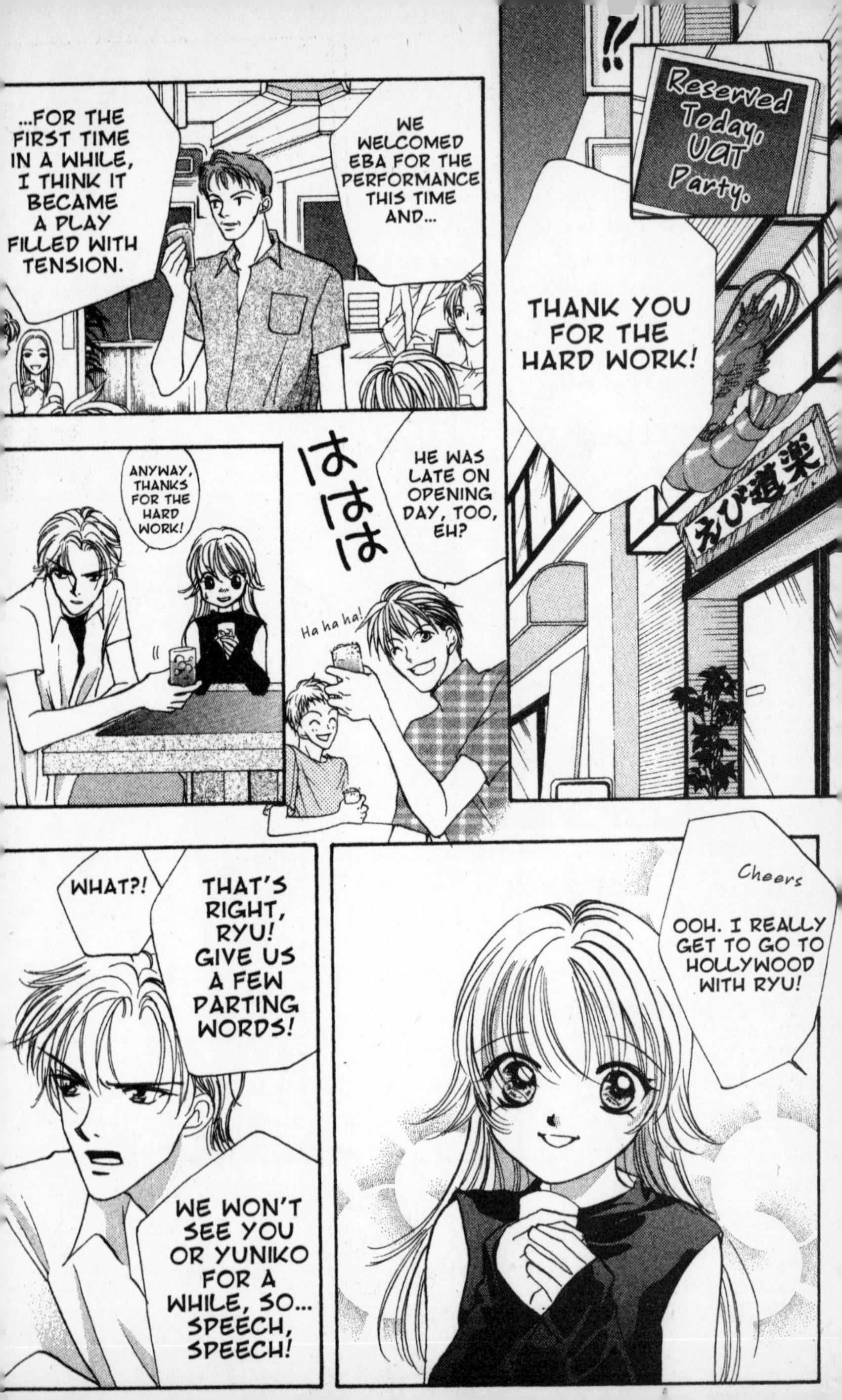
!!
Reserved Today, UAT Party.
THANK YOU FOR THE HARD WORK!
えび道楽
WE WELCOMED EBA FOR THE PERFORMANCE THIS TIME AND...
...FOR THE FIRST TIME IN A WHILE, I THINK IT BECAME A PLAY FILLED WITH TENSION.
HE WAS LATE ON OPENING DAY, TOO, EH?
ははは
Ha ha ha!
ANYWAY, THANKS FOR THE HARD WORK!
Cheers
OOH. I REALLY GET TO GO TO HOLLYWOOD WITH RYU!
THAT'S RIGHT, RYU! GIVE US A FEW PARTING WORDS!
WHAT?!
WE WON'T SEE YOU OR YUNIKO FOR A WHILE, SO... SPEECH, SPEECH!

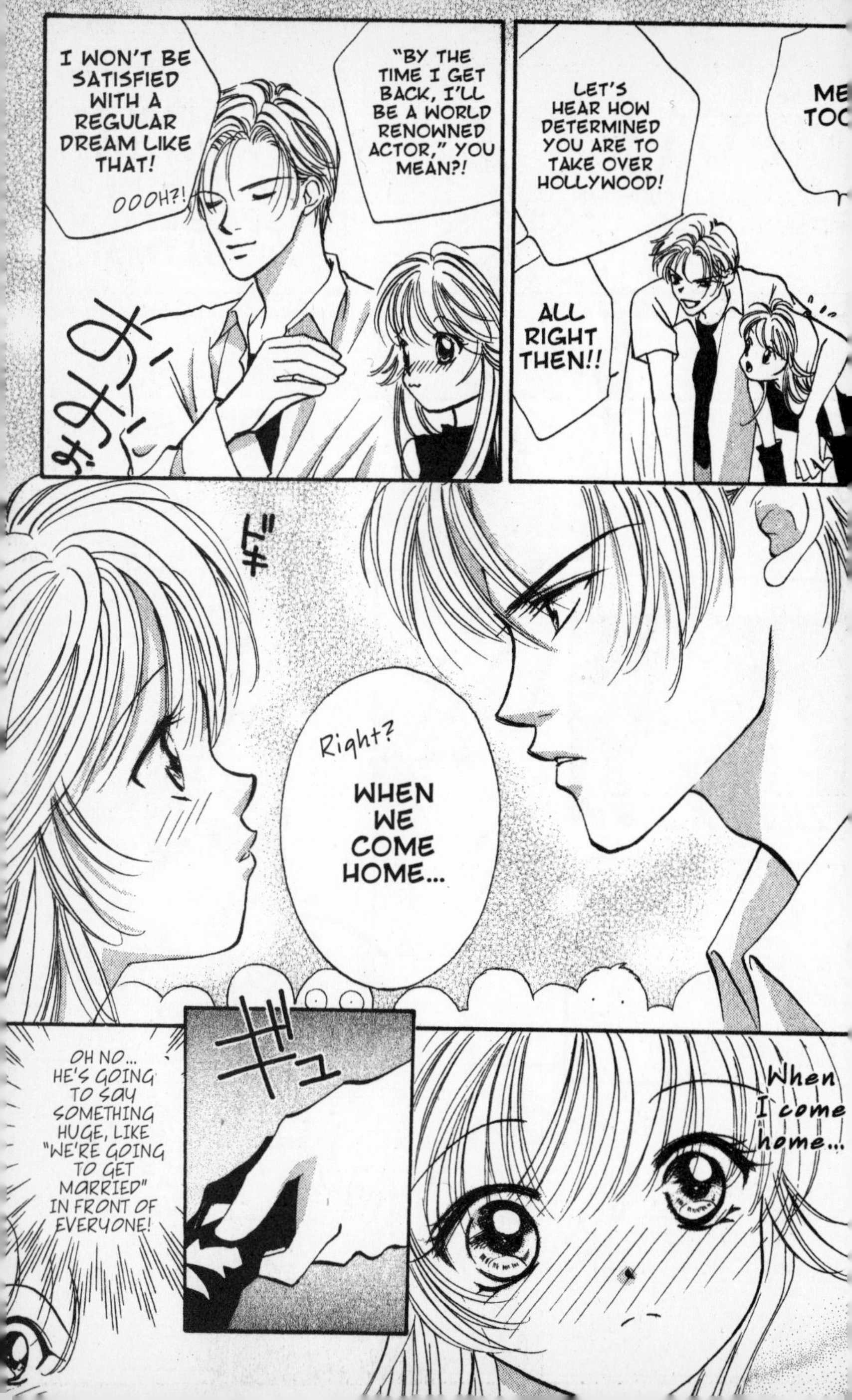
ME
LET'S HEAR HOW DETERMINED YOU ARE TO TAKE OVER HOLLYWOOD!
ALL RIGHT THEN!!
"BY THE TIME I GET BACK, I'LL BE A WORLD RENOWNED ACTOR," YOU MEAN?!
I WON'T BE SATISFIED WITH A REGULAR DREAM LIKE THAT!
OOOH?!
Right?
WHEN WE COME HOME...
When I come home...
OH NO... HE'S GOING TO SAY SOMETHING HUGE, LIKE "WE'RE GOING TO GET MARRIED" IN FRONT OF EVERYONE!

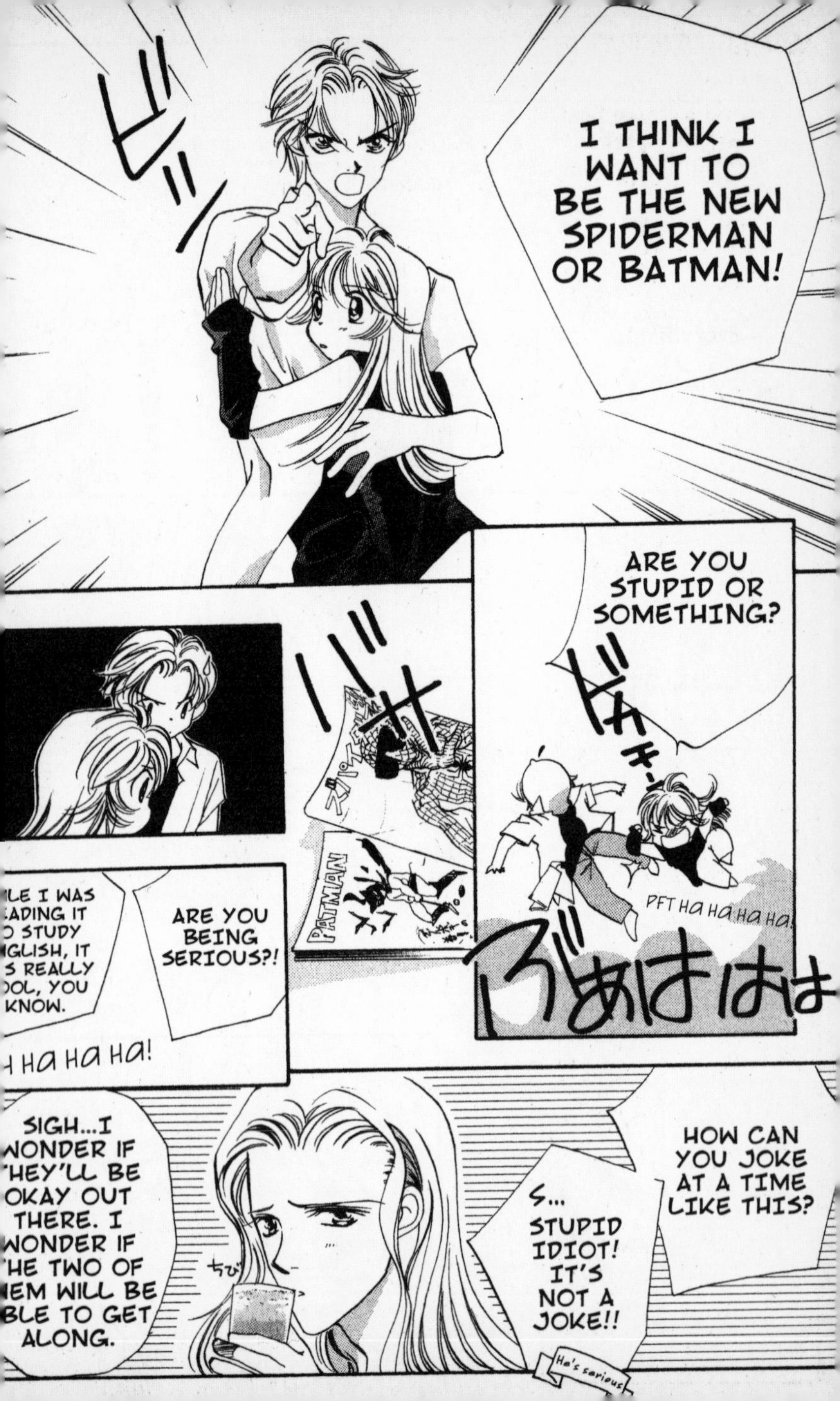
I THINK I WANT TO BE THE NEW SPIDERMAN OR BATMAN!
ARE YOU STUPID OR SOMETHING?
PFT HA HA HA HA!
ARE YOU BEING SERIOUS?!
LE I WAS ADING IT O STUDY NGLISH, IT S REALLY OL, YOU KNOW.
PATMAN
H HA HA HA!
HOW CAN YOU JOKE AT A TIME LIKE THIS?
S... STUPID IDIOT! IT'S NOT A JOKE!!
He's serious
ちび
SIGH...I WONDER IF HEY'LL BE OKAY OUT THERE. I WONDER IF HE TWO OF EM WILL BE BLE TO GET ALONG.

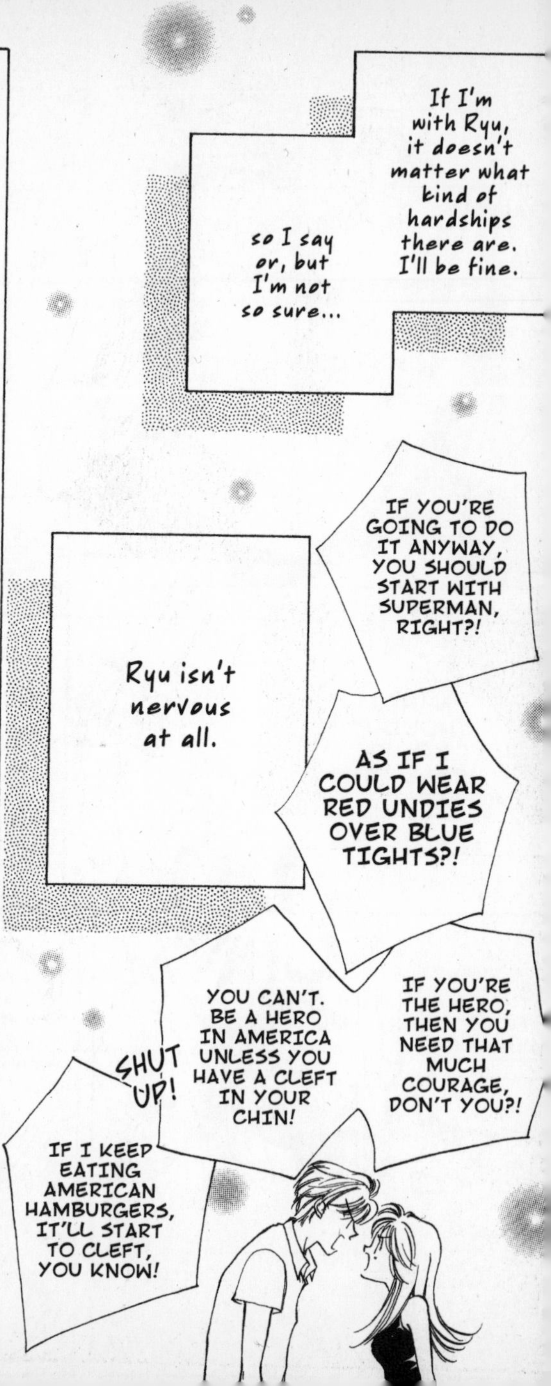
If I'm with Ryu, it doesn't matter what kind of hardships there are. I'll be fine.
so I say or, but I'm not so sure...
IF YOU'RE GOING TO DO IT ANYWAY, YOU SHOULD START WITH SUPERMAN, RIGHT?!
AS IF I COULD WEAR RED UNDIES OVER BLUE TIGHTS?!
Ryu isn't nervous at all.
IF YOU'RE THE HERO, THEN YOU NEED THAT MUCH COURAGE, DON'T YOU?!
YOU CAN'T. BE A HERO IN AMERICA UNLESS YOU HAVE A CLEFT IN YOUR CHIN!
SHUT UP!
IF I KEEP EATING AMERICAN HAMBURGERS, IT'LL START TO CLEFT, YOU KNOW!

The Thing I Like Best About Myself

Everything.

La Dee Da.

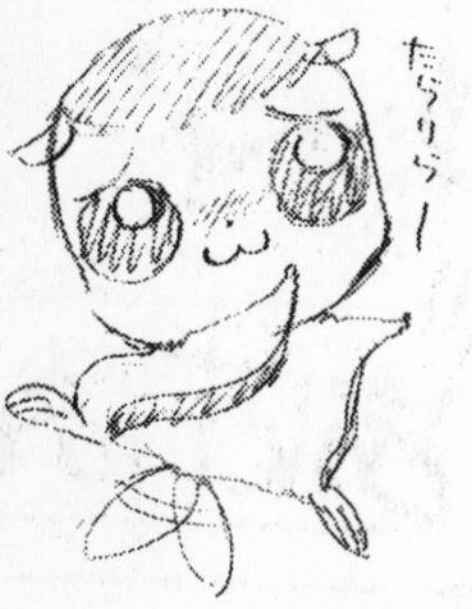

by Cinnamon

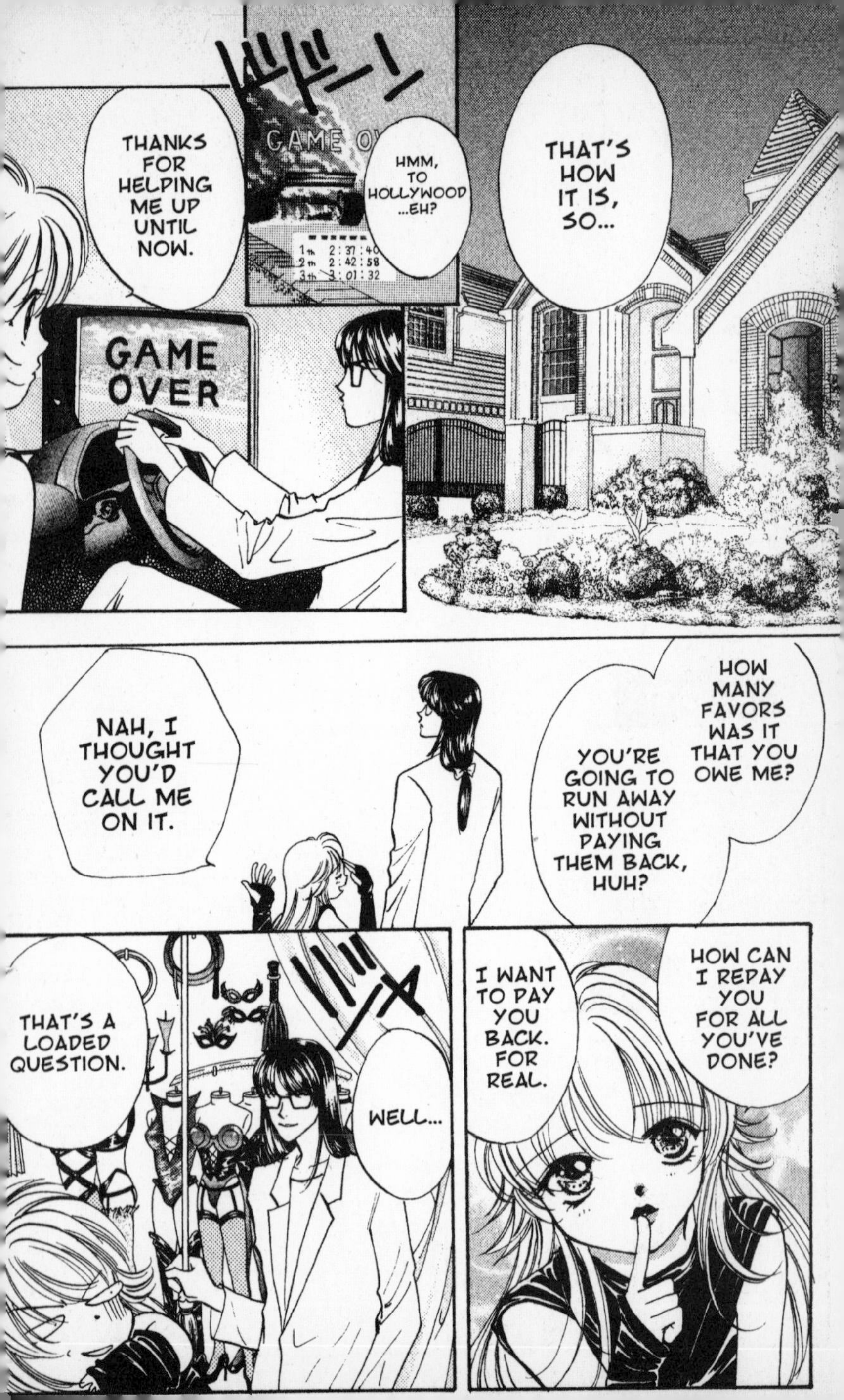
THAT'S HOW IT IS, SO...
THANKS FOR HELPING ME UP UNTIL NOW.
HMM, TO HOLLYWOOD ...EH?
GAME OVER
HOW MANY FAVORS WAS IT THAT YOU OWE ME?
YOU'RE GOING TO RUN AWAY WITHOUT PAYING THEM BACK, HUH?
NAH, I THOUGHT YOU'D CALL ME ON IT.
HOW CAN I REPAY YOU FOR ALL YOU'VE DONE?
I WANT TO PAY YOU BACK. FOR REAL.
WELL...
THAT'S A LOADED QUESTION.

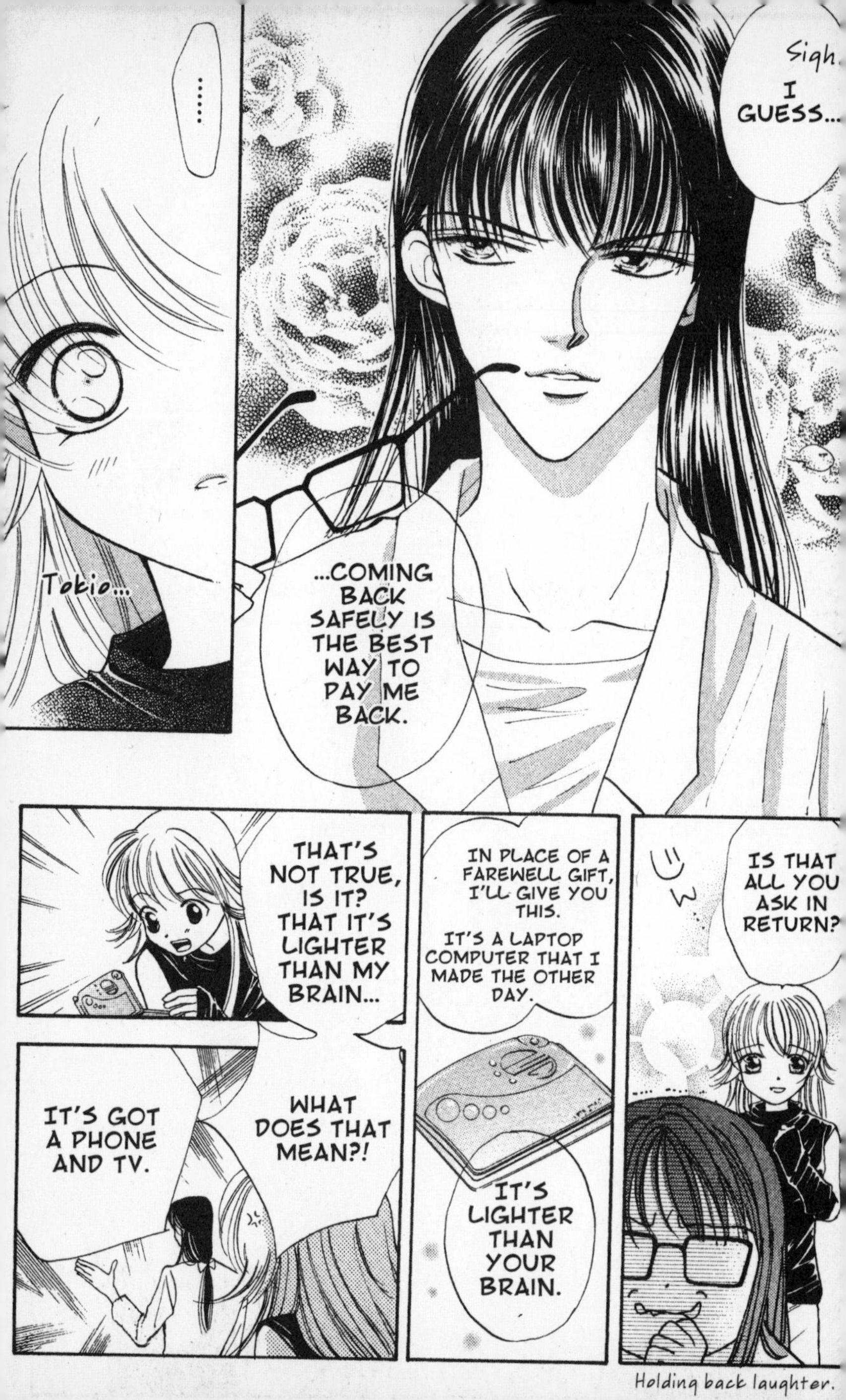
Sigh.
I GUESS...
...COMING BACK SAFELY IS THE BEST WAY TO PAY ME BACK.
......
Tokio...
IS THAT ALL YOU ASK IN RETURN?
....
Holding back laughter.
IN PLACE OF A FAREWELL GIFT, I'LL GIVE YOU THIS.
IT'S A LAPTOP COMPUTER THAT I MADE THE OTHER DAY.
IT'S LIGHTER THAN YOUR BRAIN.
THAT'S NOT TRUE, IS IT? THAT IT'S LIGHTER THAN MY BRAIN...
WHAT DOES THAT MEAN?!
IT'S GOT A PHONE AND TV.

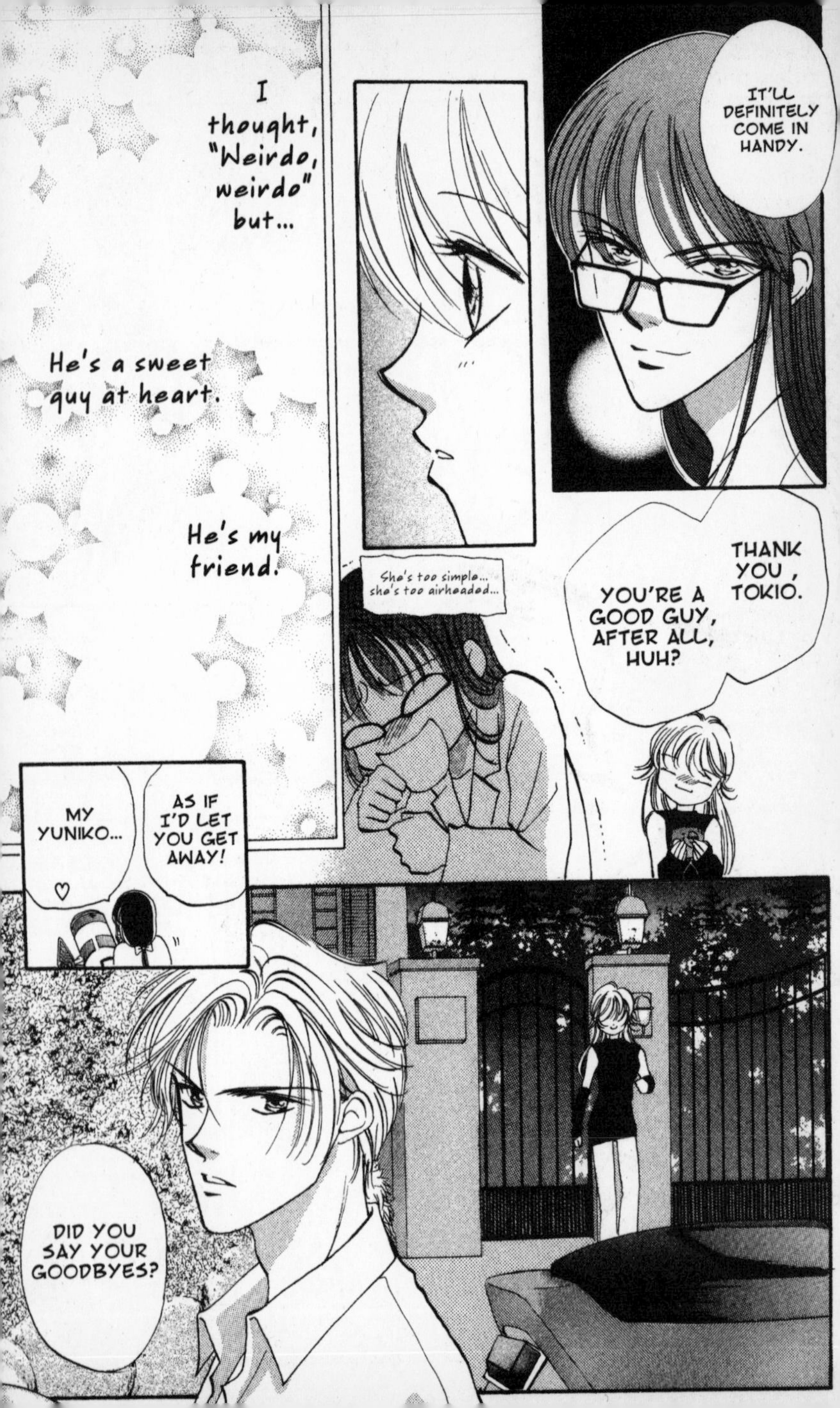
IT'LL DEFINITELY COME IN HANDY.
THANK YOU, TOKIO.
YOU'RE A GOOD GUY, AFTER ALL, HUH?
She's too simple... she's too airheaded...
I thought, "Weirdo, weirdo" but...
He's a sweet guy at heart.
He's my friend.
AS IF I'D LET YOU GET AWAY!
MY YUNIKO... ♡
DID YOU SAY YOUR GOODBYES?

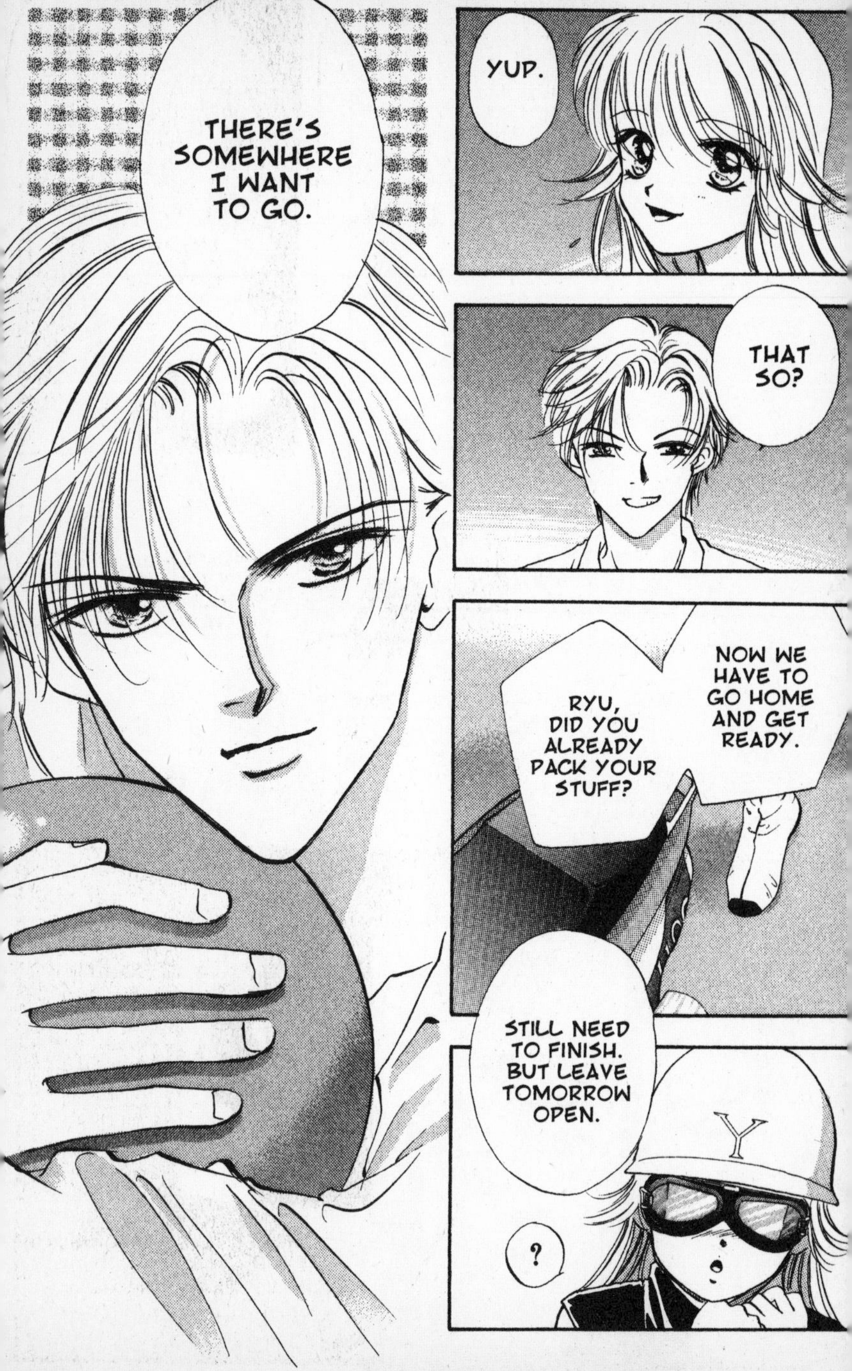
YUP.
THAT SO?
NOW WE HAVE TO GO HOME AND GET READY.
RYU, DID YOU ALREADY PACK YOUR STUFF?
STILL NEED TO FINISH. BUT LEAVE TOMORROW OPEN.
?
THERE'S SOMEWHERE I WANT TO GO.

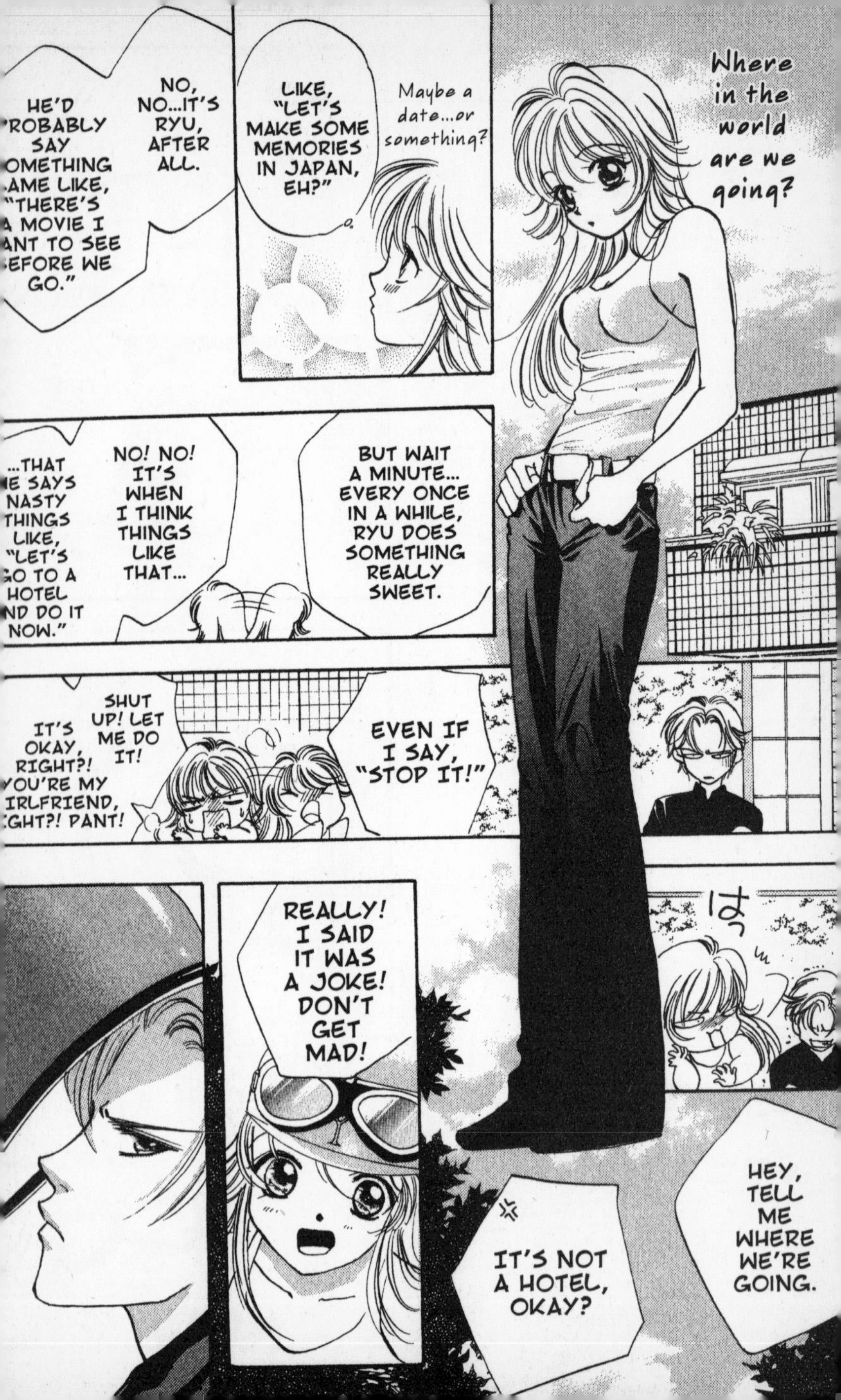

Where in the world are we going?
Maybe a date...or something?
LIKE, "LET'S MAKE SOME MEMORIES IN JAPAN, EH?"
NO, NO...IT'S RYU, AFTER ALL.
HE'D 'ROBABLY SAY OMETHING AME LIKE, "THERE'S A MOVIE I ANT TO SEE EFORE WE GO."
BUT WAIT A MINUTE... EVERY ONCE IN A WHILE, RYU DOES SOMETHING REALLY SWEET.
NO! NO! IT'S WHEN I THINK THINGS LIKE THAT...
...THAT E SAYS NASTY THINGS LIKE, "LET'S GO TO A HOTEL ND DO IT NOW."
EVEN IF I SAY, "STOP IT!"
SHUT UP! LET ME DO IT!
IT'S OKAY, RIGHT?! YOU'RE MY IRLFRIEND, GHT?! PANT!
はっ
HEY, TELL ME WHERE WE'RE GOING.
IT'S NOT A HOTEL, OKAY?
REALLY! I SAID IT WAS A JOKE! DON'T GET MAD!

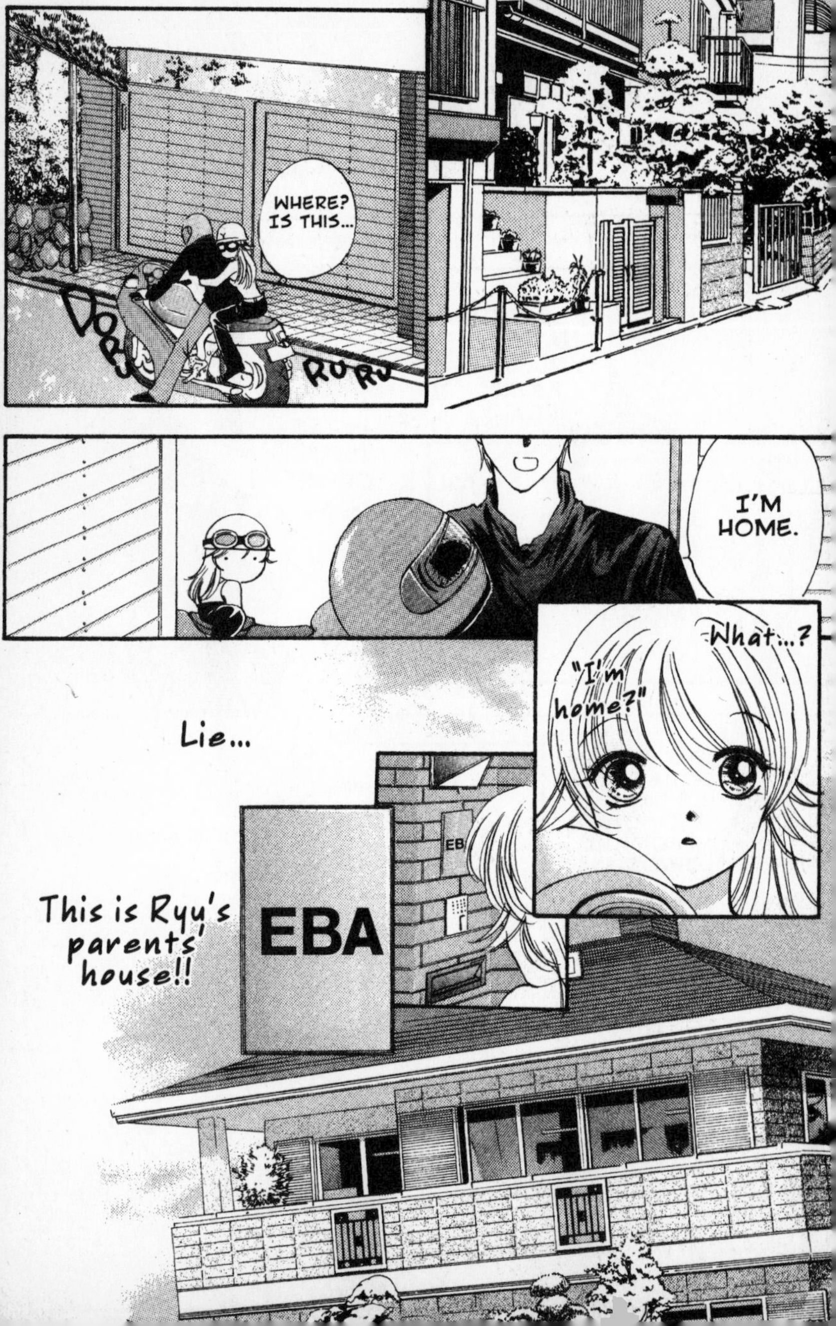
WHERE? IS THIS...
DORU
RURU
I'M HOME.
What...?
"I'm home?"
Lie...
This is Ryu's parents' house!!
EBA
EB

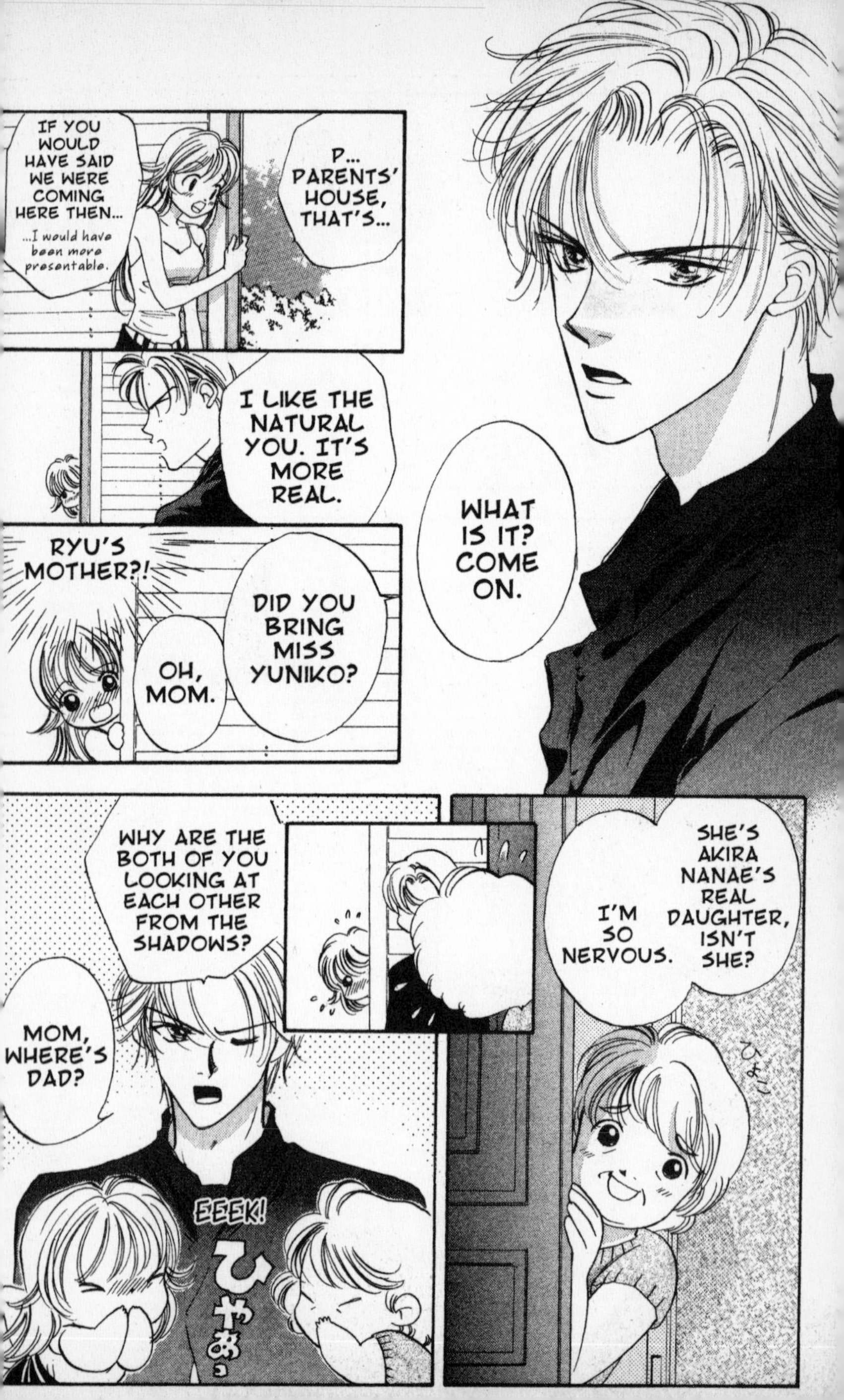
WHAT IS IT? COME ON.
P... PARENTS' HOUSE, THAT'S...
IF YOU WOULD HAVE SAID WE WERE COMING HERE THEN...
...I would have been more presentable.
I LIKE THE NATURAL YOU. IT'S MORE REAL.
DID YOU BRING MISS YUNIKO?
OH, MOM.
RYU'S MOTHER?!
SHE'S AKIRA NANAE'S REAL DAUGHTER, ISN'T SHE?
I'M SO NERVOUS.
WHY ARE THE BOTH OF YOU LOOKING AT EACH OTHER FROM THE SHADOWS?
MOM, WHERE'S DAD?
EEEK!
ひゃあっ

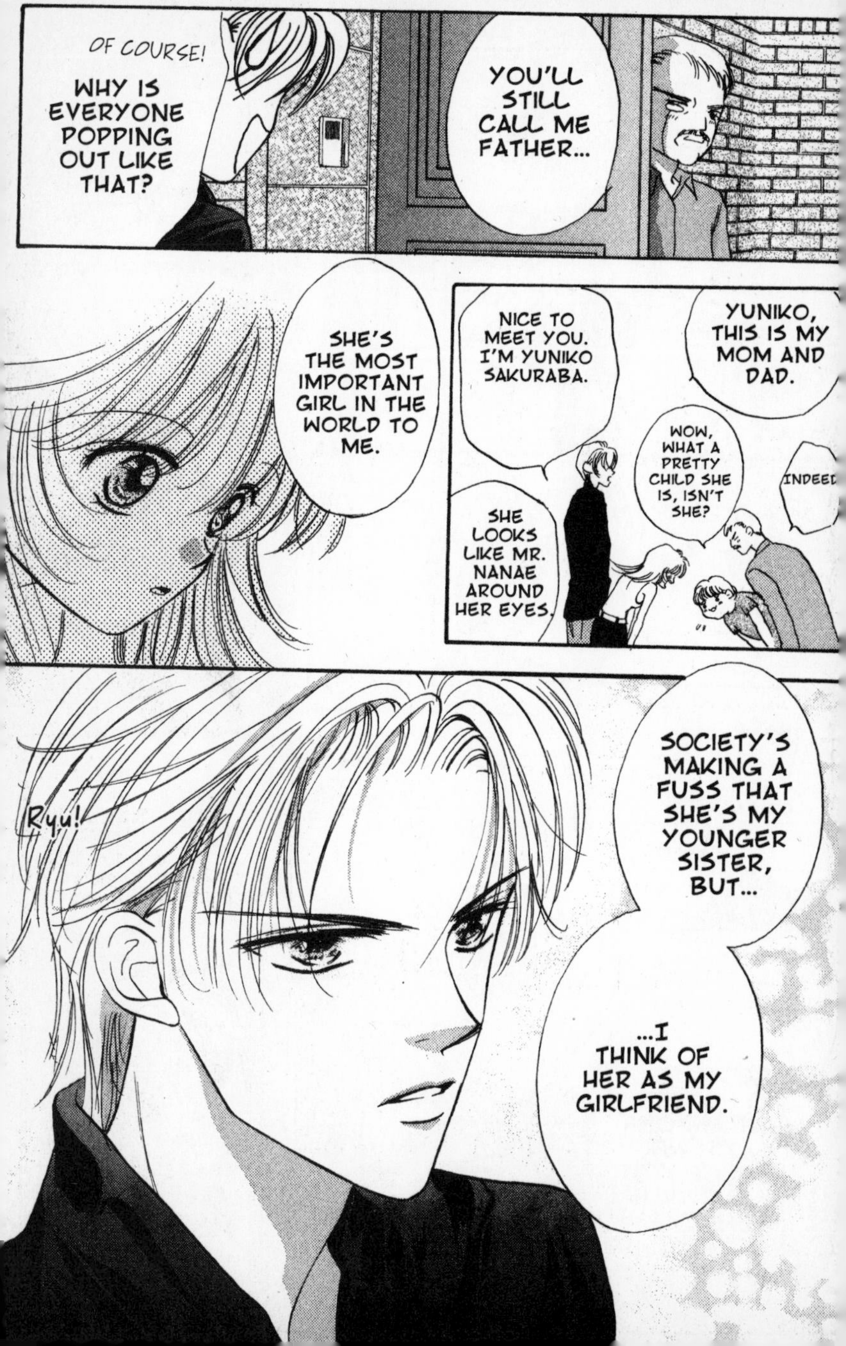
YOU'LL STILL CALL ME FATHER...
OF COURSE!
WHY IS EVERYONE POPPING OUT LIKE THAT?
YUNIKO, THIS IS MY MOM AND DAD.
NICE TO MEET YOU. I'M YUNIKO SAKURABA.
WOW, WHAT A PRETTY CHILD SHE IS, ISN'T SHE?
INDEED
SHE LOOKS LIKE MR. NANAE AROUND HER EYES.
SHE'S THE MOST IMPORTANT GIRL IN THE WORLD TO ME.
SOCIETY'S MAKING A FUSS THAT SHE'S MY YOUNGER SISTER, BUT...
Ryu!
...I THINK OF HER AS MY GIRLFRIEND.

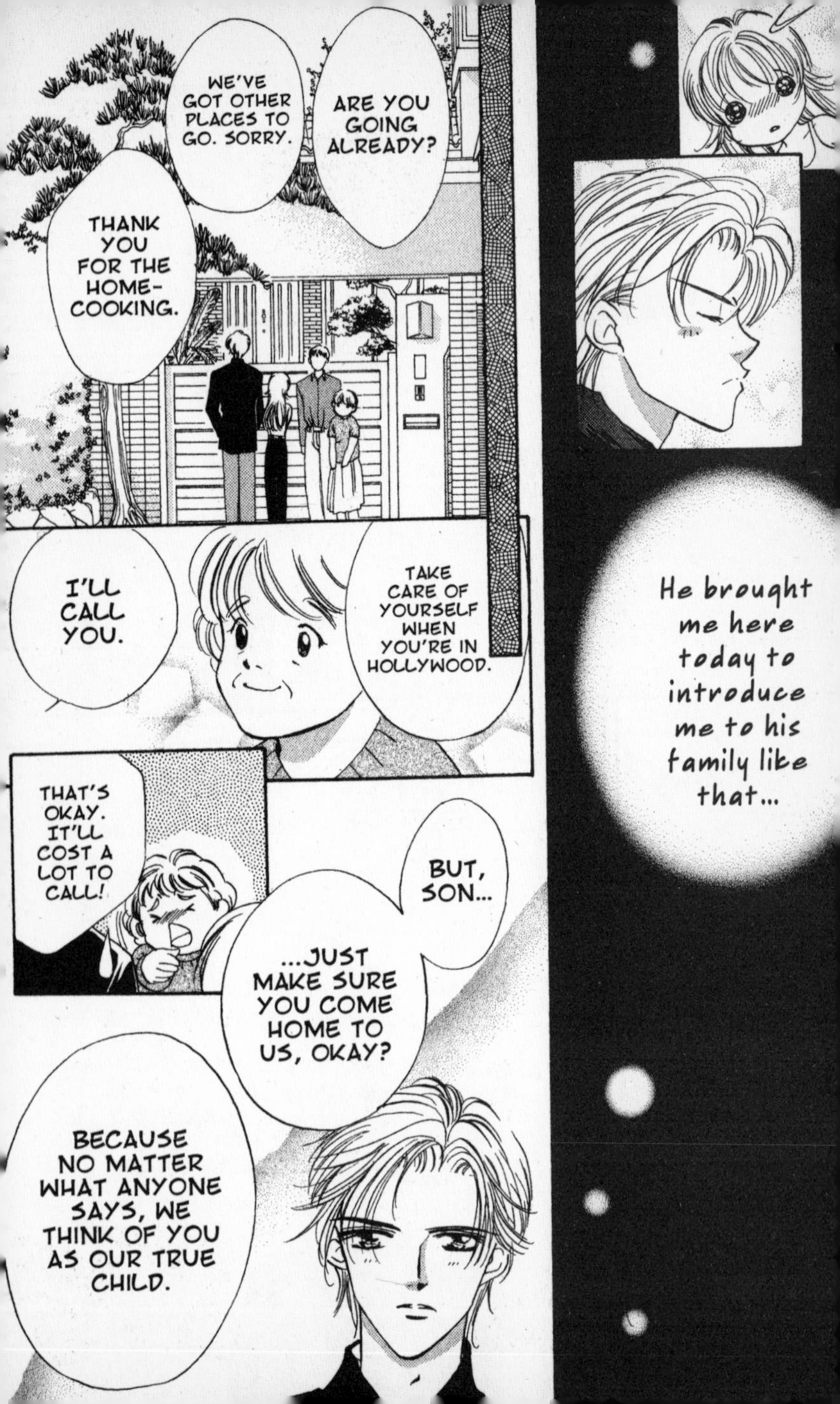
He brought me here today to introduce me to his family like that...
ARE YOU GOING ALREADY?
WE'VE GOT OTHER PLACES TO GO. SORRY.
THANK YOU FOR THE HOME-COOKING.
TAKE CARE OF YOURSELF WHEN YOU'RE IN HOLLYWOOD.
I'LL CALL YOU.
THAT'S OKAY. IT'LL COST A LOT TO CALL!
BUT, SON...
...JUST MAKE SURE YOU COME HOME TO US, OKAY?
BECAUSE NO MATTER WHAT ANYONE SAYS, WE THINK OF YOU AS OUR TRUE CHILD.

MY MOM AND DAD...

Ryu...

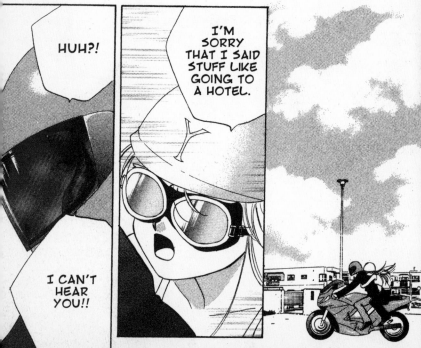

HUH?!

I'M SORRY THAT I SAID STUFF LIKE GOING TO A HOTEL.

I CAN'T HEAR YOU!!

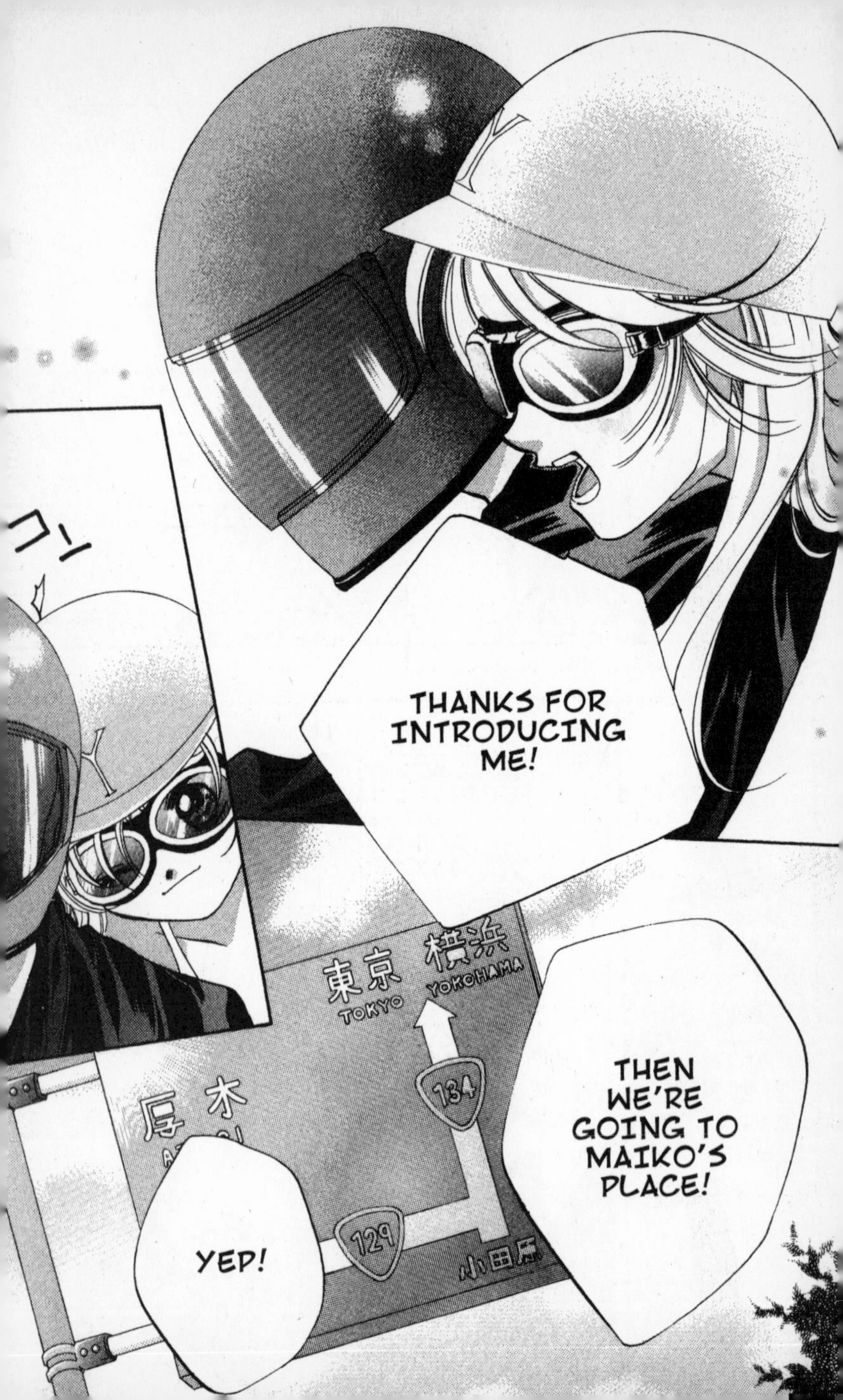
THANKS FOR INTRODUCING ME!
コン
東京 TOKYO
横浜 YOKOHAMA
134
厚木
129
小田原
THEN WE'RE GOING TO MAIKO'S PLACE!
YEP!

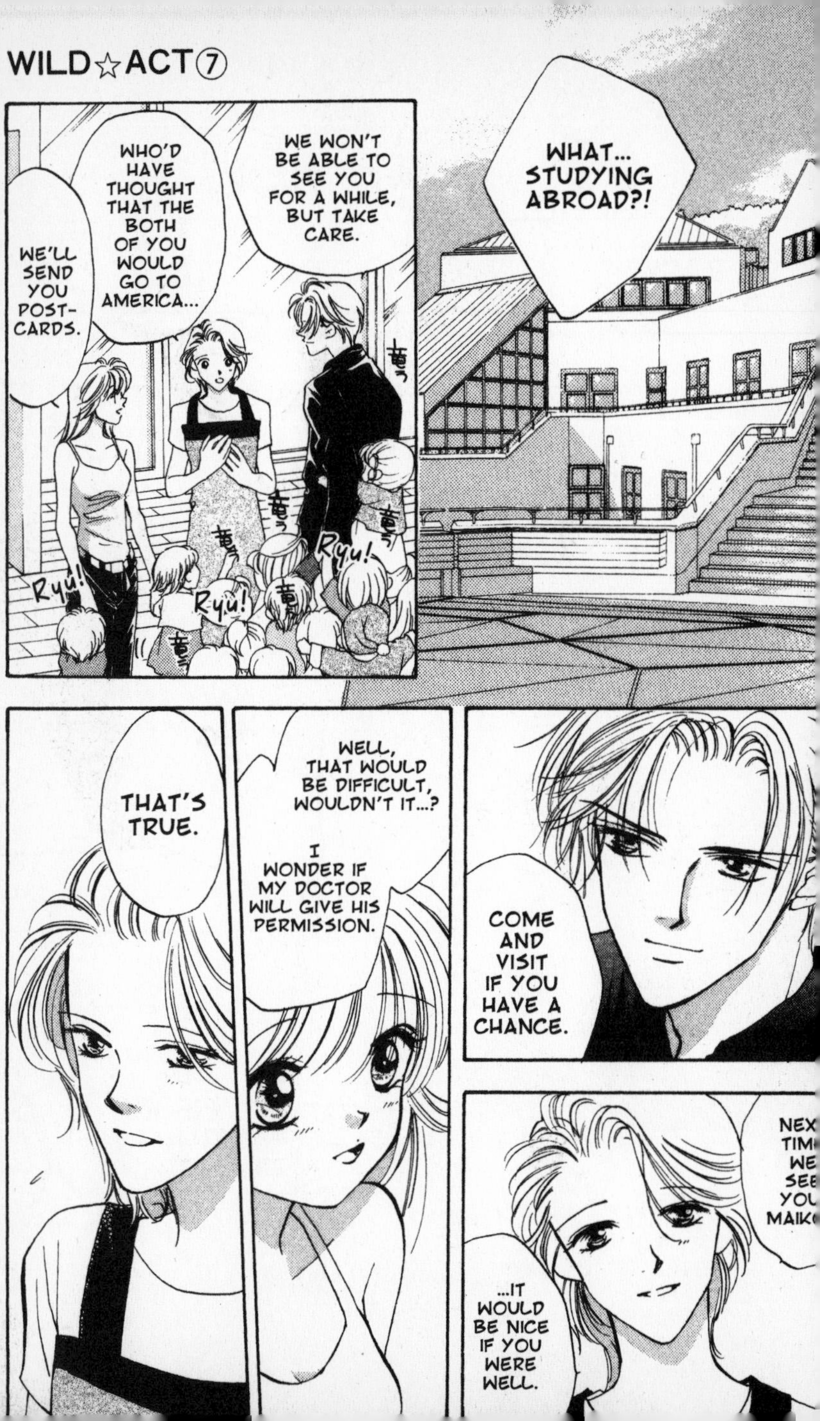
WHAT... STUDYING ABROAD?!
WE WON'T BE ABLE TO SEE YOU FOR A WHILE, BUT TAKE CARE.
WHO'D HAVE THOUGHT THAT THE BOTH OF YOU WOULD GO TO AMERICA...
WE'LL SEND YOU POST-CARDS.
Ryu!
Ryu!
Ryu!
COME AND VISIT IF YOU HAVE A CHANCE.
NEX TIM WE SEE YOU MAIK
...IT WOULD BE NICE IF YOU WERE WELL.
WELL, THAT WOULD BE DIFFICULT, WOULDN'T IT...?
I WONDER IF MY DOCTOR WILL GIVE HIS PERMISSION.
THAT'S TRUE.

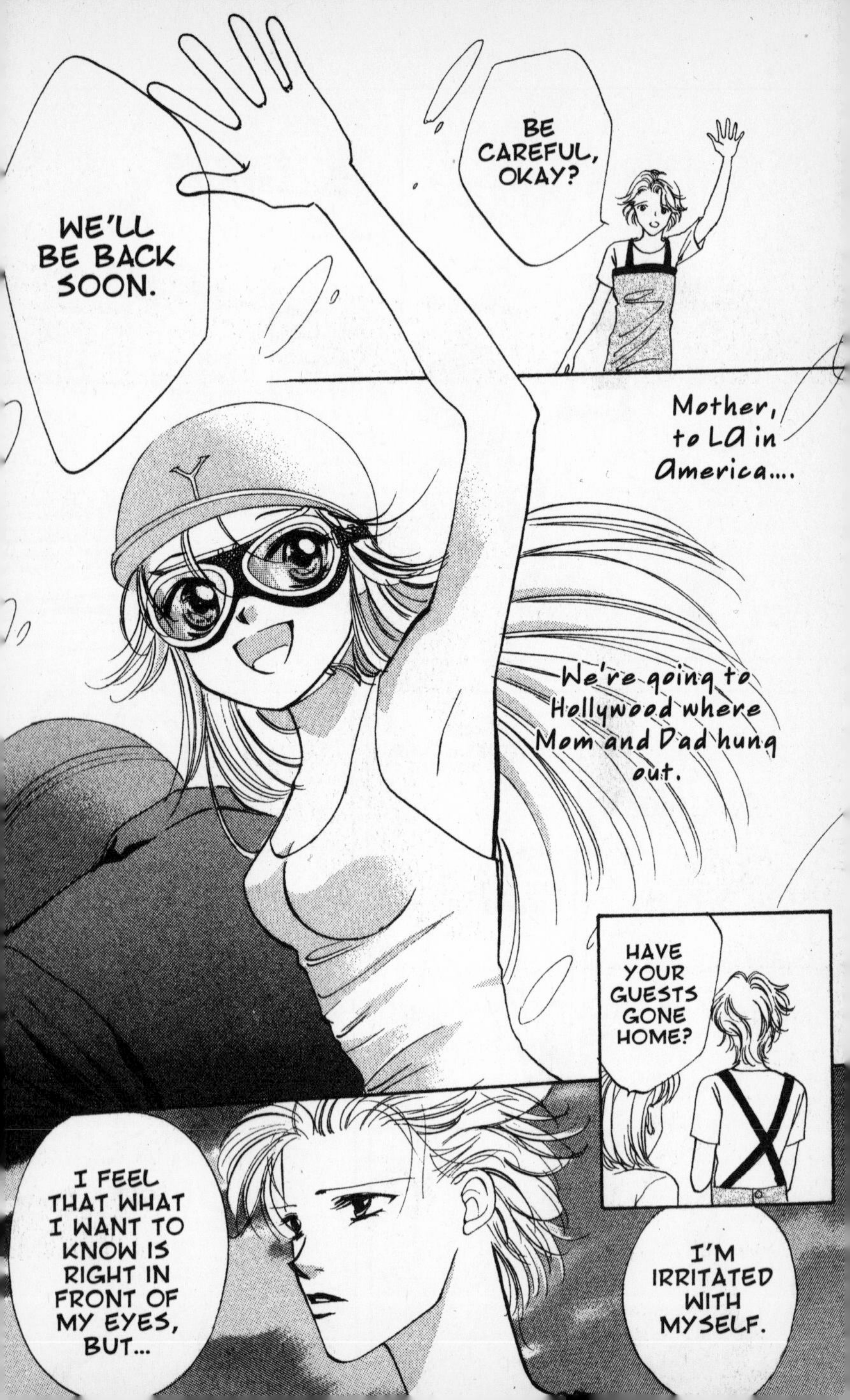
BE CAREFUL, OKAY?
WE'LL BE BACK SOON.
Mother, to LA in America....
We're going to Hollywood where Mom and Dad hung out.
HAVE YOUR GUESTS GONE HOME?
I'M IRRITATED WITH MYSELF.
I FEEL THAT WHAT I WANT TO KNOW IS RIGHT IN FRONT OF MY EYES, BUT...

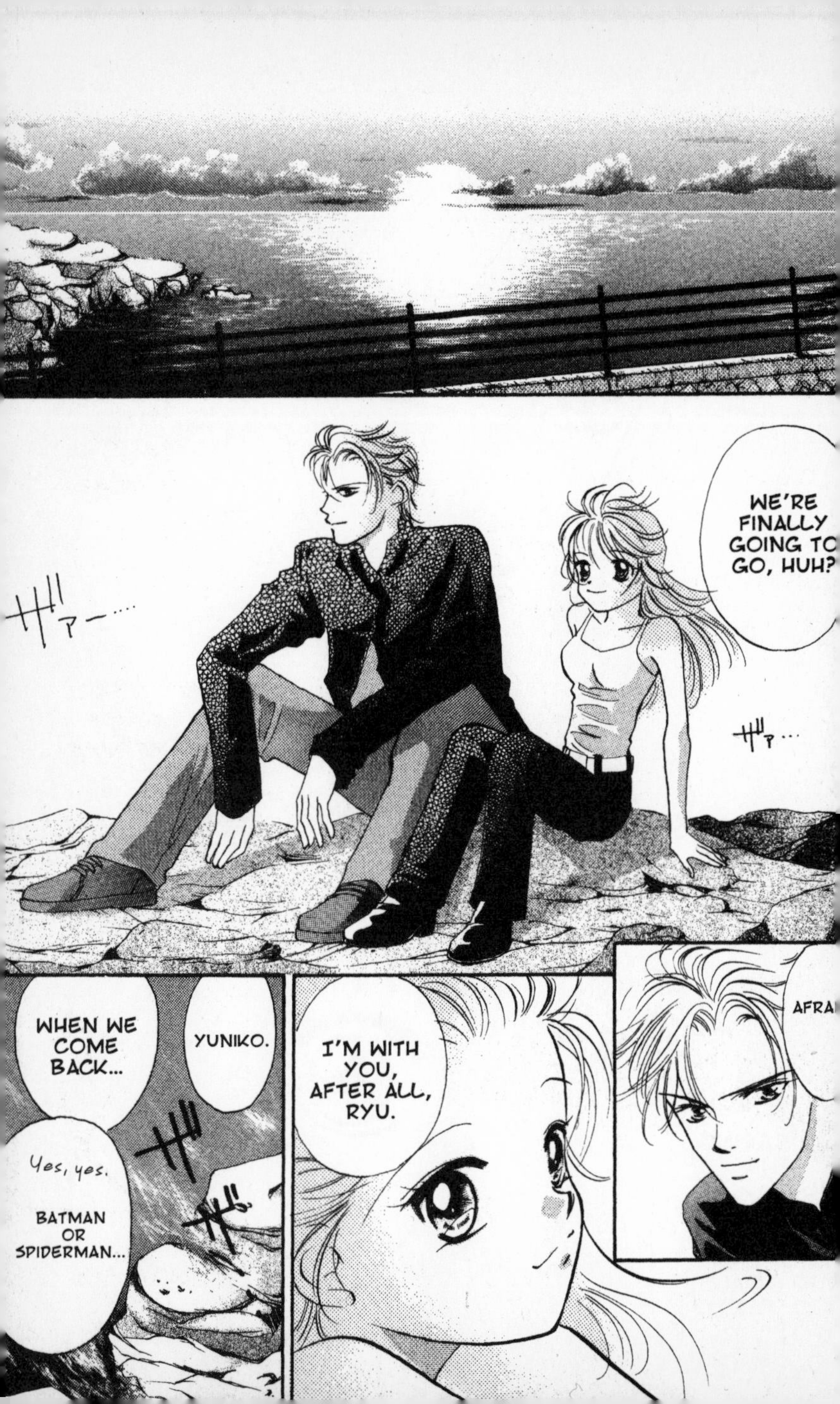
WE'RE FINALLY GOING TO GO, HUH?
ザザ…
ザザァー….
AFRA
I'M WITH YOU, AFTER ALL, RYU.
YUNIKO.
WHEN WE COME BACK...
Yes, yes.
BATMAN OR SPIDERMAN...

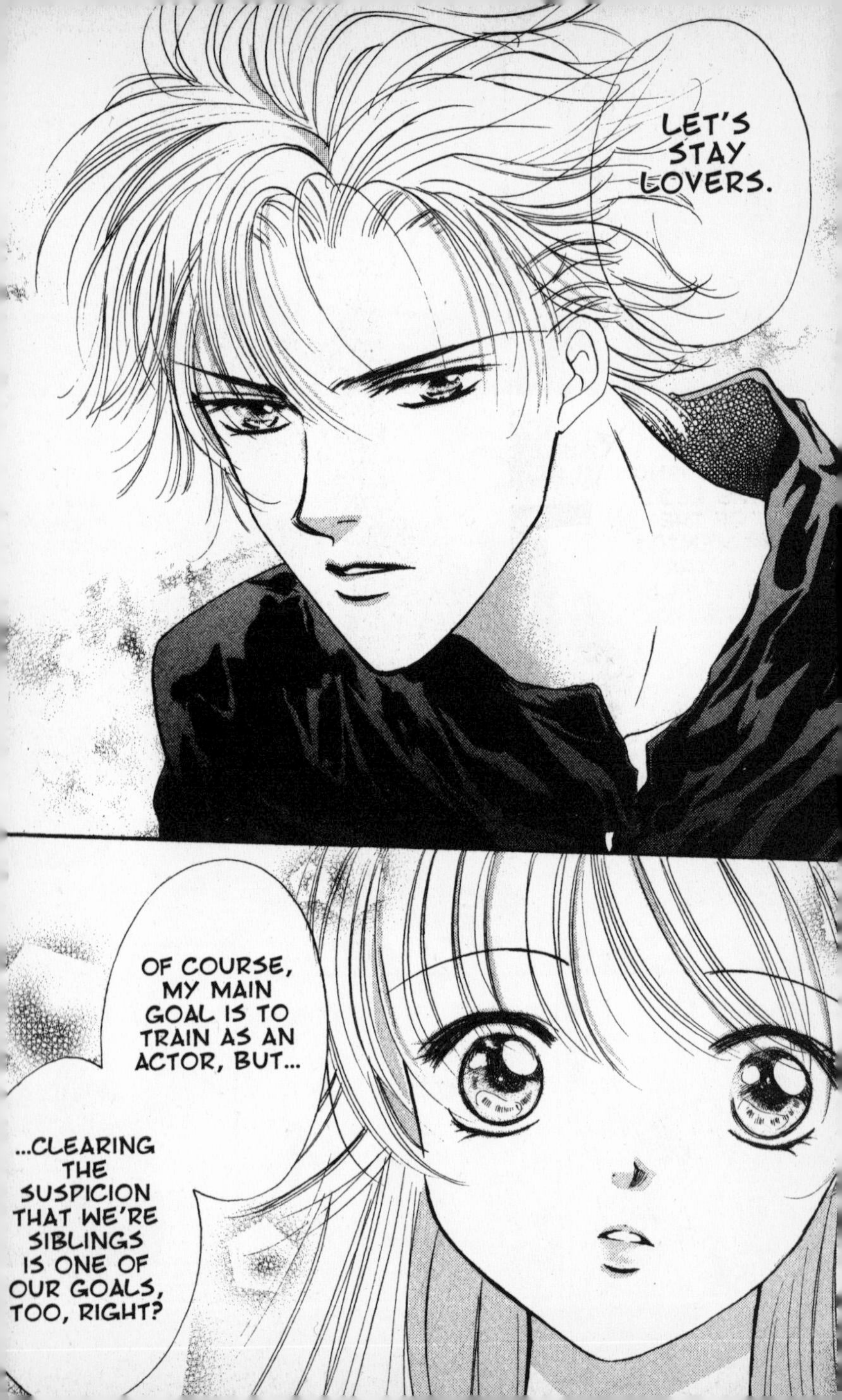
LET'S STAY LOVERS.
OF COURSE, MY MAIN GOAL IS TO TRAIN AS AN ACTOR, BUT...
...CLEARING THE SUSPICION THAT WE'RE SIBLINGS IS ONE OF OUR GOALS, TOO, RIGHT?

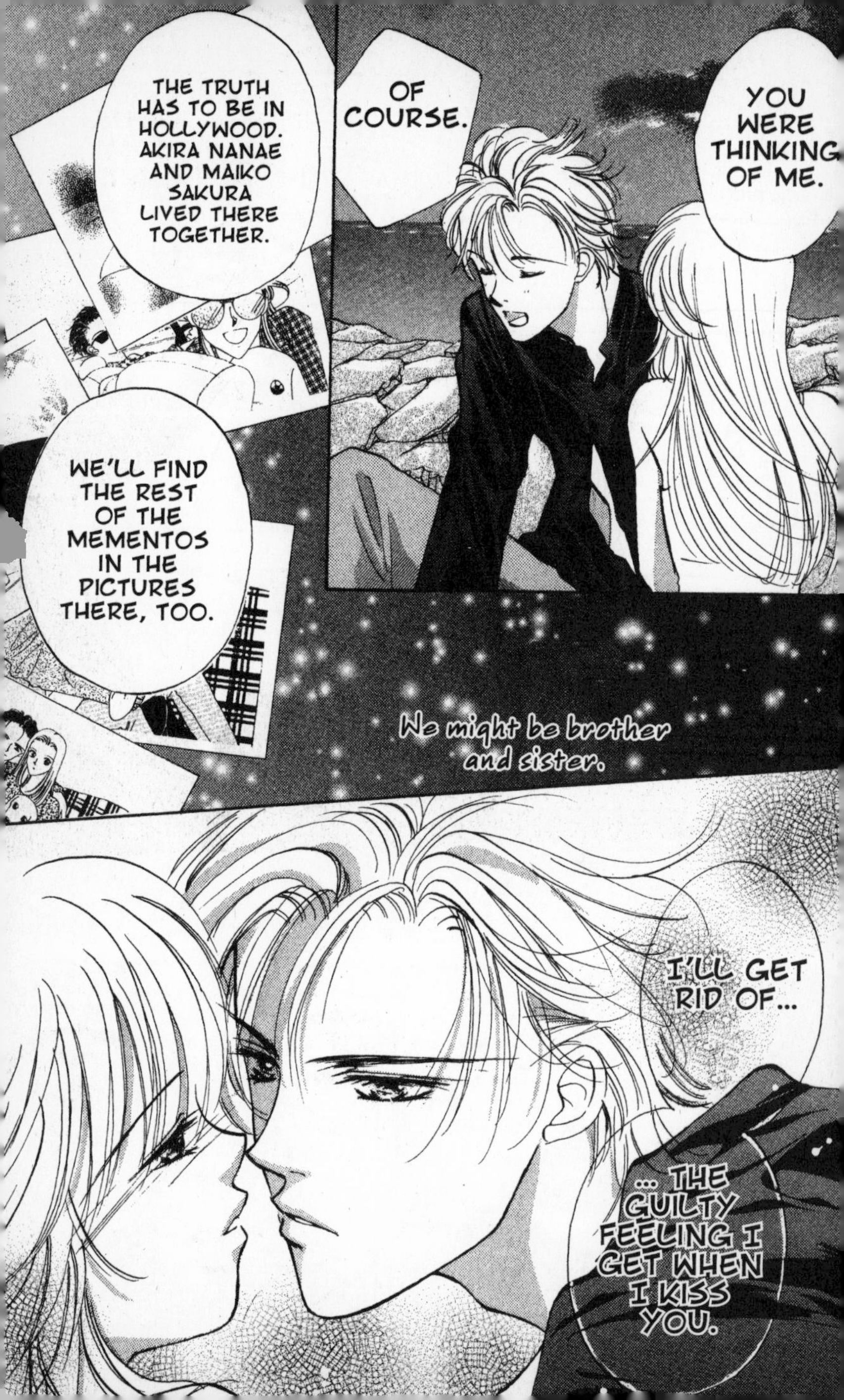
YOU WERE THINKING OF ME.
OF COURSE.
THE TRUTH HAS TO BE IN HOLLYWOOD. AKIRA NANAE AND MAIKO SAKURA LIVED THERE TOGETHER.
WE'LL FIND THE REST OF THE MEMENTOS IN THE PICTURES THERE, TOO.
We might be brother and sister.
I'LL GET RID OF...
... THE GUILTY FEELING I GET WHEN I KISS YOU.

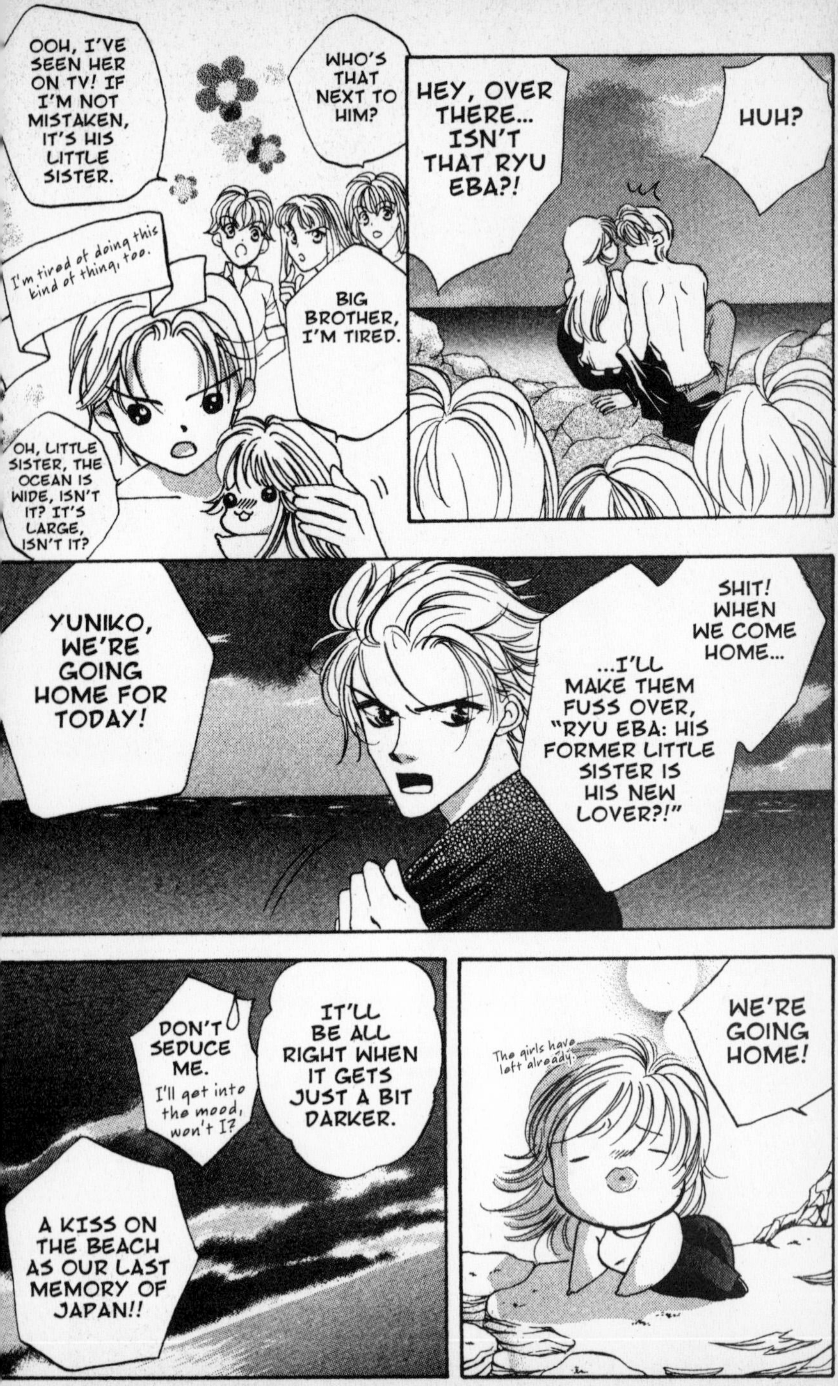
HUH?
HEY, OVER THERE... ISN'T THAT RYU EBA?!
WHO'S THAT NEXT TO HIM?
OOH, I'VE SEEN HER ON TV! IF I'M NOT MISTAKEN, IT'S HIS LITTLE SISTER.
BIG BROTHER, I'M TIRED.
I'm tired of doing this kind of thing, too.
OH, LITTLE SISTER, THE OCEAN IS WIDE, ISN'T IT? IT'S LARGE, ISN'T IT?
SHIT! WHEN WE COME HOME...
...I'LL MAKE THEM FUSS OVER, "RYU EBA: HIS FORMER LITTLE SISTER IS HIS NEW LOVER?!"
YUNIKO, WE'RE GOING HOME FOR TODAY!
WE'RE GOING HOME!
The girls have left already.
IT'LL BE ALL RIGHT WHEN IT GETS JUST A BIT DARKER.
DON'T SEDUCE ME.
I'll get into the mood, won't I?
A KISS ON THE BEACH AS OUR LAST MEMORY OF JAPAN!!

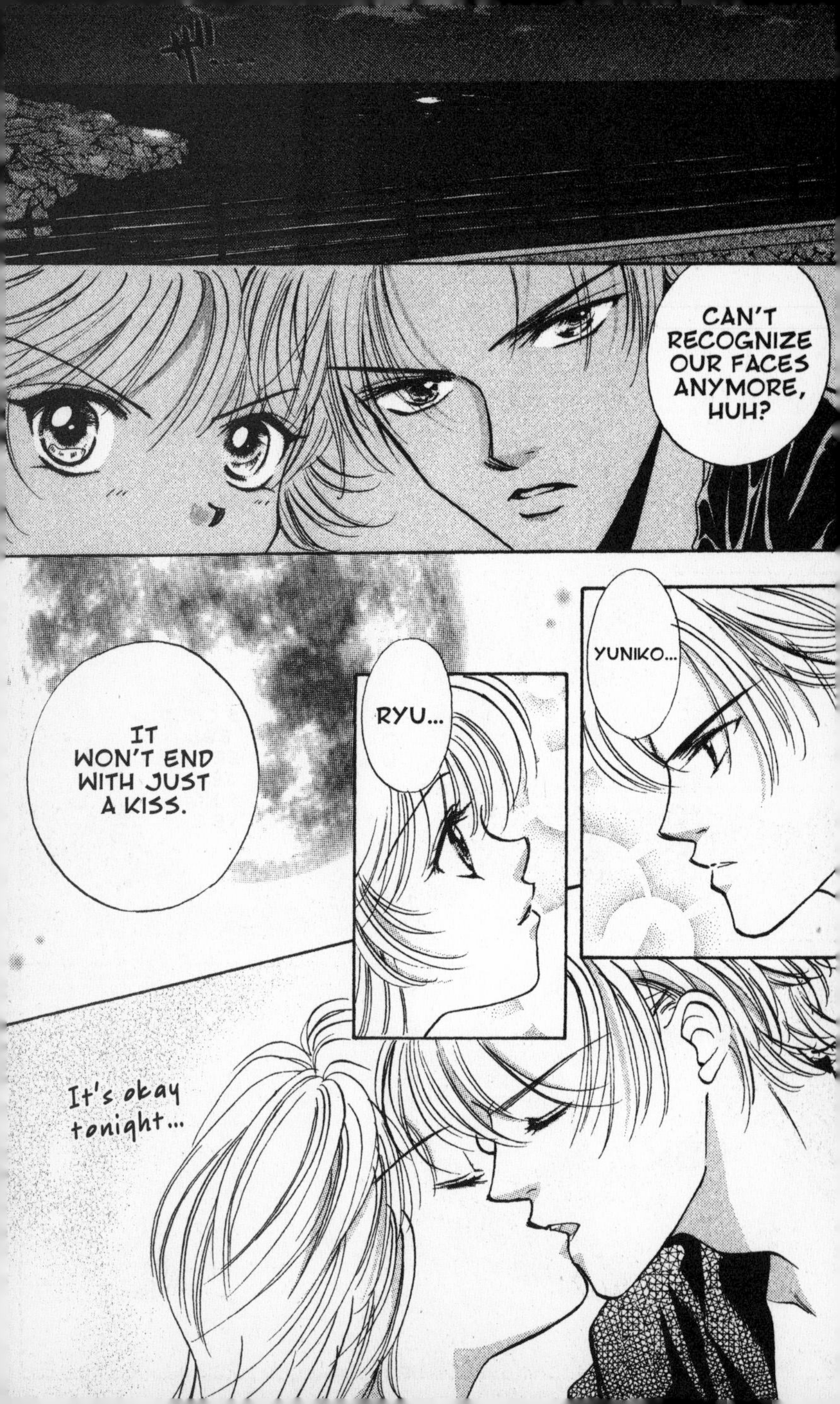
CAN'T RECOGNIZE OUR FACES ANYMORE, HUH?
YUNIKO...
RYU...
IT WON'T END WITH JUST A KISS.
It's okay tonight...

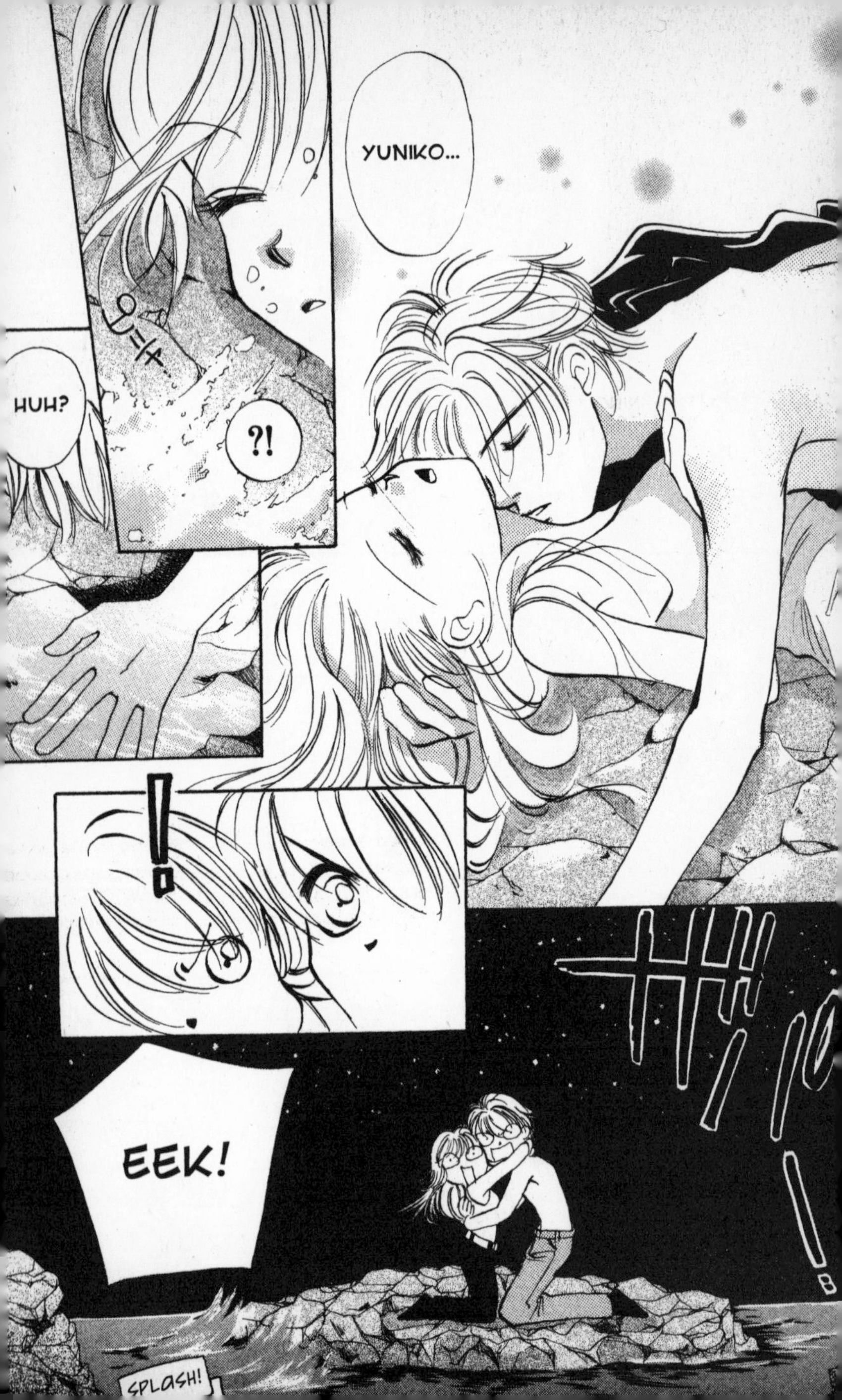
YUNIKO...
?!
HUH?
!
EEK!
SPLASH!

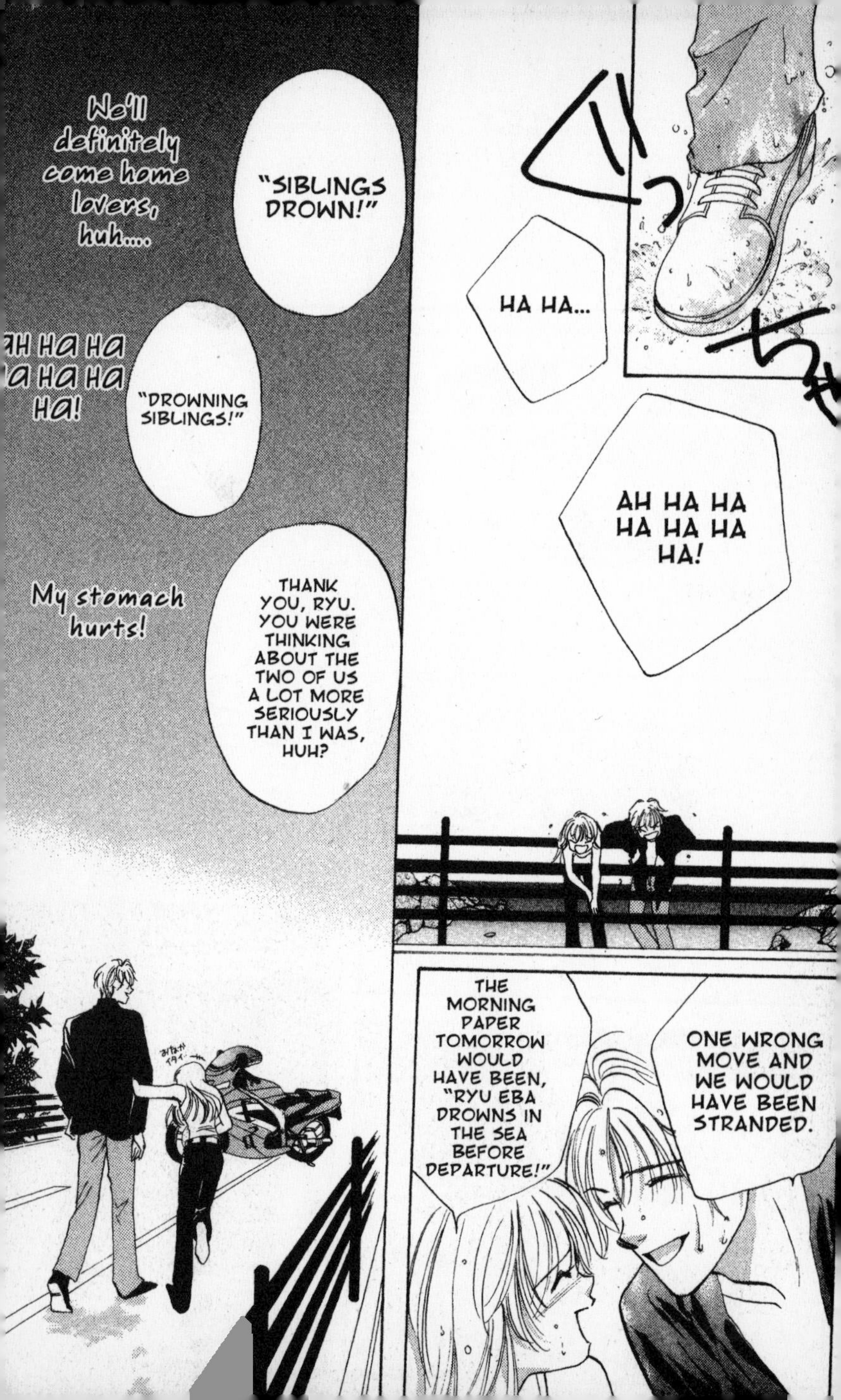
HA HA...
AH HA HA HA HA HA HA!
ONE WRONG MOVE AND WE WOULD HAVE BEEN STRANDED.
THE MORNING PAPER TOMORROW WOULD HAVE BEEN, "RYU EBA DROWNS IN THE SEA BEFORE DEPARTURE!"
"SIBLINGS DROWN!"
We'll definitely come home lovers, huh....
"DROWNING SIBLINGS!"
ah ha ha a ha ha ha!
THANK YOU, RYU. YOU WERE THINKING ABOUT THE TWO OF US A LOT MORE SERIOUSLY THAN I WAS, HUH?
My stomach hurts!

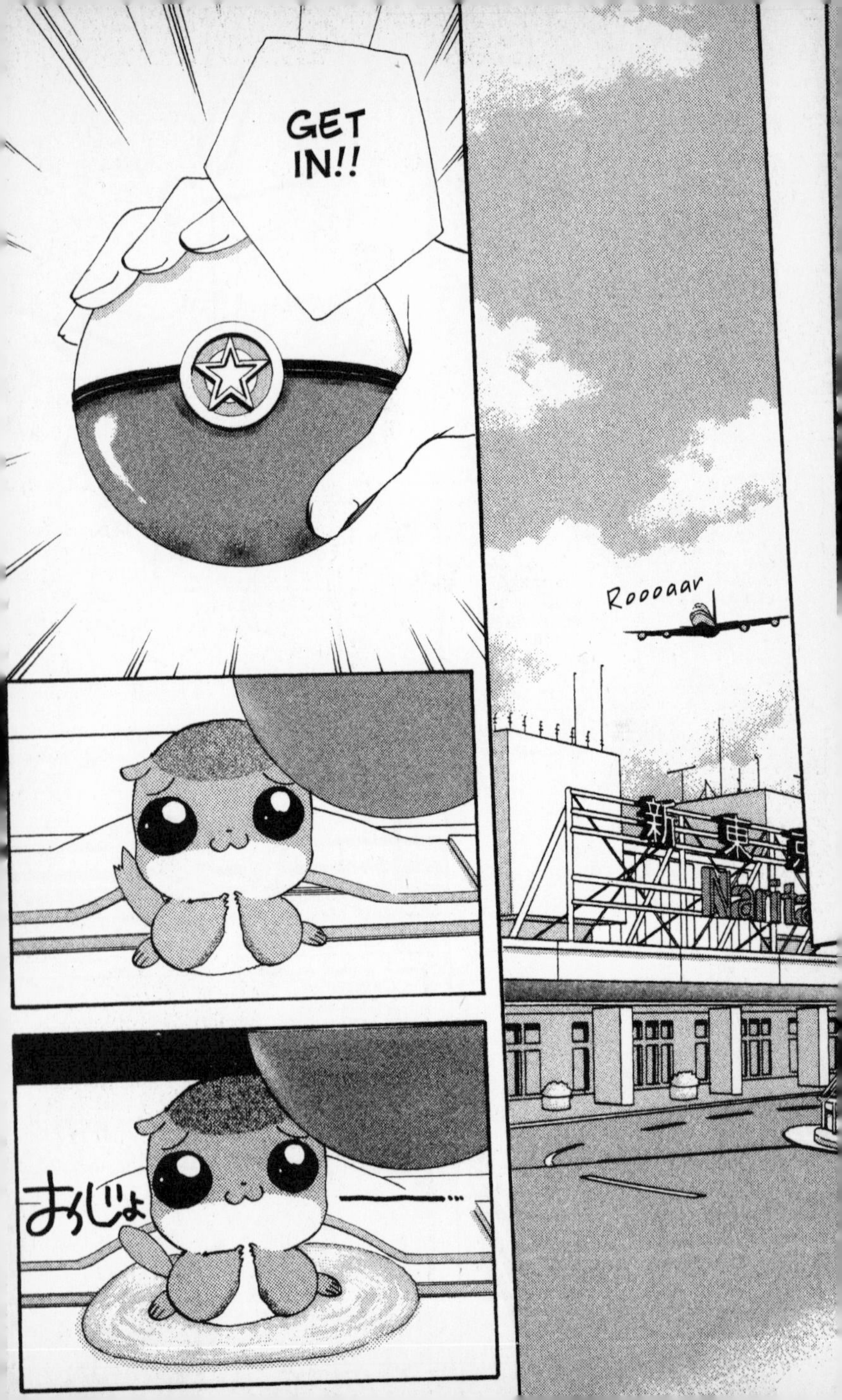
Roooaar
GET IN!!
おろじょ

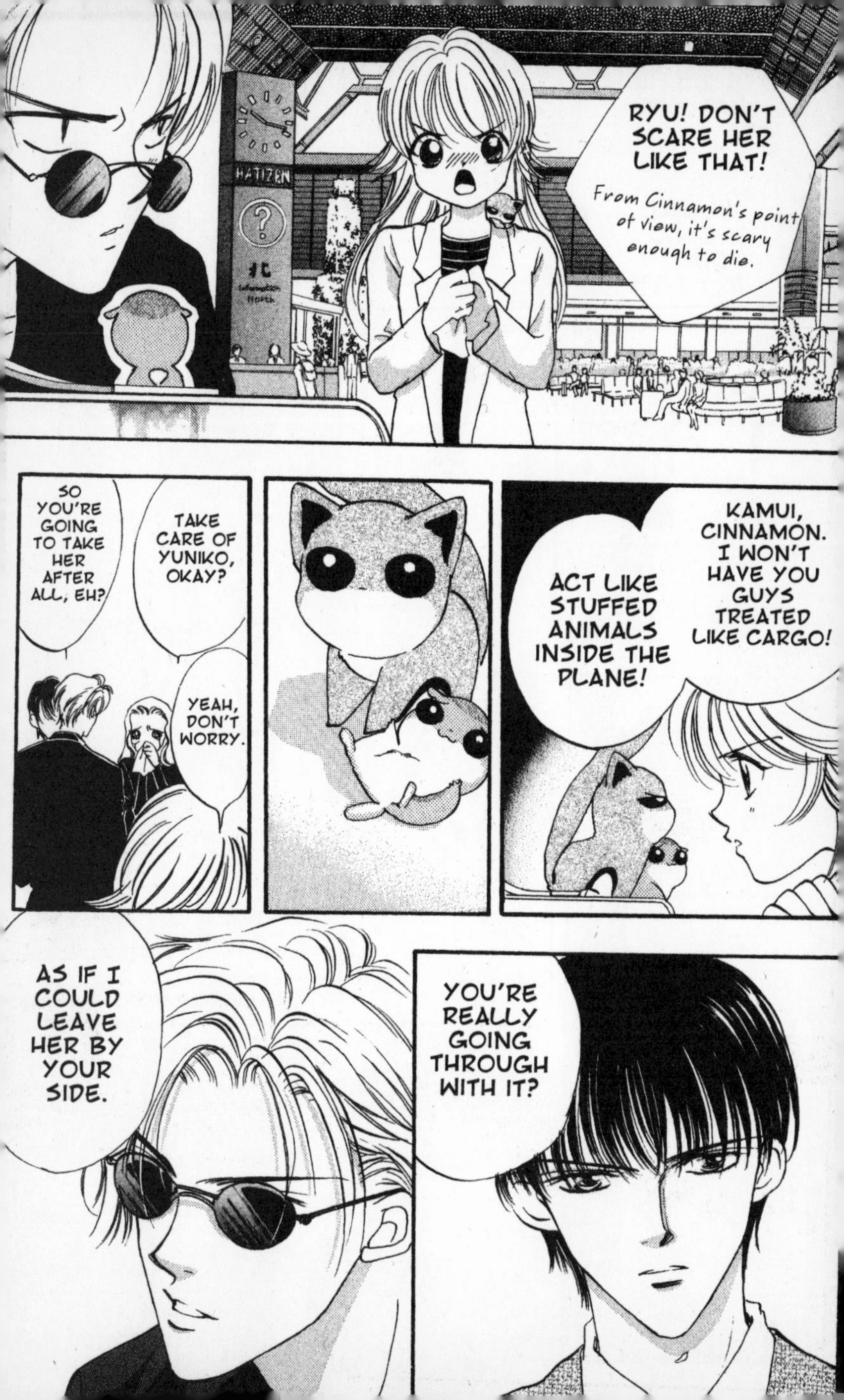
RYU! DON'T SCARE HER LIKE THAT!
From Cinnamon's point of view, it's scary enough to die.
KAMUI, CINNAMON. I WON'T HAVE YOU GUYS TREATED LIKE CARGO!
ACT LIKE STUFFED ANIMALS INSIDE THE PLANE!
TAKE CARE OF YUNIKO, OKAY?
SO YOU'RE GOING TO TAKE HER AFTER ALL, EH?
YEAH, DON'T WORRY.
YOU'RE REALLY GOING THROUGH WITH IT?
AS IF I COULD LEAVE HER BY YOUR SIDE.

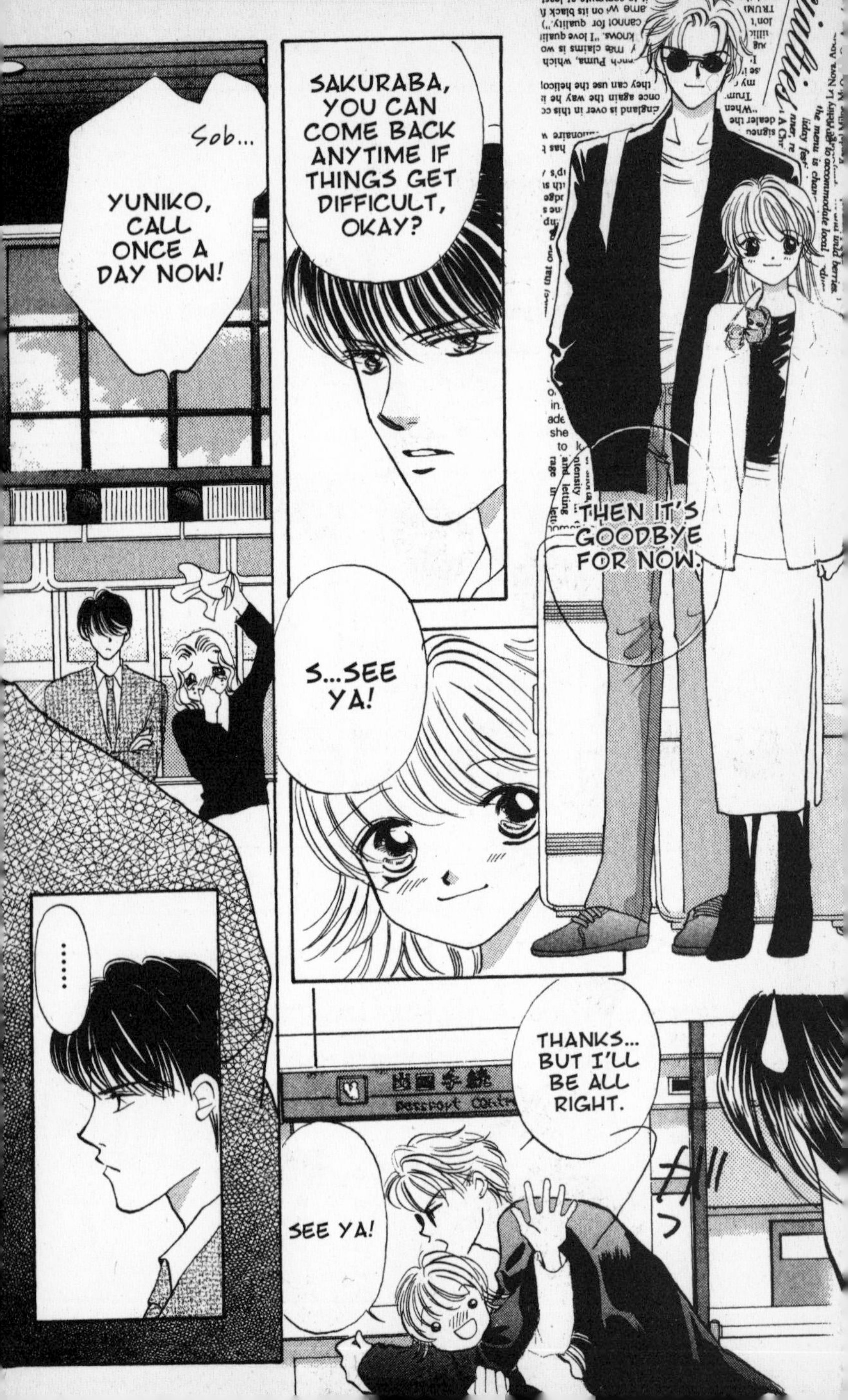
THEN IT'S GOODBYE FOR NOW.
SAKURABA, YOU CAN COME BACK ANYTIME IF THINGS GET DIFFICULT, OKAY?
S...SEE YA!
Sob...
YUNIKO, CALL ONCE A DAY NOW!
THANKS... BUT I'LL BE ALL RIGHT.
SEE YA!
......

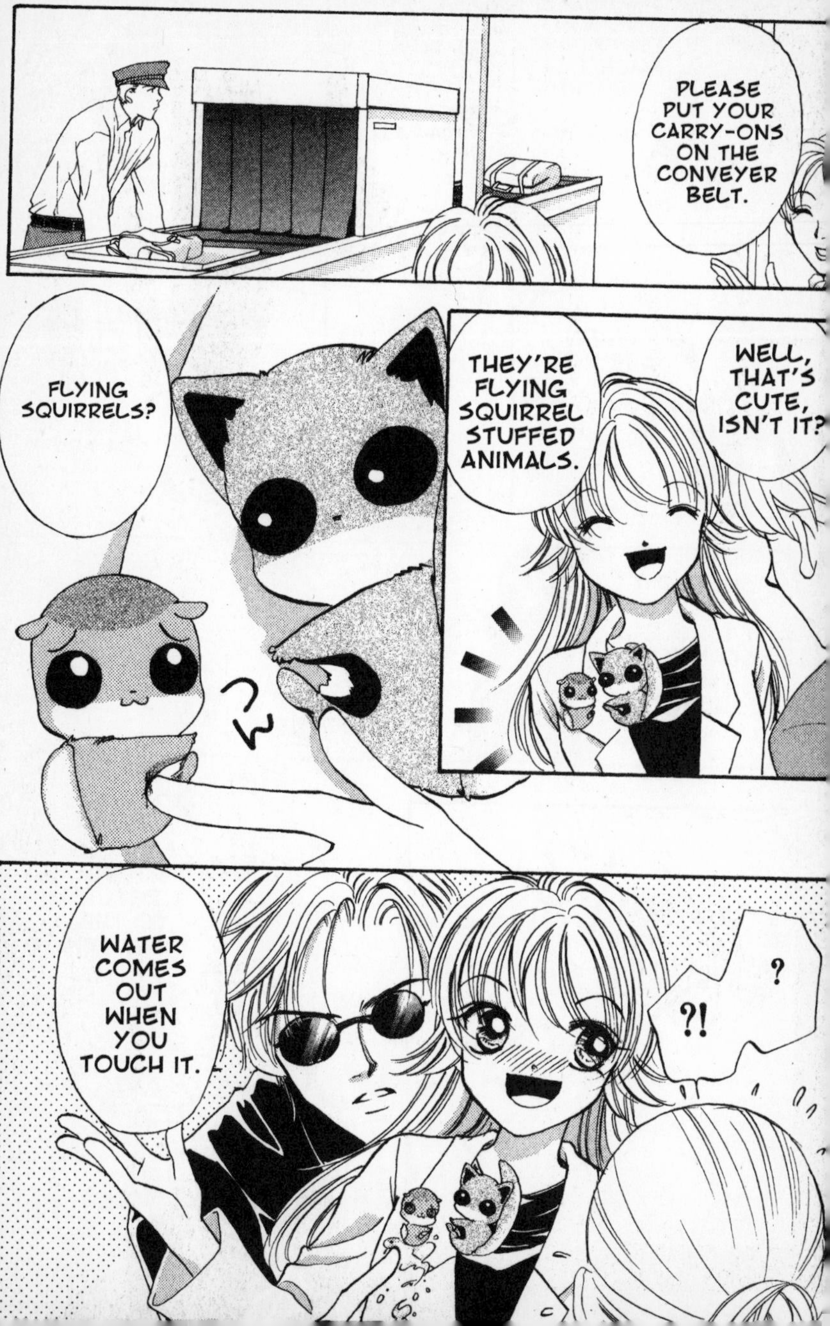
PLEASE PUT YOUR CARRY-ONS ON THE CONVEYER BELT.
WELL, THAT'S CUTE, ISN'T IT?
THEY'RE FLYING SQUIRREL STUFFED ANIMALS.
FLYING SQUIRRELS?
?
?!
WATER COMES OUT WHEN YOU TOUCH IT.

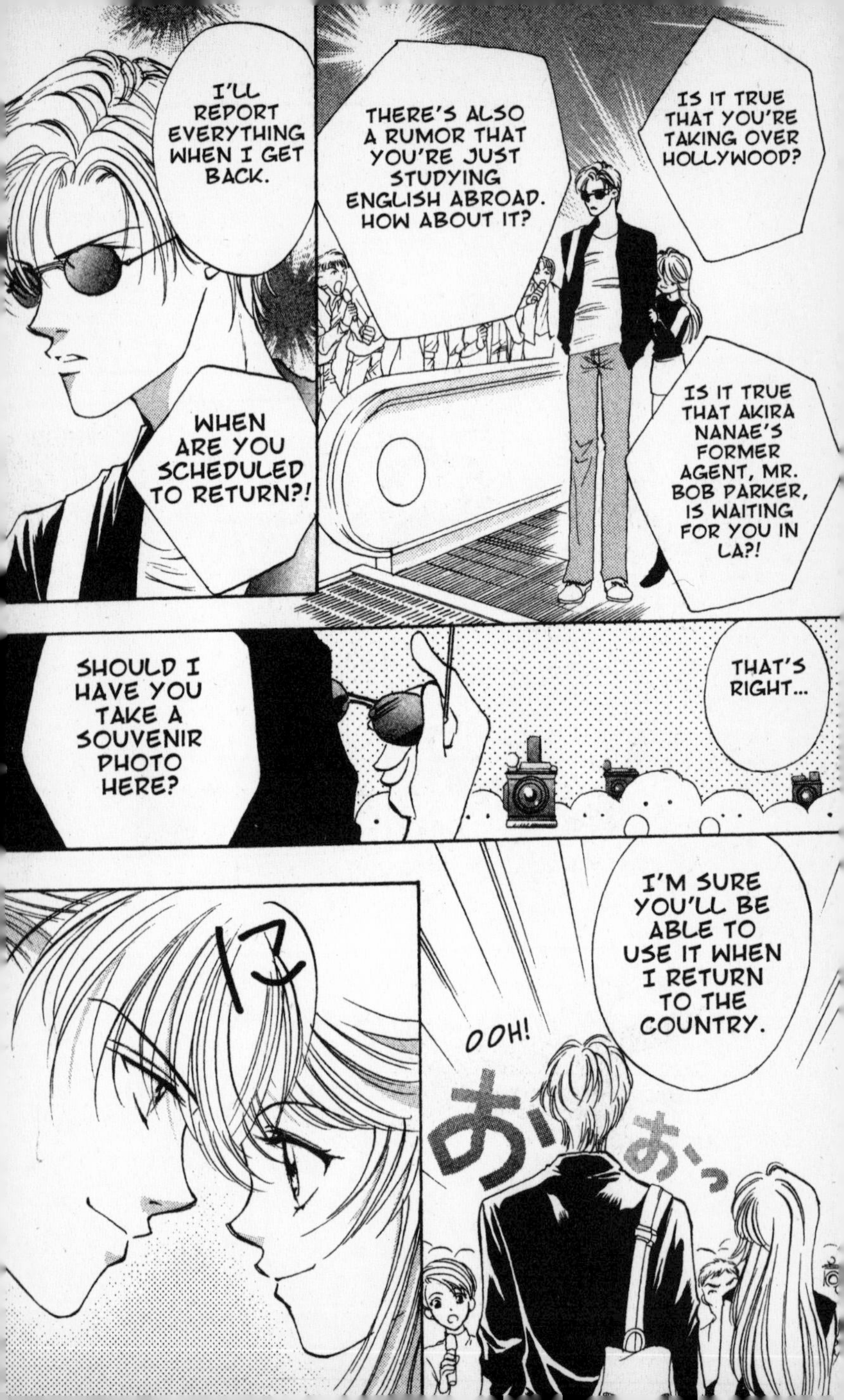
IS IT TRUE THAT YOU'RE TAKING OVER HOLLYWOOD?
THERE'S ALSO A RUMOR THAT YOU'RE JUST STUDYING ENGLISH ABROAD. HOW ABOUT IT?
IS IT TRUE THAT AKIRA NANAE'S FORMER AGENT, MR. BOB PARKER, IS WAITING FOR YOU IN LA?!
WHEN ARE YOU SCHEDULED TO RETURN?!
I'LL REPORT EVERYTHING WHEN I GET BACK.
THAT'S RIGHT...
SHOULD I HAVE YOU TAKE A SOUVENIR PHOTO HERE?
I'M SURE YOU'LL BE ABLE TO USE IT WHEN I RETURN TO THE COUNTRY.
OOH!

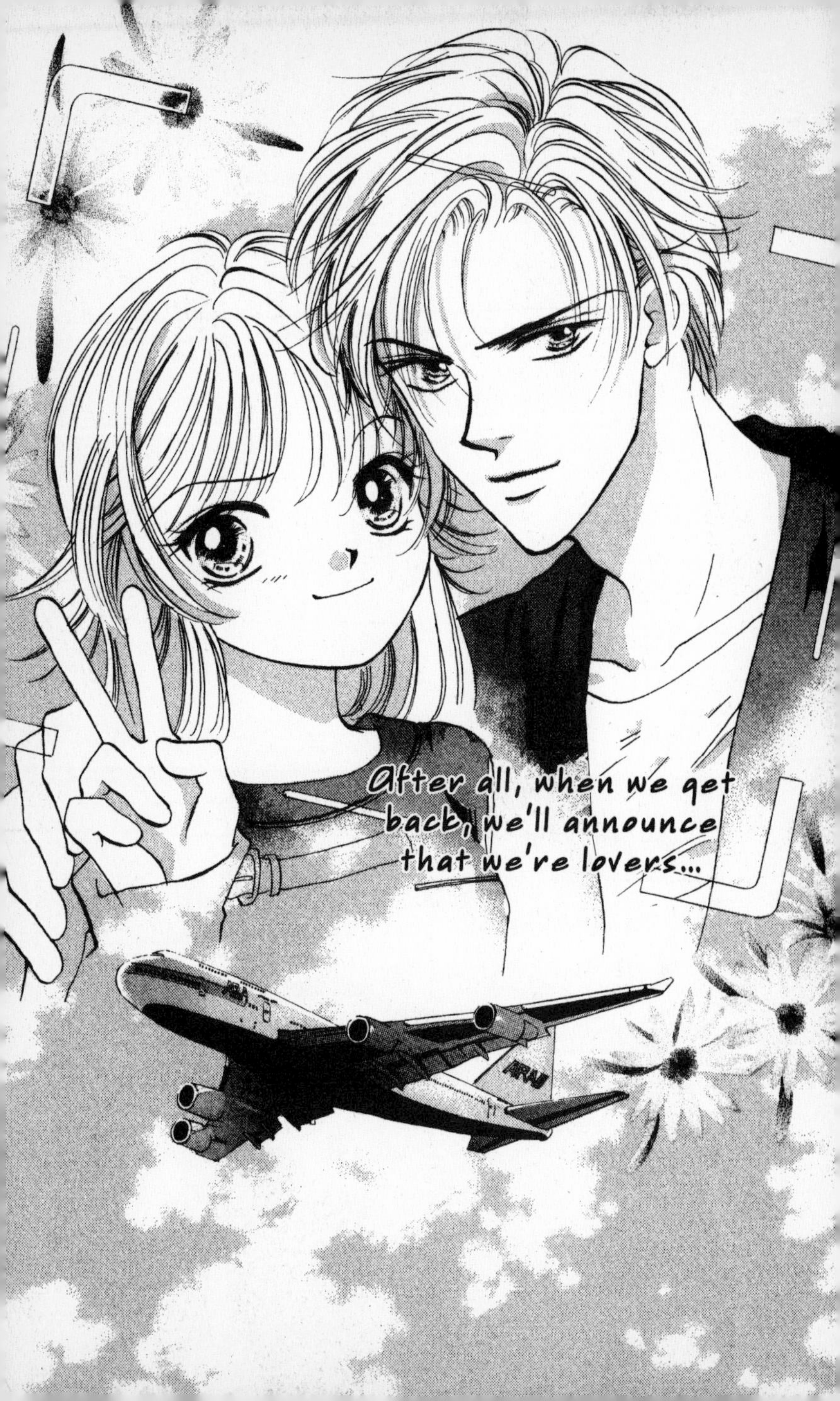
After all, when we get back, we'll announce that we're lovers...

COMING SOON

VOLUME EIGHT

When Yuniko and Ryu head to Hollywood, Yuniko is shocked to discover that Ryu's agent has signed her up at an exclusive acting school. Her life becomes filled with drama when she meets a fellow acting student named Ryu Gilliam—the two develop instant chemistry on and off stage! Now Yuniko has a starring role in the heated battle for her affection between the two Ryus!

Princess Ai

A Diva torn from Chaos...
A Savior doomed to Love

Created by
Courtney Love
and D.J. Milky

TOKYOPOP

www.TOKYOPOP.com

Going Both Ways. . .

Peach Girl
Change of Heart

& Peach Girl

By: Miwa Ueda

The continuing
story of the riveting
high school drama of
love and acceptance.

*"If you're into stories of teen
angst, if you like a good villain,
if you find complicated, misunderstanding-
riddled romance addictive, then get yourself a copy of
Peach Girl and enjoy!"* –**Animerica Magazine**

100% AUTHENTIC MANGA

Peach Girl: Change of Heart
100% Authentic Manga
Get it now *at your favorite book & comic stores!*

*The original Peach Girl Volumes 1-8
available now–***collect them all!**

TEEN
AGE 13+

WWW.TOKYOPOP.c

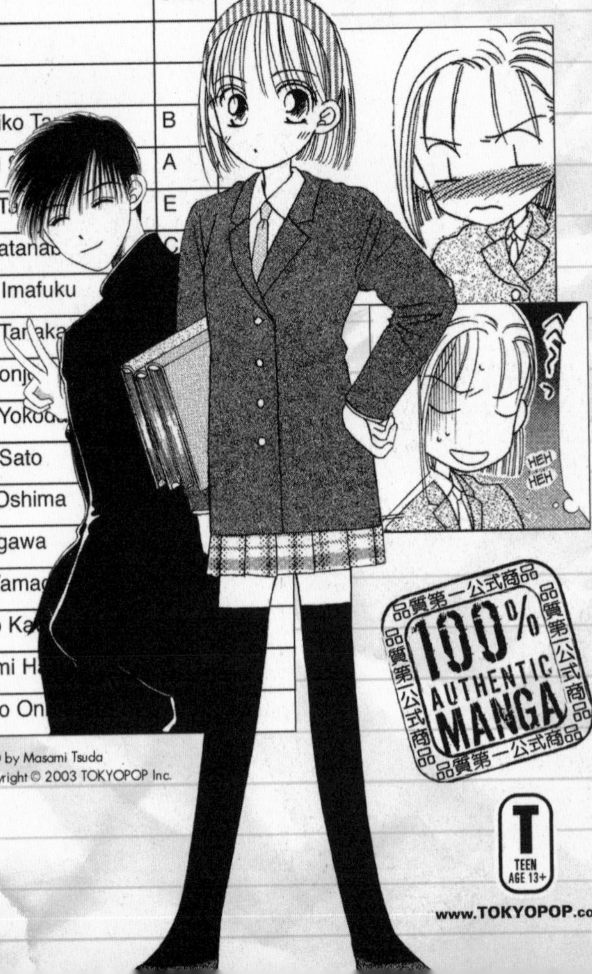
HEH
HEH

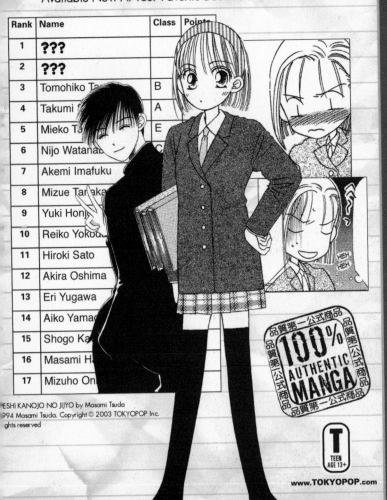

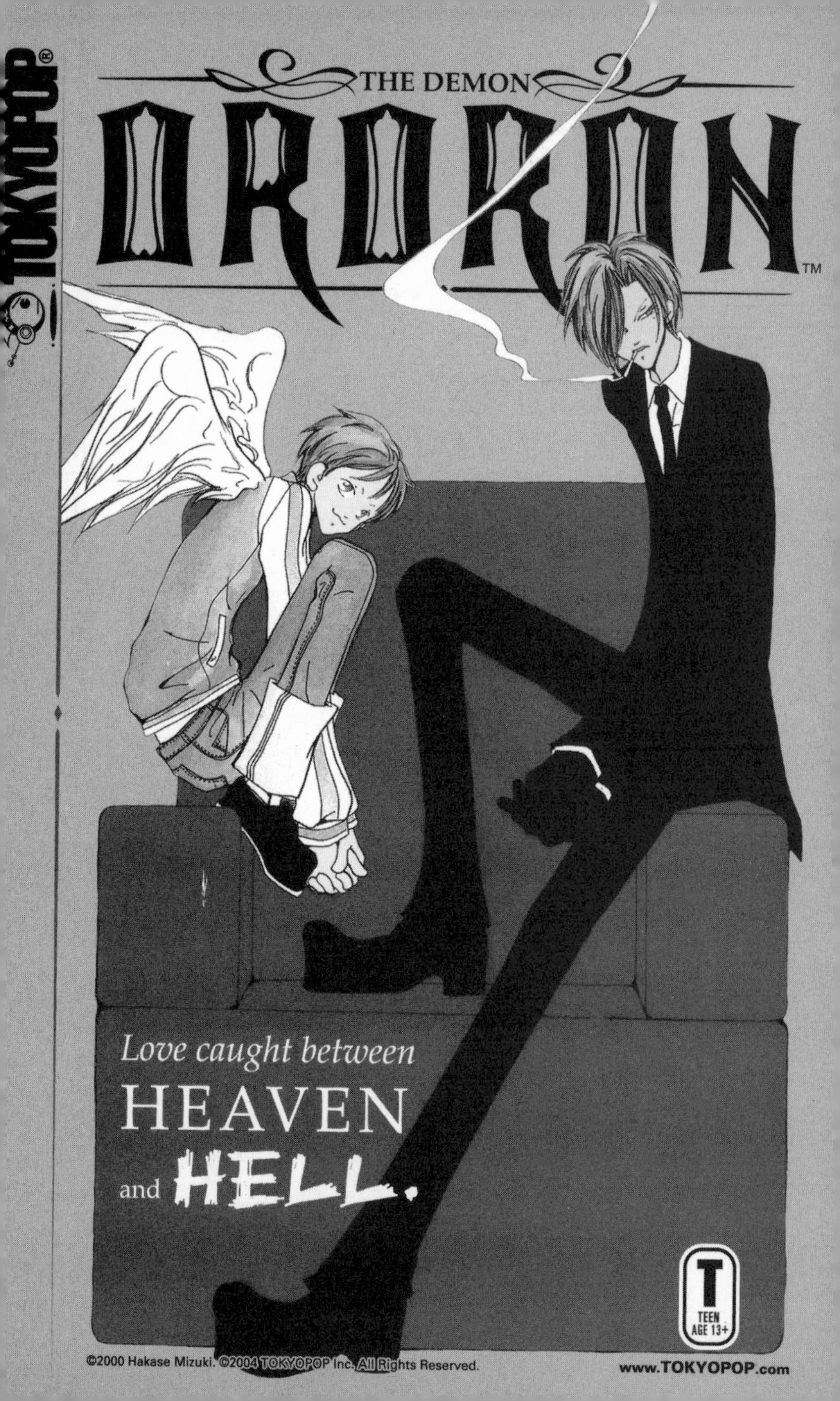
TOKYOPOP®
THE DEMON
ORORON™
Love caught between
HEAVEN
and HELL.
T
TEEN
AGE 13+
www.TOKYOPOP.com

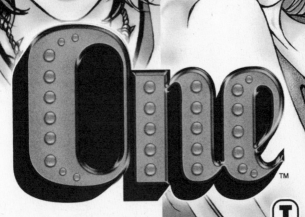

One
rocks to live.

One
lives to rock.

They've got nothing in common...except each other.

TOKYOPOP®

One™

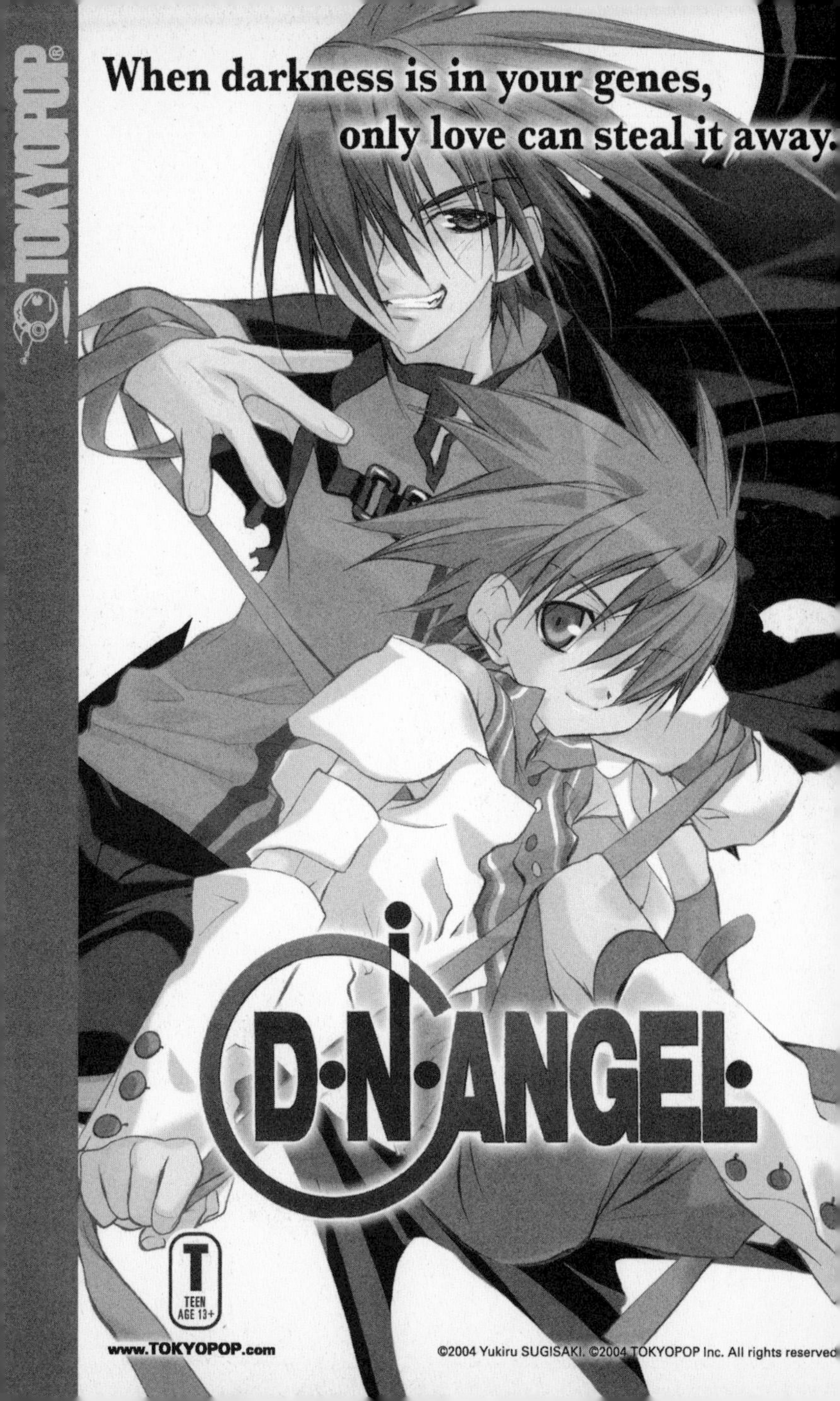

When darkness is in your genes,
only love can steal it away.
D•N•ANGEL
TOKYOPOP
T
TEEN
AGE 13+

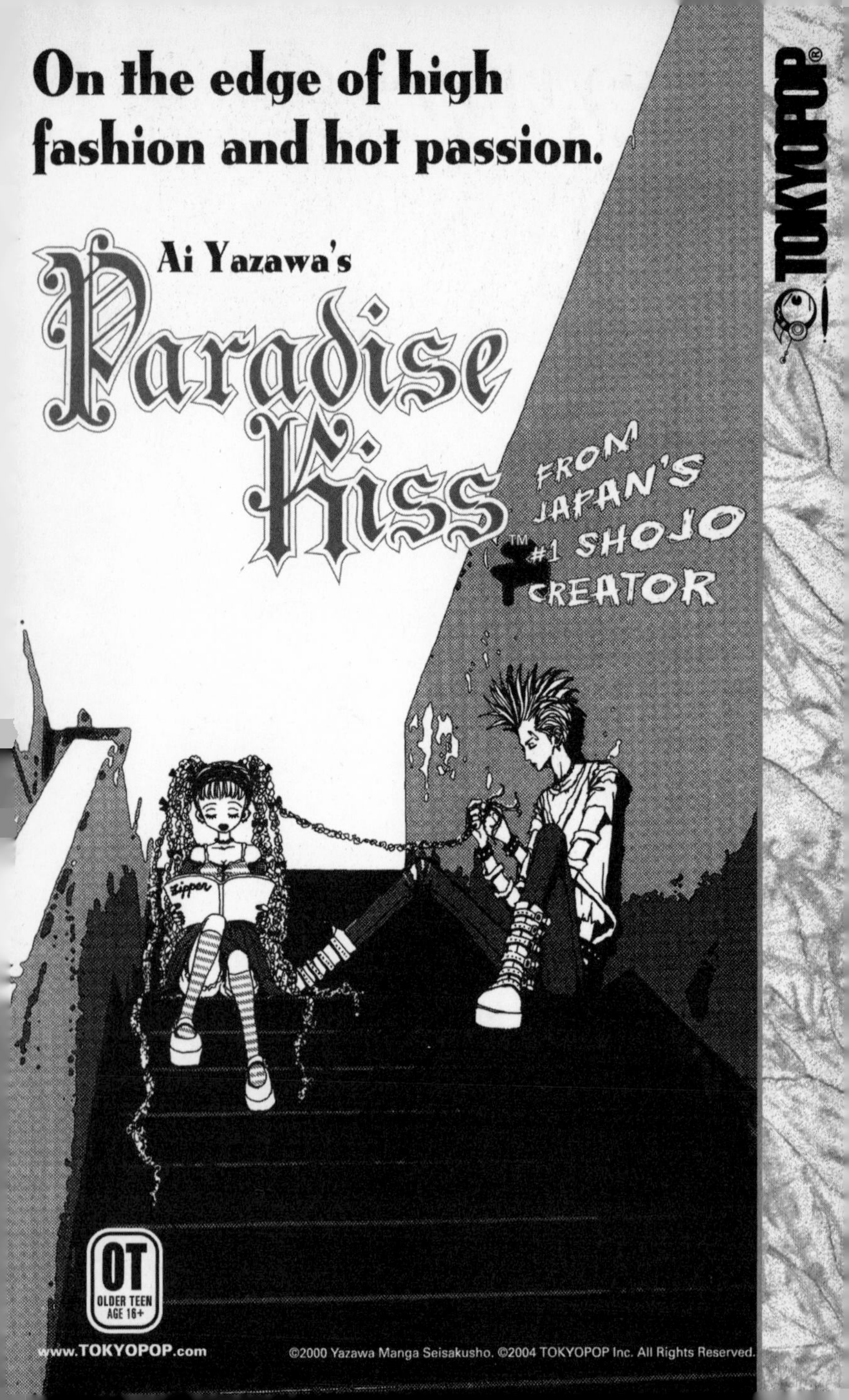
On the edge of high fashion and hot passion.
Ai Yazawa's
Paradise Kiss™
FROM JAPAN'S #1 SHOJO CREATOR
Zipper
OT OLDER TEEN AGE 16+
TOKYOPOP®
www.TOKYOPOP.com
©2000 Yazawa Manga Seisakusho. ©2004 TOKYOPOP Inc. All Rights Reserved.

Behind-the-scenes with artistic dreams and unconventional love at a comic convention

TEEN
AGE 13+

www.TOKYOPOP.com

STOP!

This is the back of the book.
You wouldn't want to spoil a great ending!

This book is printed "manga-style," in the authentic Japanese right-to-left format. Since none of the artwork has been flipped or altered, readers get to experience the story just as the creator intended. You've been asking for it, so TOKYOPOP® delivered: authentic, hot-off-the-press, and far more fun!

DIRECTIONS

If this is your first time reading manga-style, here's a quick guide to help you understand how it works.

It's easy... just start in the top right panel and follow the numbers. Have fun, and look for more 100% authentic manga from TOKYOPOP®!